GREAT MILITARY LIVES

THE TIMES

GREAT MILITARY LIVES

A CENTURY IN OBITUARIES

GENERAL EDITOR: IAN BRUNSKILL
EDITED BY GUY LIARDET AND
MICHAEL TILLOTSON

TIMES BOOKS

Published in 2008 by Times Books

HarperCollins Publishers
77–85 Fulham Palace Road
London w6 8jb

www.collins.co.uk
Visit the book lover's website

isbn 978-0-00-727670-7

British Library Cataloguing in Publication Data

A catalogue record for this book is available from the
British Library.

Designed by Heike Schüssler
Set in ff Nexus

Typeset by Rowland Phototypesetting Ltd,
Bury St Edmunds, Suffolk

Printed and bound in Great Britain by Clays Ltd, St Ives plc

CONTENTS

Foreword by William Hague vii

Introduction by Major-General Michael Tillotson xi

Wellington 1

Raglan 22

Grant 26

Lee 40

Garibaldi 43

Sitting Bull 47

Moltke 50

MacMahon 63

Cetywayo 66

Togo 72

Roberts 77

Hindenburg 95

Ludendorff 105

Fisher 111

Foch 124

Haig 135

Jellicoe 145

Beatty 156

Scheer 169

Atatürk 175

Allenby 187

Trenchard 197

Mannerheim 204

Rundstedt 208

Guderian 211

Wavell 214

Alanbrooke 221

Auchinleck 227

Cunningham 233

Horton 239

Dönitz 241

Rommel 246

Montgomery 250

Eisenhower 266

Patton 273

Kesselring 277

MacArthur 279

Nimitz 284

Manstein 288

Rokossovsky 292

Zhukov 295

Dowding 299

Galland 304

Harris 307

Slim 312

Wingate 318

Ridgway 321

Gorshkov 325

Walker 327

Fieldhouse 332

* * *

FOREWORD

WILLIAM HAGUE

Politicians should always be very careful when commenting on military matters. My own hero, William Pitt the Younger, was right to say that 'I distrust extremely any ideas of my own on military subjects', despite the fact that he was the longest serving war leader in the modern history of Britain. Even he, a statesman who built the great international coalitions against revolutionary France, found that as a man who had never seen a battlefield, his second-guessing of generals from Downing Street could lead to disaster.

This magnificent collection of obituaries of great military leaders from *The Times* offers plenty of reminders of just how tense the relations between generals and political leaders can be in wartime: Lord Alanbrooke, one of Britain's best Second World War Generals, is quoted as saying of Winston Churchill, 'He is quite the most difficult man to work with that I have ever struck, but I would not have missed the chance of working with him for anything on earth'.

Yet some of these impressive men of war went on to become the political leaders of their nations, from the Duke of Wellington and Ulysses S Grant, through to Paul von Hindenburg – his 'iron mask and rock-firm figure became an inalienable possession of the nation' – and Dwight D Eisenhower. Others used the immense stature gained from victory in war to intrude into politics whenever they fancied: I much enjoyed reading of Montgomery's 'trenchant contributions' to debates in the House of Lords in his old age, 'delivered from somewhere near the exact centre of the Conservative benches but often turning his own front bench colleagues pale with apprehension.'

For all of us who love reading history, these assessments of such pivotal figures are full of fascination, covering as they do the full sweep of military history over the last two hundred years. It is impossible to read them without reflecting on the inability of most of these extraordinary people to foretell even the immediate future. Admiral of the Fleet Lord Fisher is something of an exception with his prediction in 1910 that 'war will come in 1914 and Jellicoe will command the Grand Fleet', but it is more telling that Hindenburg initially retired in 1911 believing that he would never have the chance to serve in wartime and MacArthur confidently informed President Truman in 1950 that the Chinese were unlikely to intervene in Korea with any force. The sharp turns taken by history are often a shock to the most brilliant of minds.

These men's minds were, however, well attuned to combining the pursuit of an overall strategy with the rapid taking of decisions under extreme pressure: abilities which distinguish the mind suited to executive command from one better devoted to campaigning or commentating. This above all is why we politicians must treat these figures with reverence, as a reading of the pages devoted to Britain's military leaders in the First World War shows well. For there we find Allenby winning the war against Turkey over a vast area of the Middle East with a strategy of which 'the original conception, the patience in preparation, the rapidity and audacity in execution, prove that [he] was a true master of war'.

There too is Admiral Beatty, boldly and suddenly taking his battle-cruisers into the Heligoland Bight to achieve victory when a more cautious leader would have held back, and then his colleague Jellicoe, whose command of the Fleet gave him, according to Churchill, responsibilities on a different scale from all others: 'the only man on either side who could lose the War in an afternoon'. It is just as well, as his obituary writer notes with approval, that his life had moulded him specifically for such duty, particularly as 'he did not know in earlier years the softening influences of money or friends in high places'.

Obituaries are necessarily history as it was seen and understood at certain moments, and are often kinder than the subsequent judgement of later decades, but they have the advantage of dealing with the whole life of an individual whom we are used to reading about only at the peak of their career. Many of us will have read of the brilliance of Marshal Zhukov as he led the Soviet armies in the destruction of the Third Reich; we may have overlooked the fact that both Stalin and Krushchev rubbished his achievements and that he had to wait until 1965 before he could appear in public at a military parade and receive a 'special burst of applause'.

Whether hailed or derided by their contemporaries, these are the stories of great men. Many of them, of course, would have considered themselves such at the time. When Montgomery was asked to name the three greatest generals in history, he replied 'the other two were

Alexander the Great and Napoleon'. So as we enjoy their lives afresh, with all their fascination and inspiration, we can be sure they would have wanted and expected us to do so.

INTRODUCTION

Major-General Michael Tillotson

THIS COLLECTION OF great military lives spanning the decades from Waterloo to the South Atlantic campaign of 1982 reflects dramatic changes in the scale and much of the nature of war. It begins during the era when national armies or navies marched or sailed out to fight the army or navy of an adversary – in a manner advanced only in magnitude from when David challenged Goliath on behalf of his tribe – the outcome of the battle determining the politics of the matter, possibly for decades. Conflicts then expanded dimensionally, economically and socially to a point where the whole engine of the state became engaged, as with the Civil War in the United States – arguably the first modern *industrial* war.

Despite the speed of his defeats of Austria in 1866 and France in 1870, Field Marshal von Moltke warned Kaiser Wilhelm II in 1890 that the next war might last between seven and thirty years. He argued that the resources of modern states were so great that none would accept defeat in one campaign or major battle as fair cause for capitulation, but would fight on. He was right in the sense that the war that began in 1914 was not finally concluded until 1945. The scale of manpower involvement in land warfare increased dramatically in the years up to 1914, with the German General Staff planning to use the younger reservists – 23 to 28-year olds – to provide the strength required to envelop the French left flank under the Schlieffen Plan. Forewarned, the French looked to their younger reserves, while Britain founded the Territorial Army.

At the outset of the twentieth century the advent of the submarine, the torpedo and the mine upset the supremacy of the line-of-battle fleet that had persisted from the age of sail well into the age of steam. Naval commanders in this collection were therefore confronted with unprecedented challenges in their conduct of maritime operations. Nuclear powered attack and ballistic missile submarines, for the first time true submersibles – as they do not have to 'come up for air' – have now added a new dimension to naval warfare.

The two most significant additions to the established disciplines of war on land and sea are those of air power and the means of acquiring intelligence. In the First World War, air power was a welcome 'add-on' for observation, supporting fire and keeping the enemy air force from interfering with surface operations. In the course of a mere twenty years it had developed into a battle-winning or losing factor, as demonstrated in the 1940 German *blitzkrieg* in France, the extraordinary success of the Japanese expansionist campaign after Pearl Harbour and the critical advantage of the virtually complete Allied air-superiority over northern France in 1944.

In the field of intelligence acquisition, air reconnaissance allowed surface commanders to see the other side of the hill and over the horizon in a time scale within which they could react with profit. The targeting of aerial reconnaissance and subsequent assault onto an enemy's dispositions, deployments, industrial capacity and surface communications has been enhanced by being able to intercept and decode his strategic and tactical signal traffic. 'We had an ally,' crowed Ludendorff's Deputy Chief of Operations after victory at Tannenberg, 'The enemy. We knew all the enemy's plans.' He had had the daily intercepts of the Russian wireless messages decoded by a German professor of mathematics. The most quantum leap of all is being able to overhear an enemy's political and strategic discussions and plans, lifting intelligence to a level remote from travellers' tales and dependence on reports from agents, who could see or hear only one fragment of the plot and who might be working for the enemy.

After the two World Wars, revulsion of the prospect of more carnage and devastation led to 'limited wars', limited by geography and objective, such as were fought by the United Nations in Korea and by the United Kingdom against Argentina for the Falkland Islands, yet with the spectre of superpower conflict still hovering ominously in the background, imposing its own constraints on national manoeuvre and aspiration.

Throughout this era of change has lain the menace of 'undeclared' war, where there is no formal understanding between adversaries, no acknowledged code for the treatment of prisoners or the wounded and the civilian population is utilized – often ruthlessly – as a place of refuge, a source of support and supply or, worst of all, as hostages upon which atrocities are committed in order to apply restraint or to exact revenge. There is nothing new here and methods vary only with the terrain and the weaponry available to the antagonists. While we might applaud examples like the Spanish guerrilla attacks on the outposts of Napoleon's armies in the Iberian Peninsula and Tito's partisans against the Axis occupiers of Yugoslavia, we deplore the murder and mayhem imposed by Kenya's Mau-Mau or by communist insurgents seeking to overthrow colonial administrations or their perceived proxies in South East Asia. 'One man's terrorist is another's freedom fighter' loses none of its truth through having become a cliché. A number of the individuals whose obituaries appear here experienced conflict in several of the forms described, maintaining their reputations for success only when they adapted to change.

Change in the manner in which command is exercised has been equally dramatic. At Waterloo, where this book begins, Wellington commanded in the saddle from where he could oversee events only to the limit of visibility, while inspiring his soldiers by his overt presence. During the war for the Falklands, Admiral Fieldhouse commanded from his bunker deep below the London suburb of Northwood, from where he had access to the latest electronic and satellite intelligence, one-to-one communication with commanders at sea and eventually ashore, and with the British War Cabinet through the filter of the Service Chiefs of Staff.

The most significant aspect of the evolution of command is the extent to which political control may be applied to a commander in the field or at sea, affecting his strategic and even tactical decisions. He may jib at such restrictions, but the international nature of today's world demands he should be kept alert to political intentions and reservations. From Kitchener's 'press conference' after Omdurman ('Get out of my way, you drunken swabs') to to-day, the military commander has had to take increasing account of a pervasive, influential and technically proficient media. This raises the issue of whether one individual might any longer be able to make a critical impact on the outcome of a battle or campaign. The answer is 'probably yes, but to a lesser extent than formerly'.

These obituaries have been selected from those published in *The Times* that illustrate high command in war, long experience of armed conflict or preparation for such responsibility. Success or failure has played a smaller part than impact or influence on events at the time and in consequence on the course of history. Some who held high command also pioneered or exploited a significant aspect of war – of which Admirals Dönitz and Horton are examples for submarine warfare and Generals Guderian and Patton for fast-moving armoured penetration and encirclement. We have also included Giuseppe Garibaldi as an exponent of irregular warfare and General Walter Walker as an expert on its suppression. Chiefs Cetywayo and Sitting Bull are here for their prowess as leaders of warrior nations, their courage and methods of warfare beset and eventually defeated by technology.

Objections over omissions and even some inclusions are inevitable, but a balance of different aspects of warfare, geography and nationality had to be struck. A few who might have qualified had no obituary in *The Times*; otherwise Admiral Thomas Cochrane, Lord Dundonald, (1775–1860) would be here. While a long extract from Wellington's obituary is included, the death of his great adversary, Napoleon, occurred too early and at a time when *The Times* had not yet developed its obituary coverage. Lord Kitchener is omitted because his obituary appeared in full in *Great Lives*, published in 2005. Sadly, no woman could be found to match the criteria for inclusion.

In addition to the conduct of war, its reporting in newspapers and recording in obituaries of the participants have also evolved. News of the victory of Waterloo had to be galloped to and sailed across the Channel while only fifty years later William Russell had his reports on the failings of the staff and administrative services in the Crimea telegraphed to *The Times* for publication next day – and with little or no censorship imposed upon his copy. Such journalistic freedom, although doubtless available, was seldom exercised in the obituaries of the period. Lord Raglan, who died aged sixty-six while in command of the British Army in the Crimea, whose obituary we include, was unsuited by age and lack of command experience for the responsibilities he held, something recognised by the press and public alike. Yet his obituary concentrates chiefly on his gentlemanly personal qualities, making only the briefest genuflexion towards the awareness of his shortcomings as a field commander at the very end – and without venturing to suggest what they were.

Such courteous restraint shows signs of fraying at the edges as time wore on. First World War commanders are spared some frank criticism possibly out of consideration of the appalling circumstances they faced as well as in the interests of 'good taste'. Examples are the obituaries of Jellicoe, Beatty and Fisher whose controversies are gently alluded to but not clearly explained. The obituaries of commanders who died soon after their famous deeds tend to reflect current public perception rather than their true worth. Rommel who died in October 1944 before the end of the war in Europe was in sight is granted only grudging praise for his generalship. The treatment – in terms of detail and scope – of the lives and achievements of the selected individuals over the period shows little consistency. One is left to conclude that as much depended on the whim of the Editor of *The Times* as on the stature of the subject.

Some instances of contrasting coverage lack explanation – for example over 7,000 words for General Ulysses S. Grant against only 1,200 for his strategic equal General Robert E. Lee cannot be wholly attributed to Grant's subsequent unexciting performance as his country's eighteenth president. Astonishingly broad coverage was afforded to the Italian soldier-patriot General Giuseppe Garibaldi, over two issues of *The Times* on June 3rd and 5th 1882, seemingly reflecting the extent to which this romantic – not to say romanticised – figure had been taken into the bosom of Victorian Britain. In marked contrast, the hero of the native American people – Chief Sitting Bull, whose Prairie Sioux tribes took part in the defeat of General Custer at the Battle of the Little Big Horn – is dismissed in less than a thousand words, as is General 'Schneller Heinz' Guderian, the leading German exponent of armoured warfare in the Second World War. In several instance, for example, Wellington, Grant, Garibaldi, Moltke, MacMahon and Eisenhower, the extreme length of the published obituaries have obliged us to include only selected extracts in the book.

Political bias occasionally shows its hand. The obituary for Cetywayo – in a tract of breath-taking Victorian humbug – seeks to portray as a villain the Chief who sought only to protect his tribal lands from annexation and his proud Zulu nation from conquest. In an instance of 'political correctness', the lugubrious Field Marshal Paul von Hindenburg is accorded generous accolades as 'Father of the Fatherland' on the occasion of his death a bare eighteen months after being obliged to install Hitler as German Chancellor, causing widespread alarm across Europe. That for General Douglas MacArthur concentrates disproportionately on the Korean War and the terms of his removal, at the expense of the strategic vision of his Pacific campaign and his personal courage.

In order to provide a balanced perspective when an obituary lacks historical or strategic context, appears to fall short of the credit a subject is due, omits mention of important events or glosses over a controversy with which the subject was associated, my naval colleague – Rear-Admiral Guy Liardet – and I have added our comments. Explanations have been added when the writer of the obituary assumed the reader's familiarity with the role of persons mentioned only by name or with then recent but now largely forgotten events. Occasionally, touches of light-heartedness have been added to lift an otherwise over-solemn account.

A search for a common element or thread in the lives of those included often reveals a humble or relatively humble background, although this is by no means always so; hardship in the formative years – resulting in an enduring code of self-discipline – and most significant of all, a strong sense of public service, one that eschews personal profit or honours. Former tanner General Ulysses S. Grant, Marshal Gustaf Mannerheim – second son of a minor nobleman, as a boy obliged to speak a different European language each weekday – Admiral of the Fleet Lord Fisher, born in Ceylon, his father a junior infantry officer, entered a Victorian Navy 'penniless and forlorn' as he was fond of saying and the peasant, former cavalry sergeant Georgi Zhukov are the more obvious examples. There are exceptions: Earl Beatty combined privilege with an intense ambition.

The variation in the language of the obituaries over one and a half centuries illuminates the changes in public attitude to the great and perhaps not-so-good and in the fashion of writing structure, punctuation and use of words. In the 19th and early 20th century examples, failings are not so much left to be read between the lines as approached in the manner of 'grandmother's footsteps', with the stalker seemingly losing nerve at the last moment, leaving grandmother to reach her final destination without being openly caught out. Sentences of inordinate length, spattered with commas, colons and dashes with the generous impartiality of grape-shot were commonplace in that period. Some obituary writers had apparently never received an introduction to the paragraph, resulting in difficult-to-digest long, descending barrels of words. In the latter instances only, paragraphs have been imposed but otherwise the obituaries have been taken directly from *The Times*, retaining the original punctuation and spelling.

The sequence in which to present the obituaries allowed several options. The convenience of alphabetical order lacked imagination, while a chronology based on achievement of fame or the order of birth or death threw up awkward anomalies. Consequently, those associated with some great historical event, such as the two World Wars, have been grouped together and individuals whose names will be for ever linked – Jellicoe with Beatty over the Battle of Jutland and MacArthur with Nimitz in the war in the Pacific are put in immediate succession – all, it is hoped, without losing the possibility of a serendipitous moment as the reader casually turns the page. These lives are a part of history and their study an aid to its understanding.

WELLINGTON

Strategist and inspirational commander-in-chief

15TH SEPTEMBER 1852

This extract taken from *The Times* of 15th September 1852 describes The Duke of Wellington's conduct of the war in the Iberian Peninsula. Appreciations of his command during the Battle of Waterloo in 1815 and as Prime Minister 1828–1830 appear in the concluding commentary.

ENGLAND WAS NOW at the commencement of her greatest war. The system of small expeditions and insignificant diversions, though not yet conclusively abandoned, was soon superseded by the glories of a visible contest; and in a short time it was known and felt by a great majority of the nation that on the field of the Peninsula England was fairly pitted against France, and playing her own chosen part in the European struggle. But these convictions were not prevalent enough at the outset to facilitate in any material degree the duties of the Ministry or the work of the General; on the contrary, so complicated were the embarrassments attending the prosecution of the war on the scale required, that to surmount them demanded little less wisdom or patience than the conduct of the actual campaign. In the first instance the British nation had been extravagantly excited by the successful insurrections of the Spaniards, and the events of our experimental campaign in Portugal had so inspirited the public mind that even the evacuation of that kingdom by the French was considered, as we have seen, in the light of an imperfect result. When, however, these conditions of the struggle were rapidly exchanged for the total discomfiture of the patriots, the recapture of Madrid, and the precipitate retreat of the British army, with the loss of its commander and the salvation of little but its honour, popular opinion veered quickly towards its customary point, and it was loudly proclaimed that the French Emperor was invincible by land, and that a contest with his legions on that element must inevitably prove ruinous to Britain. But the Government of the day, originally receiving its impulse from public feeling, had gradually acquired independent convictions on this mighty question, and was now prepared to maintain the interests of the nation against the clamours of the nation itself. Accordingly, at the commencement of the year 1809, when the prospects of Spanish independence were at their very gloomiest point, the British Cabinet had proposed and concluded a comprehensive treaty of alliance with the Provisional Administration of Spain; and it was now resolved that the contest in the Peninsula should be continued on a scale more effectual than before, and that the principal, instead of the secondary, part should be borne by England. Yet this decision was not taken without much hesitation and considerable resistance; and it was clear to all observant spectators that, though the opinions of the Government, rather than those of the Opposition, might preponderate in the public mind, their ascendancy was not so complete but that the first incidents of failure, loss, or difficulty, would be turned to serious account against the promoters and conductors of the war.

Nor were these misgivings, though often pretended for the purposes of faction, without a certain warrant of truth; indeed, few can read the history of this struggle without perceiving that the single point which concluded it in our favour was the genius of that great man who has just expired. It has been attempted to show that the military forces of France and England at this period were not in reality so disproportioned as they appeared to be, but we confess our own inability to discover the balance alleged. It is beyond doubt that the national spirit remained unchanged, and that the individual excellence of the British soldier was unimpeachable. Much, too, had been done in the way of organization by the measures consequent on the protracted menace of invasion, and much in the way of encouragement by the successes in Egypt and Portugal no less than the triumphs in India. But in war numerical force must needs tell with enormous effect, and on this point England's colonial requirements left her little to show against the myriads of the continent. It was calculated at the time that 60,000 British soldiers might have been made disposable for the Peninsular service, but at no period of the war was such a force ever actually collected under the standards of Wellington, while Napoleon could maintain his 300,000 warriors in Spain, without disabling the arms of the Empire on the Danube or the Rhine. We had allies, it is true, in the troops of the country; but these at first were little better than refractory recruits, requiring all the accessories of discipline, equipment, and organization; jealous of all foreigners even as friends, and not unreasonably suspicious of supporters who could always find in their ships a refuge which was denied to themselves. But above all these difficulties was that arising from the inexperience of the Government in continental warfare. Habituated to expeditions reducible to the compass of a few transports, unaccustomed to the contingencies of regular war, and harassed by a vigilant and not always conscientious Opposition, the Ministry had to consume half its strength at home; and the commander of the army, in justifying his most skilful dispositions, or procuring needful supplies for the troops under his charge, was driven to the very extremities of expostulation and remonstrance.

When, however, with these ambiguous prospects, the Government did at length resolve on the systematic prosecution of the Peninsular war, the eyes of the nation were at once instinctively turned on Sir Arthur Wellesley as the general to conduct it. Independently of the proofs he had already given of his quality at Roliça and Vimiera this enterprising and sagacious soldier stood almost alone in his confidence respecting the undertaking on hand. Arguing from the military position of Portugal, as flanking the long territory of Spain, from the natural features of the country (which he had already studied), and from the means of reinforcement and retreat securely provided by the sea, he stoutly declared his opinion that Portugal was tenable against the Fench, even if actual possessors of Spain, and that it offered ample opportunities of influencing the great result of the war. With these views he recommended that the Portuguese army should be organized at its full strength; that it should be in part taken into British pay and under the direction of British officers, and that a force of not less than 30,000 English troops should be despatched to keep this army together. So provided, he undertook the management of the war, and such were his resources, his tenacity, and his skill, that though 280,000 French soldiers were closing round Portugal as he landed at Lisbon, and though difficulties of the most arduous kind awaited him in his task, he neither flinched nor failed until he had led his little army in triumph, not only from the Tagus to the Ebro, but across the Pyrenees into France, and returned himself by Calais to England after witnessing the downfall of the French capital.

Yet, so perilous was the conjuncture when the weight of affairs was thus thrown upon his shoulders that a few weeks' more delay must have destroyed every prospect of success. Not only was Soult, as we stated, collecting himself for a swoop on the towers of Lisbon, but the Portuguese themselves were distrustful of our support, and the English troops while daily preparing for embarkation, were compelled to assume a defensive attitude against those whose cause they were maintaining. But such was the prestige already attached to Wellesley's name that his arrival in the Tagus changed every feature of the scene. No longer suspicious of our intentions, the Portuguese Government gave prompt effect to the suggestions of the English commander; levies were decreed and organized, provisions collected, depôts established, and a spirit of confidence again pervaded the country, which was unqualified on this occasion by that jealous distrust which had formerly neutralized its effects. The command in chief of the native army was intrusted to an English officer of great distinction, General Beresford, and no time was lost in once more testing the efficacy of the British arms.

Our description of the positions relatively occupied by the contending parties at this juncture will, perhaps, be remembered. Soult, having left Ney to control the north, was at Oporto with 24,000 men, preparing to cross the Douro and descend upon Lisbon, while Victor and Lapisse, with 30,000 more, were to co-operate in the attack from the contiguous provinces of Estremadura and Leon. Of the Spanish armies we need only say that they had been repeatedly routed with more or less disgrace, though Cuesta still held a certain force together in the valley of the Tagus. There were therefore two courses open to the British commander – either to repel the menaced advance of Soult by marching on Oporto or to effect a junction with Cuesta, and try the result of a demonstration upon Madrid. The latter of these plans was wisely postponed for the moment, and, preference having been decisively given to the former, the troops at once commenced their march upon the Douro. The British force under Sir Arthur Wellesley's command amounted at this time to about 20,000 men, to which about 15,000 Portuguese in a respectable state of organization were added by the exertions of Beresford. Of these about 24,000 were now led against Soult, who, though not inferior in strength, no sooner ascertained the advance of the English commander than he arranged for a retreat by detaching Loison with 6,000 men to dislodge a Portuguese post in his left rear. Sir Arthur's intention was to envelop, if possible, the French corps by pushing forward a strong force upon its left, and then intercepting its retreat towards Ney's position, while the main body assaulted Soult in his quarters at Oporto. The former of these operations he intrusted to Beresford, the latter he directed in person. On the 12th of May the troops reached the southern bank of the Douro; the waters of which, 300 yards in width, rolled between them and their adversaries. In anticipation of the attack Soult had destroyed the floating-bridge, had collected all the boats on the opposite side, and there, with his forces well in hand for action or retreat, was looking from the window of his lodging, enjoying the presumed discomfiture of his opponent. To attempt such a passage as this in face of one of the ablest marshals of France was, indeed, an audacious stroke, but it was not beyond the daring of that genius which M. Thiers describes as calculated only for the stolid operations of defensive war. Availing himself of a point where the river by a bend in its course was not easily visible from the town, Sir Arthur determined on transporting, if possible, a few troops to the northern bank, and occupying an unfinished stone building, which he perceived was capable of affording temporary cover. The means were soon supplied by the activity of Colonel Waters – an officer whose habitual audacity rendered him one of the heroes of this memorable war. Crossing in a skiff to the opposite bank, he returned with two or three boats, and in a few minutes a company of the Buffs was established in the building. Reinforcements quickly followed, but not without discovery. The alarm was given, and presently the edifice was enveloped by the eager battalions of the French. The British, however, held their ground; a passage was effected at other points during the struggle; the French, after an ineffectual resistance, were fain to abandon the city in precipitation, and Sir Arthur, after his unexampled feat of arms, sat down that evening to the dinner which had been prepared for Soult. Nor did the disasters of the French marshal terminate here, for, though the designs of the British commander had been partially frustrated by the intelligence gained by the enemy, yet the French communications were so far intercepted, that Soult only joined Ney after losses and privations little short of those which had been experienced by Sir John Moore.

This brilliant operation being effected, Sir Arthur was now at liberty to turn to the main project of the campaign – that to which, in fact, the attack upon Soult had been subsidiary – the defeat of Victor in Estremadura; and, as the force under this marshal's command was not greater than that which had been so decisively defeated at Oporto, some confidence might naturally be entertained in calculating upon the result. But at this time the various difficulties of the English commander began to disclose themselves. Though his losses had been extremely small in the recent actions, considering the importance of their results, the troops were suffering severely from sickness, at least 4,000 being in hospital, while supplies of all kinds were miserably deficient through the imperfections of the commissariat. The soldiers were nearly barefooted, their pay was largely in arrear, and the military chest was empty. In addition to this, although the real weakness of the Spanish armies was not yet fully known, it was clearly discernible that the character of their commanders would preclude any effective concert in the joint operations of the allied force. Cuesta would take no advice, and insisted on the adoption of his own schemes with such obstinacy that Sir Arthur was compelled to frame his plans accordingly. Instead, therefore, of circumventing Victor as he had intended, he advanced into Spain at the beginning of July, to effect a junction with Cuesta and feel his way towards Madrid. The armies, when united, formed a mass of 78,000 combatants, but of these 56,000 were Spanish, and for the brunt of war Sir Arthur could only reckon on his 22,000 British troops, Beresford's Portuguese having been despatched to the north of Portugal. On the other side, Victor's force had been strengthened by the succours which Joseph Bonaparte, alarmed for the safety of Madrid, had hastily concentrated at Toledo; and when the two armies at length confronted each other at Talavera it was found that 55,000 excellent French troops were arrayed against Sir Arthur and his ally, while nearly as many more were descending from the north on the line of the British communications along the valley of the Tagus. On the 28th of July the British Commander, after making the best dispositions in his power, received the attack of the French, directed by Joseph Bonaparte in person, with Victor and Jourdan at his side, and after an engagement of great severity, in which the Spaniards were virtually inactive, he remained master of the field against double his numbers, having repulsed the enemy at all points with heavy loss, and having captured several hundred prisoners and 17 pieces of cannon in this the first great pitched battle between the French and English in the Peninsula.

In this well fought field of Talavera the French had thrown, for the first time, their whole disposable force upon the British army without success, and Sir Arthur Wellesley inferred with a justifiable confidence that the relative superiority of his troops to those of the Emperor was practically decided. Jomini, the French military historian, confesses almost as much, and the opinions of Napoleon himself, as visible in his correspondence, underwent from that moment a serious change. Yet at home the people, wholly unaccustomed to the contingencies of a real war, and the Opposition, unscrupulously employing the delusions of the people, combined in decrying the victory, denouncing the successful general, and despairing of the whole enterprise. The city of London even recorded on a petition its discontent with the 'rashness, ostentation, and useless valour' of that commander whom M. Thiers depicts as endowed solely with the sluggish and phlegmatic tenacity of his countrymen; and, though Ministers succeeded in procuring an acknowledgment of the services performed, and a warrant for persisting in the effort, both they and the British General were sadly cramped in the means of action. Sir Arthur Wellesley became, indeed, 'Baron Douro, of Wellesley, and Viscount Wellington of Talavera, and of Wellington, in the county of Somerset,' but the Government was afraid to maintain his effective means even at the moderate amount for which he had stipulated, and they gave him plainly to understand that the responsibility of the war must rest upon his own shoulders. He accepted it, and, in full reliance on his own resources and the tried valour of his troops, awaited the shock which was at hand. The battle of Talavera acted on the Emperor Napoleon exactly like the battle of Vimiera. His best soldiers had failed against those led by the 'Sepoy General,' and he became seriously alarmed for his conquest of Spain. After Vimiera he rushed, at the head of his guards, through Somosierra to Madrid; and now, after Talavera, he prepared a still more redoubtable invasion. Relieved from his continental liabilities by the campaigns of Aspern and Wagram, and from nearer apprehensions by the discomfiture of our expedition to Walcheren, he poured his now disposable legions in extraordinary numbers through the passes of the Pyrenees. Nine powerful corps, mustering fully 280,000 effective men, under Marshals Victor, Ney, Soult, Mortier, and Massena, with a crowd of aspiring generals besides, represented the force definitely charged with the final subjugation of the Peninsula. To meet the shock of this stupendous array Wellington had the 20,000 troops of Talavera augmented, besides other reinforcements, by that memorable brigade which, under the name of the Light Division, became afterwards the admiration of both armies. In addition, he had Beresford's Portuguese levies, now 30,000 strong, well disciplined, and capable, as events showed, of becoming first-rate soldiers, making a total of some 55,000 disposable troops, independent of garrisons and detachments. All hopes of effectual co-operation from Spain had now vanished. Disregarding, the sage advice of Wellington, the Spanish generals had consigned themselves and their armies to inevitable destruction, and of the whole kingdom, Gibraltar and Cadiz alone had escaped the swoop of the victorious French. The Provisional Administration displayed neither resolution nor sincerity, the British forces were suffered absolutely to starve, and Wellington was unable to extort from the leaders around him the smallest assistance for that army which was the last support of Spanish freedom. It was under such circumstances, with forces full of spirit, but numerically weak, without any assurance of sympathy at home, without money or supplies on the spot, and in the face of Napoleon's best marshal. with 80,000 troops in line, and 40,000 in reserve, that Wellington entered on the campaign of 1810 – a campaign pronounced by military critics to be inferior to none in his whole career.

Withdrawing, after the victory of Talavera, from the concentrating forces of the enemy attracted by his advance, he had at first taken post on the Guadiana, until, wearied out by Spanish insincerity and perverseness, he moved his army to the Mondego, preparatory to those encounters which he foresaw the defence of Portugal must presently bring to pass. Already had he divined by his own sagacity the character and necessities of the coming campaign. Massena, as the best representative of the Emperor himself, having under his orders Ney, Regnier, and Junot, was gathering his forces on the north-eastern frontier of Portugal to fulfil his master's commands by 'sweeping the English leopard into the sea.' Against such hosts as he brought to the assault a defensive attitude was all that could be maintained, and Wellington's eye had detected the true mode of operation. He proposed to make the immediate district of Lisbon perform that service for Portugal which Portugal itself performed for the Peninsula at large, by furnishing an impregnable fastness and a secure retreat. By carrying lines of fortification from the Atlantic coast, through Torres Vedras, to the bank of the Tagus a little above Lisbon, he succeeded in constructing an artificial stronghold within which his retiring forces would be inaccessible, and from which, as opportunities invited, he might issue at will. These provisions silently and unobtrusively made, he calmly took post on the Coa, and awaited the assault. Hesitating or undecided, from some motive or other, Massena for weeks delayed the blow, till at length, after feeling the mettle of the Light Division on the Coa, he put his army in motion after the British commander, who slowly retired to his defences. Deeming, however, that a passage of arms would tend both to inspirit his own troops in what seemed like a retreat, and to teach Massena the true quality of the antagonist before him, he deliberately halted at Busaco and offered battle. Unable to refuse the challenge, the French marshal directed his bravest troops against the British position, but they were foiled with immense loss at every point of the attack, and Wellington proved, by one of his most brilliant victories, that his retreat partook neither of discomfiture nor fear. Rapidly recovering himself, however, Massena followed on his formidable foe, and was dreaming of little less than a second evacuation of Portugal, when, to his astonishment and dismay, he found himself abruptly arrested in his course by the tremendous lines of Torres Vedras.

These prodigious intrenchments comprised a triple line of fortifications one within the other, the innermost being intended to cover the embarcation of the troops in the last resort. The main strength of the works had been thrown on the second line, at which it had been intended to make the final stand, but even the outer barrier was found in effect to be so formidable as to deter the enemy from all hopes of a successful assault. Thus checked in mid career, the French marshal chafed and fumed in front of these impregnable lines, afraid to attack, yet unwilling to retire. For a whole month did he lie here inactive, tenacious of his purpose, though aware of his defeat, and eagerly watching for the first advantage which the chances of war or the mistakes of the British general might offer him. Meantime, however, while Wellington's concentrated forces were enjoying, through his sage provisions, the utmost comfort and abundance within their lines, the French army was gradually reduced to the last extremities of destitution and disease, and Massena at length broke up in despair, to commence a retreat which was never afterwards exchanged for an advance. Confident in hope and spirit, and overjoyed to see retiring before them one of those real Imperial armies which had swept the continent from the Rhine to the Vistula, the British troops issued from their works in hot pursuit, and, though the extraordinary genius of the French commander preserved his forces from what in ordinary cases would have been the ruin of a rout, yet his sufferings were so extreme and his losses so heavy that he carried to the frontier scarcely one-half of the force with which he had plunged blindly into Portugal. Following up his wary enemy with a caution which no success was permitted to disturb, Wellington presently availed himself of his position to attempt the recovery of Almeida, a fortress which, with Ciudad Rodrigo, forms the key of north-eastern Portugal, and which had been taken by Massena in his advance. Anxious to preserve this important place, the French marshal turned with his whole force upon the foe, but Wellington met him at Fuentes d'Onoro, repulsed his attempts in a sanguinary engagement, and Almeida fell.

As at this point the tide of French conquest had been actually turned, and the British army, so lightly held by Napoleon, was now manifestly chasing his eagles from the field, it might have been presumed that popularity and support would have rewarded the unexampled successes of the English general. Yet it was not so. The reverses experienced during the same period in Spain were loudly appealed to as neutralizing the triumphs in Portugal, and at no moment was there a more vehement denunciation of the whole Peninsular war. Though Cadiz resolutely held out, and Graham, indeed, on the heights of Barossa, had emulated the glories of Busaco, yet even the strong fortress of Badajoz had now fallen before the vigorous audacity of Soult; and Suchet, a rising general of extraordinary abilities, was effecting by the reduction of hitherto impregnable strongholds the complete conquest of Catalonia and Valencia. Eagerly turning these disasters to account, and inspirited by the accession of the Prince Regent to power, the Opposition in the British Parliament so pressed the Ministry, that at the very moment when Wellington, after his unrivalled strategy, was on the track of his retreating foe, he could scarcely count for common support on the Government he was serving. He was represented in England, as his letters show us, to be 'in a scrape,' and he fought with the consciousness that all his reverses would be magnified and all his successes denied. Yet he failed neither in heart nor hand. He had verified all his own assertions respecting the defensibility of Portugal. His army had become a perfect model in discipline and daring, he was driving before him 80,000 of the best troops of the Empire, and he relied on the resources of his own genius for compensating those disadvantages to which he foresaw he must be still exposed. Such was the campaign of 1810, better conceived and worse appreciated than any which we shall have to record.

As the maintenance of Portugal was subsidiary to the great object of the war, the deliverance of the Peninsula from French domination – Wellington of course proceeded, after successfully repulsing the invaders from Portuguese soil, to assume the offensive, by carrying his arms into Spain. Thus, after defeating Junot, he had been induced to try the battle of Talavera; and now, after expelling Massena, he betook himself to similar designs, with this difference that instead of operating by the valley of the Tagus against Madrid, he now moved to the valley of the Guadiana for the purpose of recovering Badajoz, a fortress, like that of Ciudad Rodrigo, so critically situated on the frontier, that with these two places in the enemy's hands, as they now were, it became hazardous either to quit Portugal or to penetrate into Spain. At this point, therefore, were now to commence the famous sieges of the Peninsula – sieges which will always reflect immortal honour on the troops engaged, and which will always attract the interest of the English reader; but which must, nevertheless, be appealed to as illustrations of the straits to which an army may be led by want of military experience in the Government at home. By this time the repeated victories of Wellington and his colleagues had raised the renown of British soldiers to at least an equality with that of Napoleon's veterans, and the incomparable efficiency, in particular, of the light division was acknowledged to be without a parallel in any European service. But in those departments of the army where excellence is less the result of intuitive ability, the forces under Wellington were still greatly surpassed by the trained legions of the Emperor. While Napoleon had devoted his whole genius to the organization of the parks and trains which attend the march of an army in the field, the British troops had only the most imperfect resources on which to rely. The Engineer corps, though admirable in quality, was so deficient in numbers that commissions were placed at the free disposal of Cambridge mathematicians. The siege trains were weak and worthless against the solid ramparts of Peninsular strongholds, the intrenching tools were so ill made that they snapped in the hands of the workmen, and the art of sapping and mining was so little known that this branch of the siege duties was carried on by draughts from the regiments of the line, imperfectly and hastily instructed for the purpose. Unhappily, these results can only be obviated by long foresight, patient training, and costly provision; it was not in the power of a single mind, however capacious, to effect an instantaneous reform, and Wellington was compelled to supply the deficiencies by the best blood of his troops.

The command of the force commissioned to recover Badajoz had been intrusted to Marshal Beresford until Lord Wellington could repair in person to the scene, and it was against Soult, who was marching rapidly from the south to the relief of the place, that the glorious but sanguinary battle of Albuera was fought on the 16th of May. Having checked the enemy by this bloody defeat Beresford resumed the duties of the siege until he was superseded by the Commander-in-Chief. But all the efforts of Wellington and his troops were vain, for the present, against this celebrated fortress; two assaults were repulsed, and the British general determined on relinquishing the attempt, and returning to the northern frontier of Portugal for more favourable opportunities of action. He had now by his extraordinary genius so far changed the character of the war, that the British, heretofore fighting with desperate tenacity for a footing at Lisbon or Cadiz, were now openly assuming the offensive, and Napoleon had been actually compelled to direct defensive preparations along the road leading through Vittoria to Bayonne – that very road which Wellington in spite of these defences was soon to traverse in triumph. Meantime fresh troops were poured over the Pyrenees into Spain, and a new plan of operations was dictated by the

Emperor himself. One powerful army in the north was to guard Castile and Leon, and watch the road by which Wellington might be expected to advance; another, under Soult, strongly reinforced, was to maintain French interests in Andalusia and menace Portugal from the south; while Marmont, who had succeeded Massena, took post with 30,000 men in the valley of the Tagus, resting on Toledo and Madrid, and prepared to concert movements with either of his colleagues as occasion might arise. To encounter these antagonists, who could rapidly concentrate 90,000 splendid troops against him, Wellington could barely bring 50,000 into the field; and though this disparity of numbers was afterwards somewhat lessened, yet it is scarcely in reason to expect that even the genius of Wellington or the value of his troops could have ultimately prevailed against such odds but for circumstances which favoured the designs of the British and rendered the contest less unequal. In the first place, the jealousies of the French marshals, when unrepressed by the Emperor's presence, were so inveterate as to disconcert the best operations, being sometimes little less suicidal than those of the Princes of India. Next, although the Spanish armies had ceased to offer regular resistance to the invaders, yet the guerilla system of warfare, aided by interminable insurrections, acted to the incessant embarrassment of the French, whose duties, perils, and fatigues were doubled by the restless activity of these daring enemies. But the most important of Wellington's advantages was that of position. With an impregnable retreat at Lisbon, with free water carriage in his rear, and with the great arteries of the Douro and the Tagus for conducting his supplies, he could operate at will from his central fastness towards the north, east, or south. If the northern provinces were temporarily disengaged from the enemy's presence, he could issue by Almeida and Salamanca upon the great line of communication between the Pyrenees and Madrid; if the valley of the Tagus were left unguarded, he could march directly upon the capital by the well-known route of Talavera; while if Soult, by any of these demonstrations, was tempted to cross the Guadiana, he could carry his arms into Andalusia by Elvas and Badajoz. Relying, too, on the excellence of his troops, he confidently accounted himself a match for any single army of the enemy, – while he was well aware, from the exhausted state of the country and the difficulties of procuring subsistence, no concentration of the French forces could be maintained for many days together. In this way, availing himself of the far superior intelligence which he enjoyed through the agency of the guerillas, and of his own exclusive facilities for commanding supplies, he succeeded in paralysing the enormous hosts of Napoleon, by constant alarms and well-directed blows, till at length when the time of action came he advanced from cantonments and drove King Joseph and all his marshals headlong across the Pyrenees.

The position taken up by Wellington when he transferred his operations from the south to the north frontier of Portugal was at Fuente Guinaldo, a locality possessing some advantageous features in the neighbourhood of Ciudad Rodrigo. His thoughts being still occupied by the means of gaining the border fortresses, he had promptly turned to Rodrigo from Badajoz, and had arranged his plans with a double prospect of success. Knowing that the place was inadequately provisioned he conceived hopes of blockading it into submission from his post at Fuente Guinaldo, since in the presence of this force no supplies could be thrown into the town unless escorted by a convoy equal to the army under his command. Either, therefore, the French marshal must abandon Rodrigo to its fate, or he must go through the difficult operation of concentrating all his forces to form the convoy required. Marmont chose the latter alternative, and uniting his army with that of Dorsenne advanced to the relief of Rodrigo with an immense train of stores and 60,000 fighting men. By this extraordinary effort not only was the place provisioned, but Wellington himself was brought into a situation of some peril, for after successfully repulsing an attempt of the French in the memorable combat of El Bodon he found himself the next day, with only 15,000 men actually at his disposal, exposed to the attack of the entire French army. Fortunately Marmont was unaware of the chance thus offered him, and while he was occupying himself in evolutions and displays Wellington collected his troops and stood once more in security on his position. This movement, however, of the French commander destroyed all hopes of reducing Rodrigo by blockade, and the British general recurred accordingly to the alternative he nad been contemplating of an assault by force.

To comprehend the difficulties of this enterprise, it must be remembered that the superiority of strength was indisputably with the French whenever they concentrated their forces, and that it was certain such concentration would be attempted, at any risk, to save such a place as Rodrigo. Wellington, therefore, had to prepare, with such secrecy as to elude the suspicions of his enemy, the enormous mass of materials required for such a siege as that he projected. As the town stood on the opposite or Spanish bank of the river Agueda, and as the approaches were commanded by the guns of the garrison, it became necessary to construct a temporary bridge. Moreover, the heavy battering train, which alone required 5,000 bullocks to draw it, had to be brought up secretly to the spot, though it was a work almost of impossibility to get a score of cattle together. But these difficulties were surmounted by the inventive genius of the British commander. Preparing his battering train at Lisbon, he shipped it at that port as if for Cadiz, transshipped it into smaller craft at sea, and then brought it up the stream of the Douro. In the next place, he succeeded, beyond the hopes of his engineers, in rendering the Douro navigable for a space of 40 miles beyond the limit previously presumed, and at length he collected the whole necessary materials in the rear of his army without any knowledge on the part of his antagonist. He was now to reap the reward of his precaution and skill. Towards the close of the year the French armies having – conformably to directions of the Emperor, framed entirely on the supposition that Wellington had no heavy artillery – been dispersed in cantonments, the British general suddenly threw his bridge across the Agueda, and besieged Ciudad Rodrigo in force. Ten days only elapsed between the investment and the storm. On the 8th of January, 1812, the Agueda was crossed, and on the 19th the British were in the city. The loss of life greatly exceeded the limit assigned to such expenditure in the scientific calculations of military engineers; but the enterprise was undertaken in the face of a superior force, which could at once have defeated it by appearing on the scene of action; and so effectually was Marmont baffled by the vigour of the British that the place had fallen before his army was collected for its relief. The repetition of such a stroke at Badajoz, which was now Wellington's aim, presented still greater difficulties, for the vigilance of the French was alarmed, the garrison of the place had been reconstituted by equal draughts from the various armies in order to interest each marshal personally in its relief, and Soult in Andalusia, like Marmont in Castile, possessed a force competent to overwhelm any covering army which Wellington could detach. Yet on the 7th of April Badajoz likewise fell, and after opening a new campaign with these famous demonstrations of his own sagacity and the courage of his troops, he prepared for a third time to advance definitely from Portugal into Spain.

Though the forces of Napoleon in the Peninsula were presently to be somewhat weakened by the requirements of the Russian war, yet at the moment when these strongholds were wrenched from their grasp the ascendancy of the Emperor was yet uncontested, and from the Niemen to the Atlantic there was literally no resistance to his universal dominion save by this army, which was clinging with invincible tenacity to the rocks of Portugal, at the western extremity of Europe. From these well defended lines, however, they were now to emerge, and while Hill, by his surprise of Gerard at Arroyo Molinos and his brilliant capture of the forts at the bridge of Almaraz, was alarming the French for the safety of Andalusia, Wellington began his march to the Pyrenees. On this occasion he was at first unimpeded. So established was the reputation of the troops and their general that Marmont retired as he advanced, and Salamanca, after four years of oppressive occupation, was evacuated before the liberating army. But the hosts into which Wellington had thus boldly plunged with 40,000 troops still numbered fully 270,000 soldiers, and though these forces were divided by distance and jealousies, Marmont had no difficulty in collecting an army numerically superior to that of his antagonist. Returning, therefore, to the contest, and hovering about the English general for the opportunity of pouncing at an advantage upon his troops, he gave promise of a decisive battle, and, after some days of elaborate manoeuvring, the opposing armies found themselves confronted, on the 22d of July, in the vicinity of Salamanica. It was a trial of strategy, but in strategy as well as vigour the French marshal was surpassed by his redoubtable adversary. Seizing with intuitive genius an occasion which Marmont offered, Wellington fell upon his army and routed it so completely that half of its effective force was destroyed in the engagement. So decisively had the blow been dealt, and so skilfully had it been directed, that, as Napoleon had long fortold of such an event, it paralysed the entire French force in Spain, and reduced it to the relative position so long maintained by the English – that of tenacious defence. The only two considerable armies now remaining were those of Suchet in the east, and Soult in the south. Suchet, on hearing of Marmont's defeat, proposed that the French should make a Portugal of their own in Catalonia, and defend themselves in its fastnesses till aid could arrive from the Pyrenees; while Soult advocated with equal warmth a retirement into Andalusia and a concentration behind the Guadiana. There was little time for deliberation, for Wellington was hot upon his prey, but as King Joseph decamped from his capital he sent orders to Soult to evacuate Andalusia; and the victorious army of the British, after thus, by a single blow, clearing half Spain of its invaders, made its triumphant entry into Madrid.

Wellington was now in possession of the capital of Spain. He had succeeded in delivering that blow which had so long been meditated, and had signalized the crowing ascendancy of his army by the total defeat of his chief opponent in open field. But his work was far from finished, and while all around was rejoicing and triumph, his forecast was anxiously revolving the imminent contingencies of the war. In one sense, indeed, the recent victory had increased rather than lessened the dangers of his position, for it had driven his adversaries by force of common peril into a temporary concert, and Wellington well knew that any such concert would reduce him again to the defensive. Marshal Soult, it was true, had evacuated Andalusia, and King Joseph Madrid; but their forces had been carried to Suchet's quarters in Valencia, where they would thus form an overpowering concentration of strength; and in like manner, though Marmont's army had been shorn of half its numbers, it was rapidly recovering itself under Clauzel by the absorption of all the detachments which had been operating in the north. Wellington saw, therefore, that he must prepare himself for a still more decisive struggle, if not for another retreat; and conceiving it most important to disembarrass his rear, he turned round upon Clauzel with the intention of crushing him before he could be fully reinforced, and thus establishing himself securely on the line of the Douro to wait the advance of King Joseph from the east.

With these views, after leaving a strong garrison at Madrid, he put his army in motion, drove Clauzel before him from Valladolid, and on the 18th of September appeared before Burgos. This place, though not a fortification of the first rank, had been recently strengthened by the orders of Napoleon, whose sagacity had divined the use to which its defences might possibly be turned. It lay in the great road to Bayonne, and was now one of the chief depôts retained by the French in the Peninsula, for the campaign had stripped them of Rodrigo, Badajoz, Madrid, Salamanca, and Seville. It became, therefore, of great importance to effect its reduction, and Wellington sat down before it with a force which, although theoretically unequal to the work, might, perhaps, from past recollections, have warranted some expectations of success. But our Peninsular sieges supply, as we have said, rather. warnings than examples. Badajoz and Rodrigo were only won by a profuse expenditure of life, and Burgos, though attacked with equal intrepidity, was not won at all. After consuming no less than five weeks before its walls Wellington gave reluctant orders for raising the siege and retiring. It was, indeed, true for the Northern army, now under the command of Souham, mustered 44,000 men in his rear, and Soult and Joseph were advancing with fully 70,000 more upon the Tagus. To oppose these forces Wellington had only 33,000 troops, Spaniards included, under his immediate command, while Hill, with the garrison of Madrid, could only muster some 20,000 to resist the advance of Soult. The British commander determined, therefore, on recalling Hill from Madrid and resuming his former position on the Agueda – a resolution which he successfully executed in the face of the difficulties around him, though the suffering and discouragement of the troops during this unwelcome retreat were extremely severe. A detailed criticism of these operations would be beyond our province. It is enough to say that the French made a successful defence, and we have no occasion to begrudge them the single achievement against the English arms which could be contributed to the historic gallery of Versailles by the whole Peninsular War.

Such, however, was in those times the incredulity or perverseness of party spirit in England that, while no successes were rated at their true import, every incomplete operation was magnified into a disaster and describe as a warning. The retreat from Burgos was cited, like the retreat from Talavera, as a proof of the mismanagement of the war, and occasion was taken in Parliament to compare even the victory of Salamanca with the battles of Marlborough to the disparagement of Wellington and his army. Nor did any great enlightenment yet prevail on the subject of military operations; for a considerable force destined to act on the eastern coast of Spain was diverted by Lord William Bentinck to Sicily at a moment when its appearance in Valencia would have disconcerted all the plans of the French, and by providing occupation for Joseph and his marshals have relieved Wellington from that concentration of his enemies before which he was compelled to retire. But neither the wilfulness of faction nor the tenacity of folly could do more than obstruct events which were now steadily in course. Even the inherent obstinacy of Spanish character had at length yielded to the visible genius of Wellington, and the whole military force of the country was now at length, in the fifth year of the war, placed under his paramount command. But these powers were little more than nominal, and, in order to derive an effective support from the favourable dispositions of the Spanish Government, the British general availed himself of the winter season to repair in person to Cadiz.

It will be remembered that when, after the battle of Talavera and the retirement of Wellington to Portugal, the French poured their accumulated legions into Andalusia, Cadiz alone had been preserved from the deluge. Since that time the troops of Soult had environed it in vain. Secured by a British garrison, strongly fortified by nature and well supplied from the sea, it was in little danger of capture; and it discharged, indeed, a substantial service by detaining a large detachment from the general operations of the war. In fact, the French could scarcely be described as besieging it, for, though they maintained their guard with unceasing vigilance, it was at so respectful a distance that the great mortar which now stands in St. James' Park was cast especially for this extraordinary length of range, and their own position was intrenched with an anxiety sufficiently indicative of their anticipation. Exempted in this manner from many of the troubles of war while cooped in the narrow space of a single town, the Spanish patriots enjoyed ample liberty of political discussion, and the fermentation of spirits was proportionate to the occasion. It was here that the affairs of the war, as regarded the Spanish critics, were regulated by a popular assembly under the control of a licentious mob; and it was here that those democratic principles of government were first promulgated which in later times so intimately affected the fortunes of the Peninsular monarchies. 'The Cortes,' wrote Wellington, 'have framed a Constitution very much on the principle that a painter paints a picture – viz., to be looked at. I have not met any person of any description who considers that Spain either is or can be governed by such a system.' From this body, however, the British commander succeeded in temporarily obtaining the power he desired, and he returned to Portugal prepared to open with invigorated spirit and confidence the campaign of 1813.

Several circumstances now combined to promise a decisive turn in the operations of the war. The initiative, once taken by Wellington, had been never lost, and although he had retrogaded from Burgos, it was without any discomfiture at the hands of the enemy. The reinforcements despatched from England, though proportioned neither to the needs of the war nor the resources of the country, were considerable, and the effective strength of the army – a term which excludes the *Spanish* contingents – reached to full 70,000 men. On the other hand, the reverses of Napoleon in the Russian campaign had not only reduced his forces in the Peninsula, but had rendered it improbable that they could be succoured on any emergency with the same promptitude as before. Above all, Wellington himself was now unfettered in his command, for if the direction in chief of the Spanish armies brought but little direct accession of strength, it at any rate relieved him from the necessity of concerting operations with generals on whose discretion he had found it impossible to rely. These considerations, coupled with an instinctive confidence in his dispositions for the campaign, and an irresistible prestige of the success which at length awaited his patience, so inspired the British commander that, on putting his troops once more in motion for Spain, he rose in his stirrups as the frontier was passed, and waving his hat exclaimed prophetically, 'Farewell Portugal!' Events soon verified the finality of this adieu, for a few short months carried the 'Sepoy General' in triumph to Paris.

At the commencement of the famous campaign of 1813 the material superiority still lay apparently with the French, for King Joseph disposed of a force little short of 200,000 men – a strength exceeding that of the army under Wellington's command – even if all denominations of troops are included in the calculation. But the British general reasonably concluded that he had by this time experienced the worst of what the enemy could do. He knew that the difficulties of subsistence, no less than the jealousies of the several commanders, would render any large or permanent concentration impossible, and he had satisfactorily measured the power of his own army against any likely to be brought into the field against him. He confidently calculated, therefore, on making an end of the war; his troops were in the highest spirits, and the lessons of the retreat from Burgos had been turned to seasonable advantage. In comparison with his previous restrictions all might now be said to be in his own hands, and the result of the change was soon made conclusively manifest.

Hitherto, as we have seen, the offensive movements of Wellington from his Portuguese stronghold had been usually directed against Madrid by one of the two great roads of Salamanca or Talavera, and the French had been studiously led to anticipate similar dispositions on the present occasion. Under such impressions they collected their main strength on the north bank of the Douro, to defend that river to the last, intending, as Wellington moved upon Salamanca, to fall on his left flank by the bridges of Toro and Zamora. The British general, however, had conceived a very different plan of operations. Availing himself of preparations carefully made and information anxiously collected, he moved the left wing of his army through a province hitherto untraversed to the north bank of the Douro, and then, after demonstrations at Salamanca, suddenly joining it with the remainder of the army, he took the French defences in reverse, and showed himself in irresistible force on the line of their communications. The effect was decisive. Constantly menaced by the British left, which was kept steadily in advance, Joseph evacuated one position after another without hazarding an engagement, blew up the castle of Burgos in the precipitancy of his retreat, and only took post at Vittoria to experience the most conclusive defeat ever sustained by the French arms since the battle of Blenheim. His entire army was routed, with inconsiderable slaughter, but with irrecoverable discomfiture. All the plunder of the Peninsula fell into the hands of the victors. Jourdan's *baton* and Joseph's travelling carriage became the trophies of the British general, and the walls of Apsley-house display to this hour in their most precious ornaments the spoils of this memorable battle. The occasion was improved as skillfully as it had been created. Pressing on his retiring foe, Wellington drove him into the recesses of the Pyrenees, and, surrounding the frontier fortresses of St. Sebastian and Pampluna, prepared to maintain the mountain passes against a renewed invasion. His anticipations of the future proved correct. Detaching what force he could spare from his own emergencies, Napoleon sent Soult again with plenary powers to retrieve the credit and fortunes of the army. Impressed with the peril of the crisis, and not disguising the abilities of the commander opposed to him, this able 'Lieutenant of the Emperor' collected his whole strength, and suddenly poured with impetuous valour through the passes of The Pyrenees on the isolated posts of his antagonist. But at Maya and Sorauven the French were once more repulsed by the vigorous determination of the British; St. Sebastian, after a sanguinary siege, was carried by storm, and on the 9th of November, four months after the battle of Vittoria, Wellington slept, for the last time during the war, on the territory of the Peninsula. The Bidassoa and the Nivelle were successfully crossed in despite of all the resistance which Soult could oppose, and the British army, which five years before, amid the menacing hosts of the enemy and the ill-boding omens of its friends, had maintained a precarious footing on the crags of Portugal, now bivouacked in uncontested triumph on the soil of France! With these strokes the mighty gains had at length been won, for though Soult clung with convulsive tenacity to every defensible point of ground, and though at Toulouse he drew such vigour from despair as suggested an equivocal claim to the honours of the combat, yet the result of the struggle was now beyond the reach of fortune. Not only was Wellington advancing in irresistible strength, but Napoleon himself had succumbed to his more immediate antagonists; and the French marshals, discovering themselves without authority or support, desisted from hostilities which had become both gratuitous and hopeless.

Thus terminated, with unexampled glory to England and its army, the great Peninsular War – a struggle commenced with ambiguous views and prosecuted with doubtful expectations, but carried to a triumphant conclusion by the extraordinary genius of a single man.

His conduct of the war in the Peninsula confirmed Field Marshal The Duke of Wellington's outstanding reputation as a strategist. Always conscious of the enemy's strengths, capabilities, dispositions and opportunities, he advanced, withdrew and fought his almost invariably less numerous army so as to place the French at a crucial disadvantage at each decisive juncture. As a leader, he understood the nature of the British soldier of the period: capricious of good discipline – other than the Foot Guards – in moments of triumph and disaster, yet tenacious in battle when led by competent officers careful with the lives of their men. He encouraged them by his words before and after battle and, his reputation established, inspired them by his imperturbable presence in the saddle at the centre of the fight.

The Waterloo campaign of 1815 provided him with scant opportunity to show his strategic skill. Having gathered his army during the Hundred Days since returning from Elba, Napoleon had the strategic initiative but was hindered by the need to win a decisive battle for political purposes. In Wellington's words, 'It was a near run thing', during which it might be said that Napoleon relied on his presence to inspire his troops, giving virtually no directions to his key subordinates during the battle, thereby losing it for want of proper attention. Wellington fought a shrewd tactical battle at Waterloo. Aware Napoleon had to win to survive politically, he placed his main body on reverse slopes, where they could not be seen or fired upon, withdrew his forward regiments in the face of Napoleon's attack and, even when the French hesitated on seeing his force previously concealed on the reverse slopes, held his decisive counter-attack until he saw Marshal Blücher arrive with his Prussians to give him numerical as well as – by then – the tactical advantage.

After the defeat of Napoleon at Waterloo, Wellington might have retired to the country estates that he was now able to afford, but he was only 46 years old and was to devote another 37 tears to the military and political service of his country. Throughout this period he vigorously opposed reform in the Army, such as improved education of the soldiery, abolition of flogging and the purchase of commissions by officers, arguing that the social order was the basis of military discipline. As Tory Prime Minister from 1828 to 1830, when Catholic Emancipation was a critical demand, he at first acceded to the view that it should not become a political issue but later, perceiving that delay would lead to increased violence if not war in Ireland, brought King George IV round to accept it. He also served as Foreign Secretary in Sir Robert Peel's first administration of 1834–1835 and again, as Minister without Portfolio, in his second from 1841-to 1846. He was the first commoner to be granted a state funeral on his death in 1852.

* * *

RAGLAN

British Commander-in-Chief in the Crimea

2 JULY 1855

THE FOREBODINGS WHICH we expressed in the last number of our journal respecting the work of death in this exhausting war had been but too surely verified, even before we uttered them, by the removal of one of the chief actors on the scene, Lord Raglan is no more. He succumbed to a dysenteric attack, after a few days' illness, on the evening of Thursday last; so that, at the very moment when more favourable reports were inducing a hope of his recovery, his days had closed, and the British Commander had been relieved from the duties and labours of his post by the fiat of an inexorable and all-subduing Power.

The career which has thus been terminated, if not one of the very highest order has, at all events, been, both eventful and brilliant; protracted beyond the ordinary term, and signalized by no common distinctions. Lord Raglan had been a soldier for half-a-century. When he departed to assume the command of our army in the East, he was verging towards three score and ten – that limit of human endurance – at the time when he was directing operations of enormous magnitude under circumstances of unexampled pressure.

Lord Fitzroy Somerset – to speak of him by the name which he bore through the chief part of his life – was a younger son of the fifth

Duke of Beaufort, and the influence of this distinguished family of course facilitated his early promotion in the profession of arms to which he devoted himself. The first three or four years of his service brought him to a captaincy, and it was at this period of his career that an incident occurred which determined the course of his military life. Sir Arthur Wellesley – who was himself at the time but a sepoy-general – had been intrusted with a command in the expedition despatched against Copenhagen. In selecting the staff to attend him on this service he included among the objects of his choice Lord Fitzroy Somerset, and the young captain of infantry was thus transferred from regimental duties to a sphere which he scarcely ever afterwards quitted until he became a commander-in-chief himself. It says much for his abilities that a general like Wellington should have shown him such constant and unvarying preference. From 1807 to 1852 – from the Danish expedition to the death of the Duke of Wellington – Fitzroy Somerset was the secretary and companion of Arthur Wellesley whenever the latter exercised military command. Throughout all the campaigns in the Peninsula, through that of the Hundred Days, and through that pacific administration at the Horse Guards which ended but a year or two ago, the duties of Wellington's Military Secretary were discharged by the soldier whose death is now announced. During all this period he was the Berthier of our Napoleon, nor can any more forcible testimony be given to the excellence of his qualifications than is contained in the practical acknowledgments of his sagacious chief.

It is not to be presumed, however, that he was debarred by these special avocations from the chances of peril and glory which war affords. When we said that his military career had been both eventful and brilliant, we were using the language not of vague panegyric, but of literal truth. He was present in most of the great actions of the last great war, and, indeed, even if he had not been distinguished by the preference of our famous Commander, his services would have been conspicuous enough to deserve a record.

He earned a cross and five clasps by his doings in the field. He was wounded at Busaco, he lost an arm at Waterloo, and, after the dreadful storm at Badajoz, it was to him, as he penetrated foremost into the place, that the intrepid Governor of the fortress surrendered his sword. Only the other day we drew a comparison, for the information of our readers, between the assault of that celebrated stronghold and the attack recently made upon the works of Sebastopol, and it is strange enough now to reflect that the very soldier who had taken so prominent a part in the one enterprise should be then, after more than 40 years' interval, conducting the other.

But though Lord Fitzroy Somerset, in common with others of Wellington's officers, achieved the honours which personal daring and professional gallantry secure, it was in the military cabinet that his peculiar distinctions were won. For very many years he was the Chief Secretary at the Horse Guards; in fact, as we have already observed, wherever Wellington held military rule it was Lord Fitzroy's pen which gave effect to his orders. In this capacity he became, as it were, personally identified with our military system, and was, perhaps, more conversant with its forms, more habituated to its technicalities, and better acquainted with its operation than any other man living. When the Great Duke died Lord Fitzroy Somerset was regarded, not unreasonably, as his nearest professional representative – as the officer who from long and intimate confidence must necessarily have become in some sense the depository of the great chief's views. Nor can there be a doubt that these presumptions were correct. As far as the ideas of one man admit of transfer to another Fitzroy Somerset should surely have imbibed those of Arthur Wellesley, and if this process did not include the communication of supreme military talent, the result cannot be matter of surprise to those who remember that generals, like poets, are not made, but born.

At Wellington's death Lord Fitzroy was raised to the peerage by the title, now so familiar, of Lord Raglan, and when, a short time afterwards, it was resolved to despatch an army to the succour of the Sultan, he received the command of it. How naturally this appointment was suggested by circumstances will appear from what we have remarked above, and if the expedition had proved what it was at first probably expected to be – if it had turned out a species of military demonstration, requiring, indeed, the discretion of a practised soldier and the conciliatory courtesy of a judicious commander, but without calling for the display of the highest military powers – if the operations had been even limited to such ordinary battles or *coups de main* as might have been achieved with ordinary prowess, the result might have been regarded with unalloyed satisfaction. Unfortunately, the army found itself in circumstances which might have tried the talents of a Caesar or a Turenne, and though Lord Raglan's unrivalled tact of manner and genuine kindness of disposition preserved the harmony of our alliance without a rupture throughout all these trials, they did not avail to extricate our troops from sufferings of the most terrible kind. Nothing, indeed could surpass the true amenity of his manners, and many of those whose duties compelled them to speak aloud upon the sufferings of the army found it impossible all the while to forget the generous courtesies of its chief.

In this respect, at any rate, he excelled, his old commander. Wellington could rarely, except by the sheer force of his victories, conciliate the affections of his soldiers, whereas Lord Raglan seems invariably to have inspired all those immediately around him with sentiments of unfeigned regard. In his own capacity in short or in his own sphere, his gifts were almost unequalled. With unchangeable suavity of manner he combined immense professional experience, untiring application, excellent habits of method, and singular powers of endurance. That these faculties are not sufficient to form a first-rate general is true but at the present moment it in more agreeable to think on what was given than to enlarge upon what was not forthcoming.

The author of this obituary makes no serious attempt to disguise the fact that Field Marshal The Lord Raglan was not the man to command the British Army in the Crimea but, given the 40 years of peace that had elapsed since Waterloo, there was no alternative senior officer available who might have made a better fist of it. Moreover, that same long period of peace had allowed the army to fall back on the non-essentials of elaborate uniforms and parades that inhibit rather than strengthen ability to fight, when that is the priority. In terms of tactics, communications, joint action by infantry, cavalry and artillery, logistics and care for the wounded, the army in the Crimea was woefully inadequate.

Experienced staff officer that he was, Raglan was not slow to appreciate this situation once it became clear that the campaign would be prolonged and face conditions of dreadful hardship in the Russian winter. Yet the courtesy brought about by his upbringing prevented him from setting out these critical shortcomings in his despatches with sufficient frankness to cause some effect. It took the correspondent of *The Times* in the Crimea, William Russell, through his reports to the newspaper, to expose the failings of competence, industry and lack of the necessary means for better organisation of the army to cause a national outcry and government reaction, albeit much of it too late to have real benefit on the ground.

In view of the publicity it received after the return of Major-General The Lord Cardigan to England in 1855, it is surprising that no mention is made in this obituary of the part played by Lord Raglan in the saga of the charge of the Light Cavalry Brigade – commanded by Cardigan – at the Battle of Balaclava on October 25, 1855. That six hundred horseman charged down a valley held on both sides by the enemy towards a concentration of field artillery at the far end was due, of course, to a misunderstanding. Raglan's order, 'Lord Raglan wishes the cavalry to advance rapidly to the front, follow the enemy and try to prevent the enemy carrying away the guns,' was clear to him on the heights overlooking the valley, from where he could see Russians about to drag away some captured artillery pieces, a sensible target for light cavalry supported by horse artillery, which he authorised. Unfortunately, on the valley floor only the Russian guns at the far end of the valley were visible. Raglan might have anticipated this and made clear to which guns he referred, but his chief of Staff, Sir Richard Airey, who wrote the message and the galloper who carried it, Captain Nolan, were chiefly responsible for what occurred.

Raglan cared deeply for the loss of any of his men and worked long into the night writing letters to the families of officers who lost their lives in the fighting or through disease.

* * *

GRANT

Master strategist of the Union Army

24 JULY 1885

ULYSSES S. GRANT, GENERAL ON the retired list of the United States Army, and eighteenth President of the United States, who died yesterday morning after a long illness at Mount M'Gregor, near Saratoga, New York, was born in the State of Ohio, at a small village called Point Pleasant, April 27, 1822. His ancestry was Scotch, and his parents were in humble circumstances. He was named Hiram Ulysses Grant, and during his infancy his parents removed to Georgetown, Ohio, where his boyhood was passed. He had but moderate opportunities for education in early life, and when 17 years of age the member of Congress from the district in which he lived appointed him a cadet at the United States' Military Academy at West Point, New York. By a blunder his name in the appointment was written 'Ulysses S. Grant,' and this name he had to adopt.

He served the usual four years' military course at the Academy without special distinction, although he showed some proficiency in mathematics, and in 1843 graduated number 21 in a class of 39. His first commission was brevet second lieutenant of infantry in the army, and he was sent to join a regiment guarding, and sometimes fighting the Indians on the Missouri frontier, where he continued for two years, when the war between the United States and Mexico began, and his regiment was sent to the Texan frontier to join the army corps then forming under the command of General Zachary Taylor, who afterwards became President of the United States. On September 30, 1845, young Grant was commissioned second lieutenant, and he entered with ardour upon the campaign of invasion of Mexico, which began the following spring. He developed fine soldierly qualities, and first saw bloodshed at the opening battle of that invasion at Palo Alto in May, 1846. He took part in all the battles of that active campaign, which included the capture of Monterey and the siege and capture of Vera Cruz.

In April, 1847, Grant was made the quartermaster of his regiment, the 4th Infantry, and he participated in the battles fought by the American troops on their victorious advance into the interior after the capture of Vera Cruz. For his gallantry at the battle of Molino del Rey, in September, he was made a first lieutenant on the field, and at Chapultepec, a few days later, he commanded his regiment, and did such good service that he was brevetted captain. Colonel Garland, who commanded the brigade to which his regiment was attached, called especial attention to Grant in his report describing the operations of the day, and said, 'I must not omit to call attention to Lieutenant Grant, 4th Infantry, who acquitted himself most nobly upon several occasions under my own observation.' The subsequent capture of the city of Mexico and the dictation of terms of peace by the victors ended the war.

When the United States troops were withdrawn, Captain Grant returned with his regiment, and was afterwards located at various posts on the Canadian border. He married in 1848, his wife being the sister of a classmate, Miss Julia T. Dent, who is still living. For several years his life was without special feature. His regiment was ordered to the Pacific coast, and he accompanied it, being for two years in California and Oregon, where he was commissioned a full captain, August 5, 1853. In July, 1854, he resigned from the army and settled at St. Louis as a farmer and real estate agent. His business talents were poor and he had ill-success, and for a few years he tried various occupations in civilian life at various places, finally going to Galena, Illinois, in 1859, to join his father, who was a tanner.

When the American civil war began, in the spring of 1861, Grant's fortunes were at a low ebb and he was ready for almost anything that promised an improvement. The opening of the civil war found the country without an army, and the entire North aflame to raise a volunteer soldiery. The few men in different parts of the States who had been officers of the regular army, and particularly those who had seen active service in Mexico and on the frontier, at once advanced to a high place in the popular estimation, as the main reliance in officering the new force. A company of volunteer troops was formed at Galena and selected Grant for its captain. He was 39 years of age when, a day or two after the firing upon Fort Sumter, he marched his company to Springfield, the capital of Illinois, and offered his services to the Governor of the State.

The next few weeks saw a remarkable uprising, military organizations forming and drilling all over the country, and being made up into regiments and sent to the seat of war. Governor Yates selected Captain Grant as his aide-de-camp and mustering officer to organize the State troops of Illinois, and this service occupied him nearly two months. He organized 21 regiments, and on June 1, 1861, was commissioned as colonel of the 21st Illinois Regiment. During the remainder of this month he drilled his regiment, and in July crossed over the Mississippi river and was ordered to guard the Hannibal and St. Joseph Railroad, which crosses the northern part of the State of Missouri, and was in constant danger of destruction by guerilla raids. Promotion was rapid in the early part of the civil war, especially for veteran officers, and August found him practically in command of all the troops in Northern Missouri, a part of the force under General John Pope, and on August 23 he was made brigadier-general of volunteers, his commission being dated May 17, 1861.

The qualities of General Grant, both as a fighter and as a strategist, were early recognized, and his remarkable military career may be regarded as beginning in August, when he was sent to take command at Cairo, the point of junction of the Ohio and Mississippi rivers. This important post was threatened by Confederates in Kentucky, and also by a disaffected element in Southern Illinois and Missouri; and a large force of Union troops was concentrated there. Grant had not been there long before he made up his mind that safety would be best assured by holding the strategic points of the Mississippi river below the Ohio river, and also those on the Kentucky shore of the latter stream. In September he seized and garrisoned Paducah, at the mouth of the Tennessee river, and Smithland, at the mouth of the Cumberland river, and thus got control of Western Kentucky. His firm, straightforward, and sententious character was shown in his proclamation to the citizens of Paducah, in which he said, 'I have nothing to do with opinions, and shall deal only with armed rebellion and its aiders and abettors.' Having thus cared for the Confederates on the eastern side of the Mississippi, in October he began a campaign against those on the western shore, where General Jeff Thompson had assembled a formidable force.

Grant sent out a detachment from Cairo to check their advance, which was done in a battle at Fredericktown, Missouri, and then, taking the field in person, he fought on November 7, with two brigades. the battle of Belmont, Missouri, his first contest of the war, having a horse shot under him. This movement effectually demoralized the Confederates in the southern counties of Missouri. Grant, who was in every sense a fighter, then began preparing for an active campaign further southward, and made Paducah his base.

Here he gathered a force of 15,000 men, and also assembled a fleet of western river steamboats, sheathed with iron as a bullet-proof protection, and known as 'tin-clads.' The enemy had strongly garrisoned posts near the boundary line between Kentucky and Tennessee, known as Forts Henry and Donelson, the former controlling the Tennessee river and the latter the Cumberland. With his troops and steamers on February 3 he left Paducah to attack them. Fort Henry was first invested, and on February 6 surrendered, its capture being mainly the work of the boats. Fort Donelson, commanded by General Buckner, made a stubborn resistance, and Grant gradually increased his force besieging it to 30,000 men, who fought a severe battle on February 15, losing 2,300 killed and wounded. The fort was shattered, and Buckner proposed that Commissioners be appointed to arrange terms of capitulation.

Grant promptly wrote in reply:- 'No terms other than an unconditional and immediate surrender can be accepted. I propose to move immediately upon your works.' On the 16th the fort, with its defenders, surrendered, being the first great victory that had crowned tho Union arms, which had been generally unfortunate in the campaign east of the Alleghanies. The victor at once became a national celebrity, and the sobriquet of 'Unconditional Surrender Grant' was given him as the popular testimony of admiration of his terse demand for the surrender that had given so much gratification. He was commissioned Major-General, dating from February 16, 1862.

Grant's subsequent career became practically the history of the war for the suppression of the rebellion. General Halleck had been placed in general command of all the troops west of the Alleghanies, and he had been collecting a force of about 40,000 men to make an expedition up the Tennessee river, under General Smith; but soon after it started General Smith died, and the command fell upon General Grant. An attack upon Corinth, in Northern Mississippi, had been contemplated, and part of the force in anticipation of this had been lying some time at Pittsburg Landing, when at daylight on April 6 General Albert Sydney Johnston, with an overwhelming Confederate army, surprised and routed them with great loss. Grant arrived on the field in the morning and re-formed the broken lines, after which heavy reinforcements, under General Buell, were ordered up, and, arriving in the night, the battle was renewed next day; and the enemy, being defeated, withdrew behind the intrenchment at Corinth.

These were the bloodiest conflicts that had taken place down to that time, the killed and wounded numbering 12,000 in each army, and Grant being slightly wounded. The Confederates were followed to Corinth, and General Halleck arriving assumed command, and began a siege of the place. This continued several weeks, the enemy subsequently evacuating their works. Halleck was called to Washington in July, after M'Clellan's disastrous retreat from before Richmond, and Grant was given command of the Department of West Tennessee. The country looked to him as the hero of the western active campaign, the defeats and disasters in Virginia having caused general dismay. He made his headquarters at Corinth, which was a post of strategic importance in Northern Mississippi, and for two months devoted his attention to suppressing guerrillas and spies and strengthening his force preparatory to a new campaign.

He took possession of Memphis, and severely disciplined a newspaper there which published treasonable articles. In September he sent out an expedition which attacked and defeated the Confederates under General Price at Iuka, gaining a substantial victory. In the meantime General Bragg, with another Confederate force, began pushing northwards towards the Ohio river through the country to the eastward, and the better to check this advance Grant removed his headquarters to Jackson, Tennessee, with part of his guns. He left about 20,000 men, under General Rosecrans, at Corinth, and the enemy, under Price and van Dorn, hoping to beat him in detail, attacked Corinth with 40,000 men on October 3. After a desperate battle, continuing two days, Rosecrans successfully repulsed them, while General Buell, with an auxiliary force, moved out to intercept Bragg, and forced the latter to give up his advance towards the Ohio river and retreat towards East Tennessee.

General Grant was thus left free for a march further southward, and in the middle of October his department was expanded to include Vicksburg, his troops being constituted the Thirteenth Army Corps. Vicksburg was the great Confederate stronghold on the Mississippi river, and the active and energetic commander soon conceived the idea of trying to capture it. This occupied his attention for several months. He first approached it from the north, but the enemy outmanoeuvred him, and inflicted serious losses in December by capturing and destroying much of his stores at Holly Springs, in Mississippi. He then determined to make his attack from the southward. When the severity of the winter had passed he crossed over with his army to the western bank of the Mississippi river, moved down, and re-crossed at a point below Vicksburg on April 30, 1863. Vicksburg was commanded by Pemberton, and, as soon as he divined Grant's movement, he sent for reinforcements, which General J. Johnston tried to give him. In a series of brilliant minor engagements, Grant during the early part of May prevented this, and on May 18 he began the siege of Vicksburg. For fully a year this 'Gibraltar' had obstructed the navigation of the Mississippi by the Union forces, whose gun-boats had control of the river both above and below, although at Port Hudson, 120 miles further down, the Confederates were building extensive fortifications. General Pemberton had about 25,000 effective men, but was deficient in small ammunition, and had only 60 days' rations. He contracted his lines, concentrating all his forces in the immediate defences of the town, and abandoned Haines's Bluff. Johnston advised Pemberton to evacuate Vicksberg if the bluff was untenable, and march to the north-east, he himself moving so as to expedite a junction of their forces. Pemberton replied that it was impossible to withdraw, and that he had decided to hold Vicksburg as long as possible, conceiving it to be the most important point in the Confederacy.

Grant no sooner began the siege than he tried on May 19 to carry the place by a *coup de main*, but he was repulsed, and then made a regular investiture. His force was soon increased to 70,000 men, and he maintained the siege until July 3, when Pemberton sent him a note stating that he was fully able to hold his defensive position for an indefinite period, but proposing that Commissioners should be named to arrange a capitulation. Grant met Pemberton personally in the afternoon to arrange the terms, and the actual surrender followed next morning, July 4, 1863. There were 27,000 prisoners paroled altogether, of whom about 15,000 were fit for duty, the others being sick or wounded. From the time he crossed the Mississippi, Grant had lost 8,567 killed and wounded, half of them in the immediate siege. The Confederate loss during the same period was about 10,000. This victory caused a great sensation throughout the country, which had been depressed by repeated defeats in Virginia and by Lee's march northward into Pennsylvania until checked by General Meade at Gettysburg; and Grant from that time became the great hero of the war. He had been a Major-General of Volunteers and was promoted to Major-General in the Regular Army, the highest rank he could attain as the law then existed.

General Grant was in October given the supreme command west of the mountains, his territory being called the 'Military Division of the Mississippi,' with departments under him, commanded respectively by Generals Sherman, Thomas, Burnside, and Hooker. After Vicksburg fell, his troops had driven Johnston's forces eastward, and they with Bragg's troops, which had gone into East Tennessee, began threatening Chattanooga. This picturesque town nestles among the Alleghany Mountains near the southern border of Tennessee, and Bragg occupied formidable positions nearby on Missionary Ridge and Lookout Mountain. Grant, in November, concentrated troops for the defence of Chattanooga, and on the 24th and 25th Bragg's strongholds were carried by assault, and he abandoned that portion of the mountain district, retreating into Georgia. The Union troops pursued him some distance and then turned to relieve Burnside at Knoxville in East Tennessee, whom the Confederates had besieged, General Longstreet commanding them. These were the last active movements in the west which General Grant personally directed.

The successive failures in the east, in the campaigns made in Virginia by various generals for the capture of the Confederate capital at

Richmond, caused a popular demand that the young commander who had so distinguished himself in the west should be placed in charge of what was regarded as the chief theatre of the war. When Congress convened in December, 1863, the first measure passed was a resolution ordering a gold medal to be struck for Grant, and returning thanks to him and his army. His name was on every tongue, and preparatory to giving him control of all the armies, Congress in March, 1804, created the rank of Lieutenant-General of the Army, and President Lincoln immediately appointed him. When his appointment was announced he at once went to Washington, arriving March 9, and received his commission.

He was given entire control as Commander-in-Chief of all the campaigns against the Confederacy. Never before during the war had any general in the field commanded all the Union armies. All previous generals in Virginia had been trammelled and thwarted by the powers in Washington. This political interference was thenceforward to cease; and it did cease in reality, Grant during the remaining year of the war being an autocrat whose will was the supreme law in military affairs. He returned to the west, and at Nashville, March 17, issued his order taking command, announcing that his headquarters would be in the field and with the 'Army of the Potomac.' He had nearly 700,000 men in active service under him.

At Nashville, in connexion with General Sherman, he planned two campaigns, east and west of the mountains. Sherman was to operate against Johnston's forces at Atlanta, Georgia; and Meade was to move against Lee at Richmond, the latter movement being supervised by General Grant in person. Returning to the east he got his troops in readiness to advance as soon as the opening of spring permitted. The movement against Richmond began May 3, 1864, Grant crossing the Rapidan river with the Army of the Potomac, and a few days later being reinforced by Burnside's troops, who were brought from the west, so that he had a force of nearly 150,000 men. His object was to turn Lee's right flank by pushing through the desolate region known as the 'Wilderness,' and thus to place the Union army between Lee's forces and Richmond. This quickly resulted in a bloody contest, for Lee on the 4th of May learned Grant's movement, immediately took the offensive, and marching eastward into the 'Wilderness' struck Grant's advancing forces on the flank. The region was a difficult one to move in, being filled with scrub timber and in many places an impenetrable jungle. The battle began on the 5th and, each side being reinforced, was continued on the 6th.

The fighting was almost exclusively with musketry, the nature of the ground making artillery useless. Grant's numbers were at all points superior to Lee's, and though the two days' contest was generally regarded as a drawn battle Grant had secured the roads by which Lee was to pass out of the 'Wilderness' towards the southward, and after a day's rest was able to resume the march towards Richmond. On the night of May 7 the Union army was put in motion towards Spottsylvania, a few miles to the south-eastward, moving in two columns. The advance was slow and difficult, being obstructed at all points by felled trees and constant skirmishes on front and flanks. Lee had evidently anticipated Grant's movement, for he was pushing forward by a parallel road, and his advance had reached and was intrenched at Spottsylvania before Grant's advance came up. Lee got his entire force in position there during the 8th, facing north and east. Both armies strengthened their positions on the 9th, and on the 10th Grant made a succession of attacks, losing about 5,000 men and being repulsed, the enemy having comparatively but small loss.

The battle was renewed on the 11th and again on the 12th, when, before daybreak, General Hancock. stormed and captured Lee's outer works with 4,000 prisoners. Lee, from his inner citadel, made five unsuccessful attempts to recapture this work. Grant in the meantime made repeated attacks upon Lee's flanks, which were repulsed, and finding the enemy's position practically unassailable, Grant during the next week gradually developed his left flank by withdrawing troops from the right under cover of the remainder of the army. By this movement Grant hoped to outflank the Confederates, but Lee discovered the process and made similar movements to meet it, moving at the same time on a somewhat shorter line. When, on May 23, the Union army arrived at the northern bank of the North Anna river the enemy were found posted on the southern bank. Hancock on the left, and Warren leading the Union right, crossed over, the latter being furiously assailed. Warren repulsed the assault with a loss of about 350, and took 1,000 prisoners. The Union flanks held their positions, but Lee prevented their centre from crossing, and Grant, seeing the danger of his position, determined to abandon it. On the night of May 26 the Union army was withdrawn and started by a wide circuit eastward and then southward towards the Pamunkey river, one of the affluents of the York river, Lee again making a similar movement by a shorter line. This series of 'Battles of the Wilderness,' continuing about three weeks, were the bloodiest of the war, Grant's losses being 41,398, while no trustworthy report was made of Lee's losses, which estimates place at 20,000.

It was during this series of battles that Grant sent the despatch to the Government containing the famous sentence: 'I propose to fight it out on this line if it takes all summer.' After crossing the Pamunkey, Grant's troops advanced to Cold Harbor, a few miles northward from Richmond, on the edge of the swamps of the Chickahominy region, where Lee's forces were found intrenched in an impregnable position. Grant had got his army reinforced up to 150,000 men, while Lee had about 50,000. Grant determined to advance against the intrenchments, and in the grey, rainy dawn of June 3 the rush was made, the Union troops being, however, everywhere repulsed with heavy losses. A desultory contest was kept up during the day, but the attack was not renewed, Grant having lost 7,000 killed and wounded, the Confederate loss being less than half that number. For nearly two weeks the armies lay in position watching each other, when Grant made up his mind to abandon this plan of attack and to adopt a new one, by which Richmond, like Vicksburg, might be outflanked and taken from the rear.

These successive contests, which aggregated Union losses of about 55,000 men and Confederate losses of 32,000, showed the character of Grant's military tactics. He knew that in the tottering condition of the Confederacy it must ultimately succumb to starvation and the waste of battle, and so long as men enough were given him to throw upon the enemy he would keep it up. The Government gave him everything he asked, and sent constant reinforcements to Virginia, which was then the principal theatre of the war. To prevent the Confederates from getting reinforcements, other detachments of Union troops were being advanced in the Shenandoah Valley and along the Kanawha, in West Virginia, while the Confederates west of the mountains were fully engaged in caring for Sherman's advance to Atlanta. Grant had also hoped that General Butler, south of the James, might have captured Petersburg, so as to invest Richmond from the southern side. Butler had been foiled, however, and, crossing the James river in June, Grant personally began the siege of Petersburg.

The crossing of the James river, which was the beginning of the operations against Petersburg as directed by General Grant personally, was made upon June 12, 1864, and the army encamped at City Point, the junction of the Appomattox river with the James. Butler's troops were at Bermuda Hundred, a peninsula formed by a bend of the James above City Point. Lee withdrew his forces into Richmond and took new positions east and south of the city, his force, with the men he found at Richmond, being about 70,000, while Grant had 100,000. Grant immediately began attacks upon the enemy's position. On June 15 a corps of Butler's forces made an unsuccessful assault, and on the 16th a combined attack was made by Hancock's, Burnside's, and Butler's troops, which was repulsed with great slaughter. These preliminary engagements, Grant reported, had only the result that 'the enemy was merely forced into an interior position,' yet they cost the Union army the loss of 10,203 men. Grant then proceeded to invest Petersburg, which is about six miles south-west up the Appomattox from City Point, and the siege began on the 19th of June.

Lee, leaving about half his force at Richmond, went with the remainder to defend Petersburg, establishing strong lines around the town east, south, and south-west. Grant approached from the east, and on the 21st made a movement to seize the Weldon Railroad, which runs southward from the town. This attack, was repulsed, but Grant's cavalry, about 8,000 strong, made an extensive raid through the country south and south-west of Petersburg for many miles, tearing up this and other railroads, so that Lee was reduced to sore straits for want of supplies. Thus matters rested during July, when Grant made a new plan. He sent a force across the James and up the eastern bank to a place called Deep Bottom, near Richmond, to threaten an attack, in the hope that Lee would withdraw part of his force from Petersburg to meet this new movement. In the meantime a mine had been dug under a fort occupying an advanced position in the Confederate defensive lines, directly behind which was Cemetery hill, the most commanding ground in Petersburg.

This mine was a gallery 520ft. long, terminating in lateral branches 40ft. long in each direction, and it was charged with 8,000 pounds of powder. General Burnside had it in charge, and if the Confederate works were blown up by the explosion other troops were disposed so as to quickly reinforce him. The Deep Bottom expedition having reached its post, the mine was exploded on July 30 about daybreak, blowing up the fort and its garrison of about 500 Confederates, belonging to a South Carolina Regiment. The explosion made a crater about 30ft. deep, 200ft. long, and 60ft. wide, and the Confederates fled from their works on either hand. The sides of the crater were rough and steep, so that they could not be mounted in military order. A single Union regiment managed to climb up, and made for Cemetery Hill; but, others not following, they faltered and finally fell back into the crater. The Confederates quickly rallied, poured in shells, and planted guns to command the approach. Four hours were spent in this ineffectual effort, and then the Union forces were withdrawn, leaving 1,900, prisoners, their entire loss being about 4,000, while the Confederates lost about 1,000.

This result was disheartening, and a long period of comparative inaction followed, Grant making movements to get possession of the railways south and west of Petersburg, which Lee steadily foiled. Butler tried to cut the Dutch Gap Canal across a narrow neck of land to divert the James, but this was also unsuccessful. Nothing of interest occurred in the autumn or winter, the two armies watching each other, although movements elsewhere were gradually enclosing the Confederacy in narrower limits, until, when spring opened and Sherman's march from Atlanta had come out to the sea, it was practically reduced to southern Virginia and northern North Carolina. Lee and Johnston, all told, then had less than 100,000 rebels, while Grant, Sherman, and others were pressing them in all directions. Petersburg and Richmond were successfully held, but their supplies were endangered, and at times cut off.

Lee in March planned to abandon Petersburg and Richmond, and to unite with Johnston, who was on the Carolina border. Lee to facilitate his withdrawal threw an offensive movement against the Union right. On the morning of March 25, squads of Confederates announcing themselves as deserters approached the Union lines, and this being a common occurrence no suspicion was aroused. Suddenly, however, these squads overpowered the pickets, and a Confederate column 5,000 strong rushed out and seized a fort. In a few minutes the Union guns from all sides began playing upon the fort, and it was speedily retaken, less than half the Confederates being able to regain their lines. The contest extended, and the Confederates lost altogether 4,500 and the Union army 2,000. Grant then began a movement westward to turn the Confederate right, the troops being in full motion by March 29. The moving columns were about 50,000, including 10,000 cavalry under Sheridan. Lee had an intrenched line at Petersburg about 10 miles long, and leaving 10,000 men to defend it, collected all his remaining force, not 20,000 men, to oppose this flanking movement.

A furious storm next day made the roads almost impassable, but on the 31st the two forces met at Five Forks, about eight miles south-west of Petersburg, and had a severe conflict. Lee gained some advantage, and on April the 1st drove the Union advance about three miles southward to Dinwiddie. Reinforcements coming up, Sheridan, who was in command, forced the Confederates back to Five Forks and then beyond it, routing them at Hatcher's Run and the cavalry pursuing them for miles. This broke up the two corps of Lee's army upon which he had placed the most reliance, the Confederates losing 6,000 prisoners, besides large numbers killed and wounded. Simultaneously with this movement a heavy bombardment was made upon the works at Petersburg and a general assault was ordered on April 2, the outposts being captured. Lee that night abandoned both Petersburg and Richmond. The Confederates still had 40,000 men, but they were widely scattered and the only forlorn hope was in concentration. Before daybreak on April 3 the Confederates had all withdrawn from Petersburg, crossed the Appomattox and burnt the bridges behind them, at the same time blowing up the magazines on the whole line to Richmond. The Union troops immediately advanced, and were met by the Mayor of Petersburg, who surrendered the city. To unite their forces, Lee moved north-west from Petersburg and Longstreet south-west from Richmond, and they came together at Chesterfield. Thence they moved westward, Grant pursuing on parallel roads to the southward. Lee had ordered a provision train to meet him at Amelia, but through mistake of orders it went on to Richmond without unloading, so that when he arrived he found no rations for the famishing troops and had to halt and send out foraging parties. This delay was fatal, for Grant's troops came up and surrounded him, so that further resistance was useless. On April 8 Grant sent Lee a message to the effect that there was no hope of any further successful resistance and demanding surrender in order to avoid further shedding of blood.

Lee replied, asking the terms upon which a surrender would be received. Grant named as the sole condition that 'the men and officers surrendered shall be disqualified from taking up arms again against the Government of the United States until properly discharged.' Lee, on the 9th, met Grant near Appomattox Court-house, and the terms of surrender were agreed upon. The list of paroled prisoners was 27,805, but of these barely one third had any arms, there being only 10,000 muskets and 30 cannon found. All the rest of Lee's army had been killed or captured, or had deserted during the operations around Richmond and Petersburg.

Thus ended the great civil war, and Grant became a hero of world-wide renown.

Grant was himself partly responsible for confusion over his names. Christened Hiram Ulysses, he wished to avoid being nick-named 'Hug' and so reversed the sequence on his application for West Point, but the congressman through whom the application passed mistakenly entered him as Ulysses Simpson. A fine horseman since boyhood, it was his hope to join the cavalry, in which he would doubtless have done well, as his understanding of manoeuvre and pursuit during the Civil War was to demonstrate, but lack of a cavalry vacancy resulted in him being commissioned into the 4th Infantry. His reason for leaving the army in 1854 is attributed to a rebuke for heavy drinking, through boredom, while in command of a small isolated fort on the California frontier.

There are indications of some intellectual laziness, not only in his failed business ventures but also in his conduct of set-piece battles where much careful thought is required. In fluid warfare, opportunities to exploit the enemy's situation suggest themselves, so long as the commander has a working grasp of the ground, but frontal attacks such as he made at Corinth in 1862 and against Lee in Richmond in 1864 brought only a terrible 'butcher's bill' of casualties to the Union Army. His slow and deliberate speech was consistent with his real military strength as a strategist, as was his lack of outward concern for the losses his mistakes incurred, a concern usually associated with the thinking of a tactician.

The American Civil War was the first fought in a nation-wide industrial context and Grant appreciated that from well before he became commander-in-chief of the Union armies. His strategies were designed to destroy the Confederate capability and will to continue the struggle, although the idea of Sherman's 'March to the Sea' devastating the wheatlands of Georgia, came from Sherman. Grant was initially opposed to the plan and even as complete success was in prospect, urged Sherman to caution. A straight comparison between Grant and his Confederate opponent Robert E. Lee is complicated by their different troop strengths and politico-strategic objectives. Given an even contest, Lee would probably have won.

LEE

American soldier: 'one of the noblest soldiers who have ever drawn
a sword in a cause which they believed just.'

12 OCTOBER 1870

EVEN AMID THE turmoil of the great European struggle the intelligence from America announcing that General Robert E. Lee is dead will bs received with deep sorrow by many in this country, as well as by his followers and fellow-soldiers in America. It is but a few years since Robert Lee ranked among the great men of the present Time. He was the able soldier of the Southern Confederacy, the bulwark of her northern frontier, the obstacle to the advance of the Federal armies and the leader who twice threatened by the capture of Washington, to turn the tide of success, and to accomplish a revolution which would have changed the destiny of the United States.

Six years passed by, and then we heard that he was dying at an obscure town in Virginia where since the collapse of the Confederacy, he had seen acting as a schoolmaster. When at the head of the last 8,000 of his valiant army – the remnants which battle, sickness, and famine had left him – he delivered up his sword to General Grant at Appomattox Court House, his public career ended; he passed away from men's thoughts; and few in Europe cared to inquire the fate of the General whose exploits had aroused the wonder of neutrals and belligerents, and whose noble character had excited the admiration of even the most bitter of his political enemies. If, however, success is not always to be accounted as the sole foundation of renown, General Lee's life and career deserve to he held in reverence by all who admire the talents of a General and the noblest qualities of a soldier.

His family were well known in Virginia. Descended from the Cavaliers who first colonized that State, they had produced more than one man who fought with distinction for their country. They were allied by marriage to Washington, and previous to the present war were possessed of much wealth; General, then Colonel Robert Lee residing, when not employed with his regiment, at Arlington Heights, one of the most beautiful places in the neighbourhood of Washington.

When the civil war first broke out he was a colonel in the United

States' army, who had served with distinction in Mexico, and was recounted among the best of the American officers. To him, as to others, the difficult choice presented itself whether to take the side of his State, which had joined in the secession of the South, or to support the Central Government. It is said that Lee debated the matter with General Scott, then commander-in-chief, that both agreed that their first duty lay with their State, but that the former only put in practice what each held in theory. It was not until the second year of the war that Lee came prominently forward, when, at the indecisive battle of Fairoaks, in front of Richmond, General Johnston having been wounded, he took command of the army; and subsequently drove McClennan, with great loss, to the banks of the James river. From that time he became the recognized leader of the Confederate army of Virginia.

He repulsed wave after wave of invasion, army after army being hurled against him only to be thrown back beaten and in disorder. The Government at Washington were kept in constant alarm by the near vicinity of his troops, and witnessed more than once the entry into their entrenchments of a defeated and disorganized rabble which a few days previous had left there a confident host. Twice he entered the Northern States at the head of a successful army, and twice indecisive battles alone preserved from destruction the Confederate Government and turned the fortune of the war.

He impressed his character on those who acted under him. Ambition for him had no charms; duty alone was his guide. His simplicity of life checked luxury and display among his officers, while his disregard of hardships silenced the murmurs of his harassed soldiery. By the troops he was loved as a father as well as admired as a general; and his deeply religious character impressed itself on all who were brought in contact with him and made itself felt through the ranks of the Virginian army. It is said. that during four years of war he never slept in a house, but in winter and summer shared the hardships of his soldiers. Such was the man who in mature age, at a period of life when few generals have acquired renown, fought against overwhelming odds for the cause which he believed just. He saw many of his bravest generals and dearest friends fall around him, but although constantly exposed to fire, escaped without a wound.

The battles which prolonged and finally decided the issue of the contest are now little more than names. Atnietam, Fredericksburg, Chancellorsville and Gettysburg are forgotten in Europe by all excepting those who study recent wars as lessons for the future and would collect from the deeds of other armies experience which they may apply to their own. To them the boldness of Lee's tactics at Chancellorsville will ever be a subject of admiration; while even those who least sympathize with his cause will feel for the General who saw the repulse of Long-street's charge at Gettysburg, and beheld the failure of an attempt to convert a defensive war into one of attack, together with the consequent abandonment of the bold stroke which he had hoped would terminate the contest.

Quietly he rallied the broken troops; taking all the blame on himself, he encouraged the officers dispirited by the reverse, and in person formed up the scattered detachments. Again, when fortune had turned against the Confederacy, when overwhelming forces from all sides pressed back her defenders, Lee for a year held his ground with a constantly diminishing army, fighting battle after battle in the forests and swamps around Richmond. No reverses seemed to dispirit him, no misfortune appeared to ruffle his calm, brave temperament. Only at last, when he saw the remnants of his noble army about to be ridden down by Sheridan's cavalry, when 8,000 men, half-starved and broken with fatigue, were surrounded by the vast net which Grant and Sherman had spread around them, did he yield: his fortitude for the moment gave way: he took a last farewell of his soldiers. and, giving himself up as a prisoner retired a ruined man, into private life, gaining his bread by the hard and uncongenial work of governing Lexington College.

When political animosity has calmed down and when Americans can look back on those years of war with feelings unbiased by party strife, then will General Lee's character be appreciated by all his countryman as it now by a part, and his name will be honoured as one of the noblest soldiers who have ever drawn a sword in a cause which they believed just, and at the sacrifice of all personal considerations have fought manfully . Even amid the excitement of the terrible war now raging in Europe, some may still care to carry their thoughts back to the career of the great and good man who now lies dead in Virginia, and to turn a retrospective glance over the scenes in which a short time ago he bore so prominent a part.

In a letter to *The Times*, Lieutenant-Colonel Arthur Fremantle of the Coldstream Guards suggested that Lee was 'the greatest soldier America has produced'. The present obituary, printed after Fremantle's letter on 15 October 1870, three days after Lee's death, appeared as the Franco-Prussian War was drawing to a bloody close and as the Communards were defeated in Paris.

Arguably, Lee was as skilled a strategist as his Union adversary Ulysses S. Grant, whose army and that of Sheridan he successfully manoeuvred against until far outnumbered and, with his own force critically depleted, he was forced to surrender. He had far greater regard for his men than had Grant and, by his tactics, spared them the scale of battle casualties that appeared of less concern to Grant.

* * *

GARIBALDI

Italian Patriot and Soldier of Fortune

3 AND 5 JUNE 1882

GARIBALDI IS DEAD. The spell attached to his name has partly been broken by the prolongation of his life beyond its sphere of possible usefulness; but the worth of his character will bear inspection, even when sober criticism had done its utmost to strip it of all the glitter with which popular enthusiasm had invested it.

In the first place, this hero of a hundred fights has been made almost too much of as a warrior, but justice has hardly, perhaps, been done to his abilities as a leader. Garibaldi was no strategist. He knew little and cared less about organisation, equipment, or discipline; never looked to means of transport or commissariat, but simply marched at the head of a few officers, hardly turning to see how the troops would follow. He never had a competent head of the staff. He thought he had found one in his friend Anzani, at Montevideo, a man of whose abilities and actual genius Garibaldi had the most transcendent ideas, who had often brought order in the Legion where before his arrival all was confusion, and of whom Garibaldi said that 'had such a genius as Anzani's conducted the Lombard campaign of 1848 or commanded at the battle of

43

Novara or the siege of Rome the stranger would from that moment have ceased to tread with impunity the bones of Italy's bravest combatants.' But Anzani died, as we have seen, on his landing at Genoa in 1848, and Garibaldi was left only with valiant and heroic, but inexperienced and incapable men.

The army which conquered Naples in 1860 trailed up a long straggling line from Reggio to Salerno, picking up the arms with which the fugitive Neapolitans strewed the fields, living as they could on the grapes and fruits providentially at that season ripening everywhere on the roadside. At Varese and Como, in the previous year, the Italian guerrillero astonished Urban by appearing before him where the Austrian was sure Garibaldi could not be, and where, indeed, the Volunteer Chief was almost alone; 'his 2,000 volunteers,' as he said, 'straggling behind, while his adversary had 14,000 men at hand.' What was mere rash confidence of the Italian struck the Austrian as deep stratagem, and he was put to flight by a mere trick of audacity analogous to that which had served the purposes of Bonaparte and compelled the Austrian commanders of his own time to surrender, 62 years before, in those same North Italian districts and only a little more to the east.

Garibaldi, however, was a tactician. and would have creditably handled an army had a ready-made one, well-armed and trained and led, been placed under his orders on the eve of battle. He had the sure glance, the quick resolution, the prompt resource of that *Enfant gâté de la victoire*, his townsman Massena. As the Lombard volunteer, Emilio Dandolo, quoted by Dumas, graphically paints his chief – 'On the approach of a foe, Garibaldi would ride up to a culminating point in the landscape, survey the ground for hours with the spy-glass in brooding silence, and come down with a swoop on the enemy, acting upon some well-contrived combination of movements by which advantage had been taken of all circumstances in his favour.'

And he possessed, besides in a supreme degree that glamour which enslaved his volunteers' minds and hearts to his will. Though there was no order or discipline in his army, there was always the most blind and passsive obedience wherever he was. Even with his crew on board his privateer sloop at Rio Grande he tells us he had ordered the life, honour, and property of the passengers of a vessel he had captured to be respected – 'I was almost saying under the penalty of death,' he adds, 'but it would have been wrong to say that for nobody ever disputed my orders. There was never anybody to be punished.' A great craven must he be who would not fire up at sight of that calm and secure lion-face.

Garibaldi had faith in himself. He looked upon that handful of 'the Thousand,' who had been a match for 60,000 Neapolitans, as equally fit to cope with all the hosts of France and Austria, singly or conjointly. To make anything possible he had only to will it, to order it, and he never failed to find men ready and willing to attempt it. He called out in one instance in Rome for '40 volunteers wanted for an operation in which half of them would be sure to be killed and the other half mortally wounded.' 'The whole battalion,' he adds 'rushed forward to offer themselves, and we had to draw lots.' On another occasion, also at Rome, he 'called all well-disposed men to follow him.' 'Officers and soldiers instantly sprang up as if the ground had brought them forth.' At the close of the siege, when, upon the surrender being voted by the Assembly, he had made up his mind to depart, he put forth this singular order of the day – 'Whoever chooses to follow me will be received among my own men. All I ask of them is a heart full of love for our country. They will have no pay, no rest. They will get bread and water when chance may supply them. Whoever likes not this may remain behind. Once out of the gates of Rome every step will be one step nearer to death.' Four thousand infantry and 500 horsemen, two-thirds of what was left of the defenders of Rome, accepted these conditions.

And it was in peace as in war. In leisure hours in his wanderings, and more in his solitude at Caprera, Garibaldi read a good deal, and accumulated an ill-digested mass of knowledge, of which the utopian mysticisms of Mazzini and the paradoxical vagaries of Victor Hugo constituted the chief ingredients. But, in politics as in arms, his mind lacked the basis of a rudimental education. He rushed to conclusions without troubling his head about arguments. His crude notions of Democracy, of Communism, of Cosmopolitanism, of Positivism, were jumbled together in his brain and jostled one another in hopeless confusion, involving him in unconscious contradiction notwithstanding all his efforts to maintain a character for consistency.

In sober moments he seemed to acknowledge his intellectual deficiencies, his imperfect education, the facility with which he allowed his own fancy or the advice of dangerous friends to run away with his better judgment; but presently he would lay aside all diffidence, harangue, indite letters, preside at meetings, address multitudes, talk with the greatest boldness about what he least understood, and put his friends to the blush by his emphatic, trenchant, absolute tone, by his wild theories and sweeping assertions, as he did at Geneva at one of the Peace Society Congresses, when, before a bigoted Calvinistic audience, he settled the question whether St. Peter ever had or had not been in Rome – 'a futile question,' he said, 'for I can tell you no such person as Peter has ever existed.'

His sword was a fine cavalry blade, forged in England and the gift of English friends. The sabre did good slashing work at need, and at Milazzo, in Sicily, it bore him out safely from a knot of Neopolitan troopers who caught him by surprise and fancied they had him at their discretion. Garibaldi carried no other weapons, though the officers in his suite had pistols and daggers at their belts; and his negro groom, by name Aguyar, who for a long time followed him as his shadow, like Napoleon's Mameluke, and was shot dead by his side at Rome, was armed with a long lance with a crimson pennon, used as his chief's banner. His staff officers were a numerous, quaint, and motley crew, men of all ages and conditions, mostly devoted personal friends – not all of them available for personal strength or technical knowledge but all to be relied upon for their readiness to die with or for him. Some of the most distinguished, like Nino Bixio, Medici, Sirtori, Cosenz, &c, had all the headlong bravery of their General – more than that no man could boast – and were his superiors in intelligence and in professional experience, ably conducting as his lieutenants field operations which he was, from some cause or other, unable to attend.

The veterans he brought with him from Montevideo, a Genoese battalion whom his friend Augusto Vecchi helped to enlist, and the Lombard Legion, under Manara, were all men of tried valour, well trained to the use of the rifle, inured to hardships and privations, and they constituted the nucleus of the Garibaldian force throughout its campaigns. The remainder was a shapeless mass of raw recruits from all parts of Italy, joining or leaving the band almost at their pleasure – mere boys from the Universities, youths of noble and rich family, lean artisans from the towns, stout peasants and labourers from the country, adventurers of indifferent character, deserters from the army, and the like, all marching in loose companies, like Falstaff's recruits, under improvised officers and non-commissioned officers; but all, or most of them, entirely disinterested about pay or promotion, putting up with long fasts and heavy marches, only asking to be brought face to face with the enemy, and when under the immediate influence of Garibaldi himself or of his trusty friends seldom guilty of soldierly excesses or of any breach of discipline. The effect the presence of the hero had among them was surprising. A word addressed to them in his clear, ringing, silver voice electrified even the dullest. An order coming from him was never questioned, never disregarded. No one waited for a second bidding or an explanation. 'Your business is not to inquire how you are to storm that position. You must only go and do it.' And it was done.

This extract from the obituary of Garibaldi published in *The Times* of 3rd and 5th June 1882 deals with his life as a military commander. He had two great qualities that every soldier yearns to see in his leader: he knew what to do in every situation that confronted him – and he won.

* * *

SITTING BULL

Chief of the Prairie Sioux

17 DECEMBER 1890

SITTING BULL IS DEAD. He has fallen as dramatically as he has lived, in conflict with the hated whites, or their Indian mercenaries. Were the Red Indians a people possessed of vitality sufficient to throw off fresh legends, the old chief might figure in ages to come as the hero of some wild saga, credited with stupendous victories against the advancing hordes of white men, and with a miraculous translation to the happy hunting grounds of the Great Spirit. In truth Sitting Bull approaches nearer to the ideal of a national hero than any Indian of recent times. For all we know, he may have worn trousers and a stove- pipe hat. These are weaknesses from which the greatest modern braves are not exempt.

There would be, moreover, according to civilized ideas, some difficulty in allowing the quality of heroism to a chief who dissects the writhing bodies of his captives in war, drives splinters under their finger-nails, and lights slow fires upon their stomachs. But we must not expect to find the Red Indian – of all savages the most unteachable and the most impervious to civilized influences – endowed with Christian virtues. It would even be unfair to compare Sitting Bull and his athletic son, who headed his father's rescue and shared his father's fate, with Tecumseh and Uncas, or any other of Fenimore Cooper's redskin heroes. There is a tolerably general opinion among those who have studied the Indian character in later days that Tecumseh and Uncas were impossible Indians. With all his craftiness and vindictiveness – faults that are virtues in savage codes of morality – Sitting Bull has been a very picturesque figure in American history for twenty years past as one of the last champions of a decaying race. His career will some day fill a page of romance.

The romancer, let us hope, will discreetly forget that his hero allowed himself to be dragged at the tail of Colonel Cody's 'Wild West Show.' That reminiscence would rather jar upon the rest of the story. But let us not make too much of what seems to us a humiliation. The Indian stoic sees these things with different eyes. For him there is no more ignominy in exhibiting himself for hire in a circus than in wearing the hats and trousers of the white man, or begging for rum or rations. Whether herein he be a philosopher or a child, it is not for us to say.

President Harrison is reported to have expressed a confident hope that, the prime disturber of the peace being out of the way, the Indian difficulty would be settled without bloodshed. Those who know the Indians well are not equally hopeful. The skirmish or affray in which Sitting Bull lost his life – whether by the bullets of the Indian police. or of his rescuers – may prove to have precipitated the conflict which has been for a long time impending. Very probably Sitting Bull had, as the authorities allege, made up his mind to join the band of Sioux who were raiding settlers' cattle from their strongholds in the 'Bad Lands,' and, if so, then it was right and expedient to arrest him, although not with the inadequate force despatched for the purpose. But, whatever his intentions, Sitting Bull can by no stretch of imagination be said to be the cause of the Messianic craze which is now inflaming the imaginations of not only Sioux, but Cheyennes, Arapahoes, Apaches, Utes, and other tribes. Although physical exhaustion and hard weather have apparently stopped the 'ghost-dances,' the exaltation and unrest arising from the predicted appearance of a deliverer from the whites still continue and have to be reckoned with. In this very combustible state of Indian feeling there is a danger that the fight near Sitting Bull's camp may kindle a serious conflagration. The braves who attempted to rescue Sitting Bull have tasted blood.

Through the injudicious action of the authorities they were allowed to score a decided advantage over the arresting party before the arrival of cavalry armed with Gatlings made further conflict impossible. The Americans call it a victory; but it was a victory in which their own side seems to have suffered as severely as the Sioux, and to have brought away from the field a very lively appreciation of the accuracy of the rebels' shooting: Moreover, no attempt was made to follow up the defeated party, who made good their retreat to the hostile camp in the 'Bad Lands.' It is certain that if the rebel Sioux, thus reinforced, think it worth while to resist, their subjugation will be a more serious business than GENERAL BROOKE's telegram represents it, and, in the meanwhile, a general uprising of the Indians might change the situation altogether. The Americans owe it to their credit as a humane nation to see that the war of extermination to which some of their Generals look forward with complacency is not provoked by the 'energetic treatment' so popular in American military circles. The saying current among United States soldiers that 'the only good Indian is a dead Indian' expresses a sentiment which is responsible for many atrocious massacres and needless wars.

The information provided to the American press was that that Sitting Bull and his son had been killed when the Indian police arrested Sitting Bull, as they had heard that he intended going to 'Badlands'. A troop of cavalry followed the police, and upon their arrival at Sitting Bull's camp, it was evident that arrangements had already been made for his departure. The police started back with Sitting Bull in custody. His followers rallied, however, and attempted a rescue. A mêlée ensued, in the course of which Sitting Bull, his son, and several Indians, as well as five of the Indian police, were killed.

Sitting Bull was one of the most cunning Indians who ever ruled a tribe. He will be best remembered in connection with the Indian rising of 1876, when he held the best troops of the United States at bay. He was not so much a fighting man as a statesman and although nominally in command of the Indian tribes when Colonel Custer with the 7th Cavalry was annihilated, it was really his fighting chief, Crazy Horse, to whom the credit of the Indian victory was due.

After the great Indian war, Sitting Bull escaped to Canada, where he lived until pardoned, though he never regained the position of chief of the six tribes forming the Sioux nation. Despite all the efforts of the United States authorities, Sitting Bull would never look upon the white men as other than his natural enemies. He declared that the white men were always secretly goading them into violence in order to have a pretext for shooting them down and seizing their lands. He took the bounty offered by the Government agents at the Indian Reservations, but with an ill grace. For some time he travelled in America witb Colonel Cody in his Wild West Show, but, though he took an intelligent interest in many things he saw, he remained to the last a typical Indian of the plains, untamed and untamable.

* * *

MOLTKE

'Organizer of victory'

25 AND 27 APRIL 1891

A GREAT SOLDIER HAS passed away. A foremost name has faded from contemporary history. The genius and skill of Moltke became apparent to the world only when he was 66 years old, for he was born in the first year of this century, and has thus lived on into his 91st year. His was a long, patient, and silent career of toil and of duty before suddenly his fame burst forth and the excellence of his labour was made manifest. Peace, hardly ruffled save by the campaign in the Elbe duchies, had been the fortune of Prussia for fifty years since Blücher hurled out of Belgium the columns of the first Napoleon after their repulse at Waterloo.

The startling victory of Königgrätz in 1866 surprised the world and woke it to the fact that one of the greatest strategists known to history was chief of the Prussian General Staff. Count Moltke had counselled King William to order the dispositions which allowed the three armies of the Crown Prince, Prince Frederick Charles, and Herwarth to strike a concentrated and crushing blow against the Austrian forces on the

Upper Elbe. The war had endured but a few days. It was only on the morning of the 16th of June that the first Prussian corps stepped across the Saxon frontier, and war became inevitable. On the evening of the 3d of July the shattered battalions of Austria were hurrying in disordered flight along rain-sodden tracks to seek shelter under the guns of Olmütz. This sudden victory practically concluded the war between Austria and Prussia. The prize won was the unity of North Germany; and on that day the foundation-stone was laid of the modern German Empire. The military plans which led to this rapid and brilliant success were confessedly due to the inspiration of Moltke, and when the Emperor William some years later received the Crown of all Germany, his early thought was to thank the strategist to whom so much was due.

The war of 1866 made Count Moltke famous. This fame was won through hard work, constant perseverance, and rigid self-denial. Officers of every army can take no brighter example as their model than Helmuth Karl Bernhard von Moltke. He was born on the 26th of October, 1800, at Parchim, in Mecklenburg. His parents were of good family, but poor, and he was their third son. His father, who had been a captain in the Prussian service, in 1801 inherited the family estate in Mecklenburg, but sold it in 1803 and retired to Lübeck. When nine years old young Helmuth was sent to school near Kiel, where he made rapid progress. He and his brother were in 1811 sent to Copenhagen, and in the following year were admitted as cadets into the Royal Military Academy there. In the beginning of 1818 young Moltke passed his examination for his commission as best of the candidates and in March, 1819, was appointed lieutenant in the Oldenburg Regiment, which was then stationed at Rendsburg.

Promotion was slow in the Danish service. Norway had been severed from the arms of Denmark, and the Danish army had to be reduced. The Prussian army had gained renown on the Continent by its gallant action in the war of liberation and the campaign of the hundred days. Moltke determined to transfer himself to Prussia. He obtained leave from his colonel, went to Berlin, passed a brilliant examination for the rank of officer, and at the age of 22 became second lieutenant in the 5th Infantry Regiment, then quartered at Frankfort-on-Main.

In the following year he joined the Staff College at Berlin, and after three years of study there passed an excellent examination on leaving. He returned for a short time to his regiment at Frankfort, but in the following year was detached from regimental duty to staff employment, and never did a regimental duty afterwards. It is noteworthy how little regimental duty was done by the three great strategists of this century –

Napoleon, Wellington, or Moltke. Moltke was first appointed to the Topographical Department, and took part in the surveys of Silesia and Posen. About this time it would appear that he became an author, as a pamphlet appeared at Berlin, which is little known, but which bore the title 'Holland and Belgium, by H. von Moltke.' In 1835 he obtained longer leave, and then began the part of his life spent in the East.

He lived in the dominions of the Sultan for more than three years. In 1839 war, broke out between the Sultan Mahmud the Second and Mehemet Ali, Viceroy of Egypt, who claimed the right to name his successor. The army of the Sultan was little ready for war, but the Porte appreciated the military talent of Moltke, who was staying as a guest at Constantinople. He and his companion Mühlbach were sent as military advisers to the head-quarters of Hafiz Pasha, in the Valley of the Euphrates, near Kharput. In April, 1839, the Turkish army, 70,000 strong, commenced its advance towards Syria. It was divided into three corps, but consisted chiefly of recruits and was speedily reduced by sickness and desertion. The Egyptian army was at Aleppo under Ibrahim Pasha. In this advance Moltke commanded the Turkish artillery. In vain Moltke pointed out how unprepared for an active campaign was the Turkish army. The Mollahs insisted on offensive operations. Consequently on the 22d Moltke resigned his post as counsellor of the Commander-in-Chief. On the 24th Ibrahim Pasha attacked the Turkish position, the army fled and dispersed, although it had lost only 1,000 and Hafiz Pasha himself only escaped with difficulty. Moltke and his German comrades then returned to Constantinople. There he found the Sultan dead.

Moltke then returned to Berlin, where he was again occupied on the General Staff, and for his services in the Egypto-Turkish campaign received the Prussian order 'Pour le Mérite' In the following year, 1840, he was removed from Berlin to the Staff of the 4th Corps d'Armée at Magdeburg. Here, in the following year, he published his well-known work. 'Letters from Turkey, 1835–39.' He also drew and issued some valuable maps, the materials for which he had collected in the East, of the Bosphorus, Constantinople, and Asia Minor. The letters from Turkey, when first written, before they were made public, had been addressed to one of his sisters, who was married to an English gentleman, named Burt, then resident in Holstein. Mrs. Burt had a step-daughter on whom this correspondence made an impression which ripened into affection when Captain Moltke, after his return was a visitor in her father's house. They were soon engaged, and Moltke was married to his English step-niece in April, 1842, a few days after he had been made a major. The marriage proved most happy, and for a quarter of a century Moltke's domestic life was unruffled by any trouble.

Promoted in 1850 to the rank of lieutenant-colonel, and in the following year to that of full colonel, Moltke was selected to fill the important post of first aide-de-camp to Prince Frederick William of Prussia, afterwards the Emperor Frederick. In 1856 he became a Major-General. In 1856, Prince Frederick William was appointed Colonel of the Second Silesian Regiment, and when not travelling lived with his Staff chiefly at Breslau. In the following year the Prince was made Commander of the First Brigade of Guards. A few days later Generial Reyher, the chief of the Staff of the Army, died, and shortly afterwards Moltke, one of the youngest general officers in the service, was temporarily intrusted with the duties, and in May, 1859, was made permanent Chief of the Staff, with the rank of Lieutenant-General. Moltke thus rose to the post in the Prussian Army which under the great Frederick had been held by Schmettau and Levin; after Jena, by Scharnhorst; and in the war of liberation by Gneisenau, and on his death by Müffling. Great were these names, but Germany regards now Moltke as greatest of them all.

The duty of the Chief of a Staff is, above all things, to prepare in peace for war. He must consider and regulate the measures for the mobilization of the army down to the most minute detail, the plan of operations, and the means of concentration. He must have a thorough knowledge of his own and of foreign armies, and be intimately acquainted with railways, roads, and bridges. Under the administration of Moltke the Prussian Army became rapidly more ready for war in every particular. Its mobilization, which on his accession to office was calculated to require 21 days, can now be effected in ten days.

Moltke had not long to wait before his services were called into active play. On account of the advance of the French Army through Lombardy in 1859 towards German soil the Prussian Army was mobilized, and he drew up the regulations for the advance of the Prussian Army and its railway transport to the Rhine. The manner in which he accomplished this then original task showed the Government and the Army that a wise step had been taken in placing him in the most responsible military position in the country.

Almost at the same time as Moltke took up the duties of Chief of the Staff of the Army, great political changes occurred in Prussia. In 1857 in consequence of the severe illness of King Frederic William IV, the Prince of Prussia, afterwards the Emperor William I. was entrusted with the Regency of the kingdom. In 1861 the King died and William succeeded to the Throne. He determined to gain for Prussia a leading position among European Powers. The first step necessary to carry out this great project was the reorganization of the army. The King was determined that the land forces should be put in thorough working order. By 1863 the reorganization was complete. Events soon came to show how necessary the work was and how well it had been done. In 1863 the Prussian Staff was active, for the turmoils in Russian Poland made it doubtful whether Prussian troops might not be required to take the field.

In the following year the war with Denmark on account of the Elbe Duchies broke out. In it Prussia on account of her geographical position took the leading part, and it fell to Moltke to draw out the plan of operations for the combined Prussian and Austrian armies. Thus his first active service was against the same army in which he had borne a commission as a youth. He directed the advance of the armies which under Field-Marshal von Wrangel invaded the duchies, and after the storming of Düppal in 1864 accompanied the King to the theatre of war and as Chief of the Staff directed the further operations. For a moment England thought of saving Denmark single-handed from Prussia, but most fortunately wiser counsels prevailed, and British troops were not sent to prove the terrible efficacy of the Prussian needle gun. A conference was, indeed, held to consider the matter at London; but it separated without result. England folded her hands and allowed the war to proceed. Prince Frederick Charles, with Moltke as his Chief of the Staff, took the command of the allied forces. On the 30th of October peace was signed, and Holstein, Lauenburg and Schleswig were annexed to Germany. To these results the talents of Moltke largely contributed. They were much aided by the breech-loading rifle of the Prussian infantry and by a portion of the artillery also consisting of breech-loading guns. But in Europe at large little attention was paid to these mechanical improvements, and even in Germany they were not thoroughly appreciated.

A larger field in which to prove his strategical genius was opened to Moltke in the war of 1866. Austria and Prussia found cause of quarrel in the newly acquired Elbe Duchies. By the middle of June, 1866, the armies on both sides were concentrating on the common frontier. The Prussian forces consisted of three armies, which by Moltke's combination advanced concentrically into Bohemia, and by carefully calculated marches and skilful manoeuvres exposed the Austrian forces to a simultaneous attack in front and rear. It had hitherto been considered exceedingly hazardous to advance into an enemy's country in different independent columns, especially through mountain passes, as two columns might be checked by small forces, while an overwhelming weight was thrown on the third, and then the columns might be destroyed in detail. But this danger Moltke perceived would be averted if each column could communicate almost instantly with the others. He called science to his aid. The military field telegraph was instituted and each column could communicate in a few seconds with the others, though a hundred miles distant, and tell exactly the hostile forces in its front.

Aided thus, Moltke perfected plans by which the army of Prince Frederick Charles, joined with that of Herwarth, burst into Bohemia through Saxony, swept away the detachments left to bar their progress, and threatened the flank and rear of the main force with which Benedek hoped to check the Crown Prince. The latter, fighting hard, pushed his way through the Silesian hills. His breech-loaders swept away the badly-armed Austrian columns opposed to him, and Benedek, thus assailed and threatened, fell back perforce to a rearward position on the Bistritz. Once through the mountains, the junction of the Crown Prince with Prince Frederick Charles was assured, and on the night of the 1st of July their horsemen communicated with each other near Gitschin. The next day the King, with Moltke, arrived at Gitschin. Prince Frederick Charles felt the Austrian army on the Bistritz, and, fearing that it might retreat beyond the Elbe, determined to attack and hold it fast till the Crown Prince could come up within striking distance and smite it heavily in flank and rear. The consent of the King, by Moltke's advice, was given to this bold but wise view of Prince Frederick Charles. The battle of Königgrätz was the result, where the Austrian army was so utterly defeated that Benedek telegraphed immediately to his Sovereign, 'Sire, you must make peace.'

An armistice was then agreed upon, and the Peace of Prague definitely concluded on the 23d of August. At the close of the war Moltke wrote, 'It is beautiful when God gives to man such a result to his life as He has vouchsafed to the King and many of his Generals. I am now 66 years old and for my work I received much reward. We have made a campaign which for Prussia, for Germany, and the world is of inestimable importance.' But there was a great sorrow in store for the General. In December, 1866, Madame von Moltke fell ill, and Christmas Eve, which brings gladness to so many hearts, was sad to Moltke. Before the dawn of Christmas Day his wife lay dead. They had had no children, and his life would have been very lonely had not the kindly King appointed his nephew, Lieutenant von Burt, to be his permanent aide-de-camp; his only surviving sister, Madame von Burt, took charge of his house, and thus he was not left quite alone. But he ever cherished a most lasting and tender affection for his wife. She was buried on his property in Silesia, and whenever the General went home from Berlin his first action was to visit her grave.

But there was hard work to distract his mind from private sorrow. The main results of the war of 1866 were the formation of the new North German Confederation, under the Sovereign of Prussia, and the disappearance of Austria as a Germanic Power. The Treaty of Prague was, however, but the stepping-stone, not the keystone, of German unity. North Germany was, indeed, linked with Prussia, which now held the command of the German forces and the power of peace and war north of the Main. The treaties with Baden and Wurtemberg were of the same tenor. On account of the representations of the Emperor of the French, Saxony was not so completely absorbed into the union. The Saxon King retained the power of nominating his civil and military officers, and the Saxon army was not merged in that of the Confederation. France, by an attitude of desire to interfere in the internal arrangements of Germany, facilitated the conclusion of those treaties; and the fact that on the 6th of August, 1866, she demanded the fortress of Mainz from Prussia under threat of war, though known to but few, had doubtless an important effect.

Moltke's answer to the demand was the rapid march of 60,000 men to the Rhine; and when it was seen that Prussia was resolute, the threat was not carried out, but an excuse made that the demand was wrung from the Emperor while suffering from severe illness. But those who looked below the surface saw that France was brooding, and pushing forward armaments and military organization. Moltke well knew this. His system of intelligence from France was excellent; every change in armament and every movement of battalions was known to him. The war which he had long foreseen broke out, indeed, suddenly, but found him prepared. In England it caused great surprise, although in the spring of 1870 French agents were abroad in all our southern counties buying corn and forage. The excuses for enormous purchases of this description were that the season had been so dry that no harvest was expected in France. But these excuses were transparent, for had forage been so very scarce in France French dealers would not have cared, simultaneously with an enormous rise in the price of forage, to largely export horses to France.

At the same time, a flotilla was secretly collected in the northern

French ports, capable of transporting 40,000 men and 12,000 horses. These things were carefully noted by Moltke's agents, but the British Government, against which the arrangements might have been equally directed, remained in happy ignorance of any danger of war, and within a few hours of the outbreak of hostilities our Secretary of State for Foreign Affairs, as he himself stated in Parliament, 'believed that there was not a cloud on the political horizon of Europe.'

Careful precautions were taken on the Prussian side, and already in December, 1867, Moltke worked out and laid before the King a plan for the railway transport of the armies of Germany to the Rhine and a plan of campaign against France. So carefully were the details of the transport arranged that when war broke out more than two years afterwards they had hardly to be altered. The key of Moltke's plan of campaign as exposed in his history of this war which was published from the office of the German staff in 1874, was 'to find the main body of the enemy and to attack it wherever found.' The mobilization of the army was prepared in every detail, and Moltke, with a keen but bold strategy, fixed the point of concentration in the Bavarian palatinate, between the Rhine and the Moselle. The assembly of the whole German force here protected the upper as well as the lower Rhine, and allowed for an offensive movement into France which would probably prevent any invasion of German territory.

It might appear hazardous to concentrate the armies on the French side of the Rhine, where they might be attacked before they were united, but his calculations were so perfect and his arrangements so complete, that under his magician's hand this danger disappeared. For every detachment, the day and hour of its departure from its garrison and arrival near the frontier was laid down. On the 10th day after mobilization was ordered, the first troops would descend from their railway carriages close by the French frontier, and on the 13th day 60,000 combatants would be there in position and on the 18th day this force would be swelled to 300,000 men. He calculated that only on the eighth day, in most favourable circumstances, could the French cross the frontier with 150,000 men, when there was time for the Prussian staff to stop their railway transport at the Rhine and there disembark their forces. To move from the frontier at Saarlouis to the Rhine the French would require at least six marches, and could only reach the river on the 14th day to find the passages occupied by overwhelming German forces. For on the German side there were ready to take the field, as soon as their rapid mobilization was complete, the 12 corps of the North German

Confederation, mustering at least 360,000 men; and the armies of Bavaria, Würtemberg, Darmstadt, Saxony and Baden, which were under the supreme command of the King of Prussia in virtue of the treaties concluded after the campaign of 1866, raised the field forces of that Sovereign to over 500,000 combatants.

The German soldier was more suitably equipped for European war than the French. Discarding the cumbrous equipage necessary for the formation of camps or the refinements of cooking, the German troops were prepared during a campaign to trust to the shelter which villages nearly always afford in Western Europe, or, in case of necessity, to bivouac in the open air, while a small mess-tin carried by each soldier sufficed for his culinary wants. The French soldier, on the contrary, was weighed down with *tentes d'abri*, heavy cooking apparatus, and an enormous kit. These were generally useless, frequently lost, always incumbrances; but an army accustomed to African or Asiatic war clings pertinaciously to the idea of canvas covering, fails to realize the different conditions under which campaigns must be conducted in Europe, and shudders at the idea of an exposure in war to which every true sportsman will willingly consent for pleasure.

The plans matured in peace by Moltke were now to be tested. They were not found wanting. Late at night, on the 15th of July, the King of Prussia ordered the mobilization of the whole German army. The 16th was the first day of mobilization; on the 26th the mobilization was complete; and on the 3d of August three army corps stood formed in order of battle south of the Moselle, between the Saar and the Rhine, and ready to advance into France. While the German army was being mobilized the French lost all advantage which their hasty declaration of war should have given. Their army, instead of having been ready before the declaration of war, was unprepared to advance, and instead of dashing boldly into Germany lay inactive on the frontier. Thus the German army was able unhindered to assume the offensive with superior numbers.

Moltke's plan of the campaign was that the army of the Crown Prince should advance on the east of the Vosges Mountains, on the German left, that of Prince Frederick Charles in the centre, and that of Steinmetz on the right, to the west of the Vosges. Moltke expected to find the united French army on the Moselle between Nancy and Metz, but his cavalry soon informed him that they were not even concentrated, but in scattered corps. On the 4th of August the French corps which occupied St. Avold, a small town on the road from Metz to the frontier line of the

Saar at Saarbruck, made a movement towards the latter place. The Emperor and Prince Imperial were present, and the French soldiery thought that the advance had at last really begun, and that they were upon the high road to Berlin. The movement was not, however, pushed; the French did not even cross the frontier in force, but occupied the strong heights of Spicheren.

Meanwhile the German troops had drawn swiftly and silently down to the frontier. In the early morning of the 6th of August, the Crown Prince had massed his forces behind the dark woods which lie north of Weissemburg. Thence, soon after day-break, he sprang upon the unsuspecting advanced guard of the corps of Marshal MacMahon, and drove them back with great loss on Wörth. The same day Prince Frederick Charles and Steinmetz stormed the heights of Spicheren and drove the French occupants of that position in full retreat towards Metz. On the 8th the Crown Prince came upon Marshal MacMahon at Wörth, and after a severe battle, in which the French leader showed much tactical resource, overthrew him completely, and the Marshal retreated in great confusion on Nancy. The future Emperor Frederick, at Wörth, tore from the brows of tho French army the laurels which a too credulous world had uncritically accorded to it, and proved that the army of France, however much animated by enthusiasm and gallantry, was unable to withstand the stern onset of the German soldiery directed with judgment and conducted with skill.

Reports soon came in which showed that the whole French army contemplated a retreat from the line of the Moselle towards Châlons. Then Moltke conceived the daring plan of throwing the German force between Bazaine and Châlons and cutting off the French retreat. Prince Frederick Charles crossed the Moselle and engaged Bazaine's retreating columns in the bloody battle of Mars-la-Tour. Here he held the French General, who had 180,000 men, with his 90,000, and although he lost heavily he gripped him tight and prevented his further retreat. Other German corps hurried up in support; and on the 18th the main German army, with its rear to Paris, engaged Bazaine at Gravelotte and, after a severe fight, drove him back into Metz, where his force was quickly surrounded by Prince Frederick Charles was shut up from all further participation in the war, and was finally compelled to capitulate in the latter part of October.

While the German cavalry hurried forward in front of the armies of the two Crown Princes to gather news of the French movements, the Chief of the Staff joined the head-quarters of the Crown Prince of Prussia on the 24th of August at Ligny. A council of war was held. It was known that the French army was near Rheims, and rumours gathered by the cavalry from the country people told that MacMahon contemplated a march to Metz. It was then determined to continue the march towards Châlons. On his arrival at Bar-le-Duc General Moltke went to walk on the ancient walls of that once fortified town. He meditated on the state of the campaign, and then for the first time the thought struck him of what MacMahon really was doing, and he saw that it was possible that the French leader might endeavour to throw himself into Metz behind the advancing German armies and at the same time threaten their lines of communication. He went to his quarters and there studied the possibility of such a movement and the measures to be taken to counter-act it. He found that the proposed French march could be carried out, and that to defeat it the enemy's columns must at the latest be stopped on the right bank of the Meuse and attacked, and that the position of the German armies allowed them to be attacked there by the fourth army in front and the third army on their right flank with overwhelming force. In the course of the evening, reports from the advanced cavalry showed that the enemy was moving from Rheims in an easterly direction towards Metz. Moltke studied the reports by aid of his maps, in which each detachment of troops was marked with a pin, and soon concluded that there could be no doubt that the French General was marching on Metz. He at once laid his views before the King, and obtained his permission that the march on Paris should be given up, and that the third and fourth armies, wheeled to the right, should march towards the north.

These movements brought on the battle of Sedan. On the 30th of August, the Crown Prince of Saxony, moving down the right bank of the Meuse, surprised the French advance at Mouzon; for the French army, instead of making forced marches of about 20 miles a day, on account of want of discipline among the new levies and the failure of transport arrangements, was only able to make about six. On the same day the Crown Prince of Prussia also engaged the heads of Marshal MacMahon's columns at Beaumont and Donchery and drove them in. On the 1st of September the two armies, under the eyes of the King of Prussia, attacked the position which the French had taken up at Sedan. The Crown Prince threw his left completely round the French army. All day the battle raged. The French fought gallantly, even desperately, but, pressed upon by the better disciplined legions of Germany, they were pushed closer and closer to the ramparts of the fortress, while their adversaries gained a firm footing on all the heights which command and overlook the basin in which Sedan is situate. At last, hemmed in, surrounded, and exposed to the commanding fire of a numerous and superior artillery, no resource was left to the French army but capitulation.

After the halt of a few days necessary for the completion of arrangements at Sedan, the armies of the Crown Princes marched direct for Paris, where alone the war could be ended. There was no French army worthy of mention now in the field. Bazaine, with the Army of the Rhine, was invested in Metz, the Emperor and MacMahon were prisoners on the road to Germany. The few troops that escaped from the general catastrophe at Sedan, or had been on the way to reinforce Marshal MacMahon, were hurried back to Paris to man the defences of the capital. The German movements were, in Moltke's fashion, at once rapid and deliberate. On the 19th of September the investment of Paris was, in a sense, completed, though much had to be done to fix the grasp securely on the doomed victim.

Here opened a second stage of the war, which for several months was directed from Moltke's quarters at Versailles. There can be little question that, in the first instance, the Germans were led away by a miscalculation, and for a time, undoubtedly, Moltke's schemes had to embrace, not only offensive operations against the enemy, but a safe retreat in case of disaster. The resources of Paris, the strength of the fortifications, and the spirit of the people had been underrated. If the Germans had not reckoned on the immediate surrender of the city, as in 1814 and 1815, they would hardly have risked an advance while Bazaine's army was still safe in Metz and while the fortresses of Alsace and Lorraine threatened their main lines of communication. When Moltke saw that Paris was not to be captured by a *coup de main*, but that it must be regularly invested, he must have passed some uneasy days and nights until Toul and Strasburg fell; nor could his anxieties have been greatly relieved before Metz capitulated on the 28th of October. Then the problem became a comparatively simple one, for even if the German armies had been compelled to raise the siege they could have retired in perfect order and kept their hold upon the occupied departments. But, at the very outset, Moltke stood firm, and, even while the security of his communications was doubtful, a vast double line of intrenchments, thrown up by the spade, hemmed in the Parisians.

Thenceforward the issue of the siege was only a matter of time. Paris fell by the pressure of hunger. Even Moltke had not truly estimated the strength of the fortifications, which remained unbroken when the gates were opened to the investing armies; and the struggle might have been prolonged for months if there had been any means of getting supplies of food. Perhaps no part of Moltke's work was more remarkable than the complete success with which he solved a problem only one degree less difficult than that of victualling Paris – the provision of supplies during the winter for the investing armies, in a country to a great extent stripped of its resources and where a prolonged siege had not been contemplated. It is curious that those who planned the fortifications had calculated that no investing army could subsist outside the walls for more than two months, whereas the German investment lasted for five months. Versailles became thus the scene of the most important part of Moltke's life work.

This extract from the extensive obituary of Field Marshal Count Helmuth von Moltke published in *The Times* on 25th and 27th April 1891 deals with the key points of his career, in particular those during the Austro-Prussian and Franco-Prussian Wars.

Moltke was a general who fought the *next* war with his every breath. Recognising that the railways could cut the time for national mobilization to provide a decisive strategic advantage over France, he studied the system in immense detail. His mobilization plan worked perfectly in 1870 but when his nephew, Moltke the Younger, as Chief of Staff in 1914, was asked by Kaiser Wilhelm II whether the plan could be changed to deliver the bulk of the German Army to face Russia in the east, rather than to face France in the west, Moltke said the complexity of the railway schedules made it impossible. In fact, it could have been done, as was later conceded, as an alternative plan for that contingency had been prepared in 1913.

Moltke's grasp of the importance of co-ordination and communication, using the telegraph, gave his armies another decisive advantage once they reached the battlefield and, like Napoleon, he instinctively anticipated his enemy's intentions and interpreted his movements.

MACMAHON

Descendant of a distinguished Irish family
in the service of France.

18 OCTOBER 1893

MARIE EDMÉ PATRICE MAURICE DE MACMAHON, Marshal of France, Duc de Magenta, was descended from an Irish family of distinction. In the time of James II its representatives ruined themselves in his service and went with him into exile.

The late Marshal was born in the Château of Sully, near Autun, July 13, 1808. He entered the army and plunged with ardour into the campaign of conquest undertaken by the French in Algeria. He exhibited such talent and bravery that he speedily won renown. As a lieutenant he acquired fame and the Cross of the Legion of Honour by fighting the Kabyles along the slope of the Atlas.

The Crimea furnished the great field for the display of his indomitable courage. In 1855, when General Canrobert left the scene of war, MacMahon was selected by the Emperor to succeed him in the command of a division. When the chiefs of the Allied Armies resolved on assaulting Sebastopol, September 8, he was assigned the most perilous position in the grand final attack on the Malakoff Redoubt. MacMahon said to Marshal Niel, 'I will enter it, and you may be certain that I shall not be removed from it living!' Then ensued a colossal and terrible struggle, which will redound for ever to the military credit of the French.

In the Italian campaign of 1859 MacMahon greatly distinguished himself. At the battle of Magenta his conduct was particularly bold and sagacious. When Europe was startled in 1870 by the news of the declaration of war between France and Prussia, Marshal MacMahon was appointed to the command of the First Army Corps. His mission was the defence of Alsace. Although the declaration of war was made only on the 15th of July, by the 30th of the same month the Germans had three armies in the field. The French, on the contrary, had with difficulty collected 270,000 men with 925 guns by the beginning of August. The Emperor assumed the chief command, and had 128,000 men between Metz and the frontier at Saarbrück, some 47,000 under Marshal

MacMahon on the eastern slopes of the Vosges Mountains, and 35,000 in reserve at Châlons.

The first engagement took place on August 2nd, when General Frossard's corps drove out the weak German detachment in Saarbrück, but did not follow up its success, and the Germans took the offensive the next day. On the 4th the Third German Army, under the command of the Crown Prince, met General Douay's advanced brigade near Wissembourg, defeated it, and then pressed forward. On the 6th the Crown Prince attacked the united Army Corps of Generals MacMahon, Failly, and Canrobert, drawn up in position at Woerth. MacMahon was in chief command, having under him some 50,000 men in all, and he occupied a strong defensive position on the slopes of the Vosges. The Marshal fought courageously against tremendous odds (the Germans having about 120,000 men), and he braved death in the most reckless manner, wringing testimonials of admiration from his enemies. But the display was powerless against the well-laid plans and superior force of the Germans. He was compelled to fall back upon Nancy, leaving in the enemy's hands 4,000 prisoners, 36 cannon, and two standards.

MacMahon's retreat was so ably conducted, however, that the Emperor confided to him the supreme command of the new levies which he was mustering at Châlons. This new army was the last hope of France. The Marshal was ordered to effect a junction with Bazaine's forces at Metz. To effect this MacMahon began a northerly march on the 21st of August, without intelligence reaching the Germans, part of whose Second Army was again in motion towards Paris. On the 25th the Germans learned, as it was alleged, through a telegram in a foreign newspaper, of MacMahon's movements, and they at once changed the direction of their march so as to intercept him. Finally, on the 30th, the 5th Corps, under De Failly, was surprised and driven northwards on Sedan. MacMahon here collected his dispirited troops, but only to find that the enemy had surrounded him, and by vigorous forward movements had captured the bridges over the Meuse and the commanding positions round the town. The fierce and decisive battle of Sedan commenced early on the 1st of September by the attack on Bazeilles. This village was captured by the Bavarians and recaptured by the French and ultimately burned. By noon MacMahon had been dangerously wounded in the thigh, and he resigned his command to General Wimpffen.

When M. Thiers resigned the Presidency of the Republic, May 24, 1873, Marshal MacMahon was elected to the vacant office by the Assembly. While MacMahon himself was unwilling to accept the office, it is said that his ambitious wife was determined that he should receive the Presidential office. She had put his name about, chiefly through the *Figaro*, as the champion of order, so that the Marshal, after considerable persuasion, accepted the Headship of the Executive.

This extract from the extensive obituary published in *The Times* on 18 October 1893 concentrates on MacMahon's exploits in the Crimean and Franco-Prussian wars. At his death, a Paris newspaper proclaimed, 'He was the last but one of the French Marshals, (Canrobert was still alive) identified with the old monarchy and not likely to be revived', but the honour of Marshal of France was bestowed on French commanders of the First World War and subsequently.

On the battlefield, MacMahon displayed coolness but also impetuosity, reflecting the cavalry tradition, although his early service was as an infantry officer. He lacked the intellect and temperament to be a commander-in-chief, succumbing as he did to the strategy of Moltke in 1870.

As a politician he was well-intentioned, in particular for the benefit of the poorer classes, but artless and easily out-manoeuvred by the professionals. It was a weakness he almost certainly recognised but shouldered political responsibility – when no other suitable candidate was available – as a matter of patriotism and soldierly honour.

His devotion to the large family his wife, a lady of the ducal house of Caraman, bore him was a consistent feature of his life.

CETYWAYO

Cetywayo, King of the Zulus.

11 FEBRUARY 1884.

CETYWAYO, WHOSE SUDDEN death is announced by telegram on 10 February, was the son of King Umpanda, who for many years ruled over Zululand. In 1856 Cetywayo's ambitious designs on the throne led to family quarrels, which before long broke forth into open war. In one of the battles six of the King's sons were slain, and as the result of Cetywayo's victories he virtually superseded his father and became King. A year or two later an ingenious compromise was arrived at. King Umpanda was declared to be too old to work or fight; but not too old to think. Cetywayo was therefore called in to share the Royal dignities and duties. The father was styled the head, while the son was said to be the feet of the nation.

Umpanda, however, lived for many years after this compact had robbed him of most of his power. It was not until 1873, after a reign of 35 years, that the old King was laid to rest. Cetywayo then succeeded to the throne, his coronation taking place in the presence ot the Secretary for Native Affairs, Mr. afterwards Sir, Theophilus Shepstone. Five years later, Sir Bartle Frere, Governor of Cape Colony, visited Natal in his capacity of the Queen's High Commissioner for South Africa. He regarded Cetywayo's military power with suspicion as a standing menace, in his opinion, to Natal and the Transvaal. So he despatched to Cetywayo in December, 1878, an ultimatum, calling upon him to make reparation for alleged outrages on British subjects, to disband his formidable army, to abandon his tyrannical system of Government, and to accept a British Resident. Cetywayo was in no mood to accede and treated this communication with contemptuous silence.

The days of grace having elapsed, Lord Chelmsford, on January 11, 1879, entered Zululand, at the head of 13,000 British troops. The early weeks of the campaign were signalised by the disaster of Isandlana, followed by the gallant defence of the post at Rorke's Drift. At Ulundi. on July 4, Lord Chelmsford completely routed the Zulus, and Cetywayo, taking to flight, sought a hiding place in the bush, where, however, on August 28 he was captured by Major Marter. By this time Sir Garnet

Wolseley had succeeded Lord Chelmsford, and to him fell the task of re-organizing the country.

He divided it into 13 separate governments, with a British Resident exercising control over all. Cetwayo himself was taken to Cape Town, where he was kept as a prisoner. Here he received all reasonable indulgence and freedom, subject to such regulations as were necessary for his safe detention. The ex-King constantly petitioned to be released, and also, as an alternative, to be brought to England. This latter request having been granted he arrived at Plymouth on August 3, 1882, and immediately came to London, where he occupied a private house in Melbury road, Kensington, which had been specially prepared for him by the Government. During his stay in England he visited the Earl of Kimberley at the Colonial Office, Mr. Gladstone in Downing street, the Prince and Princess of Wales at Marlborough House, and had an interview with the Queen at Osborne.

On the 15th of August the Government announced that they had decided to restore Cetywayo, and he left England on the 1st of September to resume, as he thought, the throne of Zululand. His subsequent disappointments and defeats are still fresh in the public mind. The latest definite news with reference to Cetywayo previous to the announcement of his death was contained in a telegram from South Africa mentioning that on Sunday the 27th ult. the ex-King with a number of his followers surreptitiously left Ekowe, where he had been living under British protection. His destination and intentions were not known, but he was pursued by the military, captured on the following day, and brought back to Ekowe. There was no doubt, however, that Cetywayo still nourished a hope of regaining his throne. This is confirmed by a telegram so late as Wednesday last, which stated, in connexion with the movement of Boers into Zululand, that Cetywayo, Zibebu, and Oham were each offering inducements to the Boers in the shape of land grants in return for active service in aid of their respective claims. The reason for his flight was also probably partly to be found in the dissatisfaction with which the late King regarded his treatment by the authorities while in the Reserve Territory. It was recently stated by a Natal paper, although it was most hostile to Cetywayo, that 'all the King's chiefs who were staying with him got notice to leave Ekowe, and on refusing to do so had their hut burnt down.' This statement was confirmed from other sources, so that the number of chiefs who were forced from their homes in July last, and had since been in personal attendance upon him, were turned out of Ekowe; the followers allowed to remain with Cetywayo being limited to ten. In addition to this be was not permitted to have the presence of an English adviser, and he had been compelled to fall back upon his native counsellor.

The death of Cetywayo at Ekowe relieves the Cabinet of one of its minor embarrassments. It was pointed out in the House of Commons last week that his presence in the Reserve was a standing menace to the peace of Zululand, and Mr. Chamberlain admitted that the difficulty of disposing of him in a satisfactory way would have to be dealt with by the Government. Decent burial is now all that the deposed monarch can require at our hands. On a former occasion his death was confidently announced, though our own Correspondent never gave any countenance to the rumour. But the scope for conjecture which existed when Cetywayo was beaten in a struggle of his own seeking exists no longer. As a refugee under British protection, jealously watched by British officials, all his movements must be authentically known and there can be no doubt that his turbulent and chequered career is really at an end.

Cetywayo has played a much more important part than usually falls to the lot of a savage potentate, whatever his natural ability, and has succeeded in linking his name with the domestic no less than with the colonial history of England. For nearly a quarter of a century he wielded supreme power in Zululand, and by the extent of his military preparations and the unscrupulous character of his policy made himself the most conspicuous figure in South Africa. In the struggle which brought about his fall a serious defeat was inflicted upon a British army, the well-deserved reputation of Sir Bartle Frere, whose dangerous illness now excites the interest and sympathy of the country, received a shock, and the Conservative Cabinet suffered one of the blows which brought about its downfall. The policy which led up to the Zulu war as well as that subsequently followed in respect alike of Cetywayo and his country has not commanded the fervent admiration of any section of politicians. Considered as the centre and origin of long and bitter political controversy in England, Cetywayo will probably hold a position unique in the history of our dealings with barbarous races.

In 1856 Cetywayo arrived at the conclusion that his father, Umpanda, ought to make provision for the succession to the throne. The King was old and feeble, and probably feared to excite the hostility of the unsuccessful candidates by nominating any one of his sons to succeed him. He accordingly made answer that with the Zulus the strongest man is king, thus practically inviting his unruly children to fight out the question among them. They were not slow to take the hint, and after several

pitched battles between the rival factions Umeularte, the most formidable of Cetywayo's antagonists, was defeated, and his adherents
mercilessly slaughtered. Three of the brothers escaped into Natal and
one into the Transvaal, leaving Cetywayo practically king. His father's
submission probably saved his life. Cetywayo graciously admitted that,
though too old to fight or govern, he was still capable of thought, and
thus he remained as a sort of privy councillor until his death in 1872.

Cetywayo then thought that his position required the sanction of
the white men in his vicinity, especially as it was open to the Natal
Government or the Transvaal to recognize one of the other claimants to
the succession. He accordingly asked both Natal and the Transvaal
formally to assist at his installation as king, and Sir Theophilus Shepstone went on behalf of the Natal Government to confirm him in his
position. It was stipulated, however, that in return for recognition he was
to cease the murderous practices to which he was given, and that no Zulu
should in future be condemned without fair trial, Considering the terms
upon which he was received in this country in 1882, it would be agreeable
to think that he adhered to the solemn promises by which he purchased
English support. But, unhappily, after every allowance has been made for
exaggeration, there is too good ground for believing that he broke faith
in the most unblushing manner, and carried on his government with
that total disregard for human life shown in his original usurpation.

Far from reciprocating our friendship, he intrigued against us in
every possible way, his machinations having been traced even on the
borders of Cape Colony itself. However, he hated the Boers not less
cordially than ourselves, and, notwithstanding all that can be said about
the danger arising from his numerous and well drilled army, it has never
been satisfactorily shown that our colonies were in any immediate peril.
Unfortunately, we concentrated upon ourselves the hostility of the
Zulus by taking over the government of the Transvaal, thus depriving
them of an enemy who would have usefully diverted their attacks. From
this step, prompted beyond doubt by the most humane desire to promote the well-being alike of Boers and English colonists, flowed the
mischiefs which have since perplexed successive Governments in South
Africa. If anything could have reconciled the Boers to the loss of their
independence it would have been the perpetual fear of Zulu invasion.
But that fear was allowed to influence our own policy to such an extent
that the destruction of the Zulu power came to be regarded as indispensable. The annexation of the Transvaal had undoubtedly increased
the dangers to which Natal was exposed, but it has never been shown as

clearly as such an undertaking required that we had no alternative but to fight Cetywayo.

We did fight him, however, broke up his army, took him prisoner, and finally divided Zululand into thirteen portions, each under the rule of a separate chief, and all supervised by a British Resident. This arrangement had hardly been made when it began to be vehemently assailed. Cetywayo in captivity at Cape Town, became an object of extraordinary and inexplicable interest to a great many good people at home. Impassioned speeches were made about him, accounts were telegraphed home showing the dignity, intelligence, and nobility of his demeanour, and philanthropists in no long time persuaded themselves that nothing but his restoration to the throne of his ancestors could wipe away the guilt of the Zula war. Some astute observer of the ways of men at length started the idea of bringing Cetywayo to England to have an interview with the Queen and to plead his right in person. He came over in the autumn of 1882. and took up his abode in Kensington. The British public received him with the greatest cordiality, and followed his movements with as much interest as if he had been a white elephant. By some process of reasoning which we confess our inability to elucidate, it came to be regarded as an indisputable political truth that, after receiving him in this effusive manner, we were bound in honour to restore him to his kingdom. His people were said to long for his return, the destruction of their national unity was represented as a crime, and sanguine philanthropists pointed to a golden future in which a monarch civilized by the gracious influences of Melbury Road should exercise his mild and beneficent sway over a regenerated nation. In January last year, accordingly, Cetywayo returned to his own land under the patronage of England, a certain number of chiefs being dispossessed of their brief authority in order to furnish him with a kingdom.

He at once began to scheme for the restoration of his old position, and the state of Zululand became, in the language of the Queen's Speech, 'unsettled.' In less than six months matters came to a crisis, and Cetywayo, notwithstanding the love of his people, was completely vanquished by his rival, and compelled to seek refuge in the Reserve territory, which had been prudently retained to act as a buffer. It was stated by the Under-Secretary of State for the Colonies that even after this disaster he has never ceased to cherish hopes of recovering his kingdom or to carry on intrigues for that end, and it is even said that he recently ran away and had to be recaptured by a party of soldiers. Tried by European standards of morality, it must be admitted by all except very ardent lovers of aboriginal humanity that there were serious flaws in Cetywayo's character, but we may cheerfully recognize the rude abilities required in his position, and an indomitable energy and courage. It is matter for regret that circumstances have made it impossible to think of his demise except in connexion with the relief it brings to our administrators in South Africa.

This example of Victorian hypocrisy and humbug tries to shield the reader from the background of British colonial expansion in South Africa that led to conflict with the proud and warlike Zulu race. Cetywayo's system of tribal laws, trials and judgements were a far cry from the principles for the same in England and much of Europe at the time, but they were the accepted way of his people and no excuse – per se – for deposing him as the ruler of an independent nation.

There is no doubt that the Zulus were a serious obstacle to British expansion. They were utterly fearless warriors, obliged to be celibate until after killing or wounding an enemy, and trained to fight in strictly disciplined groups called 'impis'. No tactical skill was required to defeat Lord Chelsford at Isandhlwana in January 1879. After pitching camp in an open plain, he led half his force off in search of the main Zula army, leaving the remainder to be slaughtered at the camp site when Cetywayo's 20,000 warriors stormed over the Isandhlwana ridge chanting his war-cry 'Usuthu, Usuthu!'

In battle, Cetywayo used 'impis' of stronger, older warriors to fix the enemy in frontal confrontation, while the younger warriors raced round the flanks to encircle them. Unfortunately for him, he was no strategist. After Isandhlwana, he might have led his army on a devastating raid into Natal, but instead he allowed 7,000 warriors to throw themselves on the unimportant outpost of Rorke's Drift, which they failed to subdue. Chelmsford returned with a reorganised force, brought Cetywayo to battle at Ulundi and decimated his warriors with systematic rifle fire from infantry squares with Gatling guns at each corner.

TOGO

Japan's Nelson

30 MAY 1934

WE ANNOUNCE WITH great regret this morning the death, at the age of 86, of Japan's greatest naval hero, Admiral of the Fleet Marquis Togo, who was created a Marquis on his death-bed.

Not until he reached his forty-seventh year did Heihachiro Togo become in any sense a marked man. Born in December, 1847. at Kagoshima, the son of Togo Kichizaemon, a humble *samurai* of the Satsuma clan, he made his career without adventitious aid of any kind, and his diffidence and reticence were so marked that the great qualities underlying these characteristics were for long unsuspected. He first went to school at a naval academy at the Heigaku-ryo, where Baron Yamamoto, Minister of Marine in the Russo-Japanese War, and Admiral Ito, of Yalu fame, also attended.

At the age of 16 he began his sea service on board a warship belonging to his feudal chief, and five years later (1865) he was transferred to the Imperial Navy, then in its embryonic condition. With the exception of unfailing though absolutely unostentatious devotion to duty there was nothing to distinguish him from his fellows, but his superiors had sufficient discernment to include him in a batch of 14 young officers who were sent to England in 1871 to study the art and science of warfare. Togo himself joined the nautical school ship *Worcester* on the Thames. He devoted seven years to his studies, a part of the time being occupied in a voyage to and from Australia on board a sailing ship, and the last year being passed under a Greenwich professor of naval science

Thus the young officer's knowledge may be said to have been acquired wholly in England. He returned to his country in the *Hiyei*, one of the first vessels built to the order of the Japanese Government in an English dockyard. This was in 1878, and thereafter for 16 years the public heard nothing whatever of the name of Togo, nor did any special rapidity of promotion distinguish his career. He had absorbed, as he himself frequently said, the 'tradition' idea of Great Britain, and he was anxious that the Japanese Navy should be so closely modelled on that of the 'mistress of the seas' that there should be no visible distinction between them. So unobtrusive were his efforts in this direction that in 1894 he was still in a fairly lowly post, having the command of the *Naniwa*, one of Japan's crack cruisers.

THE NANIWA'S ACTION

On July 25 the *Naniwa*, accompanied by the *Itsukushima* and the *Yashima*, was cruising in the Yellow Sea off the coast of the Korean Peninsula when a steamer hove in sight flying the Union Jack and the Yellow Dragon, and escorted by three Chinese cruisers. She proved to be the *Kowshing*, a British vessel chartered by the Chinese Government as a military transport, and she carried 1,100 soldiers destined to reinforce the body of troops then encamped at Yashan in Korea. The relations between China and Japan were then severely strained, though not severed. Tokyo had formally notified Peking that any further dispatch of troops to the Korean Peninsula would be deemed an act of war, and thus in the *Kowshing*, laden with troops and steaming for Yashan, Commander Togo recognized a constructive declaration of hostilities on China's part. His duty seemed perfectly clear. He summoned the *Kowshing* to surrender, and on her refusal to haul down the Dragon flag he made signal that all persons of foreign nationality on board the steamer should leave her, after which preface fire was opened. The Chinese cruisers stood by their convoy for a few minutes, but finding themselves out-classed in speed and armament they finally deserted the Kowshing and fled. The transport was sunk. Her gallant officers kept her colours flying to the last, and at the supreme moment the *Naniwa's* boats were lowered to save life, but most of the Chinese soldiers preferred death to realization of the wild fears they had been taught to harbour about the fate of prisoners falling into Japanese hands. Naturally the incident created profound excitement. It meant not only inevitable war between China and Japan, but also probable complications with England. Togo's detractors were clamorous. Nobody had looked for such a display of supreme resolution on the part of an officer so taciturn and seemingly so insignificant. Soon, however, it was universally recognized that had Togo acted differently the honour of his Government would have been sullied, and when the war closed he was promoted to be rear-admiral, his Sovereign bestowing on him the much-coveted Order of the Golden Kite. No one was more surprised than Togo at the way in which his action was regarded. All his reading and all his experience of the British 'tradition' indicated that his was the only possible course, and he was not at all concerned with the criticisms of his detractors.

THE RUSSIAN WAR

During the next nine years Togo's name was not associated with any signal incident, and the public felt some surprise when the outbreak of war with Russia in 1904 found Vice-Admiral Togo in command of the combined squadrons of his country's Navy. Lord Fisher, in his 'Records,' related how Yamamoto told him that just before the outbreak of war he (Yamamoto) had superseded a splendid admiral, loved by all his fleet, because Togo was 'just a little better!' The superseded man was the Minister's own *protégé*, but the results amply vindicated the wisdom of this selection. Togo's operations were invariably crowned with success, sometimes signal, sometimes partial, but never equivocal. His strategy showed an excellent combination of prudent reserve and resolute daring. Two objects had always to be kept in view: the destruction or complete crippling of the Russian Fleet in the East and the maintenance of a residuum of strength to meet the Russian Fleet coming from the West. The former was accomplished by holding the enemy's ships closely blockaded in Port Arthur until they became a target for the heavy guns of the investing army and the laying down of a wide minefield in traversing which many Russian ships met their doom; and the latter by such a careful husbanding of strength throughout the long struggle of 15 months that, when the final encounter took place in the Japan Sea, the Baltic Fleet was wiped out of existence. Togo's great achievements were those of his utter identification of himself with his fleet. To him no personality ever existed in the Japanese Navy: the Navy was the Navy and that was all. The Battle of Tsushima victory did not mean that Togo's strategy was greater than Rozhdestvenski's, but that the Japanese Navy was better than that of the Russians. This complete impersonality hid Togo from the people most effectively but not from his superiors. He was anxious always that there should be as much lack of feeling among his officers and men as among the varied parts of a perfect, smooth-running machine. Exultation in victory had no place in his conceptions.

It was in his dispositions to meet the Russian Baltic Fleet that Togo had to make the second great decision of his career. Two avenues were available for the Russian ships to reach Vladivostok. Togo had not strength to guard them both. A choice had to be made, and a wrong choice would have reversed the whole situation. It seemed that Togo never hesitated. He selected the Tsushima avenue, and remained there for weeks, quietly on the watch. Contrasting this calm assurance with the magnitude of the issues at stake, onlookers were disposed to attribute to Togo some occult aids to foresight. His own explanation was of the simplest. He argued that all the Russian admiral's circumstances dictated the shortest and easiest route as essential, and he felt that he himself would have chosen the southern avenue had he been in Rozhdestvenski's place. It was all very easy and straightforward, as great problems generally are when great hands undertake to solve them.

MODESTY AND SIMPLICITY

Togo became the idol of his country. His reserved, self-effacing habits, combined with the highest fighting qualities, constituted Japan's ideal leader, and when in 1907 his Sovereign raised him to the rank of Admiral, bestowed on him the First Class of the Golden Kite, and ennobled him with the title of Count, there was universal satisfaction. Subsequently Count Togo was nominated Chief of the Naval Staff; and he ultimately became Admiral of the Fleet, which title corresponds in Japan, as with us, to that of field-marshal.

An incident which occurred shortly after the war was thoroughly characteristic. The officers and men who had served under him, seeing that, after his promotion in the service and elevation to the peerage, he continued to live in the humble dwelling of his subaltern days, subscribed to present him with a suitable residence. When the money was offered to Togo he earnestly begged that it should be devoted to erecting bronze statues of the men whom Japan regarded as the fathers of her modern Navy, Admirals Kawamura, Nirei, and Saigo. His wishes were obeyed and he himself continued to lead his old life of frugality and retirement. At the time of the battle of Tsushima, in May, 1905, a son of Count Matsukata, the Elder Statesman, who was at the head of the Kawasaki dockyard at Kobe, had to send some spares urgently needed by the Japanese fleet, and with them he sent three pieces of silk, requesting that Admiral Togo would write on them. Later, in 1906, Mr. Matsukata presented one of the pieces to a Correspondent of *The Times*. The writing on it is difficult to translate, but it may be rendered. 'Cultivate virtue, faithful to calling (i.e., profession or vocation). Summer, 1905, At the front. Written by Togo.' The sense is not unlike Togo's signal before the battle, which is usually given as 'Let every man do his utmost.'

One who had served under Togo pictured him as 'gentle of voice and gentler of his expressions, rare of words, the very model of saintly dignity.' Of his great modesty many anecdotes might be told. Lord Fisher stated in his Records 'that Togo was extremely diffident about accepting the British Order of Merit, conferred upon him by King Edward in 1906, and even when he did so he wore the Order the wrong side out, so that the inscription 'For Merit' should not be seen, a few years after the war in the Far East he visited England, where he was received with every mark of respect and honour. Among the societies and institutions which entertained him was the Royal Navy Club of 1765–1785, membership of which is strictly limited to naval officers of and above commander's rank, and which only once before in its long history had entertained a foreign officer, Admiral Mahan, the American historian. While in England he also visited his old training ship, the *Worcester*. The Navy Club's compliment he appreciated the more by reason of its great traditions and the fact that Nelson had once been a member. For the great English admiral he had a profound veneration, and one of his most treasured possessions was a little bust of the victor of Trafalgar, made of wood and copper from the Victory, which was sent to him by some of his English admirers.

There's a large picture on the wall of the museum of the US Naval War College, Newport, Rhode Island, painted by a Japanese artist and depicting the arrival of Commodore Perry's four 'Black Ships' in Tokyo Bay on 8 July, 1853. It is clear that the eye and brain of this artist were quite unable to comprehend the shape, size, detail and function of these strange smoke-breathing monstrosities, in marked contrast to a cultural ability accurately to depict fishermen, fans and flowers. Togo was by then six years old.

There can be a no more telling an illustration of the consequences of Commodore Perry's historic visit – the Meiji Restoration, the fall of the Tokugawa shogunate and the extraordinarily rapid opening up of medieval Japan to an industrial revolution which soon made her a great military power.

Togo's career and the British honours that he received exemplify the friendship that then existed between Great Britain and Japan and which, no doubt, contributed to the strange incident when, on the way to the Far East and defeat at Tsushima, Admiral Rozhdestvenski's Baltic-based ships fired on British fishermen in the North Sea, believing them to be Japanese torpedo craft.

It is often forgotten that Japan declared war on Germany on 23 August 1914, capturing the German base of Tsingtao in November. From April 1917, fourteen Japanese destroyers were based at Malta, playing an efficient part in convoy escort.

In 1932 during the Sino-Japanese war and two years before Togo's death, Vice-Admiral Sir Howard Kelly, backed by four powerful cruisers, brokered a cease-fire at Shanghai in the interests of some £150 millions worth of British trading interests. When Kelly and his flagship steamed out of Shanghai, the Japanese ships manned sides and cheered him. This was the last Japanese salute to British power in the Far East.

* * *

ROBERTS

'He may be tiny, but he's wise,
He's a terror for his size.'

15 NOVEMBER 1914

FREDERICK SLEIGH ROBERTS was born at Cawnpore on September 30, 1832. His father, who lived to become General Sir Abraham Roberts, GCB, and died in his 90th year at the end of 1873, was at that time commanding the Bengal European Regiment, now known as the Munster Fusiliers. He came of a family long settled in County Waterford, and had a trace of Huguenot blood, his father's mother being a daughter of Major Francis Sautelle, who fought under King William at the Boyne.

He married, on May 17th, 1859, Nora Henrietta, daughter of Capt. Bews, 73rd Foot Rcgt. Lord Roberts, besides widow, leaves two daughters, Lady Aileen Mary, and Lady Ada Edwina Stewart Lewin, who was married on February 20, 1913, to Major Henry Lewin, RFA. There were also two other daughters Nora Frederica (died 1861) and Eveleau Sautelle (died 1869). Lord Roberts had two sons, Frederick Henry, who died in 1869, and Frederick Hugh Sherston. The latter entered the Army, and had a gallant career. Born in 1872, he served in the Waziristan Expedition in 1894–5 and was mentioned in dispatches; with the Chitral Relief Force in 1895, Nile Expedition 1898, and in South Africa during the following year as a lieutenant in the Kings Royal Rifles. Lieutenant Roberts died of wounds received while endeavouring to save the guns at the battle of Colenso, on

December 17 of that year, and was awarded, after his death, the Victoria Cross for conspicuous bravery.

Frederick Roberts was taken home by his parents when he was two years old, and was left at Clifton when they went back to India. At 13 he was sent to Eton for a year, and in January, 1847, he entered Sandhurst. His father, having obtained a nomination for him to Addiscombe, withdrew him from Sandhurst at the end of 18 months, but he had to wait a year and a half for a vacancy, and spent the time at Wimbledon. On December 12, 1851, after two years at Addiscombe, he gained his commission as second lieutenant in the Bengal Artillery, being placed ninth in his batch. Of those above him, afterwards General Sir Aeneas Perkins, was his chief engineer in Afghanistan. Roberts was a delicate boy with a weak heart, but was noted for his high spirits and resolute character.

IN THE INDIAN ARMY

He landed at Calcutta on April 1, 1852, and in the autumn went up to the Punjab to join his father, who was commanding the Peshawar Division. For 12 months he did double duty there as aide-de-camp and battery officer; but General Roberts was obliged to go home at the end of 1853, owing to ill-health. Father and son had hitherto seen little of one another, and this year of close intercourse was welcome to both. General Roberts knew the Afghans well, and shared the views of Herbert Edwardes as to the advantage of cultivating more friendly relations with them. It was fortunate for the man who was afterwards to have so much to do with them to have so sound a mentor at the outset of his career.

It was Roberts's ardent wish to belong to that famous corps, the Bengal Horse Artillery, and in 1854 he obtained the coveted jacket. He made the most of his opportunities. As he afterwards wrote:-

'The stud horses used for artillery purposes at that time were not the quiet, well-broken animals of the present day. I used to try my hand at riding them in turn, and thus learnt to understand and appreciate the amount of nerve, patience, and skill necessary to the making of a good Horse Artillery "driver," with the additional advantage that I was brought into constant contact with the men.'

He had the advantage, too, of serving at Peshawar under an exceptional brigadier, Sydney Cotton, who liked to turn his back on the drill ground and make his men practise in peace what they would have to do in war.

THE MUTINY

On May 12, 1857, news reached Peshawar of the outbreak at Meerut, and, thanks to his staff appointment, Roberts was present next day at the eventful council which settled the measures to be taken to prevent the spread of the Mutiny to the Punjab. He was staff officer to Neville Chamberlain, who at first commanded the movable column, and to Nicholson, who succeeded Chamberlain; but hearing that artillery officers were badly needed in the army before Delhi, he hurried there at the end of June. During the siege he again did double duty; he took part in the bombardment as a battery officer, but he was now definitely appointed a deputy-assistant-quartermaster general, and was mainly employed on staff duties.

He had some narrow escapes. While he was laying a gun a shot came through the embrasure and took off the arm of the gunner who was serving the vent. In repulsing a sortie on July 14 he was hit close to the spine by a bullet, and though the blow was partly deadened by a leather pouch, it was severe enough to prevent his mounting a horse for more than a month. A few days after the fall of Delhi he saw a sepoy taking deliberate aim at him in a *mêlée* but his horse reared opportunely and intercepted the bullet.

INTIMACY WITH NICHOLSON

This animal had belonged to John Nicholson, a man who impressed Roberts as no other man ever did, and whose intimacy he was proud of gaining. Nicholson confided to him his intention of proposing that Archdale Wilson, the commander of the Delhi field force, should be displaced if he hesitated any longer to order an assault. Roberts not only thought Nicholson right at the time, but was of the same opinion in his old age.

Good fortune, going hand in hand with merit, gave Roberts a share, and not an insignificant one, in the relief of Lucknow. Hardly more than a boy, he was chosen by Sir Colin Campbell to guide the relieving force from Alambagh to the Dilkusha. He had, too, the more arduous task of finding his way back to the Alambagh at night to bring up fresh ammunition. When the Moti Mahal, the last obstacle to a junction with the Residency garrison, was taken, Sir Colin told Roberts to hoist a colour on one of its turrets as a signal to Outram. Twice the colour was shot away, but he propped it up a third time, and it was not hit again.

HIS VICTORIA CROSS

After the relief Roberts was attached to Hope Grant's cavalry division, and it was in a cavalry charge at Khudaganj in January, 1858, that he won his Victoria Cross. He saved the life of a *sowar* who was overmatched by a *sepoy*, and he took a standard from two other *sepoys*. While he was struggling with one of them, the other tried to shoot him, but the musket missed fire. He was with Hope Grant during the siege of Lucknow, but by the time it was over, hard work and exposure had told so severely on his health that the doctor decided he must go to England. On April 1 – exactly six years after his arrival in India – he handed over his office to Major Wolseley, his future rival on the road to fame.

He returned to India in June of the following year, taking with him a wife; for on May 17 he had married Miss Nora Bews, daughter of Captain John Bews, formerly of the 73rd Regiment.

Roberts was sent up to Umbeyla during the operations against the Sitana fanatics in 1863; otherwise he saw no active service for several years. He had charge of the Viceroy's camps when Lord Canning made his progresses through Northern India, being recommended by Lord Clyde as 'a particularly gentlemanlike, intelligent, and agreeable young officer.'

In the Abyssinian Expedition of 1868 he was Assistant Quartermaster General with the Bengal Brigade; but he was left behind at Zula, the port of disembarcation, and had to spend four months landing and afterwards reshipping men, animals, and stores, with a temperature of 117 deg. But the time was not wasted. He learnt the organization of transport from Sir Robert Napier. In recognition of his exertions, Napier sent him to England with his final dispatches and he received a brevet lieutenant-colonelcy. He had been made brevet major in 1860.

He served in the Lushai Expedition of 1871–2, which met with serious obstacles from the country and the climate rather than from the inhabitants. These difficulties pressed especially on the department which Roberts represented, and the CB that was given to him was well earned. In January, 1875, he became brevet colonel, and was made quartermaster-general, having already officiated as such for several months. The office carried with it the temporary rank of major-general.

During these years Russia was making rapid progress in the subjugation of Central Asia. The capture of Samarkand in 1868 had brought her within 500 miles of Peshawar; the conquest of Khiva in 1873 consolidated her acquisitions, and paved the way for a future advance along the northern border of Persia. While the Russian Ambassador in London was giving assurances that Afghanistan was regarded as entirely outside the Russian sphere of action, the Governor-General of Turkestan was making repeated overtures to the Ameer. Shere Ali was at first alarmed at these overtures and reported them to the Indian Government. But he could get no definite promise of support; he had grievances of his own, and his attitude became more and more equivocal.

THE AFGHAN MENACE

As to the grave danger to British rule in India which would result from the establishment of Russian influence in Afghanistan, there were no two opinions. How the danger should be met was the point on which men differed. The Lawrence policy is misdescribed as one of 'masterly inactivity'. It proposed to warn Russia that advance beyond a certain point would entail war with England all over the world. It was a policy of indirect defence, shifting the burden from the Indian to the British taxpayer. But the warning would lose its efficacy if at any time Russia should be driven by her interests elsewhere to face the risk of war with England. When the Conservatives came into office in 1874 there were already signs that such a situation might soon be brought about by the revival of the Eastern question.

The defence of India had to be dealt with, therefore, as an Indian problem, and on the assumption of an unfriendly Ameer. It was a problem which specially concerned Roberts as Quartermaster-General. He shared the 'Mervousness' which the Duke of Argyll made light of, and he thought that our haphazard frontier required rectification, so that we might gain command of the passes instead of waiting blindfold behind them. A paper written by him was sent home by the Commander-in-Chief, Lord Napier of Magdala, and was given by Disraeli to Lord Lytton when he went out as Viceroy in 1876. It formed the starting-point of an intimacy which soon gave Roberts great opportunities; for Lytton saw that he was the sort of man he needed, and was glad of his support against older and more cautious soldiers. In March, 1878, Roberts was offered and accepted the command of the Punjab Frontier Force. It was a step downward in the military hierarchy, but it offered unequalled chances of active service. He knew, too, that Lytton intended to detach all the trans-Indus borderland from the Punjab and to make him Chief Commissioner of it.

A few months later, the repulse of Sir Neville Chamberlain's mission, following upon the welcome given to General Stolietoff at Kabul, brought matters to a rupture with the Ameer. Three columns were formed: one to advance on Kandahar by the Bolan, one to make a demonstration in the Khyber, and the third to occupy the Kuram and Khost valleys and threaten Kabul from the Shutargardan. This last column was entrusted to Roberts, and consisted of about 1,300 British and 4,000 native soldiers, with 13 guns. On November 20 orders were given to advance. Roberts had to leave one-third of his men behind as he moved up the Kuram Valley. Near the head of it he found eight Afghan regiments in a strong position, with 18 guns, and with swarms of tribesmen in support of them. They were holding about four miles of a precipitous range, clothed with dense pine forests barring the pass known as the Peiwar Kotal. Seeing the hopelessness of a front attack, Roberts decided to turn the position by a night march with two thirds of his available force. This he accomplished on December 1, though the usual hazards of a night march were aggravated by the treachery of some Pathans in a Punjab regiment. There was some sharp fighting, but the Afghans fled when they found their line of retreat threatened, abandoning their guns and baggage. The pass was won at the cost of less than 100 men killed and wounded.

Roberts pushed on to the Shutargardan, and then did what could be done with his small force to settle the Khost and Kuram valleys. Shere Ali had fled to Turkestan on the news of the forcing of the Peiwar Kotal, and died there in February. Yakub Khan succeeded him at Kabul, and on May 26 signed the Treaty of Gandamak, conceding all the British demands. Roberts thought the peace insecure, for the Afghans did not reckon themselves beaten; and it was with much misgiving that he took leave of Cavagnari in July on the summit of the Shutargardan. Cavagnari went on to Kabul, and Roberts went to Simla to serve on a Commission for reducing Army expenditure. He had been promoted major-general at the end of 1878, and he received the thanks of Parliament, and was made K C B.

THE MARCH ON KABUL

On September 5 news reached Simla of the massacre of Cavagnari and his party at Kabul. By the evening of the next day Roberts was on his way back to Kuram. His force there was the only one available for a prompt advance on Kabul, and it was to be raised to a strength of 7,500 men, with 22 guns. It was essential that he should push on rapidly before Yakub Khan should have succeeded in stirring up the tribes to resistance, as it was known he was trying to do. But, as usual, transport was lacking. It was near the end of the month before Roberts was ready to cross the

Shutargardan, and even then he had to move his two brigades forward on alternate days that the animals might serve for each in turn.

Roberts met with no opposition till he reached Charasia, about 12 miles south of Kabul. There he found the enemy in force and in a strong position in either side of the gorge through which his road lay. Demonstrating towards the defile with a small force under Major (afterwards Sir George) White, who here won his Victoria Cross, Roberts sent most of his men against the enemy's right and rolled up their line. With a loss of only 88 men he routed them so thoroughly that Kabul fell into his hands without further fighting. On October 12 he went to the Bala Hissar, and read his proclamation to a large gathering of Sirdars. A fine was imposed on the city, and parts of it were to be levelled; the carrying of weapons, whether knives or firearms, was forbidden; and all persons concerned in the late outbreak were to receive their deserts. Two Courts were instituted, one to investigate the circumstances of the outbreak, the other to try the accused.

In November communication was opened through the Khyber, where a second division had been assembled and placed under Roberts's orders. This gave him the control of 20,000 men, but of these only 8,000 were in the neighbourhood of Kabul. Some explosions at the Bala Hissar, where great quantities of powder were stored, made him decide to withdraw his men from it; and he gave orders for its demolition, as the scene of the massacre. He made arrangements for the concentration of his troops at Sherpur, in the vast cantonment built by Shere Ali; and his preparations were already well advanced when, on December 11, a storm burst upon him for which he was not unprepared, but which far surpassed his anticipations. For four days he tried to make head against the swarms of Afghans that were pouring in from all quarters by striking at them in detail before they could combine. But local successes were costly and ineffectual against such numbers, estimated at 100,000 men. He decided to confine himself to the defence of Sherpur, while waiting for a brigade which he had summoned from the Khyber line. For ten days he was shut in, and on the tenth day a furious assault was made upon the camp. But though delivered with reckless bravery, it had no chance of success. By the middle of the day the Afghans were in full flight, and by next morning their whole gathering had melted away.

TO KANDAHAR

In the latter part of July the recognition of Abdur Rahman was announced at Kabul, and orders were issued for the British troops to return to India. A few days afterwards came news of the disaster of Maiwand. Ayub Khan, the younger brother of Yakub, had marched on Kandahar from Herat and had routed a British brigade on his way. The garrison of Kandahar was weak, and there were not troops enough at Quetta for its early relief. Roberts had by this time brought his transport to a state of admirable efficiency, and he at once proposed that he should lead a column from Kabul The proposal, supported by Stewart, was approved by Lard Ripon, the new Viceroy; and on August 9 Roberts began his famous march with a carefully-selected and well-equipped force of 10,000 men. Ho took with him only 18 guns, and these mountain guns, that he might not be delayed by wheeled artillery in a country without roads; but he had 8,000 followers and more than 10,000 animals.

He met with no opposition, and there was no want of food and forage; but the hardships inseparable from a rapid march were aggravated by want of water and extreme variations of temperature. In the first fortnight he covered 225 miles, to Kolat-i-Ghilzai. There he learnt that Kandahar was in no immediate danger, and he was able to allow eight days to the remaining 88 miles. On August 31 he entered Kandahar, and next day he defeated and dispersed Ayub Khan's army. It was a brilliant achievement. The fruit of careful forethought, boldness, and vigour; and the English people's appreciation of it was heightened by the shock of Maiwand and the subsequent suspense. But Roberts himself had pointed out that, with such a force as he had, his task was really much less arduous than the march on Kabul in the previous autumn. He again received the thanks of Parliament, and was rewarded with a baronetcy and the GCB. He was appointed to the command of the Madras Army, but his health had suffered so much that he was obliged to go to England in October. He was abundantly fêted and honoured, but he did not succeed in persuading the Government to retain Kandahar.

INDIAN ARMY ORGANIZATION

He had been little more than three months at home when he was sent to South Africa on the news of the Majuba disaster and the death of Colley. But he reached the Cape only to find terms of peace agreed upon, and in 24 hours he was on his way back to England. In the autumn of 1881 he returned to India, and held the command at Madras till the end of 1885, when he succeeded Sir Donald Stewart as Commander-in-Chief in India. During his tenure of this office he did much for the military strength of the country and for the welfare of the individual soldier. He revised the schemes for fortifying Quetta and other points on the north-west frontier and pressed forward their execution, but passive defence was not much to his taste, and he was more intent on improving communications and establishing an adequate transport. His chief care was to render the Indian Army as perfect a fighting machine as it was possible to make it. He took great pains to improve the shooting, both of infantry and artillery, and to practise field firing under conditions as like those of actual service as might be. He found a zealous instrument in Colonel Ian Hamilton, afterwards one of his best lieutenants in South Africa.

In 1881 Mr. Childers had offered him the post of Quartermaster-General at the Horse Guards, although he was an outspoken critic of the short-service system, and thought that 'the Army was being sacrificed to obtain a Reserve, which was one only in name.' At that time he preferred to remain in India; but when he was invited, in 1890, to succeed Lord Wolseley as Adjutant-General, he accepted the offer. Three months afterwards it was somehow found that he could not be spared just then from India. He was asked to remain there two years more, and Lord Wolseley was succeeded by Sir Redvers Buller. On January 1, 1892, Roberts was given a peerage, and a further extension of his term of command was offered him; but he needed rest and change of climate, and in the spring of 1893 he finally left India, amid universal expressions of regret and regard.

After his return to England he had two years of leisure, which enabled him to tell the story of his 'Forty-one years in India.' There are few better records of a soldier's life. He offered it only as 'a plain, unvarnished tale of Indian life and adventure,' and it was occasionally careless in style and wanting in literary finish. But there was singular charm about its simplicity and directness and its modest and generous tone.

In May, 1895, he was made Field-Marshal, and in October he became Commander-in-Chief in Ireland. There, as in India, he tried to improve the shooting of the troops, being convinced that 'one good shot is nowadays equal to at least half a dozen bad ones'; and he laid stress on combining effective fire-control with a high standard of individual marksmanship. He did not at that time accept the prevailing German opinion that at the decisive ranges volleys are no longer possible. 'Once launched to the attack, men will, no doubt, get out of hand occasionally, but if they have been carefully trained, it should not be difficult to pull them together, and if this can be done sufficiently to enable them to fire even one volley it will give them a new lease of courage and steadiness'; so he told the All Ireland Rifle Meeting at the Curragh in 1897. His various speeches on 'Musketry Training and Artillery Practice' from 1884 onward were reprinted (though not published) in the autumn of 1899, and were noticed at some length in *The Times* of September 23.

THE BOER WAR

When the Government decided to send an army corps to the Cape they might well have given the command of it to the man who had been hurried out there 18 years before and hurried home again. But his age and his rank were against him; and Sir Redvers Buller seemed to be marked out for the task by his knowledge of the country and the people, as well as by other qualifications. By the time he reached the Cape the first flashes of success at Talana Hill and Elandslaagto had been replaced by the gloom of Nicholson's Nek, and the force which was to protect Natal was itself shut up in Ladysmith. These Dutch farmers were plainly more formidable than we had anticipated, not in mere number of men and guns, but in the use they could make of them. Few doubted, however, that when the troops already on their way should arrive the tide would turn.

Six weeks of expectation followed, and then came even worse news. Gatacre at Stormberg, Methuen at Magersfontein, Buller himself at Colenso, had met with reverses which were disquieting out of all proportion to the actual loss incurred. In South Africa, as in Spain, there was need of a man with grasp of the situation to give unity of direction to our widely-scattered force. Few were at that time aware that the General on the spot was suggesting that he should 'let Ladysmith go'; but nevertheless it was with a deep sense of relief that the British public learnt on December 18 that Lord Roberts was going out to take command, with Lord Kitchener as Chief of the Staff.

Among those who sacrificed their lives in endeavouring to save the guns at Colenso was Lieutenant Frederick Hugh Sherston Roberts, Lord Roberts's only son, who was on the staff of General Clery. Only 28 years of age, he had already served in three Indian expeditions and in the Nile Campaign of 1898. He lived long enough to be recommended for the Victoria Cross. There was singular pathos in the summons to the veteran Field-Marshal to take the field himself following so closely upon such a blow, and the wife who bravely bore this two-fold trial deserved well of her country.

POSITION IN SOUTH AFRICA

Roberts saw from the first that the only course which promised any real success was to concentrate the British forces and carry the war into the Free State – to revert, in fact, to the original plan of campaign. But he would have to guard an ever-lengthening line of communications, and must wait for large reinforcements from England or Natal. He also needed a transport service that would allow him to operate freely, for to be tied to the railway lines was to give the enemy the choice of battlefields. The existing transport was not only insufficient in quantity, it was on the regimental system; that is to say, it was attached to the several units for their own special use. Such appropriation, however convenient, is an expensive luxury.

Setting this system aside as far as possible, Roberts with Kitchener's help organized a transport available for general use, comprising more than 20,000 mules and oxen, and he found an able Director of Transport in his military secretary, Sir William Nicholson, who had been chief of the staff in the Tirah Campaign. The local Volunteers had hitherto felt themselves slighted. Roberts made much of them, drew his own bodyguard from them, and formed a separate Colonial Division of some 3,000 mounted men under the command of a tried soldier and stanch loyalist, Colonel Brabant.

Troops arrived at the Cape in a full and steady stream, and at the beginning of February Mr. Wyndham was able to tell the House of Commons that, including those who were on their way or under orders, the total was no fewer than 180,000. But the effective fighting strength was not more than half that number and of this two-fifths were in Natal. The force there still found itself unequal to its task, and on February 7 Sir Redvers Buller abandoned his third attempt to reach Ladysmith. The attempt and its abandonment were alike against Roberts's wish. Kimberley was becoming clamorous for relief; the Boers about Colesberg were showing themselves more aggressive and Sir Alfred Milner feared that there would be a general rising of disloyal Dutch throughout Cape Colony as soon as the British troops left it behind them. But Roberts held fast to his plan, and was deaf to all solicitations to fritter away his forces, while careful to conceal the point where he was massing them. Risks must be run in war: but he was confident that his advance would draw the Boers to him, and would not only relieve Kimberley, but lessen the strain in Cape Colony and Natal. He chose the western line rather than the line leading direct to Bloemfontein, not only because it was the road to Kimberley, but because it led through less difficult country, and he would not be exposed to attack on both flanks.

On February 8 he arrived at Modder River camp, and three days afterwards he began to turn Cronje's position. It was a wide *detour*, as if one should go from London to Hatfield by way of Reigate, Guildford, and Windsor. But this devious course perplexed the enemy as to his object and gave him a comparatively clear road. His army numbered 40,000 combatants, of which nearly 10,000 were mounted, and he had 100 guns. French's cavalry division led the way, nearly 15,000 strong, with seven batteries of Horse Artillery. On the 12th it seized Dekiel's Drift on the Riet river, and on the 13th it reached Klip Drift on the Modder. French had to wait there a day for infantry to come up to guard the drift; but on the 15th he rode into Kimberley, after charging through a gap between two bodies of the enemy. In four days of intense heat his division had marched nearly 100 miles.

CAPTURE OF CRONJE

Cronje was slow to believe that the British Army was enveloping him, but on the morning of the 10th he was found to be in full retreat eastward from Magersfontein. All that day and the next the Sixth Division, which had relieved the Cavalry at Klip Drift, hung upon his rear. French was engaged with a retreating column of the enemy to the north of Kimberley on the 16th, but on the 17th he appeared on Cronje's left flank, and gained a position commanding the drift by which the Boer general meant to pass the Modder. Cronje might still have saved his men by sacrificing his guns and wagons, but he decided to entrench himself and hold out in hope of succour. He formed a laager on the north bank and occupied some miles of the deep bed of the river, a little above Paardeberg Drift. He was vigorously attacked on the 18th by Kelly-Kenny and Kitchener, in the hope that his camp might be stormed before he could strengthen it, but the British troops had to be drawn off after losing 1,200 men.

Roberts himself arrived at Paardeberg on the 19th. He decided not to renew the attack, but to tighten his grip of the Boer camp, shell it day after day, and drive away the parties that came to its assistance. Cronje held out with rare tenacity, but his position was hopeless and became intolerable. On the morning of February 27 (Majuba Day) he surrendered with 4,000 men. Nor was this all. The invasion of the Free State had the effect, which Roberts reckoned on, of drawing some 10,000 men from the Boer forces in Natal, and after a fortnight's hard fighting the relief of Ladysmith was accomplished on the day after Cronje's surrender.

Hard work and starvation had worn out the horses. A week's rest was imperative for them, and was also needed for the bringing up of troops and supplies. It allowed the enemy to muster in considerable force for the defence of Bloemfontein, but when Roberts advanced they made no stand. He moved on a front of many miles, turning positions instead of attacking them, and with the fate of Cronje before their eyes the Boers did not wait for him to complete his movements. If his Cavalry had been in better condition, he might have captured at Poplar Grove not only guns and stores, but the two Presidents, for they were on the field, vainly exhorting their burghers to stand firm. Preparations were made for such a stand at Bains Vlei, 10 miles west of Bloemfontein; but Roberts, turning southward from the direct road, avoided this position, and on the 13th he entered the capital of the Free State.

At the beginning of May the 10th Division, under Hunter, crossed the Vaal near Kimberley and fought its way up the right bank till it joined hands with the 1st Division at Fourteen Streams. At the same time Roberts began his own advance on Pretoria. His army had latterly been echeloned on the Upper Modder, from Karreo siding on the railway to Wepener, on the Basuto border. Leaving the 8th and 3rd Divisions with Brabant's Colonial corps to guard his communication and to prevent the Boers in the eastern districts of the Free State from going south again, he moved rapidly forward with the 7th and 11th Divisions. The Cavalry under French were in advance on his left, and on his right was a newly-formed division under Ian Hamilton, with the Highland Brigade in support of it. His advance was made on so broad a front as to outflank the Boers. They meant to dispute the Zand river, and as his telegram put it, 'They occupied a position 20 miles in length; ours was necessarily longer.' By these tactics, always enveloping, instead of allowing himself to be enveloped, he forced back the enemy with small loss of men or time, and on May 12 he reached Kroonstad.

He was obliged to wait there about 10 days while the railway was being repaired and supplies were coming up. During this time he had the satisfaction of learning that Mafeking, after crowning its gallant defence by the repulse of a determined assault and the capture of more than a hundred prisoners, had been relieved on the 17th; and that on the same day Buller had reoccupied Newcastle, after skilfully turning the Biggarsberg positions and driving the enemy back to Laing's Nek.

THE MARCH TO PRETORIA

On the 22nd Roberts resumed his advance. His mounted infantry were already at Heilbron, and on the Queen's birthday they crossed the Vaal. On the same day a proclamation was issued annexing the Free State, to be known henceforward as the Orange River Colony. In the north-east of it there were still several thousand burghers in arms, and Roberts was advised by some of his staff to subdue the country more thoroughly before he entered the Transvaal But while fully alive to the risk he ran, he felt that it was worth running. Delay would not only enable the enemy to prepare for a more obstinate defence of Pretoria; it would allow them to remove some 4,000 British prisoners, and perhaps to commit wholesale destruction of mines and buildings at Johannesburg.

Pressing forward with a rapidity which took the Boers aback, he seized the railway junction of Germiston on the 29th, and on the 31st he entered Johannesburg. His swift approach caused panic at Pretoria, the Boer resistance collapsed, and the war bade fair to come to an end. President Kruger fled eastward with all the gold on which he could lay hands, and the burghers under General Botha melted away to a few hundreds. But at this crisis the Free State leaders showed more backbone than those of the Transvaal. It was settled that guerilla tactics should be tried and they soon met with a success which put fresh heart into the burghers and swelled the strength of their commandoes.

Only a feeble stand was made in front of Pretoria. Kruger, Botha, and other prominent men were leaving wives or property there, and had no wish to provoke a bombardment of the city; and on June 5 the British flag was once more hoisted there.

In his conduct of these operations Roberts had shown a happy mixture of judgment and vigour, of suavity and strength. His Afghan campaigns had given ample evidence of the dash, insight, and decision which made a successful leader in Indian warfare; but as Algeria proved a bad school in some respects for French officers, so victories won over Asiatics might have habituated him to a style of fighting ill-suited to so different an enemy. If age was likely to cool his ardour, it was even more likely to rob him of that suppleness of mind which instantly recognizes and adapts itself to new factors in war. It had done neither one nor the other. 'For 19 years I have led an abstemious life in the hope of this day,' is said to have been his answer to Lord Lansdowne's appeal to him to go out, and he had kept his mind as fit as his body. Again, his tact and kindliness were well known. 'Bobs' had won the heart of the British soldier in an unexampled degree. But he did not shrink from making great demands upon his men or from plain speaking and strong action in cases that called for them.

President Kruger had shifted his Government to Machadodorp, on the Delagoa Bay railway, which afforded means of supply and a way of escape. Botha, with a force which soon grew to 5,000 men, remained west of Middelburg, covering the new capital and at the same time threatening the neighbourhood of the old one. He was driven back on June 12 after an obstinate fight at Diamond Hill. To guard against being outflanked he had extended his front so widely that his centre was weak, and Roberts had an opportunity of showing that turning movements were not his only resource.

To bring the war to an end it was plainly necessary to push eastward up to the Portuguese frontier, forcing the Boers off the railway or over the border. But two things had to be done first – an additional line of communication must be opened between Pretoria and Natal, which would also serve to separate the Orange from the Transvaal Boers; and the Orange Boers must be more effectively subdued. The former was accomplished early in July. Sir Redvers Buller had gained possession of Laing's Nek on June 12; by the 23rd he was at Standerton; and by July 4 the Natal army was in touch with the main army near Heidelberg. The subjugation of the Orange Boers proved more difficult. Columns from north, west, and south, amounting to something liko 30,000 men, converged upon the Bethlehem district and drove the Boers before them into Brandwater basin, on the Basuto border. Out of some 7,000 Boers 4,000 surrendered with Prinsloo at the end of July; but De Wet and Steyn had broken through the cordon, and a fresh attempt to surround them on the Vaal in August failed. Circling round Pretoria, Steyn went to Machadodorp to join Kruger, while De Wet returned to his own country to keep the guerrilla warfare alive.

THE TRANSVAAL ANNEXED

By this time Roberts's preparations for dealing a final blow to the organized forces of the Transvaal were well advanced. In the latter part of July he had occupied Middelburg, and early in August Buller had begun his march northward with 10,000 men of the Natal army to cooperate with 15,000 men moving eastward along the Delagoa Bay railway. On the 24th Roberts left Pretoria for Belfast, and on the 28th, after two days' hard fighting, Machadodorp was occupied and the Boer commandoes scattered. Nearly all the British prisoners were released, and on September 1 the annexation of the Transvaal was proclaimed.

While Buller followed up the retreating burghers to Lydenburg and Pilgrim's Rest and French made his way to Barberton, Pole-Carew and Ian Hamilton followed the line of railway to Komati Poort, which was reached on September 24. Lourenço Marques ceased to be a Boer port of supply, Kruger had taken refuge there on the 11th, and on October 19 he left South Africa in a Dutch man-of-war.

Roberts returned to Pretoria before the end of September. Circumstances kept him two months longer in the Transvaal, but his task was done, and he was wanted at home to succeed Lord Wolseley as Commander-in-Chief.

Lord Roberts reached England on January 2, 1901, in time to receive the personal thanks of Queen Victoria and to be rewarded by her with an earldom and the Garter. Three weeks later he was charged with the military arrangements for her funeral. He was warmly welcomed on all sides, but he asked that all public demonstrations should be postponed till the end of the war. He entered at once upon his duties at the War Office.

The changes in Army administration during the latter half of the 19th century had made the position of the Commander-in-Chief an anomalous one. The 'dual system' had been gradually superseded by the unquestioned predominance of the Secretary of State. The real power of the Commander-in-Chief fell short of the dignity of the office and the associations which hung about it. After 1895, when Lord Wolseley succeeded the Duke of Cambridge, the other military chiefs at the War Office became, in fact, his colleagues, while his title implied that they were his Staff officers. Owing to the bitter complaints made by Lord Wolseley this state of things was altered to some extent after Roberts's appointment. The Adjutant-General was made the subordinate of the Commander-in-Chief, like the Military Secretary and the head of the Intelligence Branch. The Commander-in-Chief had a certain responsibility and control also in regard to the Ordnance and Supply services, but his functions were vague, and he was liable to be overruled.

TRAINING A MODERN ARMY

But if friction was inevitable from a false position, much valuable work was done during the three years of his association with Mr. Brodrick. He declared it to be the most important duty of general officers to maintain a high standard of efficiency in musketry, since straight shooting counts for as much as tactical combinations on the modern battlefield. He recognized that even for cavalry the firearm is now the principal weapon, and he had the boldness to discard the lance in the teeth of cavalry sentiment.

The encouragement of intelligence and initiative, both for horse and foot, was a matter on which he laid stress on every opportunity, and in the preface to the new drill book (significantly called Infantry Training) he said: 'It is forbidden to limit or restrict the freedom granted in these regulations to battalion and company commanders, both as regards methods of instruction and the leading of their men in action. Nor are the men to be allowed to degenerate into mere machines.' He set his face against all playing at soldiers, and did what he could to raise the standard of the Militia, Yeomanry, and Volunteers, provoking some discontent by his requirements. He made a serious effort to cut down officers' expenses, especially in the cavalry, and to open that arm to fit men who had hitherto been debarred from it. He dwelt much on the importance of good horsemanship. A 'service dress' was introduced, suited to modern warfare and aiming at invisibility instead of showiness. Efficiency for war was in fact kept steadily in view in all the changes that were made. Staff appointments were reduced to three years and young men who had done well in South Africa were given high commands.

It might be expected to be one advantage of having a renowned soldier at the War Office that his decisions in matters of discipline would ordinarily he accepted as final. But the widespread interest in personal questions and the growing tendency of Parliament to meddle with executive details annul this advantage. As Commander-in-Chief Roberts had two troublesome cases to deal with – the repeated fires which occurred at Sandhurst, and the 'ragging' in the Grenadier Guards. In both cases the course which he took met with general approval, but in both he was called upon, or found it advisable, to defend himself in the House of Lards against irresponsible critics.

CREATION OF ARMY COUNCIL

In the autumn of 1903 the Commission on the War in South Africa made its report. It showed how unsatisfactory was the *status* of the Commander-in-Chief, and how the country had failed to benefit to such an extent as might have been anticipated from having an experienced soldier in that capacity at the beginning of the war. Who was to blame was a moot point, but it was agreed on all hands that something must be done. Lord Wolseley' suggestion was that the Minister of War should be a soldier, as in foreign countries, or else that the Commander-in-Chief should be in the Cabinet. Lord Roberts advised a reversion to something like the Cardwell system, a division of the War Office into three branches – military, spending, and finance, each with its responsible head. The War Commission as a whole made no recommendation, but Lord Esher (with the concurrence of some of his colleagues) proposed that the War

Office should be remodelled on the lines of the Admiralty, and the office of Commander-in-Chief be abolished, as the Hartington Commission had advised in 1890. The Government wisely took this course to which public opinion had long been tending.

On February 18 the retirement of Lord Roberts was officially announced, and at the same time King Edward publicly expressed his thanks to the Field-Marshal for his services of over 50 years in India, in Africa, and at home. 'During that long period,' his Majesty wrote, 'he has performed every duty entrusted to him with unswerving zeal and unfailing success.' A higher tribute could not have been desired or better deserved by any man.

Lord Roberts's official career thus ended nearly 11 years ago, but his activities, as everyone knows, continued to the day of his death. He followed the reorganization of the Army which Lord (then Mr.) Haldane undertook with perhaps more anxiety than sympathy, but when once the reforms had been decided upon he was not slow to give his support to the new Territorial Force and do his best to make it a success. At the same time he did not fear to criticize the weakness of the whole scheme and when, after the lapse of several years, it became evident to him that by no possibility could the new organization meet national needs, he opened the last and not the least glorious of his campaigns. He had then attained the ago of 79, but it was with equal vigour end enthusiasm that he set out upon a tour of the country for the purpose of awakening it to the danger that threatened. In Manchester, Bristol, Leeds, Glasgow, and elsewhere he urged the necessity of national service, and henceforth his whole life was devoted to that cause.

The present crisis found Lord Roberts as alert, vigorous, and resolute as ever. He followed every turn of the war with the keenest interest, plunged into a vast correspondence with the innumerable friends in the Army and elsewhere who always turned to him for advice and sympathy, was a constant visitor to the Government Departments, and in particular lent his name and active support to the work of collecting field-glasses, saddles, and other additional equipment for the troops. Up to the moment of his leaving England he was at the height of his remarkable powers, and it is a consolation on to those who mourn his loss that he should have been spared what to him would have been the supreme terror of a decline into useless inactivity.

Seldom if ever can a commander have enjoyed the confidence and trust of his soldiers as did Field Marshal Earl Roberts of Kandahar,

Pretoria and Waterford, VC, KG, GCB, OM. He had the unique quality of knowing what to do in crisis or emergency, the quality that every serviceman seeks in those responsible for his life and the success of his mission. Above all, he could reorganize his force quickly and move it swiftly to where it could seize the best advantage and win the battle.

Known to his British and Indian soldiers as 'Bobs Bahadur', from the days when he led the way on his lively pony from Kabul to Kandahar, he was a small but fiery man. As the couplet put it after his victory in South Africa:

> He may be tiny, but he's wise,
> He's a terror for his size.

He died in France, where he had gone to welcome Indian troops, within the sound of the guns. To date, he is the only man to win the Victoria Cross, be appointed a Knight of the Garter and receive the Order of Merit.

* * *

HINDENBURG

'Father Of The Fatherland'

3 AUGUST 1934

WHETHER FIELD-MARSHAL von Hindenburg, President of the German Reich, whose death in his eighty-seventh year we announce on another page, will be recognized by history as the greatest soldier of the Great War of 1914–1918 is questionable; but he may well stand out in the perspective of time as one of the greatest men of the chaotic period which was opened by the War and continued in its shadow.

There were other soldiers, even on the German side, who may have surpassed Hindenburg in military brilliance; politicians who rose to European and world prominence during and after the War may have surpassed him in statesmanship; but it is hard to think of any man who, combining high qualities both of military leadership and of statesmanship with an outstanding strength and simplicity of character, achieved so much for his own country in difficult circumstances, so long as he was in fully conscious and unfettered exercise of his functions as head of the State. It was in crises where strategy, military or political, was of little avail without character that Hindenburg's finest work was done. He was, in the long period of his fully active life, a leader in the highest sense of the term, not always in the van, but, wherever duties placed him, an outstanding figure, imperturbable, firm as a rock, inspiring trust, and always ready unhesitatingly to take responsibility.

It may be assumed with some confidence that, without this unfailing reserve of moral strength, the military achievements of Germany in the War, the conception of which has been attributed in large measure to Ludendorff and other Staff officers, would have been less remarkable than they were. It can be assumed, too, that without it Stresemann and others would have met with even greater obstacles in their political efforts to save Germany from chaos after the War and restore her to a place of consideration among the Powers. It is, indeed, almost impossible to imagine the course German Republican history would have taken during the first decade after the War without Hindenburg's Presidency; and quite impossible without what was perhaps the greatest service of all, the simple decision, in November, 1918, to stand by the country when the Kaiser had fled and to lead the German Army home.

FOUR PHASES

On October 2, 1927, when Germans united, as they had not united in anything for nine years, to honour their President on the occasion of his eightieth birthday, there emerged from all the hundreds of tributes a sketch of his life in four clear-cut phases which may be recalled because it was an epitome of nearly a century of German history and conveyed the essence of a character in which honesty and simplicity dominated other qualities. That there was to be a distinct fifth phase, somewhat puzzling in comparison with the others and attributable partly, perhaps, to advanced age, was not then foreseen.

The first four phases were these:- Paul von Beneckendorf und von Hindenburg, of old Junker stock, served four Kings of Prussia and three German Emperors as an able officer. General Beneckendorf von

Hindenburg, having, in his own words, 'done better in his military career than he had ever dared to hope,' and having retired to make room for younger blood, was asked to command an army in 1914, replied, 'Am ready,' and stopped the 'Russian steam-roller.'

Field-Marshal von Hindenburg, Chief of the General Staff, left his Imperial master, on the bitterest day of his life, to face a topsy-turvy world of which, he wrote afterwards, his one longing was to know no more, allied himself – his own words – with the Socialist saddler-President Ebert 'to save our people from the threatening collapse,' and led the Army, back from the War to a German Republic; 'I remained at my post,' he wrote in his simple way in his memoirs. Lastly, the old soldier, 'Our Hindenburg,' as he was affectionately called, once again in retirement plunged at the age of 77 into the turmoil of a Presidential Election in the hope of preserving unity in a country torn by political passions stimulated by the sufferings of the inflation period, and, as President von Hindenburg, carried out his constitutional duties with noteworthy correctness. Such was the record which, on the President's eightieth birthday, inspired Herr Marx, then Chancellor, and formerly his opponent in the Presidential Election, to declare that the German nation gratefully acknowledged him 'Father of the Fatherland.'

THE NATIONAL IDOL

In the old Field-Marshal the German male discovered quite early in the War an incorporation of his own ideal. And so the iron mask and rock-firm figure became an inalienable possession of the nation. Germans took a pride and found fresh consolation when they spoke with affectionate familiarity of 'Our Hindenburg' or climbed the wooden colossus that during the War stood alongside the Victory Column in the Königsplatz, under the shadow of the Reichstag, and the hammering of a golden nail into its epaulettes, a silver one into the tunic seam to make the buttons, or a leaden one elsewhere, if the hammerer's means were slender, became an act of patriotic homage.

Of Hindenburg it must be said to his credit that hero-worship failed to turn his head, so that he remained one of the very few Junker-born leaders who were not *poseurs*. There was neither sham nor snobbery about him. The respect and popularity which he was able to acquire in the first flush of success afterwards survived defeat and revolution. Even the staunchest opponents of the system and the ideal in which he gave his service would have paid him to the last an ungrudging tribute. Absence of introspectiveness and genuine concentration of purpose, both of them exceptions rather than the rule in German mentality, enabled him in all his doing and thinking to conceive of no other than a single interest common to all his fellow-countrymen.

Paul von Beneckendorf und von Hindenburg was born in Posen on October 2, 1847, of a stock which had long been settled in the Eastern marches. Its elder branch, the Beneckendorfs, can trace their descent in the Altmark to the year 1280. At the age of 11 he entered the Corps of Cadets, and became a second-lieutenant in the 3rd Guard Infantry Regiment in April, 1865. During the Austrian campaign of 1866 he won distinction at the battle of Königgrätz, where he was slightly wounded in the head. In the Franco-German War Hindenburg fought with the same regiment, and was seriously engaged for the first time on August 18, 1870, at St. Privat, the village which was afterwards called 'the graveyard of the Prussian Guard.' Hindenburg again distinguished himself, and was later present at Sedan, although only in the role of a spectator. He was with the besieging army outside Paris, and saw the proclamation of the German Empire at Versailles. Thus at a very early age he had twice enjoyed the privilege of entering Berlin as a member of the victorious Army, in a triumphal march through the Brandenburger Tor.

Shortly after he returned from the Franco-Prussian War Hindenburg passed the entrance examination to the *Kriegs Akademie*, which he entered in 1873. From that time onward he passed with unfailing regularity through the various grades of staff appointment, with periodical intervals as a regimental officer in accordance with the Prussian usage. At the age of 46 he was promoted colonel and took over command of the 91st Infantry Regiment at Oldenburg, where he remained until 1896, when he became major-general and Chief of Staff to the VIII Army Corps at Coblenz. In 1900 he was again promoted, and took over the command of the 28th Baden Infantry Division at Karlsruhe, an appointment which he vacated three years later on succeeding to the command of the IV Army Corps at Magdeburg, one of the most important peace-time commands. He retired in 1911, when he was 64, and went to live in Hanover. He explained that he did not think he would ever see the day of war, and therefore desired to clear the path for younger minds.

THE GREAT WAR
LIBERATION OF EAST PRUSSIA

Hindenburg himself gave a vivid picture of the anxious days of waiting after the outbreak of war in August, 1914, before he received the call to service. His doctors had always certified him, in the German phrase, 'core-healthy.' On August 23 the suspense was ended by a tele-gram received from General Headquarters asking whether he was ready for immediate employment in a high command. Before his laconic answer 'Am ready' could have arrived he had received a further telegram informing him of his appointment as GOC Eighth Army, which was then in retreat on the Eastern frontier. His Chief of Staff, General Ludendorff, was already named, and the first meeting of the two men whose partner-ship was to remain unbroken till the end of the War occurred at Hanover railway station during the small hours, of the following morning.

The retreat of the Eighth Army in East Prussia had made it necessary to find a new commander who could be relied on to save the situation by bold measures. Such a one was believed to have been found in General Erich Ludendorff, taken fresh from the storming of Liege. Ludendorff, however, was a relatively junior officer. He was also an uncommonly self-willed and difficult subordinate. In this emergency the choice of a superior fell on General von Hindenburg, who combined an un-tarnished military record with the necessary gifts of personality. His intimate knowledge of the East Prussian terrain was naturally regarded as a strong supplementary recommendation.

A 'HAPPY MARRIAGE'

Hindenburg, in his memoirs, described the comradeship-in-arms with General Ludendorff thus established as a 'happy marriage,' whereas Ludendorff was prone always to employ the pronoun 'I' when narrating those actions and decisions which nominally required the sanction of his immediate superior. Undoubtedly Hindenburg may be judged a competent military expert, untrammelled with false notions, who could comprehend and appreciate the inspirations of a talented subordinate. The implication of Ludendorff's 'I' that the Field-Marshal lacked creative genius is not in itself misleading. Nevertheless, the whole truth would have to take equal account of Hindenburg's capacity to adjust and conciliate.

The Eighth Army was in evil case. Its front and its right flank were threatened by two Russian armies, and General Prittwitz, its first commander, had proposed a withdrawal to the Lower Vistula, which would have meant the abandonment of East Prussia. Hindenburg, who was sent to prevent the retreat and if possible to open an offensive, was able by exploiting the palpable shortcomings of the Russians to feint against one army with an insignificant force and concentrate the whole of his remaining troops against the other, inflicting a heavy defeat at

Tannenberg on August 28–29. He then turned against the first Russian Army, and by fighting the first battle of the Masurian lakes pushed it back on to the lower waters, of the Niemen. East Prussia was liberated, and at the same time the campaign had cost the Russians an exceedingly heavy toll of prisoners, guns, and ammunition. Hindenburg was advanced to the rank of Colonel-General, and was decorated with the first class of the Iron Cross. It was not long before he became 'Our Hindenburg,' not only for the Eighth Army but for all the armies, and ultimately for the entire nation.

FALKENHAYN'S DECISION

The campaign had directed the attention of the Higher Command to the possibilities of striking victories over the Russians just at the moment when the hope of a short Western campaign was proved mistaken. Moreover the duumvirate in the East steadily pressed forward their conviction that 'the war must be won in the East.' Falkenhayn, who had succeeded Moltke as Chief of the General Staff after the Battle of the Marne, was faced with the failure of his Flanders offensive at the end of 1914, but before this was manifest took a decision in favour of extensive operations on the Polish front in view of the necessity for supporting the Austrian Army in Galicia.

Accordingly, Hindenburg was placed at the head of an Army Group of two armies – the Eighth and Ninth. His plan was to bring the Russian forces in Poland to a standstill by directing an offensive against their northern flank, while the Eighth Army neutralized the threat of a second descent on the East Prussian frontier bastion: Falkenhayn found himself in substantial disagreement with the Eastern Army Group Command, because to his mind support of the Austrians was far more urgent. He accordingly ordered the advance of the Ninth Army in the neighbourhood of Cracow in closest cooperation with the Austrians.

The October campaign in Southern Poland, although it saw an initial advance by the Germans almost to the gates of Warsaw and by the Austrian forces to the River San, ended in a retreat. An outflanking movement was executed by the Russian Army based on Warsaw, which threatened the German left, and the Eighth Army had in consequence to make its second retirement to the Masurian lakes. Hindenburg was nevertheless promoted to be Field-Marshal.

A LOST OPPORTUNITY

Winter was rapidly approaching, but the Eastern Command returned with that resourceful energy which was its characteristic and without a moment's delay to carry out the original intention. A rapid advance in November culminated in an encircling movement on Lodz. But the reinforcements which were required to consolidate the new positions and which had been begged for at the outset from the German High Command, as well, as from the Austrians, were not forthcoming, although the Austrian line on the Carpathians was more than adequately held and the massed formations on the Western front were at this time still beating vainly against the iron wall which defended Ypres.

In the result, the opportunity was not only lost, but lost ignominiously. The three German Army Corps which had been attacking Lodz on the North and East escaped only by the skin of their teeth from complete encirclement. At the end of 1914 the Ninth Army still stood, on Russian soil, but the successes of its campaign had so far been purely transient. The Russian flood had been stemmed, but a dangerously weak Eighth Army was still astride of the Masurian lakes leaving considerable tracts of German territory under hostile occupation when the two sides passed from the rapid movements of open warfare to the task of entrenching for the winter.

SUCCESS AND FAILURE

Neither winter nor disappointment served to daunt the old Field-Marshal in his determination to push back the enemy at the earliest opportunity beyond the East Prussian border. Reinforcements had reached him and a new army – the Tenth – had come up on the Baltic flank, so that the Eighth now held the centre. He was equally determined, for the attainment of this aim, that the operative plans of his own command should at length be brought to fruition. Not only did the second Masurian victory free East Prussia, but the reverberating success made certain the encirclement of a large Russian force in the forests of Augustow, and advanced the line of battle in enemy territory.

The effect of this campaign performed in the depth of winter made, however, little difference in the general situation; but the fame of Hindenburg and his Chief of Staff became even greater, and both received special tokens of the Imperial favour. Far more portentous was the enthusiasm which acclaimed the Field-Marshal as the idol of the public. Nevertheless, the Austro-German forces operating from Gorlice-Tarnow, which in the course of the summer of 1915 drove the Russians from Galicia and Poland, were under the command of Mackensen.

If 1915 was for Germany a year of victory sufficient to disguise a stalemate, 1916 brought disillusionment and crisis. The High Command appears to have assumed that Russia had been heavily defeated. It therefore concentrated its forces in the West, where were begun in February those costly attacks upon Verdun which failed utterly after an all-promising beginning. In June the Russians, under Brussiloff, suddenly awoke from their winter slumber, defeated the Austrians from the Bukovina to the Pripet, and even attacked .the Germans so far north as Riga. The position of the German High Command was especially critical because the summer campaign, which had begun in July with the Battle of the Somme, precluded the withdrawal of any Western divisions.

THE FINAL EFFORT

By the end of August the situation had become more precarious. The last German reserves, and even a Turkish Army Corps, had been rushed to the assistance of the Austrians, who were confronted on the 27th of that month by a declaration of war from Rumania. The losses in the West, the false estimate of the real strength of Russia, and the consequent depression of German opinion would have been enough to cost Falkenhayn his position without the network of secret intrigue woven against him. On August 28 Hindenburg was informed by the Chief of the Military Cabinet that the situation was serious and bidden to present himself at Pless, the seat of the Imperial Headquarters, on the 29th. Arriving in the company of General Ludendorff, he was notified without delay that he had been appointed Chief of the Great General Staff and Ludendorff First Quarter-master-General.

The first anxiety of the new duumvirate was to establish in its own interest unity of command over the whole forces of the Quadruple Alliance. Certain subsidiary fronts in Italy and Albania remained under the control of the Austrians, but in reality for the rest of the War there was no weighty decision in which the controlling voice was not with Hindenburg and Ludendorff. Hindenburg ceased to act even as a titular commander, and became to a far greater degree than before the chairman of a military directorate. At the same time he remained for the four allied peoples the great military leader, and for his enemies something more than the figure-head of a national tradition. Without the strength of character and reputation he possessed, it is doubtful whether the High

Command would have been able to evoke an organized unison of effort and long hold the ultimate issue in the balance.

The offensive against Verdun had to be abandoned and the Germans had to stand on the defensive in the West. while a campaign against Rumania was successful. An attempt was made to ease the strain by the intensive submarine campaign, but the strangle-hold of the blockade persisted. In 1917 the Italians were defeated and after the Russia of the Kerensky regime had been severely hammered Bolshevist Russia made peace. But in the West France and England remained entrenched. The great German offensives which began on both sides of St. Quentin in March, 1918, were planned to be a decisive blow before the full weight of the Americans could be thrown into the conflict. They had their tactical successes, but brought no decisive advantage and proved to be the beginning of the end.

In July the second battle of the Marne lifted the initiative from the Germans; it was followed by Haig's attack before Amiens on August 8, Ludendorff's 'black day.' Then the Allied Armies from Flanders to the Argonne made converging attacks which definitely spelt disaster to the German arms. The defection of Bulgaria hastened the final victory, and. at the beginning of October Hindenburg demanded that a request for an armistice be made. On November 11, after the collapse of Turkey and Austria, hostilities came to an end. Hindenburg led his army home a beaten commander, but with his spirit unbroken and by his firmness saved the country from chaos.

A RUTHLESS SYSTEM

The plane on which Hindenburg stood was one whence a virtual dictatorship in the political field could easily be wielded. The Siegfried line, or Hindenburg line as the Allies knew it, the decision in favour of submarine warfare, and the enforced resignation of two Chancellors, Bethmann-Hollweg and Michaelis, signify particular episodes in a ruthless system. It is unlikely that either the Kaiser or Ludendorff, essentially contentious characters, would alone have maintained it. In the end, while other 'war-lords' took to ignominious flight, Hindenburg, the plain patriot, remained to conduct the retreat and demobilization of his armies. For them he was Father of his country to the last.

In assessing Hindenburg's reputation as a commander, it must be remembered how much every German general depended upon the work of the General Staff; educated in a common doctrine and entrusted with the working out of strategical plans. A brilliant strategist he was not, and his opinion, obviously unsound, that a decision should be sought in 1915 on the Russian front was doubtless the result of his greater familiarity with that theatre. But he possessed that clarity of aim and steadfastness of character which often bring success in the field; moreover, he knew how to utilize the talents of his subordinates. When called to the supreme direction of the War he, like Falkenhayn before him, found that he was not the master of events; but he may be regarded as the incarnation of the spirit of the old German Army, and he knew how to preserve his soldierly dignity in defeat.

When, in 1919, he retired from active service, the Revolutionary Government of the Republic issued a warm congratulatory manifesto. His subsequent attitude during the years of bitter controversy which saw the recrudescence of militarist parties hostile to the State was distinguished by unfailing correctness. The book of memoirs, 'Aus Meinem Leben,' which he published in 1920, was instinct with broad-mindedness and modesty.

The Hindenburg-Ludendorff partnership ended in July 1918, following the Allied successes on the Western Front, and in a manner throwing light on their contrasting characters. In a state of nervous tension, Ludendorff returned to the German headquarters at Avesnes on 18 July, where Hindenburg courteously met him at the railway station. There was disagreement between them on what should be done at lunch but the break came after dinner in the evening. Moving his hand over the high ground north-west of Soissons on the map, Hindenburg said quietly, 'This is where we must direct the counter-attack, that would solve the crisis at once,' Ludendorff stood back from the map and stormed from the room, scarlet in the face muttering 'madness, madness.' Relations between the two were never restored and Ludendorff subsequently blamed Hindenburg for the German defeat and all that followed from it.

LUDENDORFF

*Hindenburg's right hand man and
confidant in the First World War*

21 DECEMBER 1937

ERICH LUDENDORFF, WHO, as Hindenburg's Chief Staff Officer, played so conspicuous a part in the War, died in a Roman Catholic hospital at Münich yesterday at the age of 72. Born at Kruszevnia, in Posen, on April 9, 1865, the son of a minor official in the Prussian railway administration, he entered the Prussian Army in 1883. From March, 1904, to January, 1913, with one short interval, he was in the Operations Section of the General Staff, and, as the head of it, he must bear his share of responsibility for the changes made in the famous Schlieffen plan in 1908–09. He always maintained that had his advice been adopted, and three new army corps been added to the Army in 1912, the revised German plan of operations could have been worked out according to plan. He states in his 'War Memories' that he was transferred to regimental duties for his insistence on the increase of the Army on this occasion.

CAPTURE OF LIEGE

On mobilization in 1914, Ludendorff was appointed Deputy-Chief of the General Staff of the Second Army, and in this capacity was actually in command of troops for the first and only time in the War. Sent forward on the night of August 5–6 to report on the position of the troops who were attacking Liège, he found that they had been brought to a standstill. Although technically only a spectator, Ludendorff promptly took command of the centre column, and pushed forward. On the following day, although unsupported by the other attacking columns, he took the bold decision to make a dash for the citadel, which he was lucky enough to find undefended. This gallant feat of arms, in which he was able 'to fight just like any soldier of the rank and file who proves his worth in battle,' was, so he states in his 'War Memories,' his favourite recollection of his life as a soldier.

TANNENBERG

He did not remain long on the Western Front, for on August 22 he was appointed Chief of Staff of the Eighth Army in East Prussia, of which Hindenburg was given the command. The two men were then personally unknown to each other, but thenceforward they formed an association to which military history furnishes few, if any, exact parallels. Each was the needful complement of the other. Ludendorff was the motive force in the partnership: Hindenburg the balancing factor, his calmer nature serving as a corrective of his more brilliant assistant's eager and nervous temperament. Ludendorff could stand the strain of responsibility when things went well, but was liable to become unduly excited in adverse circumstances.

Their combined reputation was established by the great victory at Tannenberg, but the impartial student may well come to the conclusion that for the strategy which led to the Russian disaster the staff of von Prittwitz, the general whom Hindenburg succeeded, was really responsible, especially Lieutenant-Colonel Hoffmann; that had the initial orders given by Ludendorff been carried out the German victory would not have been so striking; that General von François, who commanded the I German Army Corps, was the vigorous tactician who actually brought about the Russian surrender, and that had he strictly obeyed Ludendorff's instructions most of the Russian forces would have escaped. But popular legend is little affected by historical research, and the names of Hindenburg and Ludendorff are likely to be associated for all time with the crushing defeat of Samsonoff's Army at Tannenberg, which was followed up a month later by the rout of Rennenkampf 's Army at the battle of the Masurian Lakes. By these strategic successes East Prussia was freed for the time being of the Russian invaders, and the German Eastern Army was rendered available for the support of the Austro-Hungarian armies, which were in sore need of help.

The campaign that followed in Poland in October and November after various vicissitudes of fortune, brought the capture of Lodz, which led to a general retirement of the Russian forces. This added considerably to the growing prestige of the Hindenburg-Ludendorff combination, few critics bearing in mind the weakness of the Russians in arms and munitions. The tactical results gained were followed up in the summer, but although by the month of September their front had been forced back as far as Vilna, the Russians succeeded in escaping the enveloping movement with which they were threatened. and no great strategic success, as Ludendorff himself admitted, had been gained.

The plan advocated by Hindenburg and Ludendorff was a movement to the north upon Minsk, designed to cut the Russian railway communications. This was rejected by von Falkenhayn, then Chief of the German General Staff. The withdrawal of the troops and guns from the Eastern Front that was rendered necessary in 1916 by the Verdun offensive prevented any further advance by Hindenburg and Ludendorff. They were unable to prevent the great Russian victories over the Austrians between the Pripet (marshes) and the Carpathians, hut they succeeded in holding their own line inviolate.

On August 27, 1916. Rumania declared war on Austria-Hungary, and two days later Hindenburg was appointed Chief of the German General Staff in succession to von Falkcnhayn, and Ludendorff became second chief with the title of First Quarter-master-General. The two men thus became responsible for the conduct of the whole of the German operations in the field. The successful campaign against the Rumanians in the autumn and winter of 1916 did something to relieve the serious economic situation in Germany, while the cessation of the German attacks on Verdun and the withdrawal to the Siegfried line in the spring of 1917 eased the position of the German forces on the Western Front, where they had suffered heavy pressure from the Franco-British offensive on the Somme.

THE OFFENSIVE OF 1918
'THE BRITISH MUST BE DEFEATED'

It now became the great object of the Germans to force a decision in the West before the United States of America could throw effective forces into Europe. The collapse of Russia, as a result of the revolution in the spring of 1917, the subsequent rise of the Bolshevists, and the sweeping successes against Italy in the autumn of the same year considerably assisted Ludendorff's plans for his great offensive in the spring of 1918. He laid down that 'the British must be defeated,' and, with this object in view, he eventually decided upon the great 'Michael' attack on either side of St. Quentin which, both in direction and method, departed from the ideas of his strategic adviser, Wetzell. The objections to this were amply borne out by events.

On March 23, as a result of the stubborn defence of the British First and Third Armies, he decided to abandon his attempt to roll up the British forces in a north-westerly direction, and tried to exploit the tactical success obtained by his flank guard on the Somme in the hope of separating the British and French. He made this change too late yet persisted in it too long. Then with his forces too deeply committed, Ludendorff belatedly decided to try the Lys offensive. Although this met with initial success, by surprise, Ludendorff's nerve faltered in the latter stages.

But he still clung obstinately to his idea of smashing the British Army, and his subsequent attacks elsewhere were only conceived as diversions, to attract reserves away from the British front. The Aisne offensive was carried too far, and its tactical success is said to have upset 'fatally' the German strategy. The attack at Rheims ended abruptly, as the French were fully prepared for it. On July 18 the Allied counterstroke was delivered against the Soissons salient, which had to be evacuated by the Germans.

Although Ludendorff on August 2 gave orders for the preparation of fresh attacks the Germans were not destined to carry them out. After the successful offensive by the British Fourth Army and the French First Army on August 8 – 'the black day of the German Army in the War,' as Ludendorff himself described it – the Allies gained the initiative, and in battle after battle drove back the Germans.

Ludendorff offered his resignation to Hindenburg and the Kaiser, after the battle of August 8, but it was refused, and he continued at his post until the pressure of political events in Germany and his differences of opinion with Prince Max of Baden and his Government on the armistice question led to his resignation on October 28. His career after the War did nothing to add to his reputation, and, after becoming involved in several abortive Nationalist risings, he ceased to take any important part in public life.

CHARACTERISTICS

Ludendorff was an energetic and resolute soldier, but it is doubtful whether he ever fully deserved the immense prestige which he enjoyed during the War, both among his own countrymen and abroad. On the Eastern Front he had a comparatively easy task against the Russians: on the Western Front he failed largely because he did not take sufficiently into account the strength of the forces arrayed against him, or fully appreciate the different conditions behind the Allied lines in France and Flanders with regard to communications, munitions, and supplies from those which prevailed in Russia. Almost to the end he believed in the possibility of a complete German victory achieved by force of arms, and refused to recognize the symptoms of the collapse of the army and of the nation when they had become apparent to political observers. He collected round him many capable officers – notably Colonels Wetzell and Bauer – but throughout the War he took far too much on his own shoulders, and, as Prince Rupprecht has shown in his memoirs, was perpetually interfering in details which he should have left to his staff officers and army commanders. Politically, too, he was always interfering and laying down the law: he thus alienated the politicians by issuing orders to them and bullying them, rather than attempting to influence them by methods of persuasion. He was a highly trained Prussian soldier of the old school, with an infinite faith in the righteousness of his country's cause, an unlimited confidence in the invincibility of its Army, and a complete contempt for the military prowess and moral of its enemies.

A NEW PAGANISM

After 1929 Ludendorff withdrew to his tents. He lived a life of tempestuous isolation; he would appear to be brooding for months, and then would issue a savage attack on his old chief, Hindenburg, or on his new chief, Hitler, or on Christianity – especially and most frequently on Christianity. In many parts of Germany he organized shops where were displayed anti-Christian books which, perhaps because of their wild exaggerations, were not taken so seriously as the later attacks on Christianity by some of the National-Socialist leaders. But they had a morbid appeal on account of their gruesome pictures; and some of them even sold.

Ludendorff never forgave Hindenburg for signing the Young Plan. The two men had fought together at Tannenberg – an accident of chance for which Ludendorff 'apologized to posterity' in his magazine, *Volksvarte*. He also apologized for having presented Hindenburg as a national hero, 'a misrepresentation only possible through overwork.' Then warming to the attack, he declared that Hindenburg had been responsible for all Germany's ills, including the flight of the Kaiser, the Revolution, the Republic, the inflation. 'In fact, General Hindenburg has by the rules of the old army forfeited the right to wear the field-grey of the army and to take it with him to the grave.' It was about this time that Ludendorff's outbursts began to receive less and less serious attention in Germany. The rise of the National-Socialists, however, seemed to add power to his pen. He felt it his duty to encourage whatever was anti-Clerical in the movement, and he used to organize festivals that rather self-consciously called themselves heathen. Ludendorff himself knew no doubts: 'I am not merely an opponent of Christianity,' he declared on reaching the allotted span of life. 'I literally am anti-Christian and heathen – and proud of it. I have long since said good-bye to Christianity. Christian teaching has only one purpose, to help the Jewish people to domination.' The Germans were, he said, the people who had freed themselves the most effectively from the teachings of Christianity.

At times the National-Socialists proceeded too slowly for his volatile mind. He would criticize them and be in disgrace for a time, but he would emerge unruffled with pen unblunted. In one of his latest articles he condemned the Spanish policy of the Government: he disclosed that he thought little of General Franco, less of his troops, and less still of foreign troops pressed into service under the name of 'volunteers. The magazine was confiscated at the moment of publication.

Yet, with all his eccentricities, he had a place in German life. The National-Socialists would do him honour on his birthday, and the Reichswehr would send a platoon to salute him. Hitler, too, remembered that Ludendorff had walked at his side in the Munich 'Putsch' of 1923, and that they had faced fire together. He was a fierce old warrior, inconvenient in his fierceness at times, but yet a symbol of the military spirit. In the spring of this year he had a long conversation with Hitler, at which he later claimed to have been given State recognition of the 'Ludendorff religion,' whose members were in future to have full equality of rights with other religious and 'faith' communities in Germany.

Ludendorff was born with a logical mind and industrious personality but, as if to offset these assets, with no sense of humour. He was equally unable to detect anything remotely amusing in any situation as he was of accepting any opinion beyond his own. When appointed Chief of Staff to Hindenburg – who he had never met – on the Eastern Front facing the Russians, he sent in advance of his arrival telegrams to Hindenburg's corps commanders instructing them to concentrate against Samsonsov's 2nd Russian Army at Tannenberg. This led to the resounding defeat of Samsonov, formation of the Hindenberg-Ludendorff partnership and no damage to Ludendorff's confidence in his own opinions.

'The Ludendorff Offensive' against the southern part of the British Army sector of the Western Front in March 1918, was almost certainly taken against his better judgement. By then, he was virtually the overall German battlefield commander, as right-hand man to Hindenburg the Chief of Staff. German human and material resources were almost exhausted by the end of 1917 and the unrestricted U-boat campaign against merchant shipping, compounded by the Zimmermann telegram proposing a German alliance with Mexico against the United States, had driven President Woodrow Wilson to accept that the Americans had to join the Allies. Ludendorff had only limited time to drive Britain to a settlement negotiated on Berlin's terms before US troops arrived in Europe, to give the Allies an overwhelming manpower advantage. Hence he abandoned his successful defensive strategy for an expensive aggressive one, but it failed.

When the British counter-offensive of August 1918 breached the Hindenburg line, indicating Germany's forthcoming defeat, Ludendorff was dismissed by Prince Max of Baden, who had replaced Bethmann-Hollweg as German Chancellor. His lack of a sense of humour proved no help and his initial rage was vented against Hindenburg, who held on to his office until 1919. At the time of the November 1918 armistice, Ludendorff took refuge in Sweden, only to return to Germany to establish his special brand of religion, suggesting he had lost his judgement. Apologists blamed the penury of his upbringing for his austere nature and lack of worldliness.

* * *

FISHER

Father Of The Modern Battle-Fleet.

12 JULY, 1920

JOHN ARBUTHNOT FISHER was born on January 25, 1841, at Rambodde, in Ceylon. His father was Captain W. Fisher of the 78th Highlanders and 95th Foot, and his mother was a daughter of Mr. A. Lambe, of New Bond street, who married the niece and heiress of Alderman Boydell, sometime Lord Mayor of London and well-known in his day as a print-seller and publisher. Lord Fisher's father resided for many years in Ceylon, while serving as A.D.C. to the Governor, Sir Wilmot Horton, and to General Sir Robert Arbuthnot, Lord Fisher's godfather.

Young Fisher entered the Navy on July 12, 1854, on board the *Victory* at Portsmouth having received a nomination from Admiral Sir William Parker, the last of Nelson's captains. He was just in time to serve in the *Calcutta* in the Baltic Fleet during the war with Russia. He next served in the *Highflyer, Chesapeake,* and *Furious* during the China War, and was present at the capture of Canton and the attack on the Peiho Forts, receiving the China Medal with the Canton and Taku clasps. In passing for lieutenant, he won the Beaufort Testimonial and was confirmed in the rank 11 months after being made a mate – on November 4. 1860. Qualifying in gunnery, he joined, in 1863, the *Warrior,* our first seagoing ironclad, as gunnery lieutenant, and in 1866 was appointed to the Staff of the *Excellent,* gunnery school ship, being advanced to com-mander in August, 1869. After a commission in the China flagship, he was appointed, in 1872, to the *Excellent* 'for torpedo service.' The torpedo was then in its earlier stages of development, and Fisher was not only sent to Fiume to arrange for the purchase of the Whitehead type of torpedo, but he was also the main force in the starting of the *Vernon* as a torpedo schoolship at Portsmouth. While serving as com-mander in the *Vernon,* he compiled a short treatise on the subject, which for a time enjoyed considerable vogue in the Service. Promoted captain on October 30, 1874, he continued on instructional and ex-perimental torpedo work until 1876, and then commanded successively the *Bellerophon, Hercules,* and *Pallas* in North America and the Mediterranean.

RAPID PROMOTION

In 1879 he became president of a committee for revising the Gunnery Manual of the Fleet. His originality of mind and high conception of duty became known in the highest quarters, for, though one of the most junior captains, he was selected for the command of the Inflexible, then the biggest and most heavily armed ship in the Navy, and commanded her at the bombardment of Alexandria in 1882. During the Egyptian operations of that period, he fitted out the 'armoured train' and commanded it in several skirmishes with Arabi's troops, receiving for these services the C.B. and the British and Egyptian medals. In 1883–85 he commanded the *Excellent,* the gunnery school at Portsmouth, when

Lord Jellicoe and Sir Percy Scott were lieutenants on the Staff. It was during this time that Lord Fisher became actively associated with Mr. W. T. Stead, who, largely on Fisher's inspiration, published 'The Truth about the Navy' in 1884, which resulted in five millions sterling being at once voted for the Fleet, and paved the way for the Naval Defence Act of 1889 and other measures which gave to the nation the needed measure of sea power which saved us in 1914.

In 1886 Fisher was appointed Director of Naval Ordnance and Torpedoes, retaining that office until 1891, when, having attained flag-rank in 1890, he was appointed Admiral-Superintendent of Portsmouth Dockyard. Next, on February 1, 1892, he became Comptroller of the Navy, and for the first time took his seat at the Board of Admiralty in that capacity. He served at the Admiralty as Comptroller for five and a half years, being made a K.C.B. in 1894 and promoted to the rank of Vice-Admiral in 1896. In August, 1897, he hoisted his flag for the first time afloat in the *Renown*, to take command of the North American and West Indies Station. The Cuban War imposed on him the discharge of many delicate duties of neutrality. The relations between England and the United States at that time were not cordial; but a signal proof of change was given when, early in 1899, a squadron of American warships which had taken part in the blockade at Santiago visited Bermuda, under the command of the late Admiral Sampson. During the visit of this squadron the birthday of Washington occurred, on February 22, and perhaps for the first time in history the occasion was honoured by a salute fired from the *Renown*, Sir John Fisher's flagship, and by the other ships of his command then at Bermuda. Admiral Sampson and his officers were immensely gratified by the reception accorded to them, and especially by the honour paid to the memory of Washington by the British Commander-in-Chief. In like manner Fisher had no small share in bringing about the Entente Cordiale with France; with a zest and zeal all his own, he organized the naval visits to Brest and Portsmouth in 1905.

AT THE HAGUE

When he was Director of Naval Ordnance, Fisher, among other reforms, obtained for the Navy control of its own guns – formerly supplied through the War Office. He was unceasing in his representations to those concerned. The sequel occurred when, about 10 years later, Lord Salisbury had to nominate a Naval Delegate to the first Peace Conference at The Hague, for the man whom he favoured above all others was the one who had worried him so much about naval guns. At The Hague, perhaps,

Fisher first acquired an international reputation, for though his views on the conduct and rules of warfare were certainly rather truculent – if they were correctly reported by Mr. Stead in a 'character sketch '– yet his rare aptitude for affairs, his firm grasp of essentials, his quick perceptions, and his racy, if unconventional, mode of expression, very soon established his ascendancy in council, while his genial personality and his engaging social gifts secured for him universal popularity. 'Amongst the naval delegates,' said Mr. Stead, 'Fisher was like a little god. As he was personally most gracious, put on no airs, and danced like a middy till all hours in the morning, no man at The Hague was more popular than he.'

IN THE MEDITERRANEAN

On July 1, 1899, he took up the Mediterranean Command, and held it until the summer of 1902, having attained by seniority the rank of full Admiral in 1901. In the Mediterranean he had no fair-weather time. There was war in South Africa, and no one could tell how far the conflict might spread. 'He at once bent all his energies,' said Mr. Stead, 'to infuse something of the spirit of Nelson into his officers. He lectured them on naval strategy, and he enforced the most rigorous discipline. As one of his subordinates testified, 'Fisher infused new life into the Service and made officers think out all those momentous questions concerning strategy, tactics, and gunnery for themselves.' He brought the Fleet up to the highest level of efficiency.' Mere routine he despised. His watchword then, as always, was 'the seagoing and fighting efficiency of the Fleet and its instant readiness for war.' Whatever did not make for that kind of efficiency he had no use for. It was said of him by some of his critics that he was rather a desk-admiral than a sea-admiral. In truth he was both. No one got through so much desk-work as he, for he could work early and late. 'His officers could never tell that his eye was not upon them at any hour. He was not, perhaps, fond of sea life as such – he suffered severely from sea-sickness all through his life – but when he did go afloat he could put more work into a week's cruise than many another admiral would have put into a month's. He always manoeuvred his Fleet at high speed, and in one year of his command he rather startled the Admiralty by burning 50,000 more tons of coal in the Fleet under his command than they had allowed for. His relations with the Admiralty were at times somewhat strained. His second-in-command for the greater part of the time was Lord Charles Beresford, with whom in after years he was often – too often, perhaps – in acute personal controversy. But they worked together in the Mediterranean with no apparent friction, though perhaps their common zeal for the efficiency of the naval service was sometimes a thorn in the side of the Admiralty. It was recorded by Lord Beresford in his memoirs that the fighting efficiency of the Fleet in the Mediterranean was greatly improved under Lord Fisher. The stocks of coal at Malta and Gibraltar were increased and new breakwaters at Malta begun. From a 12-knot Fleet, with breakdowns, he made a 15-knot Fleet, without breakdowns; introduced long-range target practice; inaugurated various war practices for officers and men; and trained the Fleet for anything.

SECOND SEA LORD

In the summer of 1902 Sir John Fisher was relieved of his command in the Mediterranean on his appointment as Second Sea Lord of the Admiralty, and received the G.C.B. at the same time. At once he handed to the First Lord, Lord Selborne, an exhaustive memorandum on the entry and training of junior officers for the Fleet, a subject which had been much discussed in the Service for some time previously. This memorandum, after full discussion by the Board, resulted in the issue on Christmas Day, 1902, of what *The Times* of that date described as 'one of the most important documents ever issued by the Admiralty in time of peace.' It was signed by the First Lord on behalf of the Board and was entitled 'Memorandum on the Entry, Training, and Employment of Officers and Men of the Royal Navy, and of Officers of the Royal Marines,' and, as all the world now knows, it was based on the broad principle of common entry at an early age and common training up to the point of specialization for all executive, engineer, and marine officers. A scheme so bold, so drastic, so far-reaching. and so subversive of time-honoured traditions and sentiments naturally gave rise at once to very acute controversy. But it held its own, and though some modifications have since been introduced into it, it remained, until the-war came to disturb everything, the established system of the Naval Service. Many changes have since been introduced, some of them not at all to the taste of Lord Fisher himself, but the fundamental principle still obtains that the fighting seamen of the future, whether officer or bluejacket, must be well versed in all the mechanical appliances with which a modern warship is equipped.

AT PORTSMOUTH

The introduction and evolution of the new scheme was Fisher's great achievement as Second Sea Lord. On August 31, 1903, he hoisted his flag as Commander-in-Chief at Portsmouth. Some surprise was felt and expressed that he should have quitted the Admiralty at this critical time, but he must have desired, and doubtless the Admiralty also deemed it expedient, that the new scheme should be brought into working order under its author's superintendence. He may also have thought that the occasion was one for him *reculer pour mieux sauter*. The post of Commander-in-Chief at Portsmouth, though important, would give a man who could work as hard and as rapidly as Fisher time for pondering and maturing fresh and far-reaching schemes for promoting the efficiency of the naval service. Lord Esher has stated that Sir John Fisher's leisure at Portsmouth was actually employed in this way, and that when he returned to the Admiralty as First Sea Lord in October, 1904, he carried with him completed drafts of all the great measures of reorganization and reform which on his initiative and inspiration were subsequently adopted. Writing to Lord Esher on August 17, 1904, Fisher said:- 'I have got 60 sheets of foolscap written with all the new naval proposals and am pretty well prepared for the fray on October 21.' He had diligently wrought out, over a number of years, the schemes of naval reform which will always be associated with his name. He said in *The Times* on September 8, 1919:- 'When on Trafalgar Day, 1904, I was appointed First Sea Lord of the Admiralty, and breakfasted alone with King Edward at Buckingham Palace, though I had entered the Navy penniless, friendless, and forlorn, I was equipped with knowledge and power sufficient to say to anyone who obstructed me, "*You be damned*," and he was damned. Knowledge is power. When you have been a kitchenmaid no one can silly you as to how to boil potatoes. So I was able to introduce the wondrous turbine engine, knock out the old type of boiler, and put the fire where the water used to be and the water where the fire used to be, so that a ship could get up steam in 20 minutes instead of taking five and a half hours, make an 18in. gun that easily fired across the English Channel, double the speed of fighting ships, and clear out 19 millions sterling of parasites, animate and inanimate'.

Nor did even this arduous task of preparation exhaust his activities at Portsmouth. At the end of 1903 a committee presided over by Lord Esher was appointed by the Government to make recommendations for the reconstruction of the War Office. The other members of this committee were Sir John Fisher and Sir George S. Clarke, now Lord

Sydenham. The committee reported early in 1904, and their leading recommendations were afterwards embodied in the organization alike of the Committee of Imperial Defence and of the War Office. The report was largely permeated by Fisher's ideas. It was in the spring of this same year, 1904, that King Edward VII. spent a few days at Portsmouth as the guest of the Commander-in-Chief at Admiralty House. The relations of his late Majesty with Sir John Fisher were at all times cordial and even intimate; for besides being a great seaman and a great administrator, Fisher was an accomplished courtier, and in his lighter moments a most attractive and entertaining companion. His talk was racy, original, full of mother wit, and irradiated by a humour which was bracing and pungent as the salt of the sea itself. On Trafalgar Day, October 21, 1904, Sir John Fisher, who delighted to associate himself with great naval anniversaries, was sworn in at Whitehall as First Sea Lord of the Admiralty. On the early morning of that very day what was afterwards known as the Dogger Bank incident had occurred, when certain British trawlers peacefully engaged in fishing off the Dogger Bank were mistaken by the Russian fleet on its way to the Far East under the command of the late Admiral Rozhdestvensky for Japanese torpedo craft, and fired upon with fatal consequences by several of the Russian men-of-war. Fisher was thus confronted on the very threshold of office with a grave naval and political emergency, but the unspeakable calamity of war with Russia was happily averted. Fisher's measures were swiftly and quietly taken, and their full significance was not perhaps then perceived.

FIRST SEA LORD

Fisher's five years' tenure of the post of First Sea Lord is the most memorable in the modern history of that office. During those strenuous years, which were the consummation and crown of a long career equally strenuous, Lord Fisher, for good or for evil – and as the war proved largely for good – left an indelible mark, a mark deeper and more conspicuous than that made by any of his immediate predecessors, on the administration, organization, disposition, and equipment of the Royal Navy. It was inevitable that some reforms were introduced somewhat brusquely. It is certain, at any rate, that they aroused much bitter antagonism and much painful controversy; but much of that was involved in the very nature of the work which Lord Fisher set himself to accomplish, albeit some little of it may be due to the very characteristic, and not always, entirely commendable, methods by which he accomplished it. Be that as it may,

Lord Fisher's work remained to justify his endeavours. He was a great public servant.

First among the Fisher reforms came the initiation and organization of what is known as the 'Nucleus Crew System,' whereby the whole sea-going Fleet may be said to have been rendered as 'instantly ready for war' as was compatible with peace conditions and a peace establishment. Organically associated with this system was the elimination of ships of no fighting value from the Fleet – commonly known as the 'policy of scrapping.' A third feature of the new policy was the introduction of the Dreadnought type of warship, with results now well known to all the world. These three great strokes of policy were, as *The Times* said in 1910:-

'In reality, only ancillary and introductory to the crowning stroke of all – namely, the strategic redistribution of the Fleet and the creation in home waters of a naval force of strength alike unprecedented and unrivalled, complete in all the indispensable elements of fighting efficiency, well supplied with auxiliary vessels, and ready for immediate action, should the occasion unhappily arise.'

Such, in the briefest outline, were the leading features of what may legitimately be called the Fisher policy, though it was a policy sanctioned and adopted by several successive Boards of Admiralty, carried out by four First Lords, Lord Selborne, Lord Cawdor, Lord Tweedmouth, and Mr. McKenna in succession, further developed and expanded by a fifth, Mr.Winston Churchill, and approved by the Cabinets of three successive Prime Ministers, Mr. Balfour, Sir Henry Campbell-Bannerman, and Mr. Asquith. Lord Fisher left office in 1910 with the Navy far stronger and better organized than he found it, better equipped, and better disposed for the defence alike of the United Kingdom and of the Empire, and purged as by fire of many of 'those obese unchallenged old things that stifled and overlay' it in the past. It was a new Navy.

PLANS FOR 1914

The extraordinary foresight, or almost uncanny prevision, which Lord Fisher possessed and exercised to the advantage of his country was perhaps best illustrated by his prediction of the date of the war with Germany. Sir Maurice Hankey, Secretary to the War Cabinet, has recorded how in 1910, when on a week-end visit to Lord Fisher at Kilverstone Hall, the Admiral of the Fleet declared that 'the war will come in 1914, and Jellicoe will command the Grand Fleet.' Holding firmly this belief, Lord Fisher shaped all his plans accordingly. During 1911 and 1912 he used his influence with Mr. Churchill so that the latter disposed his patronage as First Lord to bring Sir John Jellicoe on to the right position on the Flag List that he might become Admiralissimo on the outbreak of war. Naturally this step, involving the passing over of several other worthy officers, was not accomplished without a certain amount of professional disappointment. On his appointment as First Sea Lord in 1904, Sir John Fisher was appointed by the late King First and Principal Naval Aide-de-Camp to his Majesty, in succession to Admiral of the Fleet Sir Edward Seymour. He received the Order of Merit in the next year, and at its close he was made an Admiral of the Fleet by special Order in Council, in order that his tenure of office might not be prematurely terminated by his compulsory retirement in the rank of Admiral, as it would have been on his attaining the age of 65 on January 25, 1906. In 1906 he received from the French Government the Grand Cordon of the Legion of Honour, and in 1908 the late King created him a G.C.V.O. On King Edward's last birthday, November 9, 1909, he was raised to the peerage with the title of Baron Fisher of Kilverstone, Kilverstone being the name of the estate near Thetford bequeathed to his only son by the late Mr. Joseph Vavasseur. It was his original intention to resign the office of First Sea Lord when he was made a peer; but for reasons of Departmental convenience he retained it for a few weeks longer, and finally resigned it on his 69th birthday, January 25, 1910. He remained a special member of the Imperial Committee of Defence.

A LACONIC SPEAKER

In the House of Lords he spoke only twice, and his remarks were astonishingly brief. The first speech was called for by an attack which Mr. Churchill, following his resignation from the Cabinet in November, 1915, made upon the ex-First Sea Lord for his alleged lack of clear guidance and firm support over the Dardanelles question. After a reference to Mr. Churchill's speech, Lord Fisher merely reminded the House that he had been in the service of his country for 61 years, and he said he left his record in the hands of his countrymen. 'I am content to wait,' he added. 'It is unfitting to make personal explanations affecting national interests when my country is in the midst of a great war.' Having made this utterance he walked out. Similarly, on March 21, 1917, when the Commission of Inquiry into the Dardanelles Expedition had reported, Lord Fisher rose, in an almost empty House, and said:-

'My Lords, when our country is in great jeopardy – as she now is – it is not the time to tarnish great reputations, to asperse the dead, and to discover our supposed weakness to the enemy. So I shall not discuss the Dardanelles Reports. I shall await the end of the war, when all the truth can be made known.'

In January, 1911, on reaching the age of 70, he was placed on the retired list; but his active influence on naval policy continued, and in, the anxious weeks following the Agadir incident the Government naturally turned to him for guidance, and in response to an urgent letter he returned from Switzerland to attend a secret meeting at Reigate Priory at which there were present the First Lord of the Admiralty and several members of the Ministry. At this conference were formulated plans which had a far-reaching effect on our preparations for war. Again, in May, 1912, he was consulted by the Prime Minister (Mr. Asquith) and First Lord (Mr. Churchill), who visited him at Naples for the purpose.

HIS FAITH IN OIL

In July, 1912, after 18 months' relaxation on the Continent and in the Mediterranean, he was asked to become President of a Royal Commission on Oil Fuel and Engines, and accepted the post. He entered into this work with renewed vigour and characteristic enthusiasm. Chiefly through the investigations of this Commission, the first light cruisers in the British Navy to burn oil fuel only, the Arethusa class, were about to be commissioned just as war broke out in 1914, and proved their value beyond question. Similarly, in 1913, there were launched the first oil-fired battleships in our Navy, the Queen Elizabeth class. But Fisher was not content that oil should be consumed as fuel, and he was a strong advocate for the internal combustion engine, in which it could be used with so much greater efficiency. By September 20, 1912, as he wrote to Lord Esher, he had conceived the idea of building what he called the Non-Pareil, for which all the drawings were ready. This was to be a ship with a target 33 per cent. less than any previous vessel, with no funnels, no masts, no smoke, and carrying over 5,000 tons of oil, enough to take her round the world without refuelling. He was ahead of his time. In the days when war with Germany threatened, Lord Fisher was in close consultation with the Government as to the measures to be taken. On July 30, 1914, at Mr. Churchill's request, he spent some hours with the then First Lord, and at the wish of the latter he saw Mr. Balfour to explain to him the naval situation. On September 7, when it was decided to raise a force of naval brigades for land service, Mr. Churchill appointed Lord Fisher honorary colonel of the first of these brigades, and the Admiral of the Fleet addressed a stirring message to its officers and men. When, however, towards the end of October, 1914, an unworthy popular clamour brought about the resignation of that high-minded officer the Marquess of Milford Haven, who had held the post of First Sea Lord since 1912 and discharged its duties with conspicuous ability and sagacity, the country recognized at once the man to succeed him was the great organizer and administrator who had created the modern Fleet, and whose strategic insight had inspired its efficiency and readiness for war.

THE WAR: IN OFFICE AGAIN

Lord Fisher was now nearing the close of his 74th year. But he was never younger or more vigorous; like Lord Barham of old he came back into harness with energies unabated, with resources unexhausted, and, with all the vast and varied experience of a great administrative career. So it seemed at any rate, and the country and the Service both soon felt the impress of his rare and puissant personality. He had as usual his plans fully prepared, and within a few days of taking office took the necessary steps for their resolute execution. Something like 600 vessels of all classes, many of them of entirely new design, were ordered, and for their completion a date was fixed in the spring of 1915. The precise enterprise for which these preparations were made was an invasion of the Baltic and the landing of an army within easy striking distance of Berlin on the shores of Pomerania. It has been said that Mr. Lloyd George, as Chancellor of the Exchequer, sanctioned the cost of these 612 vessels on a half-sheet of notepaper. But this fine strategic scheme, boldly but prudently conceived, which might have transferred the war to German soil was ruined in the Dardanelles. During the months needed for an adequate provision of the necessary equipment, the Government was being urged to attempt another undertaking. The report of the Dardanelles Commission affords an explanation of the substitution for Lord Fisher's carefully thought-out plan of the ill-fated Gallipoli scheme. The needs of that adventure gradually drew upon the resources which were essential to the successful execution of the alternative undertaking. Lord Fisher saw the units of his new-born armada scattered and the prospects of carrying out his project far away. His protests were disregarded, his advice rejected, and even his concessions to political exigency were misrepresented. Nevertheless he was ready to put on one side his personal predilections and loyally follow his instructions, but when he found that the drain from the North Sea forces for the Mediterranean was in his opinion jeopardizing the sea control upon which everything depended, he felt that his duty to the country demanded a further step, and he submitted his resignation to the Prime Minister. Before it was accepted the Coalition Government had been formed and the new First Lord chose as his chief adviser another naval officer. Then Fisher retired into the country. Seven weeks later, Lord Fisher was recalled for the second time to organize the newly-formed Board of Invention and Research. This post was a purely advisory one, and offered little scope for his enduring energy and undoubted genius. The man who had foretold not only that the war must come, but the approximate date when it would occur, who under successive Governments had worked and planned with consummate success to provide an adequate Fleet, to place it in the right spot and the right moment to baffle the enemy, had seen the fruit of his wonderful prevision in the first days of the war, when his successor was able to send the Fleet without a moment's delay to its war station with submarines scouting in the mouth of the Elbe and aircraft patrolling the entrance to the Channel. He was practically laid on the shelf, and although all through the succeeding months he looked on the changing fortunes of the war, conceiving fresh schemes and keeping himself ready with heart young, brain clear and a vigour unimpaired, he never received again the summons of his country which he so ardently desired and to which he was ever ready to respond.

FORCE OF PERSONALITY

It is not surprising that Lord Fisher's personality exercised a magnetic influence upon people of all sorts and conditions. His enthusiasm, his earnestness and the compelling nature of his address had a fascination for most of those with whom he was brought into contact. His deeply religious convictions appealed to many; his Biblical knowledge, although well known to his intimate friends, came as a revelation to the readers of his writings. He took as his motto on being raised to the peerage, 'Fear God, and Dread Nought,' because 'fear not' (or dread nought) was to be found, he said, over 80 times in the Bible. No man can have inspired closer or more affectionate relationships among people in as many walks of life than he did.

This comprehensive and well-written Special Memoir is a fine tribute to one of the most astonishing military personalities of the nineteenth and early twentieth centuries.

It nods towards some of the major issues which detracted from Fisher's reputation; there is no doubt that the protracted Fisher-Beresford vendetta was deeply damaging to both officers and split and soured the navy, culminating as it did in a prime ministerial committee of enquiry into Fisher's administration that at once vindicated and yet humiliated him. There is no mention of the 'fishpond', the coterie of officers who basked in Fisher's favour to the irritation of those excluded. Although he was held in much affection by his sailors — a collective well-wishing letter from the ship's company of *Inflexible* was one of his proudest possessions — and was capable of charming the birds out of the trees, professionally he was also vicious, vindictive and unfair. The enormous scope of the Fisher reforms which re-created the Royal Navy from top to bottom just in time for the war which he had long predicted would break out in the summer of 1914 required all of Fisher's energy, decisiveness and acumen — anyone who got in the way would indeed be 'damned'.

It was probably a mistake that he again took up the reins of power as First Sea Lord upon the resignation of Prince Louis of Battenberg, Marquess of Milford Haven, on account of his Germanic family name. Fisher was 73 and not as robust as painted here. Although it was his immediate decision to send two battle-cruisers to the South Atlantic to avenge the defeat of Coronel and which produced the only clear-cut surface ship victory of the war, his obsession with a plan to invade Germany over the Pomeranian coast, his quarrels with Churchill and failure fully to back the Dardanelles campaign, opposing as he did the diversion of forces that might have made the difference, were ill-judged and led to a resignation that was full of pathos and under circumstances that some have described as a desertion of his post.

He was deeply disappointed by Jutland — 'they have failed me'. When the battered, rusty and mutinous German High Seas Fleet steamed into internment in Scapa Flow, escorted by a huge Grand Fleet of stunning power and discipline, Fisher's memoirs recorded: 'Nobody said thank you'.

FOCH

The Soul Of Victory

21 MARCH 1929

THE DEATH OF Ferdinand Foch, Marshal of France and Field-Marshal in the British Army – announced on another page, deprives the French nation of the most famous soldier of his generation – the man who will for all time be regarded as the principal instrument in the defeat of the Germans in the Great War. His countrymen mourn him as the hero who brought about their national resurrection, and the people of the British Empire share in their sorrow, for it was under his supreme leadership that their troops withstood the last desperate onslaught of the German Armies, and, after a hard and bitter struggle, fought their way to the common victory.

Few generals in history achieved greater triumphs or were called upon to face greater emergencies. A marvellous vigour of mind and body, combined with an indomitable courage, a supreme confidence in himself, and a thorough mastery of his profession, enabled him to rise from a Corps Commander at the beginning of the War to the position of General-in-Chief of the Armies of the Allies on the Western Front. His reward – the greatest that could be given to any French soldier – was to avenge the defeat of 1870 and to dictate the stern terms of the Armistice on November 11, 1918, to the representatives of a beaten and demoralized Germany.

Foch was a Gascon. He was born at Tarbes, in the Pyrenees, on October 2, 1851; the third child of a minor Government official. His father's family came from Valentine, near St. Gaudens, and his mother, whose maiden name was Dupré, also belonged to the Pyrenean bourgeoisie. Both his parents were devout Catholics, and in their orderly and unpretentious home the future Marshal of France acquired a fine simplicity of character. All his life he remained attached to the religious faith of his childhood.

Having received his early education at the Jesuit School at St. Etienne, he passed his 'baccalaureat' in 1869 and was sent to Metz, to the Jesuit College of St. Clement, which was then celebrated for its success in preparing youths for St. Cyr and the Polytechnique. The following year he enlisted as a volunteer for the duration of the war against Germany, but he saw no fighting, and in July, 1871, he resumed his education, first at the Polytechnique and then at the Artillery School at Fontainebleau, from which, in 1874, he was posted to the 24th Regiment of Artillery.

Four years later he was transferred to the 10th Regiment of Artillery at Rennes. There he married, in 1883, Mlle. Bienvenue, who proved to him a devoted and lifelong comrade. Three children were born of this marriage, a son and two daughters. The former was killed in action in the early days of the War, and the news of his son's death, as well as that of his son-in-law, Captain Becourt, on the field of battle, reached Foch while he himself was engaged in the firat Battle of the Marne.

THE ECOLE DE GUERRE MILITARY DOCTRINE

In 1885 Foch went as a student to the Ecole de Guerre, and passed out fourth two years later. He returned there in 1895 as an instructor in strategy and applied tactics, after filling in the interval various minor posts on the staff and holding an artillery command. The five years during which he held this appointment formed the turning point in his career. He proved himself a brilliant lecturer, and his teaching had a profound effect in forming 'the doctrine of war' among the rising generation of French soldiers. His military opinions are embodied in two books, 'Des Principes de la Guerre,' published in 1903, and 'De la Conduite de la Guerre; La Manoeuvre pour la Bataille,' which appeared a year later.

Foch's conception of the art of war was largely formed on the teaching of Napoleon, and his books deserve the closest attention by military students. He believed that success on the field of battle depends mainly on two things – the moral factor and the influence of the commander. He held that a battle was not lost until one side had admitted itself beaten, and that it was the task of a commander to inspire his troops with such confidence in themselves that they would refuse to own themselves beaten. It was upon this theory that he based his conduct of the campaign when he was given the command of the Allied troops on the Western Front in 1918. He refused to contemplate the possibility of defeat, and set to work to check the enemy's offensive by a vigorous counter-offensive in order to deprive him of the initiative and to administer the 'coup supreme' at a time and place of his own choosing.

Despite his brilliance as a teacher, Foch was removed from his position as instructor at the Ecole de Guerre in 1900 owing to the political-religious dissensions which accompanied and followed the Dreyfus affair. In 1907, however, M. Clemenceau, who was then Prime

Minister, sent for him and offered him the post of Commandant of the Ecole. It was the first time the two men had met. Foch is said to have replied, 'I fear; Prime Minister, you are perhaps ignorant of the fact that I have a brother who is a Jesuit.' 'I don't care a damn,' said Clemenceau. 'You will make a first-rate Commandant of the School – that is all that matters to me.'

BATTLE OF THE MARNE.

Foch left the Ecole de Guerre in 1911, and, after commanding the 13th Division at Chaumont, was appointed in 1913 to command the XX Corps at Nancy. This corps formed part of de Castelnau's Second Army, which, at the commencement of hostilities in 1914, carried out the invasion of Lorraine – one of the ill-judged offensive movements which were laid down in the French plan of campaign in the event of a war against Germany. The invasion quickly ended in failure, and de Castelnau's troops, after suffering a grave reverse at Morhange on August 13, were compelled to fall back in order to cover Nancy. In the rearrangement of the French forces which followed the loss of the Battle of the Frontiers Foch was given the command of a new army – the Ninth – which was posted in the centre of the French line between the retreating. Fifth and Fourth Armies.

On September 4 Joffre issued his famous order of attack, and the great Retreat had come to an end. In the operations that followed, the task of the Ninth Army was to cover the right of the Fifth Army by holding the southern exits from the marshes of St. Gond, and, at the same time, to maintain possession of the plateau north of Sézanne. For three days, September 6, 7, and 8, Foch's troops resisted a series of desperate attacks delivered by the German Second Army, and prevented the French centre from being broken. It was during the course of this fighting that their leader sent his celebrated message to Joffre:- 'Mon centre cède et ma droite recule. Tout va bien. J'attaque.'

In 1914, and indeed throughout the great part of the War on the Western Front, the forward policy was a wrong policy for the Allies; but in 1918, when Hindenburg and Ludendorff had carried out their great offensive and exhausted their armies, the psychological moment for attack had come, and Foch was the one man at that period in the War who could make the other French commanders realize their opportunity and seize it.

THE RACE TO THE SEA

After the victory of the Marne Foch was awarded the Grand Cross of the Legion of Honour, and, on October 4, he was selected by Joffre to act as 'délégé du genéral-en-chef.' with the French forces in Flanders. 'The Race for the Sea' had begun, and the task assigned to Foch was to co-ordinate the Allied resistance on the Yser and in the Ypres salient. French writers are sometimes inclined to give the whole credit for the successful defence along the Yser and of the Ypres salient to the genius of Foch. But probably the Marshal would himself have been the first to admit that the Belgians had held their line on the Yser single-handed for a full week before Admiral Ronarch's marines and General Grossetti's infantry division came to their assistance, and that the decision to open the sluices, originally suggested on October 11 by the British Staff, was made by King Albert on his own initiative on October 25, when it was amply clear that the German advance could be checked in no other way. The main credit for the successful organization of the defence of Ypres undoubtedly belongs to Sir Douglas Haig and to General. Dubois, commanding the IX French Corps.

During the 15 months which followed their failure to break the Allied line in Flanders the Germans attempted no great offensive on the Western Front, for their gas attack at Ypres in the spring of 1915 had no weight behind it and was really only an experiment in the use of their new weapon of warfare. The Allies used this period to reorganize their line, and the arrival in France of the first divisions of Kitchener's new Armies enabled the British to take over some of the French front and thus made an Allied offensive possible in the autumn of 1915.

These operations in Champagne and Artois, which were forced on the Allied commanders largely for political and economic reasons, were not particularly successful and led to no decisive results. Foch's Army Group took a prominent part in the offensive operations in May and September, 1915, but his conduct of the operations did not enhance his reputation with his countrymen. Many thought that the results attained did not justify the heavy casualties incurred, and the politicians and the public did not in the least realize at that period in the War that strongly fortified positions held by a resolute enemy could not be captured without heavy losses among the attacking troops.

In the first Battle of the Somme in 1916, in which the British Army had the largest share of the fighting owing to the heavy French losses at Verdun, the lessons learnt in the Champagne and Artois offensives bore excellent results. The Allied leaders avoided to a great extent the errors of the previous year, and, though the casualties were heavy, the results attained were far greater, for the enemy was given no respite and the continuous pressure of the Allied advance gradually broke down the German power of resistance. The 'blood bath of the Somme,' as the Germans called it, did much, as is now known, to break down the moral of the enemy's troops.

FALL OF JOFFRE

But the true effect of the 'wearing-out battle' was not appreciated at the time. Although the results of the Somme operations were far-reaching, Joffre lost the confidence of the French Government and was removed from his active command in the field; and with him fell Foch. It was reported that the general's health had failed – he had reached the age limit on September 30, 1916 – and he was relieved of the command of the Northern Group of Armies and detailed to study matters of Inter-Allied strategy, first at Senlis and then in Paris. But in April, 1917, the great offensive, devised by Nivelle, Joffre's successor, to break through the German defences collapsed disastrously on the Chemin des Dames, and Pétain was appointed as Commander-in-Chief of the French Armies. Foch succeeded him as Chief of the Staff and thus became the technical adviser of the French Government in military matters.

The virtual retirement of Russia from the War, which followed the collapse of the offensive inaugurated by Kerensky in May, and the capture of Riga by the Germans in September, 1917, enabled the Central Powers to bring more pressure to bear in the West. Their first attack was directed against Italy, and culminated in the Italian defeat at Caporetto in October, 1917. After this disaster some French and British divisions were dispatched from France to assist the Italians in stemming the Austro-German invasion, and Foch went also as military adviser to the Italian Higher Command. He did more than anyone else to make the Franco-British assistance speedy and effective.

The Allied Conference at Rapallo in November, 1917, which followed the disaster at Caporetto, led to the establishment of the Supreme War Council at Versailles. This body was a political rather than a military organization, its functions being to bring about some single directing authority in the policy of the Allies. Nevertheless, its establishment was a step towards the unity of command which both French and British military opinion had long seen to be necessary.

An Inter-Allied Executive War Board was set up at Versailles as the military branch of the Versailles Council. The task assigned to this body, of which Foch was appointed President, was the co-ordination of the strategical plans of the Allies with a view to the maintenance of agreement between inter-Allied policy and inter-Allied strategy. The establishment of this Board was admittedly a compromise. It was a recognition by the political leaders of the Allies that some kind of unity of command was essential, but to vest the supreme control of the Allied military forces in a Committee was not a policy which commended itself to military opinion – more especially as the military representatives on the Board were empowered to give their advice to their respective Governments independently of the commanders in the field and of their General Staffs.

The difficulty of controlling the movements of armies by a body not directly responsible for their command in the field soon became apparent. The Supreme War Council decided at a meeting held at Versailles from January 30 to February 2, 1918, in view of the German offensive which was known to be imminent, to create a general reserve of the whole of the Allied forces on the Western, Italian, and Balkan fronts, and to delegate to its military branch the size, location, and movements of this reserve in consultation with the responsible commanders in the field.

UNITY OF COMMAND: FOCH AS GENERAL-IN-CHIEF

When the German offensive of 1918 began, on March 21, the direct intervention by the French on the British front was delayed because Pétain was firmly convinced that the attack on the British was in the nature of a feint and that the real German offensive would be delivered on the Aisne. This delay largely contributed to the overwhelming of Gough's Fifth Army and to the crisis which brought about the establishment of a real unity of command.

Foch's appointment to the supreme command was due more to the initiative of Lord Milner and Sir Douglas Haig than to that of anybody else. At Doullens, on March 26, Milner, with the hearty approval of Haig, urged the necessity of a single chief of the Allied forces, and designated Foch as the most suitable man for the post. Milner had the courage to accept the full responsibility of making this proposal, and it was accepted by M. Clemenceau. Foch was accordingly appointed 'to co-ordinate the action of the Allied Armies on the Western Front,' and at a subsequent conference, held at Beauvais on April 3, at which Mr. Lloyd George and M. Clemenceau were present, he was given the title of 'General-in-Chief of the Allied Armies in France.' It is interesting to recall that Lord

Hanworth, in a letter to *The Times* published on May 24, 1928, has related that Haig, after the War was over, said to him, 'I should like you to know that I asked for Foch.'

The new Generalissimo established his headquarters at Carous, near Beauvais. His staff was at first limited to what he called his 'famille' – some 10 officers who had been with him through most of the War. This staff dealt with operations only, as at this time Foch considered that any attempt to control supply and administration, would have so disturbing an effect as to bring the principle of unity of command into disrepute. His relations with the Allied Commanders-in-Chief were cordial in the extreme, and, in cases of disagreement, he was ready to listen to their arguments. He always paid particular attention to the judgment of Sir Douglas Haig, in whose military skill and experience he had great confidence, and on more than one occasion he accepted the views of the British Commander-in-Chief in preference to his own.

From the moment he assumed the command of the Allied Armies, Foch set to work with characteristic energy to organize a determined resistance to any further German advance. He did not understand such a thing as passive defence.

In an order issued on April 3 he laid down a scheme of operations by which the French were to attack south of the Somme near Montdidier with the object of driving the enemy back from the Oise, while the British were to move forward simultaneously astride the Somme from the Luce to the Ancre. He had completed, in consultation with Sir Douglas Haig, the arrangements necessary for these operations when the Germans, on April 9, suddenly shifted their offensive to the valley of the Lys, overwhelmed the Portuguese, broke through the British front between La Bassée and Neuve Eglise, and captured Armentières. Foch did his utmost in this emergency to relieve the pressure on the portion of the line held by General Plumer's Second Army. But the Germans pressed their attack with vigour, and on April 25 they captured Mount Kemmel, the defence of which had been taken over from the British by French reinforcements. The situation for a time was most serious, for the Allies, in view of the threat to the Channel ports, could not afford to lose ground on the front south of Ypres. But Foch's instructions to contest every inch of ground were successfully carried out. The German advance was brought to a standstill in front of Hazebrouck.

LUDENDORFF'S LAST BLOW

After the 'Battle of the North,' as Foch styled it, had thus been brought to an end, the Generalissimo's chief preoccupation was to accumulate reserves of fresh troops. The majority of the British divisions were worn out with continuous fighting since March 21. The casualties in the March battle had compelled G.H.Q. to reduce 10 divisions to cadres, so that their men might be used as reinforcements for the remainder. On the other hand, the greater part of the front held by the French had been untroubled by the enemy for many months; the troops holding it were intact, and by this date had recovered from the demoralizing effects of Nivelle's defeat the previous year. Foch made up his mind, therefore, to send the tired British divisions to quiet portions of the French front, and urged by every means in his power the immediate reinforcement of the British Armies in France from the vast pool of 1,400,000 men at that time under arms in Great Britain. After some hesitation, Sir Douglas Haig fell in with Foch's proposals and four divisions and the IX Corps Headquarters were sent for a rest to the French front east of Soissons.

On May 27 Ludendorff chose this particular sector of the line for his third great attack. Although our tired divisions played their part right manfully, earning the praise of Foch and the French commanders under whom they fought, the German attack swept the Allies off the formidable position of the Chemin des Dames, crossed the Aisne and the Vesle and reached the Marne between Château Thierry and Dormans. The success which at first attended this attack shook the confidence of the Supreme War Council in Foch, but Clemenceau stood by him, and, above all, he himself stood firm, unperturbed by untoward events, clear in judgment, and confident that he could and would *endiguer* the waves of the attack. Each successive day of the battle the Germans made less and less progress, and by June 13 the French front was stabilized. But the enemy's offensive was not yet at an end. On July 13 he attacked again, this time, in Champagne, where Foch was ready for him. The French dispositions were admirable, and the Germans failed to make their way through Gouraud's defences, where the Americans behaved with the utmost gallantry.

The time was now drawing near for Foch to gather the fruits of his strategy. He had foreseen that the Germans would undertake another great offensive and that they would deliver it on either side of Rheims. He had prepared an attack upon the flank of the German salient between Château-Thierry and Soissons, and had withdrawn several British and American divisions from the north for this operation. Many British soldiers and Ministers regarded this step with misgiving in view of the menace to Haig's position from Prince Rupprecht's unused troops, and Foch met with opposition both from French soldiers and from Paris. He took his risks, and Mangin's victorious counter-attack of July 18, which at last transferred the initiative to the Allies, was the splendid vindication of his confidence.

THE ALLIED OFFENSIVE: FOCH'S PLANS

On July 24 Foch assembled the only conference of Allied commanders which he summoned and outlined to them his offensive plans.

The moment had, in his opinion, arrived 'to take decisions, to face responsibilities, to enter upon sacrifice ... the initiative must be secured and the offensive launched.' He had two main objects in view. The first object was to clear the railways upon which the future movements of the Allies must depend. The second was to drive the Germans from the mining area in the north and from the Channel ports.

On August 8 Rawlinson's Fourth Army and Debeney's Tenth Army began their famous attack on the Amiens front. This was, in Ludendorff's words, 'that Black Day in Germany's history,' and it followed happily upon Foch's nomination as a Marshal of France the day before. Within five days the Allies had disengaged Amiens and the railways converging upon it. They had heavily defeated 20 German Divisions and had taken 20,000 prisoners and over 400 guns.

The offensive thus brilliantly launched was pressed forward with unremitting energy and precision. The British Third Army and then the First Army, farther to the north, joined in the attack, and the French advanced on the Montdidier front to the south-east of Amiens.

The two railways from Paris to Metz – that by Châlons sur Marne and Verdun to the north, and that by Vitry, Bar-le-Duc, and Toul to the south – had been gradually cleared. Foch now considered that the time had come to use the whole force of the Allies in a great converging movement. He directed the British and the French Armies on their immediate right to continue their advance in the St. Quentin-Cambrai direction, the French in the centre to push forward beyond the Aisne and the Ailette, and the Americans to attack the St. Mihiel salient in the Woeuvre, and, at the same time, with their right on the Meuse and their left supported by the French Fourth Army, to advance in the direction of Mezières. Foch naturally attached most importance to this last operation. He saw that an attack on the salient was unlikely to do more than lead to a local withdrawal of the Germans, while a successful advance on Mezières would menace the principal German line of communications by Namur and Liége.

The second phase of the Allied advance began on September 12 with the American and French attack on the St. Mihiel salient, which, however, the Germans did not seriously attempt to defend. It was followed on September 27 by the successful operations of the British Third and First Armies. These enabled the Fourth Army to advance farther to the south. The struggle was severe, but by October 7 the Hindenburg Line had passed into the possession of the British troops, and a wide gap had been driven through the enemy's system of defences in rear.

The effect of this magnificent series of engagements upon the subsequent course of the campaign was decisive, for the threat to the German communications now became direct and instant. There was nothing affording a system of defence between Haig's Armies and Maubeuge on the Sambre, except the natural obstacles presented by a wooded and well-watered country, and through Maubeuge runs the railway to Charleroi and Namur. Farther north the Allied advance had been equally successful, for by the same date, October 7, the First Army was in possession of the great mining centre at Lens, and the advance of the Second Army, with a French force and the Belgians under the command of King Albert, had reached a line extending from Armentières to Dadizeele, on the Lys. Everywhere Foch's strategic principles as set out in his 'Principes de Guerre' were being fully proved in the field.

The enemy was clearly demoralized although not even Foch himself realized how near the breaking point was the German power of resistance. His only object, even in the weeks immediately preceding the Armistice, was to drive back the German line as far as possible before the weather should stay further offensive operations. In fact, on September 29, after we had broken through the strongest sector of the Hindenburg line, the German Supreme Command was already insisting on an immediate armistice.

On October 10 Foch gave instructions for the British offensive to be pushed forward, in conjunction with the Allied advance in Belgium, in a north-easterly direction between the Scheldt and the Sambre so as to clear the enemy out of the Lille area, while the French First Army was to endeavour to outflank the line of the Serre, acting in combination with the French advance on the Aisne-Meuse front.

These operations progressed so favourably that on October 19 Foch issued another general order in which he outlined the future course of the campaign. The Allied troops in Belgium were to continue their march on Brussels; the British Armies south of the line Pecq-Lessines-Hal, with their right resting on Agimont, a little to the north of Givet, and acting in conjunction with King Albert's Army, were to drive the enemy towards the Ardennes; while the French First, Tenth, Fifth, and Fourth Armies, together with the American First Army, were to support this British advance by moving in the direction La Capelle-Chimay-Givet, to outflank the enemy on the line Serre-Soissons, to push forward as rapidly as possible forwards Mezières and Sedan, and to turn, if possible, the line of the Aisne by working on the left round Chaumont-Porcien and on the right towards Buzancy.

By this time the Allied troops were nearing exhaustion, the strain and exertion of this stupendous period of almost incessant fighting having told severely on all ranks. The difficulties of forwarding supplies of food and ammunition to the troops in the line were also daily becoming more and more onerous because of the destruction of roads and railways by the retreating enemy. But, although the exact objectives were not always reached, the advance continued and the German resistance was everywhere overcome.

It now became clear that the moral of the enemy's troops was completely broken and that the military collapse of Germany was at hand. But Foch never relaxed his pursuit. On November 9, two days before the Armistice was signed, he issued his final general order stating that the enemy was disorganized by the repeated attacks of the Allies, and was giving ground along his whole front. Had not the Armistice been signed on November 11 he had planned, as he himself expressed it, 'dans le plus grand mystère, dans le plus grand silence', a fresh offensive to be launched on the 13th. It was to have been carried out by 20 French and six American divisions between Metz and Strasbourg, and might well have inflicted on the Germany one of the greatest catastrophes in military history, for, if successful, it would have cut the last line of communications left open for the retreating enemy.

His own personal triumph might have been even greater than it was, had the War been continued; but Foch was satisfied. The conditions of the Armistice achieved his purpose. Once that purpose was achieved, he maintained that no one had the right 'to shed one more drop of blood.'

The fact that Foch saw no action during the Franco-Prussian War nor in France's colonial campaigns of the period, and spent three periods at the L'Ecole de Guerre, suggests the reason for his strategic insight but scant tactical ability. The French losses in the early years of the war are often attributed to his combative spirit but poor understanding of the casualties inseparable from large-scale attacks on well-prepared positions and, also, on his reluctance to release adequate reserves when their committal might well have turned the tables in his favour. Latterly, as Generalissimo on the Western Front, his will to win and comprehensive understanding of the German impending collapse brought victory.

* * *

HAIG

Master of the Field

31 JANUARY 1928

THE GREATEST SOLDIER that the Empire possessed has passed away suddenly, while still in the fullness of his powers. Lord Haig not only shouldered the heaviest military burden that any Briton has ever borne, but, when the War was over, and with the same foresight that distinguished him in his campaigns, he took up a task which probably no other could have accomplished, and devoted all his time and energy to the service of his old comrades in the field.

Haig's great characteristic was thoroughness. From his boyhood he seemed almost to foresee what destiny had in store for him and was constantly preparing himself for it. Among his contemporaries none could rival him in the knowledge of his profession. He had worked up through every grade of the Staff and had commanded every unit, so that, when he reached the position of Commander-in-Chief of the greatest Army that the Empire had ever put in the field, he was known to all his subordinates as being a master of every detail.

It is always difficult to compare one general with another of a different age, since the conditions which confronted them were so different. It would be useless, for example, to endeavour to compare the qualities of

Marlborough or of Wellington with those of Haig. It is sufficient to say that he, like them, showed himself able to use most effectively the means at his disposal, and deserves to take his place with them in the roll of fame. As a young man in South Africa, and in 1914, when he commanded the I Corps, Haig showed that he was able to manoeuvre troops in a war of movement. By the time he became an Army commander the front in France had become stabilized, and he then showed his ability to adapt himself to the changed conditions of trench warfare. It was he who was responsible for planning the operations that were to be undertaken at Neuve Chapelle, and so well did he foresee the character of the new struggle that his dispositions and orders for that battle became in their essential details the model of all future British attacks during the War, except in regard to the length of the preliminary bombardment.

To thoroughness he added coolness, optimism, and an intense tenacity of purpose. In the darkest days of the First Battle of Ypres and of the March offensive he never became ruffled, but continued to carry on his duties as though he were at manoeuvres. His judgement was sound; he never failed to appreciate the difficulties of his situation; but at the same time he saw those of his adversary, and was always able to distinguish the factors favourable to himself. His bulldog tenacity was remarkable. Once he had taken a decision nothing would move him from it, and, though at times he was severely criticized for persisting in operations long after their advantages had passed, he held strongly to the opinion, expressed in his celebrated order of April 11, 1918, that

> Victory will belong to the side which holds out the longest ... There is no other course open to us but to fight it out. Every position must be held to the last man; there must be no retirement. With our backs to the wall, and believing in the justice of our cause, each one of us must fight on to the end.

In spite of this tenacity he was always willing to listen to his allies and to cooperate with them. One of the most striking features of the First Battle of Ypres was the manner in which he worked with the French – with Dubois, who commanded the IX Corps, and with D'Urbal, the commander of the Eighth Army. Later on, too, when he was Commander-in-Chief, he was in the closest cooperation with both Foch and Pétain. He resisted, however, to the utmost all attempts to commit him to enterprises which he considered dangerous, and where he considered that the public good required it he was always willing to subordinate his own interests. He gave a notable example of this characteristic at Doullens, for it was due to him more than to anyone else that Foch was appointed without opposition and without friction to the supreme command. It was he, too, who, after Lord Milner had proposed that Foch should be appointed to co-ordinate the action of the Allied Armies on the Amiens Front, urged the inadequacy of this step, and had Foch's authority extended to cover the whole of the Western Front.

A SOLDIER'S LIFE
THE CAVALRY AND THE STAFF COLLEGE

Douglas Haig was born in Edinburgh, June 19, 1861, the youngest of the sons of John Haig, of Cameron Bridge, Fife, sixth in descent from Robert Haig, who was the second son of the 17th laird of Bemersyde, Roxburghshire. He was educated at Clifton Bank School, St. Andrews, Clifton College, where he played Rugby football, and Brasenose College, Oxford, whence, as University candidate, as was the custom then, he passed not direct into the Army but into the R.M.C., Sandhurst. There, as his contemporary, the late General Sir Walter Congreve, who occupied the same room, used to relate, he exhibited altogether exceptional zeal for a cadet, not only listening to the instruction but writing out notes of it each day. Commissioned into the 7th Hussars in 1885, he went out to India, and soon became known as a polo player and breaker of polo ponies. But sport did not interfere with his duties, and in the course of time he was appointed adjutant of his regiment. His first step on the ladder was his selection to be A.D.C. to the Inspector-General of Cavalry in India.

With his eye on the Staff College, Haig had begun to resume military study seriously. He qualified at the entrance examination for the College in 1894 and was given a nomination by the Duke of Cambridge in the following year. Thus he entered Camberley in the same class as Field-Marshal Lord Allenby and with Captain (Sir Herbert) Lawrence, his future Chief of General Staff, in the class above him. At the College Haig was remarkable for the wide view that he took of the work and the problems with which he was called upon to deal. While others were concerned with details, he would go straight for the essential points. During the second year Colonel G. F. R. Henderson, the historian, then one of the instructors, said one evening to a group of students, 'There is a fellow in your batch who will be Commander-in-Chief one of these days,' and then, without hesitation, said 'Haig.' Two who were present were able to remind Sir Douglas Haig of the prophecy when he assumed command

of the B.E.F. at St. Omer in December, 1915. And, as one of them re
marked, 'by the way Henderson said it, he meant you would be a successful one.' At all stages of his career Haig frequently referred to the debt he
owed to the Commandant of the Staff College, General Sir Henry
Hildyard, and to Colonel Henderson.

On the conclusion of the course in December, 1897, Captain Haig
was attached to the Egyptian Army and took part in the Omdurman
Campaign, receiving a brevet majority. Returning home at its close, he
was appointed Brigade Major of the Aldershot Cavalry Brigade. In
September, 1899, he was sent out to Natal and took part as Staff Officer of
Sir John French in the Natal operations, just escaping from being shut
up in Ladysmith. The Colesberg operations during the preparations for
Lord Roberts's advance were, if not conceived, worked out by him. As
Chief Staff Officer of the Cavalry Division during the advance he added
greatly to his reputation. His orders, models of their kind, are now preserved at the Staff College. In the later stages of the war he commanded a
column and a group of columns in Cape Colony. He was given a brevet
lieutenant-colonelcy and appointed to the command of the 17th Lancers,
which, however, he did not take up until the end of the war. From
October, 1903, to August, 1906, he was Inspector-General of Cavalry in
India, being promoted major-general in May, 1904, and marrying the
Hon. Dorothy Vivian, daughter of the third Lord Vivian, during a visit
home in 1905.

In 1906 he was brought home and was successively Director of
Military Training and Director of Staff Duties at the War Office, where
he was intimately concerned in the development of the General Staff,
the arrangements for mobilization, and the re-writing of the training
manuals. At the end of 1909 he returned to India as Chief of the Staff, with
later the title of Chief of the General Staff, being promoted lieutenant-
general in 1910. In February, 1912, he was brought back to England to
succeed Sir Horace Smith-Dorrien as General Officer Commanding the
Aldershot Command with the First and Second Divisions under him.
He commanded these formations as a corps at the Army Manoeuvres in
1912 and 1913, being created K.C.B. in the latter year.

THE GREAT WAR
BRITISH COMMANDER-IN-CHIEF

In August, 1914, with the same troops constituting the I Corps, he went
with the B.E.F. to France. After the First Battle of Ypres Sir Douglas Haig
was promoted full general for distinguished service, and in December,

on the formation of armies, was selected to be the commander of the First Army, then newly formed. In that command, under the orders of Sir John French, he fought Neuve Chapelle, Aubers Ridge, Festubert, and Loos.

When, on December 22, 1915, Sir Douglas Haig took over the command of the British Armies in France on the removal of Sir John French, he had many great problems to face. The Battle of Loos – though in that case he was the commander directly responsible – set many questions for the future. It was obvious from the experiences of that battle that the supply of competent Staff officers had declined to a degree dangerous to the progress of the Army, and that the subordinate officers directly in charge of the troops were not entirely proficient in the common work of the military day, the work which is a necessary step to victory. He had also the unpleasant task of assuming command in place of a commander to whom he had given loyal service through difficult days. Those who knew Haig intimately will admit that he became Commander-in-Chief in France with no great pleasure.

Once he had accepted the new duties he began his great period of service to the country. He realized the responsibility – the military prospects were none too happy – and in that attitude he showed the first essential virtue of a commander. His first efforts were directed towards the reorganization, training, and reinforcement of the British forces in the France and Flanders theatre of war. Nothing from without – political. Military, or popular – diverted his purpose from the prosecution of direct war while he remained the commander. He could be dismissed, but that was the affair of higher authority. His duty was for the day and the days to come.

THE SOMME

His powers were set to a test at an early date. The Germans, ever alive to vital points in war, began an intensive attack on Verdun, a citadel recognized as of primary importance in the War on the Western Front. In the defence of that place the French had to exert the greatest military effort they made in the War. That effort was great in every sense of the word, but it was not sufficient to avert disaster to the Allies if it was to be fought alone. A support for the French in that defence was obviously necessary and that support was promptly given by Sir Douglas Haig.

In cooperation with Joffre, with whom he was always in the closest sympathy, he began his preparations for the great series of the battles of the Somme. The sector of attack was selected with a high decree of military wisdom that relief might be given to Verdun, that the Allies in other theatres of war might be assisted, and that the German strength in front – never slight in the face of British troops – might be worn down. His former skill as a Staff officer was displayed in his direction of the very complicated preparations for battle. With a full knowledge of the great issues, he gave his firm support to those engaged in matters which those outside might consider to be minor detail, and yet are in themselves the seed of victory. There were then no solutions for the apparent deadlock of siege warfare, save, possibly, direct attack. The method of direct attack was chosen, accompanied by an artillery support previously unknown in the annals of war.

The great effort failed in many ways, but its failure was in the main due to climatic conditions. Yet the effort was in one important sense not a failure – it served to save Verdun, and it broke the spirit of the German Army, which entered the battle at the zenith of its efficiency and enthusiasm. It was a great venture, and, it cost many lives – a cost which humanity is apt to remember without admitting the profit. In the judgment of history it may be that the country will recognize the wisdom and discount the cost.

The Somme over, there was a disposition on the part of those who did not understand its effect on the enemy to criticize the Commander-in-Chief. He was accused of being reckless of life; and he was blamed for his supposedly premature use of the tanks on September 15.

ARRAS AND MESSINES

Mainly as a result of the Somme offensive, the Germans retired to the Siegfried Line, better known to the world as the Hindenburg Line. That was unexpected, but the general British plans remained constant. Immediately after the Somme, Haig began his preparations for a new offensive – with some opposition from the authorities at home and some criticism from the politicians in Paris. He still believed that a 'break-through' was possible. Nivelle had succeeded Joffre in the supreme command of the French Armies, because Joffre had unfortunately expressed a too candid opinion that the French troops were not capable of undertaking a new offensive, and that the British must for the future bear the brunt of the attack. Thus the general desire of Haig and Joffre that there should be a new vigorous offensive in 1917 was modified by the opinions of the new French commander, who was, for some time after March, 1917, in a position of power – directing the fortunes of both the British and the French Armies on the France and Flanders front. The Arras offensive, designed for the early spring in that year, was modified into a relatively minor attack over a front of 15 miles from Vimy Ridge southwards to Croisilles. The same attention to initial preparations was made, and the same early success was attained. The weather again took its share in the decision, and an early burst of success ended in a dreary series of days of heavy bombardment, in which the vast losses outweighed the territory gained.

Arras over, the long-contemplated attack on Messines was undertaken. It was admittedly a perfect battle of its kind – possibly the greatest concrete success in the war –and Lord Plumer and Sir Charles Harington deserve their meed of credit for the preliminary 18 months of preparation under very difficult conditions. But the Commander-in-Chief deserves his share of credit in an enterprise which needed the support of his authority at a time when his popular reputation was declining. Success – complete success – attended the effort, and there was a general revival of spirit throughout the armies in France.

PASSCHENDAELE.

Yet at this moment of success a period of gloom was beginning for the Allies. Certain French troops, dissatisfied with their leaders, failed, whole divisions refusing to go to the front and to obey the orders of their officers. It was an ugly episode, but it was overcome by tact and decision. In the task of maintaining the line and keeping the Germans engaged, Haig and the British troops took a great part. In June, 1917, prompt preparations were made for the series of operations now known as the Battles of Ypres, 1917. They were undertaken that a wedge might be driven into the enemy with the intention of securing the Passchendaele-Staden ridge and permitting the landing of British troops on the Belgian coast between Ostend and the Yser, and thus securing the Channel ports. Here, again, there was a minor degree of tactical success attended by very great loss. Miles of territory were nibbled away in nearly three months of action, but the German reserves were sent to the Dutch frontier to meet the expected arrival of the British from that direction. The weather again played its deadly part, the ground became a quagmire, and the mechanical weapons on which, properly, so much store was set failed in their task.

Next came Cambrai. Here the tanks were given their full opportunity, and in the first days they proved their power. But, unfortunately, the information of the clear indications of the coming German counter-attack were not passed back to G.H.Q., and the arrangements to meet it came too late, and all the advantages gained were lost.

THE GREAT TEST

In March, 1918, came the great test of the War. The Germans, aided by climatic conditions – the weather, it seemed, never failed them in the operations of war – overran large sectors of the British front. At each point the Allied troops fell back, and there was consternation among the general public. On the other hand, there was definite confidence at General Headquarters. It was known that in so swift an advance the Germans must overreach themselves, and that ultimately, after two or three such offensives, victory must be in the hands of the Allies. To ensure complete cooperation of the Allies, at Haig's suggestion Foch was now given supreme command. At the darkest hour, on April 12, in the second German offensive, on the Lys, against Kemmel, Sir Douglas issued a General Order dated April 11, in which he said:-

> Words fail me to express the admiration which I feel for the splendid resistance offered by all ranks of our Army under the most trying circumstances. Many among us now are tired. To those I would say that victory will belong to the side which holds out the longest. The French Army is moving rapidly and in great force to our support. There is no other course open to us but to fight it out. Every position must be held to the last man; there must be no retirement. With our backs to the wall, and believing in the justice of our cause, each one of us must fight on to the end. The safety of our homes and the freedom of mankind depend alike upon the conduct of each one of us at this critical moment.

Thenceforward the tale is no less complicated, but it deals with victory. Haig had his plans, and, after due consideration, in almost every case Foch adopted them in preference to his own. There was a mass of heavy fighting, but in each stage it was inspired, so far as the British troops were concerned, by Haig. There were no mistakes, and future generations may turn to the military record of that year with pride, not only in the British troops, but in their commander, who had borne without complaint the stress of the years that had passed. There will be credit for Lord Haig in the earlier years of his effort, but in military achievement in the field his reputation may well rest on his share in the history of the last months of the War, when the fate of nations was in the balance, and when he never lost heart.

AFTER THE WAR
THE BRITISH LEGION

When Haig came home after the War was over he might have claimed any appointment in the gift of his fellow-countrymen. It is well known that his name was mentioned as a possible Viceroy of India, but he had marked out the course he meant to pursue – namely, to devote himself to the interests of ex-Service officers and men. Great as were the services which he rendered to the Empire during the War, it is possible that those which he gave it after the Armistice were even greater. Some time before the Armistice he had turned his attention to the problem of ex-Service men. His governing idea was that officers of all ranks who had led the Army in the field should remain as the men's leaders, counsellors and helpers in the difficult after-war days. With this idea he founded the Officers' Association, the initials 'O.A.' serving to remind its members of the 'Operations A' Section at G.H.Q., which discharged for the Army during the War something of the same functions which it was his intention that the Officers' Association should perform towards the general ex-Service men's movement.

The idea that ex-Service men should keep together after the War, forming organizations for self-help, rapidly caught on, and by the time of the Armistice there was a number of separate organizations in existence, of which the principal were the Comrades of the Great War, the National Association of Discharged Soldiers and Sailors, the National Federation of Discharged and Demobilized Sailors and Soldiers, and the 'O.A.' Each of these associations had a character of its own. The Comrades of the Great War included a good number of officers and had fairly substantial funds. They were 'conservative' in outlook on the whole. The National Association was short of money, but had by far the largest membership, and it included a number of men holding extreme views on social and political questions and on the way in which the 'rights' of ex-Service men should be enforced. The National Federation was neither so powerful numerically nor of such pronounced views as either of its rivals. These three 'men's' associations were rivals competing for members and for influence and wasting time and a good deal of money in the process. It was inevitable that they should develop political tendencies, and during 1919 efforts were made to give the whole ex-Service men's movement a definite turn towards extremism.

These efforts Haig, then at the Horse Guards, combated by throwing into the scale his own personal influence. He saw at the Horse Guards certain of the leaders of the extremist movement, and he began a determined, and in the end successful, attempt to group together all ex-Service men into a single organization, which should be non-political and non-sectarian, and in which officers and men should find a common opportunity of serving the country in peace as they had served her together in war. He was easily able to convince the more thoughtful and sincere of the members of the men's associations that their best chance of helping themselves and each other lay in cooperation. He not only succeeded in realizing his hope of founding a single organization of ex-Service officers and men, but in doing so changed the whole course of the ex- Service men's movement. The dangers which loomed so large in 1919 have disappeared, and the British Legion exists to-day as the champion not only of the ex-Service man throughout the Empire, but of the highest national ideals.

The British Legion is essentially the work of one man, Haig. It is a work carried through in the face of no little doubt and suspicion in its early days, when partisans still feared that a single organization of ex-Service men under the lead of a soldier might have curious political consequences. That the work of demobilization, and after that the yet vaster work of absorption of the discharged millions of the Army, went through without active civil commotion is very largely due to the work that Haig did in 1919 and 1920 in giving the ex-Servicemen an object to work for; and thereafter, when the Legion had been formed, in directing its activities into right and worthy channels.

Blamed at the time and historically for the enormous British casualties through frontal attacks on strong and deep entrenchments, Field Marshal Earl Haig of Bemersyde, as he eventually became, never advocated the defensive strategy that served the Germans so well on the Western Front. This was in part due to his stubborn belief that the enemy lines could be breached, given enough artillery and manpower, but also to the failed attempts to outflank Germany strategically at Gallipoli, on the Austro-Italian front and in Salonika and his concern that standing on the defensive would allow Germany to reinforce the Western Front having defeated Russia in the east.

Ironically, the German U-boat campaign against merchant shipping, that threatened to starve Britain into negotiations, eventually swung the military balance in Haig's favour. When the Kaiser ordered an unrestricted U-boat attack against neutral shipping, the United States could no longer stand aside. This forced the March 1918 offensive on Ludendorff with the intention of defeating the British Army in France before the Americans could arrive, exhausting German resources and leaving the way open for Haig's August 1918 offensive that brought final victory.

* * *

JELLICOE

*'The only man on either side who could lose
the war in an afternoon'*

21 NOVEMBER 1935

OF ALL THE GREAT commanders on either side during the World War of 1914–18 Admiral of the Fleet Earl Jellicoe, whose death, at the age of 75, we announce with great regret, occupied a position which was unique. It has been pointed out by Mr Winston Churchill that his responsibilities were on a different scale from all others. 'It might fall to him as to no other man – Sovereign, statesman, admiral, or general – to issue orders which in the space of *two or three hours* might nakedly decide who won the War. The destruction of the British Battle Fleet was final. Jellicoe was the only man on either side who could lose the War in an afternoon.'

Looking back it would seem that from his earliest days Lord Jellicoe's career had been moulded by destiny so as to fit him for the ordeal which confronted him, at the age of 56, on that spring day and night in 1916. He came of seafaring stock. His education was carried on entirely within sight and sound of blue water. He did not know in earlier years the softening influences of money or friends in high places. In the course of one of those perennial discussions whether a junior naval officer can live on his pay, he once declared that he himself did so, with the aid of a money prize gained as a sub-lieutenant by meritorious examinations at college. Perhaps he was fortunate in the great seamen under whose notice he came in the course of his professional service and studies, men like Sir George Tryon, Sir Michael Culme-Seymour, Sir Arthur Wilson and Lord Fisher. But that he earned and deserved such fortune is undeniable. Destiny brought him through several narrow escapes from death – in risking his life in jumping overboard to save drowning men, in being shipwrecked at the loss of the *Victoria*, and in being seriously wounded in China. Self-centred but never self-absorbed, silent but never sullen, he gave the impression of strength, sagacity and serene self-confidence. His spare but well-knit figure was the very embodiment of strength, courage, and determination.

THE MODERN NAVY

Lord Jellicoe was essentially a product of the naval renaissance which dates from the passing of the Naval Defence Act of 1889. In working his way up to flag rank he kept abreast of every new development of the modern Navy. When the intensive training of the Fleet began, early in the present century, he was in it from the first. Gunnery, which had sunk to a low ebb in the Navy, was receiving a new attention, mainly owing to the efforts of the late Sir Percy Scott. Jellicoe's marked ability as a gunnery officer inevitably brought him into close association with all the problems connected with gunnery, ordnance, and material; and it was rather to the study of these important matters that his energies were directed for some years than to that of strategy and tactics. Thus he served on the Ordnance Committee, in the superintendence of ships. building by contract, as assistant to the Controller as Director of Naval Ordnance, and as Controller: in all of these the principal duties lay in the production of material. When he was appointed to the supreme command afloat his name and his qualifications were little known to or understood by the general public. It would be hardly an exaggeration to say that when the War broke out and his appointment to command the Grand Fleet was announced, he was professionally the most eminent and yet in public repute the least prominent among the senior flag officers of the Navy. He was an indefatigable worker who always acquainted himself with every detail, and was unsparing of himself in every duty that fell to him. He was ready to undertake any task. His devotion to duty was exemplified after the War by his continued service to the Empire as Governor-General of New Zealand, and by work on several patriotic bodies. Thus he succeeded Lord Haig as president of the British Legion, and he represented New Zealand at the request of that Government at the Naval Limitation Conference at Geneva in 1927.

EARLY SERVICE

John Rushworth Jellicoe was born at Southampton on December 5, 1859. His father was Captain John H. Jellicoe, who died in September, 1914, at the ripe age of 90. and who spent his life in the service of the Royal Mail Steam Packet Company, of which he was made a director on his retirement from active service afloat at the age of 70. Admiral Philip Patton, Lord Jellicoe's great-grandfather, was Second Sea Lord of the Admiralty at the time of Trafalgar, and had served afloat with distinction under Boscawen and Hawke. The late Admiral of the Fleet was not unmindful of the exploits of his ancestors; one of his daughters bears the name of Prudence Patton.

Jellicoe was educated at Rottingdean, and entered the Britannia as a cadet on July 15. 1872. On leaving he passed out first, taking all the prizes that the regulations allowed him to receive. He was rated midshipman on July 17, 1874, and afterwards joined the *Newcastle*, screw frigate, Captain R. G. Douglas, in the Detached Squadron. This was a good start for a youngster in a squadron moving to various parts of the world. In passing for lieutenant he took 'firsts' in the three branches which were then the total – seamanship, navigation, and gunnery – and was promoted to sub-lieutenant in December, 1878, and to lieutenant in August, 1880.

In February, 1881. he joined the *Agincourt* in the Channel Squadron and served in her through the Egyptian war. In September, 1882, he joined the gunnery schoolship *Excellent* to specialize in that branch, gaining the £80 prize at Greenwich in the course of his studies. He went to sea again three years later as gunnery lieutenant of the battleship *Monarch*. While in her he earned the Board of Trade silver medal in May. 1886, when he commanded a gig, manned by volunteers, which went to the rescue of the crew of a steamer stranded on a sand-bank near Gibraltar. The boat was swamped by the heavy seas, and the lieutenant and his men narrowly escaped with their lives, being washed ashore. This was one of several hairbreadth escapes which Jellicoe had from death during his career. In April, 1886, he joined the battleship *Colossus*, Captain (later Admiral Sir) Cyprian Bridge. She was the first ship in commission armed with 12 in. breech-loading guns, and the first to be lighted throughout with electric light. Admiral Bridge in his memoirs records the energetic part taken by Jellicoe in the work of the ship, and also mentions that he again saved a man from drowning.

THE LOSS OF THE VICTORIA
In June, 1891, after a period of staff duty in the *Excellent* and as assistant to the Director of Naval Ordnance, Rear-Admiral (afterwards Lord) Fisher, Jellicoe was promoted to commander. Then in February, 1892, another great seaman, Captain (later Admiral of the Fleet Sir) Arthur Knyvet Wilson, took him to the battleship *Sans Pareil* as executive officer. He left her in the spring of 1893 to join the flagship of Admiral Sir George Tryon, the *Victoria*, which was sunk in collision with the *Camperdown*, with the loss of 372 lives, on June 22 of that year. At the time, Jellicoe was in bed with fever, and was called to get up before the ship sank. Instead of looking out for himself, he went below to hurry up every one he could find there. When the ship foundered he came to the surface in a state of exhaustion. A midshipman of the ship, afterwards Commander P. D. R. West, rescued him from drowning. A few of the survivors of that disaster lost their nerve for a time, and some never completely recovered it. Jellicoe was not one of them. What he did lose was the fever, for he declared that the water had cured him of it. Among his lost effects was the medal awarded him seven years earlier by the Board of Trade! When he applied for a duplicate, he was told he could obtain a new medal by paying for it, but he preferred to go without.

In October 1893, he joined the *Ramillies*, the new flagship of Admiral Sir Michael Culme-Seymour, who became Commander-in-Chief. After three years in her he was promoted to captain on January 1, 1897. During that year he was a member of the Ordnance Committee, and in December was appointed to the *Centurion*, flagship of Vice-Admiral Sir E.H. Seymour on the China Station. When, in the summer of 1900, the Boxer rebellion broke out in China, Sir Edward Seymour sent his flag-captain to Tientsin for information, and Captain Jellicoe returned with a message from Sir Claude Macdonald, the British Minister, to say that unless help was immediate it would be too late. Upon this the Vice-Admiral landed in command of an international force, with Captain Jellicoe as his Chief Staff Officer. On June 21 the force had its hardest fight at Peitsang, where Jellicoe was very seriously wounded. Although his life was for a time despaired of, his strong constitution carried him through, and he made a complete recovery. Sir Edward Seymour recommended him in dispatches as an officer 'who was, as always, of most valuable help, both by his judgment and action, till disabled by a serious wound.' In the Honours List Captain Jellicoe was made C.B.

On his return home in 1901 he served at the Admiralty superintending the building of ships by contract, and in February, 1902, was appointed Naval Assistant to the Controller of the Navy (Rear-Admiral, later Admiral of the Fleet, Sir William May). He resumed sea duty in August, 1903, in command of H.M.S. *Drake*, in the Cruiser Squadron, and in January, 1905, returned to the Admiralty as Director of Naval Ordnance and Torpedoes.

LORD FISHER'S WAR PLANS
TRAINING A COMMANDER-IN-CHIEF

By this time Lord Fisher had become First Sea Lord, and in accordance with his settled conviction that war with Germany would come in or about 1914 was busily engaged upon plans for making the Fleet ready in all respects. These plans extended to the selection and training of a Commander-in-Chief, and it was upon Jellicoe that his choice fell. He had first come under the notice of the First Sea Lord when he was passing in gunnery and Fisher was in command of the *Excellent*. He had been an assistant to Fisher as Director of Naval Ordnance, and in 1902, when Jellicoe was again at the Admiralty, Fisher was Second Sea Lord. Now from February, 1905, to August, 1907, the two worked together upon the production of the Dreadnought, the improvement of naval marksmanship, and the evolution of the modern methods of gunlaying and fire-control. The late Admiral Sir Percy Scott, whose appointment as Inspector of Target Practice coincided with that of Jellicoe as D.N.O., declared that 1905 was a record year for gunnery in one way; the D.N.O., the Captain of the Gunnery School and the Inspector of Target Practice 'were all working harmoniously together to improve naval shooting. This friendly relation had never existed in the Navy before.' Over them all was the watchful eye and eager spirit of Lord Fisher, who supported them with all his enthusiasm.

For Jellicoe, Fisher was concerned not merely with present tasks but with training for the future, and the First Sea Lord so exerted his powers when at the Admiralty, and his influence after he left office, that Jellicoe's career was cast along lines which would not only equip him for his tremendous task in the event of war, but would also bring him on to the right position on the list with regard to seniority. An important step in this direction was that taken in 1911 by Mr. Churchill in reconstituting his Board and disposing of his patronage, on the advice of Lord Fisher in such a way that Jellicoe was made Second-in-Command of the Home Fleet, passing thus in effect over the heads of four or five of the more important senior admirals on the active list and becoming virtually designated for the supreme command in the near future.

Before this happened, however, there were years of active work. Jellicoe reached his turn for promotion to rear-admiral by seniority on February 8, 1907. Six months later he was appointed Rear. Admiral in the Atlantic Fleet, with his flag in the *Albemarle*. He served for the customary 12 months, and in October. 1908, was appointed Third Sea Lord and Controller. There followed two strenuous years, during which, as the member of the Board primarily responsible for the material of the Fleet, he was concerned with the building of the early dreadnoughts, and it was during his tenure that the programme of eight battleships and battle-cruisers in one financial year (1909–10) was authorized. In December, 1910, he was made Vice-Admiral Commanding the Atlantic Fleet, with acting rank until his substantive promotion came by seniority in the following September. His flag was flown in the battleship *Prince of Wales*, in which he was present at the Naval Review in honour of the Coronation of King George, on which occasion he was created K.C.B. He took a prominent part in the naval manoeuvres held in the summer of 1911, and again in 1912. The organization of the Fleets underwent a change from May 1, 1912, another step being taken in the direction of creating one great Fleet for duty in the North Sea, and on the absorption of the Atlantic Fleet into the Home Fleet Jellicoe became Vice-Admiral, commanding the Second Squadron of the latter, with his flag in the *Hercules*.

In December, 1912, he was recalled to the Admiralty as Second Sea Lord in succession to the late Marquess of Milford Haven, who was made First Sea Lord when Admiral Sir Francis Bridgeman left office. For the grand naval manoeuvres of 1913 an innovation was made by the appointment of Jellicoe to command the 'Red' Fleet, with his flag in the *Thunderer*, while retaining his seat as a member of the Admiralty Board. While no official account of the manoeuvres was issued, it was under-stood that Jellicoe displayed rare strategical and tactical skill, and gave his opponents a good deal of trouble and anxiety before the operations came to an end.

From the foregoing it will be seen how thorough, constant, and progressive was the experience gained by Jellicoe of the working of that great naval machine which he was destined to command in war. On July 22, 1914, it was officially announced that the King had approved of the appointment of a successor to Sir John Jellicoe, who was to vacate office on September 1, and afterwards to succeed Admiral Sir George Callaghan as Commander-in-Chief, Home Fleets. Events in the world crisis accelerated this change. On July 23, Austria presented her ultima-tum to Serbia, and the situation became an anxious one. Mr. Churchill informed Vice-Admiral Jellicoe that in the event of hostilities involving this country it was considered necessary that Admiral Callaghan should have the assistance of a Second-in-Command, and that he (the Vice-Admiral) had been selected for this post. It was arranged that he should fly his flag in the *Centurion*.

On July 31, at the Admiralty, it was intimated to Jellicoe that, in certain circumstances, he might be appointed Commander-in-Chief in succession to Admiral Callaghan. He protested against such a change on what might be the very eve of war, and left the same night for the North of Scotland, joining the Fleet at Scapa Flow on August 2. At about 4 a.m. on August 4 he received Admiralty orders to open a secret envelope which had been handed to him in the train as he was leaving London. It contained his appointment as 'Commander-in-Chief of the Grand Fleet,' with the acting rank of Admiral.

THE SUPREME COMMAND

From the outbreak of hostilities until November 28, 1916, or rather more than half the War, Jellicoe held the supreme command in the North Sea. With characteristic modesty and restraint, and yet with unimpeachable candour, he revealed to the world in 1919, in his book, 'The Grand Fleet,' the story of that command. From its War base at Scapa Flow, 'in the northern mists,' with subsidiary bases at Invergordon, on the Firth of Cromarty, and Rosyth, on the Firth of Forth, the Grand Fleet exercised a blockade of the Gerrman Fleet and Merchant Navy which increased in severity as the months passed. That it came through this trying period with comparatively few losses affords evidence of the expert handling of the Commander-in-Chief. No battleship or armoured cruiser was lost to attack by submarines, although the wholesale use of mines accounted for a few victims, the chief of which was the battleship *Audacious*.

At the first important clash in the North Sea, on August 28, 1914. when light forces penetrated into the Heligoland Bight and carried out the operation which led to the cutting off and destruction of three German light cruisers and other craft, it was at Jellicoe's suggestion that the Battle-Cruiser Squadron under Rear-Admiral Beatty was present as a supporting force, and it was these heavy ships which, appearing on the scene at the right moment, completed the enemy's destruction and extricated the British light units. Five months later, on the occasion of the Dogger Bank action on January 24, 1915, the British and German battle-cruiser forces were engaged and the *Blucher* was sunk.

THE BATTLE OF JUTLAND – A DIFFICULT DECISION

Intercepted wireless signals having shown that some movement was about to take place from Wilhelmshaven, the Grand Fleet, which was distributed between Scapa Flow, Invergordon, and Rosyth, was ordered to sea on May 30, 1916. Admiral Jellicoe gave two rendezvous, one to the main body, the other to the Battle-Cruiser Force under Vice-Admiral Beatty, about 60 miles apart. If nothing were seen by 2 p.m. on May 31, the battle-cruisers were to turn and rejoin the main body. The time for turning had actually arrived next day, when enemy light cruisers were sighted by the *Galatea*. Pursuit brought the 10 heavy ships under Vice-Admiral Beatty in contact with the five similar vessels of the First Scouting Group under Admiral Hipper, and a running action to the southward began, in the course of which two British ships, the *Indefatigable* and *Queen Mary*, were sunk. After close upon an hour's engagement, the High Sea Fleet came in view. Admiral Beatty turned to rejoin the Commander-in-Chief. The thick and hazy weather in which all the movements since leaving harbour had taken place had prevented astronomical observations, and the positions of the fleets had been calculated by dead reckoning.

The errors which arose from many causes made a difference of 11 miles between the real and the estimated positions of the two portions of the British Fleet; and these calculated positions disagreed with the indications and reports of the position of the High Sea Fleet. Admiral Jellicoe, commanding a great fleet which was approaching another at a speed of nearly 40 miles an hour, had a decision of the utmost difficulty to make as to how he should deploy: for he was uncertain as to the bearing on which the enemy at any moment might appear. He decided to deploy to port, and this action, when the enemy came in sight, brought the Grand Fleet into a position across, and partly enveloping, the head of the enemy's line. The situation in which Admiral von Scheer was then placed was perilous. He turned away and, throwing out flotillas to cover his retirement, was quickly out of sight in the mist; and though Von Scheer returned later to the attack, close action did not follow, as the German flotilla attacks caused the British Commander-in-Chief to turn away; and the German fleet returned, with the loss of two capital ships, one old and one new, to its base.

A controversy arose after the War over the tactics pursued by both Admiral Jellicoe and Vice-Admiral Beatty, largely owing to the scarcity of official information. Early in 1919, Captain John E. T. Harper was appointed to the War Staff to prepare a narrative showing the sequence of events connected with the battle. He completed this record in October.

1919, but publication was withheld on various grounds until June 1, 1927. One of the 10 appendices, No. 8, containing the signals made during the battle, was printed with the official dispatches and published on December 17, 1920. On November 15, 1923, there was published Volume Ill. of the 'Official History of the War,' containing Sir Julian Corbett's record, and on July 26, 1924, there was published a 'Narrative of Jutland,' prepared by the Naval Staff at the Admiralty.

AT THE ADMIRALTY

At the end of November, 1916, Jellicoe, to his own intense regret, gave up his command. He was invited to become First Sea Lord by Mr (later Lord) Balfour in succession to Admiral Sir Henry Jackson, and he replied expressing his willingness to do whatever was best for the Service. At the Admiralty he instituted the Anti-Submarine Division, and pursued an active policy to combat the alarming growth in the submarine menace in two ways – offensive in the direction of anti-submarine measures of all kinds, and defensive, in the direction of protective measures for trade, such as convoys. In 'The Crisis of the Naval War,' published in July, 1920, he set forth the main features of his work during the critical year of 1917. In bidding farewell to the officers and men of the *Iron Duke*, he had said that they must expect to see him the object of the same attacks as those upon his predecessor. Almost exactly a year ago, in 'The Submarine Peril,' he returned to the subject of 1917 and its lessons for the present day.

He suddenly ceased to be First Sea Lord at the end of 1917, his successor being Admiral Sir Rosslyn Wemyss. No official explanation was ever given of his abrupt dismissal – for so it was, seeing that Jellicoe himself seems to have been quite unaware that it was impending. Sir Eric Geddes, who had become First Lord, sent him a letter intimating that his term of service at the Admiralty was at an end. Admiral of the Fleet Sir A. K. Wilson, most taciturn and reticent of admirals, wrote that 'The dismissal of Sir John Jellicoe is a disgraceful concession to an unscrupulous Press agitation.' No word of complaint, however, was ever uttered by Jellicoe himself. He was raised to the peerage as Viscount Jellicoe of Scapa, and 18 months later he, in common with the leaders of the Armies and the Fleets, received the thanks of both Houses of Parliament and a grant of £50,000.

NEW ZEALAND

Throughout 1918 he remained unemployed, devoting his leisure to the preparation of his book on the creation, development, and work of the Grand Fleet. In the spring of 1919 he was invited by the Government to undertake a Mission to the Dominions to confer with their Governments on measures for the common defence of the Empire on the seas and left England on February 21 in the battle-cruiser *New Zealand*, the cruise lasting about one year, during which the vessel steamed 33,514 nautical miles, and Lord Jellicoe also travelled for 16,589 statute miles on land. He made reports to the various Dominion Governments. For the greater part of the cruise he flew the Union Flag as an Admiral of the Fleet, to which rank he was specially promoted on April 3, 1919.

In August, 1920, Jellicoe left England as Governor-General of New Zealand and served in that Dominion until the end of 1924. His term was most popular and successful, and in the New Year honours of 1925 he was created an earl. On December 5, 1924, on attaining the age of 65, he was placed on the retired list of the Navy. He had been created G.C.B. on February 8, 1915, and G.C.V.O. on June 17, 1916, in both of which months King George visited the Grand Fleet, the latter occasion after the Jutland action. He was also appointed to the Order of Merit from the date of the battle. The honours conferred upon him after the War included the Freedom of the City of London, with a sword of honour, and honorary degrees from Oxford, Cambridge, St. Andrews, and Glasgow. He was also awarded a number of decorations from foreign Governments.

Among Lord Jellicoe's various public appointments, he served as Boy Scout Commissioner for the County of London. He had previously been Chief Scout in New Zealand when Governor-General there. In 1925 he was elected chairman of the National Rifle Association, in succession to Lord Cheylesmore. He resigned this post in 1930, owing to his enlarged sphere of public work, but remained a member of the Council. It was in February, 1928, that he became president of the British Legion, in succession to Lord Haig and as such he worked whole-heartedly for the benefit of the ex-Service men, devoting the greater part of his time to the cases of distress and to speeches and schemes to help those who had suffered by the War. Ill-health compelled him to resign the presidency early in 1932. Although a member of the House of Lords since 1918, it was not until May, 1930, that he made his maiden speech there, when he declared in a debate on the Naval Treaty that 'the reductions that are now proposed go beyond the limit of security.'

Jellicoe married in 1902, as a captain, Florence Gwendoline, daughter of Sir Charles Cayzer, first baronet, the Liverpool shipowner. There were five children of the marriage, four being daughters and the last a son, the Hon. George Patrick John Rushworth Jellicoe, Viscount Brocas, who was born on April 4, 1918, and is a godson of the King and of Lady Patricia Ramsay.

Sir George Tryon is one of the great seamen who are mentioned above as having an influence on Jellicoe's early career. He is famous as the admiral who ordered the manoeuvre that caused the collision between *Camperdown* and *Victoria*, losing his own life with 371 others. Jellicoe himself was lucky to survive. The fact that the manoeuvre was more than obviously dangerous – it was impossible – was recognised by several officers, but who had such faith in Tryon as a revered fleetwork expert and senior personality that they did not question him. This tragedy has been seen as symptomatic of a deep nineteenth-century naval malaise – the senior officer is always right, do nothing unless and until he says so, initiative is not encouraged.

To a nation that needed another Trafalgar and didn't get it, the ostensibly disappointing battle of Jutland has been the subject of intense argument to the present day. Modern historical analysis agrees that Jellicoe made the correct decision in deploying into line ahead on his port wing, thus profiting from better visibility to the west and getting between Scheer and his home base. Jellicoe's difficulties were compounded by a lack of efficient scouting reports from the battlecruiser force led by Beatty – Jellicoe twice having to ask by searchlight at a very late stage; 'Where is the enemy battlefleet?'

Materiel and institutional shortcomings robbed Jellicoe of a telling victory. Based on relative losses, there was an early belief that the Germans had won. Something of this sentiment still exists here. It is not mentioned that the German strategic aim to reduce the British battleship preponderance had utterly failed and that the Grand Fleet still held the gaoler's keys.

The paragraph about the Jutland controversy and the various reports is disingenuous – it is clear that there was partisan manipulation and that Captain Harper's report was suppressed, as the facts thus exposed were critical of the handling of the battlecruiser force. Despite having allies such as Admiral Sir Reginald Bacon (*The Jutland Scandal*, Hutchinson 1925), Jellicoe found it difficult to fight his corner from New Zealand.

Despite Churchill's dictum, it is unlikely that the action off Jutland could have lost the war, but the failure to master the U-boat threat certainly could. The lack of a proper Naval Staff organisation was another institutional failure, but Jellicoe's invention of the Anti-Submarine Division was timely. The Admiralty's reluctance to adopt the convoy system had complex roots concerned with a statistical mis-appreciation of the size of the task and a belief that the tactical principles that had made centuries of sail-driven convoy work effective were not applicable to the steamship era. As First Sea Lord, Jellicoe must shoulder some of the blame; his 'abrupt dismissal' was no doubt accelerated by his 'bombshell' statement to Cabinet and others on 20 June, 1917 that owing to the great shortage of shipping, it would be impossible for Great Britain to continue the war in 1918.

Interestingly, the passage about Jellicoe's anti-submarine policies still describes convoy as 'defensive' and by implication less worthy than the 'offensive' measures which during the war were massively ineffective. Fortunately, convoy saved the nation.

* * *

BEATTY

A Great Sea Commander

11 MARCH 1936

ADMIRAL OF THE Fleet Earl Beatty, OM, whose death we announce with much regret, had a career unique in modern times. It followed no accepted routine, and brought him on to the list of flag officers at the early age of 38, the same age at which Nelson was made a Rear-Admiral of the Blue, and when he retired in January, 1936, on reaching the age limit, he was the last officer on the active list who had held substantive rank as a flag officer in the War.

When Beatty received flag rank there was a general opinion that, with so little service actually at sea, and so little even of that in a fleet, he would be wanting in the experience necessary for high command. But he possessed self-reliance and courage, both physical and moral. He was never in his earliest days fearful of taking responsibility; and, what is possibly more unusual in the Service; he was equally ready to take responsibility when he reached the highest ranks.

It was these qualities of character that brought him to the notice of those under whom he served as a youngster, and led, in the first place, to his being chosen for the first Nile Expedition. This gave him his opportunity. It was again these qualities that enabled him, when occasion thus offered her locks, to seize them; and, finally, it was these, combined with a breadth of view acquired largely by his unconventional service, and partly by escaping from the narrowing influences which dominate the life of most junior officers, that caught the attention of the First Lord, brought him the command in the Battle-Cruiser Squadron, and set him firmly on the ladder that carried him to the very top.

Beatty came of a foxhunting stock, and was himself from boyhood upwards a fearless follower of hounds and a good horseman. His grandfather, David Beatty, of Borodale, County Wexford, was Master of the County Hounds for nearly 40 years. His father, Captain D. L. Beatty, of the 4th Hussars, settled at Nantwich in Cheshire, where the boy was born on January 17, 1871, removing afterwards to the neighbourhood of Rugby. Lord Beatty had three brothers, one of whom died in India, and of the other two, both of whom served in the War, the elder, Major Charles Beatty, DSO, died of wounds.

EARLY SERVICE

Having entered the Navy in January 1884, David Beatty went to sea two years later as a naval cadet in the *Alexandra*, flagship in the Mediterranean of Vice-Admiral H.R.H. the Duke of Edinburgh, and was advanced to midshipman on May 15, 1886. The Mediterranean Station was then at its zenith as regards strength, importance, and social distinction. His gunroom messmates in the *Alexandra* included Sir Reginald Tyrwhitt, who commanded the Harwich Forces in the War, and Sir Walter Cowan, who conducted the campaign against the Bolshevists in 1919.

In 1889 Beatty joined the corvette *Ruby*, in the Training Squadron, and a year later, on passing his examination in seamanship, in which he took a second class, was promoted sub-lieutenant. In his further examinations for lieutenant he did moderately, taking a first in torpedo, a second in pilotage and gunnery, and a third in navigation. He resumed sea duty in January, 1892, in the battleship *Nile*, Captain Gerard Noel, and in the following August, having been promoted to lieutenant, he returned to his former ship, the *Ruby*. A year later he moved into the battleship *Camperdown* as watchkeeper, the same vessel which three months before had rammed and sunk the *Victoria* with large loss of life, among those saved being the future Lord Jellicoe, who was the *Victoria's* commander. In 1896 Beatty was landed as second-in-command of a naval brigade for service in a flotilla on the Nile in co-operation with the Egyptian Army under the Sirdar, Sir Herbert Kitchener. He rendered excellent service in getting the gunboats over the Cataract, and at the action of Hafiz, when the commanding officer was wounded, he took his place, and was rewarded with the DSO. Two years later he was again on the Nile in the Sudan Expedition, having in the interval commanded one of the earliest torpedo-boat destroyers, the *Ranger*, at Portsmouth. He was present at the battles of the Atbara and Khartoum, was mentioned in dispatches by the Sirdar, and, in addition to being awarded the 4th class of the Medjidieh, was promoted to commander, at the age of 27, and with six years' seniority as lieutenant.

THE BOXER REBELLION

In April 1899, he joined the *Barfleur*, Captain George Warrender, flagship of the second-in-command in China, and had the good fortune to be landed for active service again during the Boxer Rebellion. At the defence of Tientsin he was severely wounded in an attempt to capture two Chinese guns which were causing much trouble to the forces and inhabitants. He displayed great dash and gallantry on this occasion, continuing to lead his men after being hit twice. He was again mentioned in dispatches, and was promoted to captain in November 1900, after only two years as a commander. For some time after he was invalided and unemployed, and it was during this interval, in 1901, that he married Miss Ethel Field, only daughter of the Chicago millionaire, Mr. Marshall Field.

In June, 1902, he returned to duty in command of the small cruiser *Juno* in home waters, and in September, 1904, was selected to command the *Diana* in the Mediterranean, but in this appointment he did not continue, being transferred to command the new cruiser *Suffolk*. From September 1905, he again had a spell on half-pay but in 1907–8 was serving as Naval Adviser to the Army Council. It was in December, 1908, that he again went afloat in command of the battleship *Queen* in the Atlantic Fleet. His period in the *Queen* was cut short by promotion to rear-admiral on January 1, 1910. at which time advancement to the flag list was abnormally quick.

When Beatty reached the top of the list of captains he had completed but a little more than four of the six years required of command at sea. The Board, of which Lord Fisher was First Sea Lord, making a very liberal allowance for his having been unable to serve at sea for some time after his promotion, owing to the wounds he received in China, obtained an Order in Council for his promotion. The moment was certainly fortunate for Beatty, for the Board was anxious to get younger men on the flag list than they had been getting in recent years. The exceptional relaxation of a very necessary rule points, however, to Beatty's having given the impression of exceptional qualities in command.

It was recorded by Mr. Churchill in 'The World Crisis' that Beatty declined the offer of the first flag appointment suited to his rank as a junior rear-admiral in the Atlantic Fleet, 'a very serious step for a naval officer to take when appointments were few in proportion to candidates.' No reasons are mentioned, but Mr. Churchill adds:-

'I was, however; advised about him at the Admiralty in a decisively adverse sense. He had got on too fast; he had many interests ashore. His heart, it was said, was not wholly in the Service. ... It would be contrary to precedent to make a further offer'.

But, after meeting Beatty, Mr. Churchill appointed him as Naval Secretary to the First Lord:-

Working thus side by side in rooms which communicated, we perpetually discussed during the next 15 months the problems of a naval war with Germany. It became increasingly clear to me that he viewed questions of naval strategy and tactics in a different light from the average naval officer: he approached them, as it seemed to me, much more as a soldier would ... He thought of war problems in their unity by land, sea, and air. His mind had been rendered quick and supple by the situations of polo and the hunting field, and enriched by varied experiences against the enemy on Nile gunboats and ashore.

As a result, Mr. Churchill had no doubts whatever when the command of the Battle Cruiser Squadron fell vacant in the spring of 1913 in appointing him over the heads of all to 'this incomparable command.'

THE HELIGOLAND BIGHT
DECISION REWARDED

Rear-Admiral Beatty hoisted his flag on board the *Lion* on March 1, 1913. Early in the War he had his first opportunity and showed his quality. It had been learned from our submarine scouting forces in the Bight that the German flotillas and light cruisers went nightly to sea, returning at dawn. A plan was prepared to surprise them with the light forces from Harwich under Commodores Tyrwhitt and Keyes. Admiral Jellicoe, when informed of the intention, proposed to support the movement with the main fleet; he was told it was not necessary, but that he might send his battle-cruisers, and Beatty's squadron, with six light cruisers, was consequently detached.

The intended surprise miscarried. The Germans had received warning and had prepared a counter-surprise, with the result that a confused and dangerous situation resulted. During some four hours of scrambling engagements Beatty had been waiting about 50 miles to the westward of Heligoland. Then an urgent message for help reached him from Commodore Tyrwhitt.

Clearly immediate support was needed; equally clearly the risks to the great ships were considerable. Beatty boldly accepted the risks. He took his battle-cruisers into the Bight at full speed. His courageous decision was fully rewarded. Arriving in the nick of a very critical situation, he turned the tables completely, with the result that what might have been an unfortunate incident ended in a success measured by the loss to the enemy of three light cruisers and a destroyer, with about 1,000 casualties, among whom were the German Flotilla Admiral and the Destroyer Commodore. The son of Admiral von Tirpitz was among the prisoners.

Beatty received full credit for his handling of the situation. He had shown that he could take a decision promptly and was prepared to take the risks of the as yet unknown power of the new instruments, the mine and the torpedo. He had made a good start.

HARTLEPOOL AND DOGGER BANK

In December 1914, information of a coming raid upon the British coast was received. The battle-cruisers – now reduced to four – a battle squadron, and a force of light cruisers and destroyers were ordered to sea to intercept the raiders, under the command of Admiral Warrender, but a continuation of thick weather and want of information enabled the enemy, after bombarding Hartlepool and Scarborough, to escape without being brought to action. In his subordinate position Beatty showed energy and good judgment and readiness to make suggestions.

Five weeks later the warning of another raid was received, and Beatty with the battle-cruisers – now five in number – with four light cruisers, put to sea from the Firth of Forth, to be joined at a rendezvous northward of the Dogger Bank by a light force from Harwich. In the grey of the dawn of January 24 Beatty's scouts got in touch with the enemy's. Warned, the German battle-cruisers turned for home at full speed. Beatty pursued, and, gradually overhauling the enemy, he brought the rear ship of the German line, the *Blucher*, under a crushing fire, while on the other hand, the enemy simultaneously concentrated the fire of three of his ships upon the *Lion* in the British van.

Hitting soon became general, and continued for about an hour and a half. Then three events, decisive of the result, followed in quick succession. The *Blucher*, disabled, circled round to port: a report – false, as it afterwards proved – of a submarine to starboard caused Beatty to order a turn, first of eight points to port, then to N.E.; and a shell hit the *Lion*, which reduced her speed to 15 knots. She dropped astern. Beatty, intending the pursuit of the main body of the enemy to be resumed so soon as his turn had cleared his ships of the submarine, signalled 'Attack the enemy's rear,' followed by 'Keep closer to the enemy.' The first signal was misunderstood, the second was not taken in, for the wireless was disabled and flags, the only other available means of communication, could not be seen clearly. The Rear-Admiral interpreted Beatty's intention to be to attack the *Blucher*, and he therefore led the squadron to her and, concentrating his whole attention upon her, sank her. But in the meantime the remainder of the enemy had drawn far out of range, and, as there was then no probability of overtaking them, he returned to render aid to the disabled *Lion*.

Beatty, when it became clear that the *Lion* was out of action, transferred his flag to a destroyer and started in pursuit of his squadron in the hope that the battle had been fought to a conclusion, but at noon, to his unqualified disappointment, he met the returning squadron, its work unfulfilled. Like other commanders before him, he had experienced the need of taking every possible step to make his intentions clear to his officers and impressing upon them the need of acting upon their own judgment.

During the next month the battle- cruiser and light cruiser squadrons were reorganized under the title of the 'Battle-Cruiser Fleet,' in the form of three squadrons of battle-cruisers of three ships each, and three squadrons of four cruisers. In March, 1916, Beatty showed again his fearlessness of responsibility. Having taken the battle-cruisers in support of operations by the Harwich flotilla against the Zeppelin station in Schleswig, in bad weather with snow and a heavy gale, he held his station, in spite of orders from the Admiralty to withdraw, until all hopes of a general action had passed away.

JUTLAND: AN UNFORTUNATE CONTROVERSY

On the eve of the Battle of Jutland Beatty had six of the nine battle-cruisers under his command, the three oldest having been detached for service with the main body of the Fleet; in compensation he had four of the powerful *Queen Elizabeth* class attached to his Fleet. On receipt of the news of impending activity on the part of the High Sea Fleet on May 30 the battle-cruisers were ordered to proceed to a rendezvous off the Jutland Bank, and if nothing should have occurred by 2 p.m. on the 31st to rejoin the main body of the Fleet, which would sail from Scapa Flow, at a spot about 60 miles to the northward.

Beatty, after his custom, had held on for a little after the time ordered for return, and one of his light cruisers, the *Galatea*, sighted an enemy scout. Shortly afterwards the German battle-cruiser force was located, and a running action soon began in which the enemy retired at full speed upon their Battle Fleet to the southward. In this chase only six of Beatty's ten ships came into action; for, when Beatty with his battle-cruisers turned to the S.S.E. to make contact with the enemy, the signal was not passed to Admiral Evan-Thomas, commanding the battleship squadron, who was thereby left 10 miles astern. Thus, in the run to the southward Beatty began with six ships to five of the enemy. These six, however, were reduced to four. The *Queen Mary* and *Indefatigable* were sunk by lucky shells which exploded their magazines. These misfortunes Beatty accepted with courage and confidence, not relaxing his pursuit; and it was not till the High Sea Fleet was sighted by the Southampton that he turned to fall back upon the Grand Fleet.

The battle continued on the run to the northward, Evan-Thomas's battleships, which had now come into action with the van of the enemy, performing admirable service. The two main Fleets came in contact shortly after 6 p.m., and the battle-cruisers then took up their position as a fast division of the Fleet. As they had been the first to engage so they were the last ships to take part in the general action. Shortly after 8 p.m. Beatty once more sighted his old antagonist, Von Hipper: some shots were exchanged, some hits made; but in the falling light and mist the enemy was quickly lost to sight.

This indecisive battle was followed by the growth of an unfortunate division of opinion. Sides were taken in the Fleet as to the merits of the Commander-in-Chief and the Admiral Commanding the Battle-Cruisers, to the serious injury of discipline. The controversy spread to the Press, and books were written in support or condemnation of these commanders. The appearance of Sir Julian Corbett's last volume of the Official History by no means satisfied public opinion.

The controversy took a bitter turn in a book by Admiral Sir Reginald Bacon called 'The Jutland Scandal,' in which that officer roundly accused Admiral Beatty of incompetence arising from inexperience, and of want of chivalry and honour in allowing the blame for miscarriages of which he was asserted to be the cause to fall upon the shoulders of other officers – Sir Gordon Moore, his second at the Dogger Bank, Sir Hugh Evan-Thomas, and Sir John Jellicoe. Two further books, 'The Truth about Jutland,' by Admiral Harper, who had had the task of producing a report on the battle, and had been retired after doing so, and 'The Riddle of Jutland,' by Admiral Harper and Mr. Langhorne Gibson, appeared later. In these the view was expressed that the conduct of the battle by Lord Jellicoe was wise and well-judged, while Beatty was criticized for neglecting the training of his command in gunnery and signalling, and for the rashness of his handling of it in action. To these attacks Admiral Beatty refrained from replying.

COMMAND OF THE GRAND FLEET
SUBMARINE WARFARE

In November, 1916, Admiral Jellicoe was summoned to the Admiralty as First Sea Lord, and Sir David Beatty hoisted his flag as Commander-in-Chief on November 27.

One of Admiral Beatty's first acts on taking command was to issue a new set of battle instructions, in which, in a form resembling those of the 'Instructions' in the old wars, he conveyed his general intentions as to the conduct of battle. They showed that he had fully absorbed, as a result of his experiences, the need for making his subordinates aware of his ideas, and of his determination that nothing should interrupt the process of destruction of the main body of the enemy.

During the two years of his command the operations at sea were dominated by the submarine campaign. Notwithstanding the urgent need for destroyers in those waters in which the enemy submarines were operating with much alarming success, it was deemed impossible, in view of the needs of a possible battle, to make any large detachment of the flotillas from the Grand Fleet. Thus, the High Sea Fleet 'contained' the flotillas needed elsewhere for the defence of trade. Beatty, however, was confident that the enemy would never accept a decision without another battle. He was throughout this time eager to obtain new ideas, and showed himself accessible to all who had any to offer.

In the beginning of the unrestricted submarine campaign Beatty was among the first to recognize that the heavy losses were due to the want of concentration and the improper direction of the vessels used. He proposed placing one officer in control of all anti-submarine operations, with freedom to mass them where they were required, a suggestion that was adopted. He urged the mining of the Heligoland Bight, with the minefields 'watched by light cruiser and destroyer sweeps at varying intervals, with submarine patrols'; but mines then were not available in the number needed. As the campaign grew in intensity he protested against the system of patrolling areas by defensive forces of trawlers, or what was called 'offensive patrolling' by destroyers. He desired convoys to be established along the coast routes and across the North Sea. He pointed out that patrolling had given little or no security, but escorts had proved an effectual protection. As a result of his strongly expressed views – which were opposed at the Admiralty – the Scandinavian trade was placed in convoy. It was subjected to raids, as the Commander-in-Chief had fully anticipated that it would be, and the escorts grew from a few small craft to a division, or even a squadron, of battleships, with scouting and anti-submarine flotillas.

The result was an eventual sally in April 1918, by the High Sea Fleet to attack the inferior forces of an escort. Though Admiral Beatty had been assured that warning of a movement of that Fleet would be received, it sailed without the knowledge of the Admiralty. An intercepted wireless signal suddenly disclosed the presence of the enemy off the coast of Norway. Beatty, who was at short notice for steam, put to sea from Rosyth, to which base the Fleet had recently moved from Scapa Flow in order to be closer to the zone of action, to concentrate east of the Long Forties.

But though the Fleet proceeded at its utmost speed, the occasion had passed. Admiral von Hipper's stroke against the convoy had failed, and he was on his way back to harbour with the *Moltke* damaged by a torpedo from a British submarine before the Grand Fleet could interpose itself and fight the battle so long and ardently desired by the Commander-in-Chief. Want of information in time had been the cause of this disappointment.

The crowning act of Beatty's command at sea was the reception of the surrender of the German Fleet. After the signature of the Armistice Rear-Admiral von Meurer came to Rosyth, and the necessary arrangements were made with the British Admiral on November 15 and 16. On November 21 Beatty took the whole Fleet to sea to meet the surrendering vessels and escorted them into Rosyth. Having anchored them, he signalled to them: 'The German flag will be hauled down at sunset and will not be hoisted again without permission,' followed by a signal to the British Fleet, intimating his intention to hold a service of thanksgiving for the victory.

Admiral Beatty remained in command of the Grand Fleet until it was dispersed, hauling down his flag on April 8, 1919. At the same time he was promoted Admiral of the Fleet. He was the principal officer of the Navy present at the Peace celebrations in the following July, including the march through London, and was honoured in many cities and by many distinguished bodies. Among these honours was the unusual one of being the guest of the men of the Lower Deck at a dinner at Portsmouth on September 22.

FIRST SEA LORD

On November 1, 1919, he was appointed First Sea Lord. In this appointment, which he held for the unprecedented period of seven years and nine months, he had the work of reducing the fleet to a peace footing as his first task. Among the principal acts of his administration were the encouragement of scientific research, the establishment of the Fleet air arm, the development of a Fleet base at Singapore, the evolution of the Royal Indian Marine into a fighting service, and the re-establishment of the Mediterranean Fleet as the principal concentration of naval strength in peace. The executive and engineer officers' training was radically altered. Changes were also made affecting the retirements and appointments of the senior officers which, in the opinion of many officers and others, were ill-judged and would not stand the test of experience.

Lord Beatty's administration was marked by no striking measures either of principles or policy, but rather of a general care that the Navy should be maintained at the strength which the Board considered necessary for the performance of its duties, and that its personnel should receive fair and honest treatment.

In the rewards granted to the principal leaders in the War in 1919 Beatty received an earldom and a grant of £100,000. He took the titles of Earl Beatty of the North Sea and of Brooksby (his Leicestershire seat), and Viscount Borodale of Wexford, after the home of his family. He had been made a GCB for his services at Jutland to date from May 31, 1916, and a GCVO on June 25, 1917, to commemorate a visit of King George to the Grand Fleet. He was made a member of the Order of Merit on June 3, 1919. The list of foreign orders which he was authorized to wear on all occasions numbered nine. He was elected Lord Rector of Edinburgh University in 1917, and delivered the Rectorial Address on retiring in October, 1920, on the subject of 'Sea Power.' He took a practical interest in various institutions and societies connected with the naval and nautical professions. A member of the Society for Nautical Research from its inception in 1910, he was elected president on the death of Sir Doveton Sturdee in 1925. He was a Trustee of the National Maritime Museum at Greenwich. He also held office as Chief Sea Scout. He made occasional contributions to the Press on the subject of the deficiencies in the Navy, in particular with regard to the shortage of cruisers and the re-establishment of a Naval Air Service.

HUNTING AND RACING

After leaving the Admiralty Lord Beatty was able to indulge to the full his devotion to hunting and to horses, spending all the winter in the Midlands, first at Brooksby and later at Dingley Hall, near Market Harborough. It is no exaggeration to say that for his age and for his weight he was one of the best and boldest horsemen in the Shires. He had at various times some wonderful performers in his stable, and he took the greatest interest in all details connected with it. But he often rode young horses and, whatever he was riding, he was equally determined to be in the forefront of the attack. With the aid of a horse-box he hunted with all the packs in that choice but exacting country, a welcome companion wherever he chose to go. On any day he merely picked the best meet, and for many seasons he hunted regularly four or even five days a week. Nor was it often that he went home before the hounds. His cheerful disposition and unmistakable features made him easily recognized by farmers and villagers all over the Shires, and from that point of view no one, except members of the Royal Family, had latterly done more to popularize the sport of foxhunting.

Lord Beatty also bred and raced thoroughbreds, his horses in training being under the care of his brother, Major 'Vandy' Beatty, at Phantom House, Newmarket. His first success as a breeder was when the unnamed filly by Tagrag out of Cnoc Buidhe won at Lingfield Park in 1927. He became a member of the Jockey Club in April 1933, and in that year he bought from Mr. A. K. Macomber Gold Bridge, a brilliant sprinter, who had won several high-class races. For Lord Beatty, Gold Bridge won the King's Stand Stakes at Ascot (£1,290) and the Nunthorpe Sweepstakes at York (£840). Clustine, another horse which he bought from Mr Macomber, was very disappointing. He won only one of his 15 races before being sent to South Africa. Last year Lord Beatty won races with Schiehallion and Tagra filly. Schiehallion is entered in the Lincolnshire Handicap in Lord Beatty's name.

Various sporting organizations also enjoyed his patronage, and of those within the Service he was president of the RN Football Association, patron of the RN Lawn Tennis Association, and president of the RN Hunt Club. At different times he presented trophies for competition either in these or in other branches of sport.

Lord Beatty is succeeded by his elder son, Viscount Borodale, MP, who entered the Navy in May 1919. Having been promoted lieutenant in 1928, he retired in 1930 on being adopted as Unionist candidate for Peckham, and won the seat at the General Election of October, 1931. He was again successful in November 1935.

Beatty had a charisma unequalled by any British naval officer; his affectations of uniform – the cap at the 'Beatty angle', the six buttons of his reefer jacket – were famous nationally while his courageous exploits, arrogance, good looks, dynamism and marriage to a rich American divorceé were viewed with unease by many of his contemporaries who certainly thought that he had 'got on too fast'.

The Jutland controversy flourished for many years after the war. Beatty is criticised in a number of ways. Having agitated persistently for the 5th Battle Squadron consisting of four of the new fast super-dreadnought battleships of the *Queen Elizabeth* class to be added to the élite Battle-Cruiser Fleet (BCF), Beatty inexplicably failed to establish a relationship with their Rear-Admiral Hugh Evan-Thomas while in harbour at Rosyth. Nor did Evan-Thomas make it his business to call on his superior to discuss tactics. As historian Andrew Gordon has said *(The Rules of the Game (1996))* 'An hour's conversation might have saved a thousand lives'. The result, hinted at above, was a lack of understanding, an obedience to inept signalling and a failure to integrate these powerful heavily gunned ships with the rest. Partially because of this, two battlecruisers were lost in pursuit of Admiral Hipper on the way south, not to 'lucky shells' but flash in cordite routes to the magazines made less safe by relaxations aimed at increasing the rate of fire to compensate for the BCF's known poor gunnery.

When Beatty turned north towards Jellicoe, his manoeuvre exposed the 5th BS to the concentrated fire of the High Seas Fleet for over an hour and although they 'performed admirable service' they suffered much damage and many casualties; both *Warspite* and *Malaya* were nearly lost. Evan-Thomas could have avoided this himself had he had the initiative to order a 'turn-together' to the north without waiting for Beatty's ruinously delayed signal.

Beatty has been criticised for his failure to report accurately to Jellicoe the position of the enemy battlefleet, a charge equally laid at Evan-Thomas' door. Beatty has received insufficient acknowledgment for leading the High Seas Fleet into the jaws of Jellicoe's deployment, as required by his scouting role.

As CinC of the Grand Fleet, Beatty is rightly noted for instituting convoys in the North Sea area. He deserves acclaim for breaking the culture of 'obedience to orders' by introducing 'instructions' that encouraged initiative amongst subordinates. He received the surrender of the German fleet at Scapa Flow, not Rosyth. On 21 June 1919, all the German ships scuttled themselves to escape further ignominy under the terms of the Paris peace treaty.

During a stressful period of military run-down and national exhaustion, Beatty was First Sea Lord for longer than anyone, before or since. At the Washington Conference of 1922 he had to cede parity in capital ships with the USA but maintained a sufficient cruiser force for the needs of Empire. He predicted the rise of Japan and his views on the proper ownership of naval aviation were vindicated in the second world war.

SCHEER

High Seas Fleet Commander

27 NOVEMBER 1928

ADMIRAL REINHARDT SCHEER, whose death is announced on another page, was born at Oberkirchen in 1863. He was the son of a public schoolmaster, called in Germany a gymnasium professor; his early associations were, therefore, very different from those of his colleagues in later life. Tirpitz, Holtzendorff, Capelle, Muller and Ingenohl all came of fairly wealthy land-owning families. Scheer spent his boyhood in surroundings which at every minute of the day reminded him of hard work, rarely of ease, never of luxury. He entered the Navy as a cadet in 1882, and for the next 20 years he spent his life mainly at sea. His advancement was not particularly rapid, for he had put in 20 years' service before he was made second in command of the *Niobe*; and it was not until about 1900 that he was recognized as one of the rising stars of the German Navy.

He was made leader of a destroyer flotilla in 1907, and it was during this period of his service that he published his first book. It was a purely professional study of the tactical use of the torpedo arm, and is now entirely out of date, but it is marked by the characteristics of his later books. Scheer evidently learned composition from his father; then, as later, he wrote in the crabbed, academic style used by learned Germans, with more desire to say all he knew than to select and arrange his facts. But his book is orderly and forceful; it is the earnest address of a hard worker to men of his own spirit.

Between 1907 and 1914 Scheer's advancement was rapid. He was captain of the battleship *Elsass* in 1909, and chief of staff to the commander-in-chief of the High Seas Fleet in 1912, and at the outbreak of the War he was in command of the second battle squadron. His squadron was made up of older pre-Dreadnought battleships, and there was little chance that it would be seriously engaged so long as Von Pohl's cautious policy directed the movements of the High Seas Fleet. The second squadron was, none the less, at sea during the Scarborough raid; and Scheer proved to be an exceptionally capable squadron commander during the continuous battle practices that were carried out in the Bight in the first year of the War. When Ingenohl was relieved by Pohl, Scheer was promoted to the command of the third battle squadron. In January, 1916, when Pohl was stricken by a mortal sickness, Scheer was ordered to take command of the High Seas Fleet. The appointment was extremely popular; every officer in the fleet felt that the best man had been selected.

Scheer had never endorsed the opinion generally held that, in a fleet engagement, the numerically weaker fleet is certain to be utterly defeated. He was convinced that, given good tactical training and leadership, the German Fleet would be able to meet the Grand Fleet, though possibly not to fight a prolonged action; for he believed that his ships had certain points of superiority over ours, and that his captains, officers, and men were our equals. For this reason he had steadily opposed the policy of keeping the High Seas Fleet within the Horns reef-Terschelling quadrant; and as soon as he took command he started those fleet sorties and raids which culminated in the battle of Jutland.

A preliminary raid by light craft was carried out in February; Yarmouth and Lowestoft were bombarded in April; and during May he perfected his plans for a general sortie across the North Sea and a bombardment of the towns on the Northumbrian coast. Adequate Zeppelin reconnaissance was an essential part of his plan; and, when the weather made this impossible, Scheer reluctantly adopted his alternative plan of taking the fleet to the Skagerrak and operating against shipping. The project was not, in itself, very original or ambitious. Shipping between Great Britain and Scandinavia could have been attacked quite as effectively by a special concentration of U-boats; but Scheer was reckoning to turn the consequences of his plan to good advantage. When he sailed for the Skagerrak on May 30, 1916, lie hoped that some detached British squadron sent forward for reconnaissance might fall into the crushing concentration that he would have ready and waiting, between the Naze and the Jutland bank. He was disappointed; the Admiralty had no information of his real intentions, but their guesses were accurate enough to keep them from falling into the trap. Our forces sailed late on May 30, under orders which provided for a reconnaissance by the battle-cruisers, and a concentration of the whole fleet during the afternoon of May 31.

The outcome of these movements is well known. Beatty fell in with the German battle-cruisers in the early afternoon of May 31, and fought. an action without precedent in British naval history. He lost two ships to an inferior force in an hour's fighting, and retired on Jellicoe with his shattered squadron when he became aware that the High Seas Fleet was to the south of him. Scheer ran into the Grand Fleet at about 20 minutes past 6. He was taken completely by surprise, for he had no idea that Jellicoe was so near, but he extricated his fleet from a position of extraordinary danger with wonderful skill and firmness. When he reached Germany on June 1 he was able to announce that the High Seas Fleet had met and engaged the enemy, and had returned home after inflicting far greater losses than it had suffered. This was not victory, but it was a very great achievement. If fleet engagements had been the only possible gambit on the strategical chess-board in 1916, Scheer would probably have recommended that the best policy that the German Navy could adopt would be to continue its fleet sorties, and to provoke new fleet engagements as near the Heligoland Bight as possible. But since 1915 the German High Command had entertained the hope of winning a final and decisive victory at sea by unrestricted submarine war upon merchant shipping. Seheer was among those who believed that if the U-boat commanders were given a free hand Great Britain's oversea communications would be severed, and the British Islands reduced to the condition of a beleaguered city. He therefore strove to make Jutland a step towards unrestricted submarine warfare after reminding the Emperor that actions with a fleet so much more powerful as the British might end in successes, though never in victory, he made a solemn appeal for the renewal of submarine warfare.

He was compelled to wait. The German Government, with the diplomatic controversy over the Sussex incident still fresh in its mind, was not prepared to reverse its policy on the dictum of a successful admiral; and for the time being Scheer was obliged to continue his fleet sorties. On August 18 he took the fleet to sea again, to bombard Sunderland; and Jellicoe took the Grand Fleet south to meet and intercept him. By an extraordinary combination of circumstances the two fleets did not meet; and this was the last chance that was ever given to Jellicoe to try conclusions with his opponent. Both these great leaders had adhered rigidly to their conceptions of strategy and tactics. Scheer had made himself an absolute master of a system of leadership that consists in smoke screens, massed torpedo attacks, outbursts of fire, and *Kehrtwendungen*; Jellicoe, who had thoroughly divined his enemy's plan, had trained his fleet in preparation for that long artillery duel on parallel courses which he believed to be the correct counter to the German scheme of battle. Neither leader was ever allowed to put his theories to a full and conclusive test. It is said that, after the battle of Zama, Hannibal and Scipio met in a pavilion and discussed the art of war – the merits of the Roman infantry formation, the tactical use of Balearic slingers, elephants, and Numidian cavalry. It is a pity that Scheer and Jellicoe were never tempted to imitate this example of 'antient magnanimitie.'

All through the autumn and early winter of 1916 Scheer, in conjunction with other prominent members in the high naval and military commands, pressed for a renewal of unrestricted submarine war. Late in the year Bethmann-Hollweg and the civilians abandoned their resistance; and in February, 1917, the campaign that proved so fatal to Germany was begun. For over a year the High Seas Fleet was used as a mere support for the U-boat operations. In September, 1917, a powerful squadron was detached to the Baltic to support the operations against the Gulf of Riga; but that was all.

In May, 1918, Scheer took the fleet to sea on its last great enterprise. His intention was to attack and overwhelm the Scandinavian convoy, and the cruisers and battleships supporting it. If he had been better informed about the movements of the convoy that he proposed to attack, he would have scored a resounding success, for our forces put to sea far too late to interfere with the German plan. By good fortune Scheer miscalculated the date of the convoy's departure, and his last blow was struck against a zone of deserted water. In the autumn of 1918 he was appointed chief of the staff, in succession to Admiral von Holtzendorff, and he was serving in this post at the Armistice.

In the years after the War, Admiral Scheer's good sense, and freedom from the traditional prejudice of his more nobly born colleagues, saved him from committing the follies of the Tirpitzes and Ludendorffs. He had never been a rich man, and the collapse of the currency hit him hard, but he did not complain, and he gave the Republican authorities no anxiety. He kept out of political controversies, and travelled over Germany giving lectures upon the Battle of Jutland. and the achievements of the High Seas Fleet. Also, he published his two books of memoirs – 'The High Seas Fleet in the World War,' and 'From Sailing Ship to Submarine.' In other words, he re-adopted the habits of that lettered bourgeoisie in which he had passed his youth. In his books and lectures he expressed many opinions that to us seem obstinate and short-sighted; but the tone and purpose of what he wrote or what he uttered was public-spirited, honourable and modest. He did not wish that the records of his old colleagues should be obliterated by the domestic controversies of post-War Germany, so he spent his time in reminding the German people that the navy of Imperial Germany had done far more than had ever been expected of it. Naturally enough, he slurred over, or distorted, the darker side of the German naval record – the abominable cruelty of U-boat warfare, and the equally atrocious cruelty of those who practised it. He had a right to claim that, in spite of the final disaster, the German Fleet had deserved well of the Republic, and it is to his credit that he never invited to himself any echo of the applause to which he was entitled.

In 1920 much sympathy was aroused throughout Germany by the news that Admiral Scheer's wife had been murdered and his daughter dangerously wounded, at his house at Weimar, on October 9. A house-painter named Buchner, who had suffered from shell-shock and was mentally deficient, concealed himself in the cellar with the object of robbery. A maidservant who entered the cellar stumbled against Buchner in the dark, and he instantly shot her dead with a revolver. Frau Scheer, surprised at the long absence of the maid, went into the cellar, and Buchner shot her also, and Fraulein Scheer, who followed, was shot, but not killed. Before the Admiral, who was in his workroom at the top of the house, could come down, Buchner had shot himself through the head. Admiral Scheer was in time to render help to his daughter, but Frau Scheer died on the way to the hospital. She was very popular in Weimar society, and was deeply regretted.

The arrival of Britain's revolutionary battleship *Dreadnought* rendered obsolete all previous designs and threw the German naval staff into disarray. In July 1906 all work on the first all-big-gun German battleship *Nassau* was halted for a year while Germany struggled to obtain details and incorporate them into their programme. Between 1905 and 1914 the Dreadnought Arms Race produced 32 battleships for the Royal Navy but only 21 German. Production of the faster and more lightly built battlecruisers was roughly equal.

Fisher's war plans concentrated the Grand Fleet on the North Sea with bases at Scapa Flow and Rosyth. Thus outnumbered, Scheer's strategy had to be one of intermittent forays designed to nibble away at British strength; the provocative 'Boche frightful-ness' bombardments of seaside towns and the Dogger Bank engagement had this aim.

The shape of the battle of Jutland was primarily determined by the British operational capability in wireless direction-finding and crypto-analysis which gave Jellicoe the warning he needed to get his entire fleet to sea in time to meet Scheer coming north towards the

Skagerrak. Scheer had 16 dreadnoughts, but had impeded his manoeuvrability with six slower pre-dreadnought battleships – known jocularly as 'five minute ships', this being the length of time they were expected to last in battle. Many see this as a mistake.

The battlecruiser engagement described above was a victory for Admiral Hipper's superior shooting and the robustness of his ships. When Beatty sighted the High Seas Fleet (HSF) and turned away north, Scheer did not realise that he was being led into the Grand Fleet's 24 dreadnoughts and host of supporting cruisers and destroyers. As recounted above, Scheer's rapid *gefechtskehrwendung* or 'battle-turn in succession from the rear', extricated his ships from a catastrophic situation, leaving the British, who were unversed in such a manoeuvre, uncertain as to where he had gone. Scheer's subsequent battle-turn back towards the same perilous situation has been much debated, was it foolish or an expression of Scheer's combative spirit? Scheer's memoir justifies its purpose in pre-venting Jellicoe pressing on the HSF's stern, preserving 'facility of movement' as it was too early for a 'nocturnal move'.

A second turn away became necessary as dusk fell, Scheer leading his battered ships noisily home overnight through the tail-end of Jellicoe's strung-out fleet.

It is noteworthy that although Scheer and Hipper inflicted more casualties and sank more ships than they suffered themselves, Jellicoe's core fleet of dreadnoughts was unharmed; he was able to report 24 fit for battle within 48 hours, Scheer could only muster 10.

Scheer's report to the Kaiser that he believed the Grand Fleet unbeatable led to an intensified U-boat campaign that 'proved so fatal to Germany' because, with the Zimmerman telegram exposure, it brought the United States into the war.

ATATÜRK

Maker of Modern Turkey. Soldier,
Organizer and Administrator

11 NOVEMBER 1938

IN A CONFIDENTIAL report on Turkish affairs in 1926 the Ambassador of a Great Power expressed the opinion that Mustafa Kemal Pasha, whose death we announce with regret on another page, had in one respect been unfortunate in his destiny. He should have been born in the ages when the vast frontierless expanses of Central-Asia and Russia offered no political obstacle to the adventurer-conqueror, when the son of a small Mongol chief could win Empire from the Yalu to the Carpathians, and warriors like Sabutai Bahadur might be devastating Korea all one summer and riding through Hungary the next. Cast for the part of Timur or Jenghiz, he was compelled to lead a small exhausted people of 8,000,000 souls, the remnant of an Empire and of an endless succession of wars.

There has been no juster appreciation of the Ghazi: those who knew him best always recognized the fierce elemental force of the man. To a ruthless vigour and to fiery ambition, he joined a rare energy and a bold intellectual radicalism, utterly unaffected by historical tradition or religious sentiment, yet almost always tempered by political caution. The closest modern parallel to his career is that of Mohamed Ali, soldier, administrator, reformer – and Albanian. But even the founder of modern Egypt faced fewer perils than the general who defied the victors in the Great War, wrecked the careers of Venizelos and King Constantine, expelled the House of Osman, abolished the Caliphate itself and like a whirlwind swept away the cherished and ancient institutions of the Turks of Anatolia.

EARLY LIFE
Mustafa Kemal Pasha was born at Salonika in 1881. His father was a contractor in a small way of business, described by some as a Turk, by others as an Albanian: his mother, a shrewd. plucky, and energetic Albanian woman from the Tosk country in Northern Epirus, may have transmitted the Nordic type to her boy. She gave him an excellent

education after her husband's death; thus enabling him to enter the Military College at Monastir, whence he passed successfully into Pancaldi, the Sandhurst of Turkey.

It was during his cadetship that he first took an interest in politics – a dangerous interest in Abdul Hamid's despotic days. He had just taken a staff course when he was placed under arrest on a charge of conspiracy. Nothing was definitely proved against him, but he was transferred to Syria, where he founded a 'Hurriet Jemiyeti' (Liberty Society) among subaltern officers. He was then transferred to Salonika to find that the Liberty Society had been, so to speak, annexed by the nascent Committee of Union and Progress. After some regular service against the Macedonian *komitajis* he was transferred to the gendarmerie.

The Revolution of 1908 found him a junior major in that force; still nominally a member of the Union and Progress Party, he soon quarrelled with Enver Bey and other 'heroes of liberty,' who made little use of the great knowledge of Balkan affairs which he had acquired, and disliked his independent and masterful temper.

After serving against the Albanian rebels in 1909–10, he volunteered for service in Tripoli. when the Italian war broke out, made his way there in mufti through Egypt, and took part in the fighting near Benghazi as a member of Enver's staff. He quarrelled with Enver in Tripoli. Together with his friend, Fethi Bey, he criticized Enver even more fiercely after the ambitious plan of the Unionist General Staff had failed against the Bulgars at Bulair in 1913. Indeed throughout his career he was an extremely shrewd and realistic critic of military operations. But this quality did not endear Mustafa to a leader who believed in his star and played the Napoleon with an imperfect military grounding, and it was only through the intercession of some of his military friends that the critic was appointed military attaché at Sofia in 1913.

THE GREAT WAR
GALLIPOLI

It was in 1913 that the late Sir Henry Wilson, who had been visiting the scenes of the Balkan campaigns, expressed at Constantinople a rather unfavourable opinion of the capacity of the Turkish officers whom he had met, Enver and Djemal Pashas included. But he made one exception. 'There is a man called Mustafa Kemal,' he said, 'a young staff colonel. Watch him; he may go far' – and then unhappily the conversation shifted to Irish politics.

The Germans also recognized Kemal's ability. When the Great War broke out, although he had opposed the entry of Turkey into the conflict, their military mission in Turkey urged his fitness for command. He was given the command of a newly formed Division (19th) in the Fifth Army, which was assembled in March and early April, 1915, for the defence of the Dardanelles, under the command of Marshal Liman von Sanders, and his conduct of the operations of the units which he successfully commanded had such a decisive effect on the fortunes of the campaign that it deserves to be described in some detail.

Kemal's division (the 19th) contained two Arab regiments of uncertain value. On April 24 it was General Reserve for the three Turkish fighting groups in the Dardanelles theatre, and when Liman von Sanders first heard of the Australian landing at Ari Burnu (Gaba Tepe) he believed, as did the local Corps commander, that this attack was a feint, and that the main attack would be made on the isthmus of Bulair. Before 8 a.m. he was informed that a battalion of the landing force was pressing forward towards Chunuk Bair and asked Colonel Mustafa Kemal to detach a battalion as a flank guard to help to parry this stroke.

Fortunately for the Turks (says the British Official History of the Dardanelles campaign), the commander of the 19th Division was none other than Mustafa Kemal Pasha, the future President of the Republic, and the Man of Destiny was at once to show an outstanding genius for command. As soon as he heard that the enemy was making for Chunuk Bair, he realized that this could be no feint, but was a serious attack in strength. Appreciating in a flash that it constituted a threat against the heart of the Turkish defence, he at once determined to examine the situation for himself and to throw, not a battalion, but a whole regiment into the fight. Accompanied by a small advance party he at once hurried across country in the direction of Chunuk Bair. Shortly after 10 a.m. this advance party was in touch with Tulloch's small detachment in the neighbourhood of Battleship Hill. Mustafa Kemal remained on the spot long enough to issue orders for an attack by two battalions and a mountain battery, and then, having satisfied himself that the situation was temporarily in hand, he hurried back to Maidos to report to Essad Pasha.

The 57th Regiment, Kemal's best, was nearly destroyed that day, but the Turkish line held, and by holding wrecked the British Commander's plan.

SUVLA-ANZAC ATTACK

Kemal continued to distinguish himself as a Divisional Commander; his greatest services in the subsequent defence of the Turkish positions were rendered in the critical August days of the Suvla-Anzac attack. On the night of August 6–7, 1915, when Birdwood's columns broke from the northern flank of Anzac, the 19th Division was in line about Baby 700. Mustafa had early news of the advance; and, by promptly throwing in one and a half battalions, which was all he could collect, he was able to deny the crests of Chunuk Bair and Hill Q to the New Zealanders early on the morning of the 7th. The Turkish XVI Corps (7th and 12th Divisions), brought from Saros to the Suvla front, was ordered by Liman von Sanders to attack at dawn on August 8. As nothing was accomplished throughout the day, Liman replaced the corps commander (Feizi Bey) in the evening by Mustafa Kemal, in whom he had every confidence.

Mustafa arrived and took over his new command about 1 a.m. on August 9, when orders for an attack at dawn had already been issued; he was thus in command of the 7th and 12th Divisions when, on August 9, they advanced down to the Suvla plain and, in an encounter battle, stayed the belated attack of our IX Corps upon the vital Anafarta hills. Liman considered that this day's work saw another crisis safely passed. Mustafa Kemal held his line, soon reinforced, against our later August attacks. On August 17 he was appointed Commander of the Anafarta Group which included the whole Turkish line from Ejelmer Bay on the north to a point south of Chunuk Bair, and remained in command until the evacuation. No other Turkish General had served Liman von Sanders with such ability and decision in all the long campaign, but Enver remained jealous of his subordinate.

CAUCASUS AND PALESTINE

Late in 1916 Kemal was sent to the Caucasus front to command the Turkish Army. The situation was unfavourable The amateur strategists at Turkish headquarters had botched the campaign; which was to recover Trebizond and Erzurum. German lorries just kept Kemal's army from starving to death, but it lost most of its transport animals and a third of its men from cold and disease in the winter of 1916–1917. Mustafa's complaints were unheeded, and the support given them by Liman von Sanders only made matters worse, for Enver and the German Marshal were now at daggers drawn. Finally, Enver removed Kemal from his command and Staff.

During the last months of 1917 and the spring of 1918 Kemal was in

Germany and Austria, first in the suite of the Heir-Apparent, and later in a hospital at Vienna. In June. 1918, he was offered the command of the VII Army in Palestine; he accepted it, but, true to his past reputation, indulged in sharp criticisms, which he committed to official reports, of German interference in Turkey's Arab policy, and implicitly of Enver's subservience to his Teutonic masters. In the battle of Sharon-Esdraelon, which destroyed the Turkish armies in Palestine, he could do nothing to enhance his military reputation, but he rallied his troops sufficiently to form a front west of Aleppo against the relentless British pursuit.

THE NATIONALIST MOVEMENT
A PATRIOTIC TURK

In May, 1919, shortly after the Greek landing at Smyrna, Kemal was sent by Damad Ferid Pasha as Inspector-General of the Forces in Eastern Anatolia. Damad Ferid knew that Kemal was a bitter enemy of the Committee of Union and Progress, and believed that his personal animosity would lead him to suppress the beginnings of the Nationalist movement because Unionists, such as Rauf Bey, were engaged in promoting it. He forgot that Kemal was for all practical purposes a patriotic Turk.

At Samsun the Inspector-General found the country startled by the news from Smyrna, the local Greeks talking wildly of a Republic, the Turks angry and excited, the British garrisons too small for any efficient garrisoning of the country. Under the eyes of the Intelligence Department of the British Army of thc Black Sea, Kemal prepared a movement which gained ground rapidly among the Anatolian garrisons. By December, 1919, it had led to a Conference at Sivas, where Kemal, Rauf Bey, and other chiefs drew up the 'National Pact.' The Constantinople Government outlawed him, but Kemal was none the worse.

POPULAR HERO.

Then came the ill-omened Treaty of Sèvres. Its stipulations concerning Ionia made Kemal a popular hero; public opinion supported him, and henceforth he was the embodiment of Turkish resistance to the Greek. Yet the difficulties which confronted him were immense. In parts of the country brigand chiefs professing allegiance to the Nationalists maltreated Turks and Christians equally and made the Nationalist Government, which had moved from Sivas to Angora, as unpopular as the Greeks. In Konia the old Seljuk particularism showed itself in an unsuccessful rising; the Kurds were untrustworthy; the Circassian colonies often openly rebellious. Geography, indeed, fought for the Turks, but their only other ally was Soviet Russia, and Kemal, while ready to accept arms and subventions from Moscow, refused even to discuss the admission of Bolshevist troops. But he and his supporters held their ground. The fall of Venizelos isolated Greece, and the French, weary of a long guerrilla struggle in Cilicia, moved towards a separate peace.

TREATY OF LAUSANNE

Then came the Sakaria campaign. Kemal and Ismet Pashas were at first out-gencralled by Pallis and Sariyannis, who planned the Greek summer offensive, and during the greater part of the battle of the Sakaria Kemal himself was incapacitated by injuries received during the retreat from Eski-Shchir. But geography and the stubbornness of the Turkish soldier saved Angora. A year later the Greek army went to pieces. Great Britain was isolated by the defection of France and the way was clear for the triumph of Lausanne.

Victory did not obscure his judgment. He might, indeed, have prevented the burning and massacres of Smyrna: his attitude towards those Turks who had stood by the unfortunate Sultan who fled to Malta in November, 1922, was one of pitiless hatred and contempt. But he was too shrewd a soldier and politician to hazard his astonishing success by excessive claims. He refused to entertain demands for the retrocession of Western Thrace, to insist upon the refortification of Adrianople and Kirk-Kilisse or to link his fortunes too closely to those of the Soviets. Russia had been useful, but the public execution of a party of Communist conspirators on the day of the arrival of the new Russian Minister at Angora was a warning to Moscow not to presume upon past services. The Mosul question remained unsettled, and here Kemal Pasha, who had now been acclaimed Ghazi, preferred propaganda to action.

THE FALL OF THE CALIPHATE
REPUBLIC PROCLAIMED

On November 1, 1922, the Grand National Assembly abolished the Sultanate. On November 17 Sultan Mehmed Vahi-uddin fled on board H.M.S. *Malaya* at Constantinople and left Turkey for ever. The Assembly had already announced its intention of electing the 'best qualified' member of the House of Osman as Caliph, and on November 18 it elected Abdul Majid Effendi Caliph of Islam.

These revolutionary proceedings aroused alarmed protests throughout the Moslem world. Turkish Conservatives who held that the spiritual

Caliphate could not be separated from the temporal Sultanate, and members of the Committee of Union and Progress who could not forgive the Ghazi for stealing their thunder began to murmur and to combine against him, fearing his severity and foreseeing his dictatorship.

He soon found the situation intolerable. The Caliphate was either a temporal power or it was nothing, and Mustafa, furiously anti-clerical, anti-Moslem at heart, like so many of his antinomian kinsmen in Albania, saw in this survival of the theocracy an obstacle to his designs, and a rallying point of the growing political opposition. The Lausanne negotiations kept Turkey outwardly united, but after their successful conclusion the new regime, though it had won a military success over the Greeks, and an even more remarkable diplomatic success against Western Europe, had to face increasing criticism at home.

On October 29, 1923, the Assembly proclaimed Turkey a Republic with the Ghazi as its first President and 'Chief of the State,' thus affirming lay supremacy. It incidentally declared Islam to be the religion of the State, a concession to Anatolian conservatism, as Kemal affirmed in his six days' speech at Angora four years later, when he unmasked his hatred of Islam. Next spring the publication in three Constantinople newspapers both of an appeal for the strengthening of the Caliphate, signed by H.H. the Aga Khan and by the Right Hon. Sayyid Ameer Ali; enabled the President to carry out his design. On March 31 the 'Popular Party,' which he led and which was in a majority in the Assembly, passed a law abolishing the Caliphate and ordering the banishment of all members of the House of Osman. On the same night the unoffending Abdul Majid was unceremoniously bidden to leave Turkey. He left at dawn, and within a few days all the other members of that ancient House were exiled and the greater part of their property confiscated.

SOCIAL REFORMS

The Caliphate once abolished, the Ghazi turned with ardour to the secularization of his country and to the destruction of his political rivals. He ruled as a dictator, combining the offices of President of the Republic, President of the Council of Ministers, President of the Grand National Assembly, and Leader of the Popular Party, and made no secret of his intention to deal severely with any opposition.

In the early spring of 1925 came a Kurdish rebellion, which was suppressed after some arduous fighting. It was inspired by religious leaders, and its suppression was followed by the closing of all Moslem religious houses and the abolition of all religious orders in Turkey; the prohibition of the distinctive dress of the orders of Dervishes, and the imposition of European head-dresses and raiment, 'the ordinary clothes in use among the civilized nations of the world,' upon all officials. A month later the Assembly passed a law making the wearing of hats compulsory for all male citizens. The wearing of the hat had always been regarded as impious by old-fashioned Moslems, since the brim prevented worshippers from touching the ground with their foreheads, and this was no doubt one of the reasons why the President, who shunned mosques like the plague, determined to strike at turban, fez, and kalpak.

To the surprise of Europe, and to the horror of pious Moslems in other lands, the law was generally obeyed. A few clerics and rustics rioted and were hanged or imprisoned. It was not generally realized that the Turkish peasant had lost much of his religious conservatism and that he was grateful to the new Government for lightening his taxes and killing off the brigands who had been a scourge since the War. Most Turkish women were also grateful to the new régime for its legislative removal of the restrictions which hampered female education, for the abolition of polygamy, and for other concessions to feminist demands.

THE MOSUL QUESTION
NEGOTIATIONS WITH BRITAIN

The Progressive Party remained alive and dangerous. The Mosul question was alive too: the refusal of the British Government to be stampeded from Iraq by a section of the Press, and the fear that the Dictators of Italy and Greece might join England if the Turks attacked, persuaded the Ghazi and his advisers, after the League had provisionally awarded Mosul to Iraq, to open direct negotiations with Great Britain. These terminated in an agreement, signed on June 6, whereby both parties accepted the frontier suggested by the League.

A few days later came the news that a plot to murder the Ghazi had been discovered, and that many members of the Opposition had been arrested. Two trials were held; the first at Smyrna, where the Tribunal of Independence gave short-shrift to the group of conspirators who had undoubtedly planned the Ghazi's murder. Their leader, 'Kara' Kemal, once a leading light in the Committee of Union and Progress, shot himself. Their arrest resulted in the production of evidence which purported to show that ex-Unionist members of the Progressive Party had been implicated in a plot to change the form of government. Javid

Bey, the former Finance Minister of the Young Turks, who was favoured in international financial circles, and Dr. Nazim, the most ruthless of the persecutors of the Armenians, were arraigned at Angora on this charge. Rauf Bey and other opponents had left the country. The Tribunal was merciless, as was expected, and Nazim and Javid were hanged.

MASTER OF ANATOLIA

So the Dictator paid off his old scores against the C.U.P., and, with the opposition in exile or underground, could feel that at last he was undisputed master of Anatolia. Next year he celebrated his triumph by a visit to long-neglected Constantinople, and by giving orders to his party to select a number of young and active candidates for the coming General Election. The candidates were duly elected – in fact, the Popular Party won 315 seats out of 315, and the only Opposition candidate obtained one vote, which may have been his own. The Ghazi followed up the victory by a six-days' speech, describing the struggles and victories of Turkish Nationalism and his own contribution thereto, in a style that seemed to have been modelled on Caesar's 'De Bello Gallico.'

Thenceforth he and his Ministers marched from one successful reform to another. They had already introduced a civil code based upon the Swiss model as a substitute for the Moslem Sacred Law. On April 10, 1928, the Assembly gave unanimous consent to modification in the Constitution by which Islam ceased to be the State religion. Later in that year he led the movement for the substitution of the Latin for the Arabic alphabet, a remarkable change which caused some temporary embarrassment but proved to be most beneficial to education and letters. A brief experiment in the formation of a Liberal Republican Party was dropped after three months in November, 1930, and in a General Election held next year the Popular Party swept the board and the Ghazi was elected President for the fourth time in succession.

In 1932 came a movement for the 'purification' of the language from Arabic and Persian words, and the President with some impetuosity publicly supported various philological and linguistic theories at which the experts looked askance. 1934 saw the adoption of a Five-Year Plan, the abolition of the time-honoured titles of Pasha, Bey, and Effendi, the granting of the franchise to women, 17 of whom were elected to the Grand National Assembly, now the Kamutay, in 1935, and the compulsory adoption of surnames, the lack of which had caused endless confusion in Moslem countries. The President himself was given the appropriate surname of Atatürk, i.e. Chief Turk, by a special law passed by the

Assembly. During all this period Government was steadily improving agriculture, communications, public health, and education in every province; Kurdish risings were crushed, and the retirement of the Prime Minister, General Ismet Inönü, the President's old friend and political ally since the days of the Greek War, in the winter of 1937 hardly left a ripple on the quiet surface of Turkish politics.

Meanwhile Turkish foreign policy had undergone a remarkable change. In Dr. Tewfik Rushdi, now Dr. Rustü Aras, the Ghazi found a most competent Minister of Foreign Affairs. The understanding with Russia was still the sheet-anchor of Turkish foreign policy, but once the Ghazi and his Ministers realized that the British had abandoned all ideas of supporting Kurdish independence and that the Iraq Agreement was working well Anglo-Turkish relations improved. So did the relations between Turkey and her Balkan and Near Eastern neighbours.

The Ghazi and his lieutenants, and M. Venizelos too, recognized that the persistence of the Turco-Greek quarrel after the exchange of populations effected by the Treaty of Lausanne was an anachronism. In 1930 M. Venizelos visited Angora, where, aided by Turkish statesmanship, he inaugurated the Turco-Greek Entente, which developed into a virtual alliance in 1933. In 1932 Turkey, entered the League of Nations. By a Balkan pact signed at Athens on February 9, 1934, Turkey, Greece, Rumania, and Yugoslavia guaranteed the inviolability of their respective Balkan frontiers. Turco-Bulgarian relations were distant until this year, when King Boris's tactful diplomacy and the desire of the Turks to link the Balkan States more closely in the face of any possible threat from the totalitarian States brought about an agreement. It freed Bulgaria from the shackles of the Treaty of Neuilly, and Turkey and Greece from the last of the limitations to their sovereignty which had been imposed by the demilitarization of parts of their European frontier by the Treaty of Lausanne.

THE DARDANELLES

But before this the Turkish Republic had won a signal diplomatic triumph at Montreux in 1936, where they regained full sovereignty over the Dardanelles and Bosporus from the Powers which had signed the Straits Convention of 1923. The Ghazi, who had become a warm supporter of Anglo-Turkish friendship, who never fully trusted Italy, and resented Russian attempts to dictate Turkish foreign policy – although he desired to remain on good terms with the Soviet Republic – supported British policy over sanctions during the Abyssinian crisis and again at the Anti-Piracy Conference at Nyon. The Pact of Saadabad with Iran, Iraq and Afghanistan helped to stabilize conditions in Western Asia and to guarantee the Republic against any Asiatic support of the Kurds.

In all these negotiations the attitude of the Turkish Government was conciliatory and correct, and only on one occasion was the President of the Republic known to have intervened personally in the conduct of the policy which he had so largely inspired. This was in an early stage of the Alexandretta dispute, when he countered the French unwillingness to fall in with Turkish claims that the Turks of Alexandretta should obtain full autonomy by travelling in a special train to an Army Corps head-quarters near the frontier. An adroit mixture of threats and diplomacy finally gave Turkey all that she had demanded and made it almost certain that Alexandretta would fall into her hands whenever she wished.

This was the Dictator's last success. He had lived hard, he had never been temperate, and this year cirrhosis of the liver declared itself. He spent his last months quietly, but on October 16 his illness grew suddenly desperate.

A CHARACTER SKETCH

So died this astonishing man, whose decision, courage, and ruthless vigour first saved Turkey from her enemies, and then imposed upon her people social and political changes only comparable to those forced upon Russia by Peter the Great and by Lenin. As a soldier, an organizer, and an administrator, he had no rivals among modern Turks, and few even among the fighting Sultans of antiquity. His achievements made Turkey a European nation, changed the history of the Near East and may yet prove to have had a decisive effect on the evolution of Islam.

His character was strangely compounded; he had no trace of sentimentality: his mind was clear, his speech precise and trenchant. For all his charm of manner, he could give way to tempestuous outbreaks of brutality; his hatreds were inveterate and deadly to the end. An in-defatigable student of war and politics, he would now and again fling history and strategy to the winds to indulge in a long and furious drink-ing bout, to dance the night through, or to play cards till morning. If at the end of a long card party he had lost, he paid his debts. If he won, he sent his winnings back to the loser with a curt compliment, for he would not win from his friends and subjects. It was his desire to leave the table without debt or credit that often made him prolong the game till midday.

Women had little part in his life. After marrying an accomplished Turkish lady in 1923, he suddenly came to the conclusion that she was trying to influence his political decisions and forthwith divorced her, signing his own decree of divorce, like our Henry VIII. He subsequently adopted as his daughters several respectable young women, orphans of the wars, whose modest demeanour silenced the whispers of scandal.

Farming was one of his interests: he liked the Anatolian peasant and the model farm which he purchased and equipped out of a grant of fT.1,000,000 voted him was an example to the land-owners of Angora. He had few friends, and gave his full confidence to none save Fethi Okyar, now Turkish Ambassador to Great Britain, and though he had great personal magnetism and the gift of inspiring men with an unquestioning trust in his leadership, his chief affection was perhaps given to his ideal of a secularized State-disciplined modernized Turkey. The criticism of a Turkish lady – 'A marvellous leader, incapable of love for anything' may have been biased: but it did, at least, emphasize the strange, steely hardness of this Cromwell of the Near East.

It is worth a moment's speculation of the outcome had Enver Pasha been able somehow to dispose of his military subordinate, of whom he was deeply jealous, and himself survived the Turkish conflict with the Bolsheviks in Turkestan in 1922. While a dynamic political leader of the 'Young Turks', Enver proved incompetent as a military commander. He and Mustafa Kemal differed sharply on almost every topic; for example, Enver encouraged German involvement in Turkish affairs, while Mustafa argued for Turkish neutrality in the First World War. Atatürk's rule was dictatorial but he saw that as the only route to the modernization of Turkey. Privately, he was impressed by Western parliamentary systems and at no time indicated he did not foresee Turkey eventually emerging as a parliamentary democracy.

ALLENBY

Great Soldier and Administrator

15 MAY 1936

PALESTINE AND EGYPT

Both as soldier and as administrator Lord Allenby, whose death we announce to-day, rendered invaluable service to his country. From a regimental officer, possessing no advantages beyond those of his own character and personality, he steadily attained to the highest office in his own mounted arm. Then came the campaign in France, which rapidly brought him forward as a gifted leader of men, and before long he was in command of an Army. From the trenches in Picardy he was transferred as an independent commander-in-chief to Egypt and to the open warfare of Palestine, where he won a reputation of a far higher order.

Even with the close of the victorious advance into Syria his services were not at an end. As the representative of Great Britain it fell to his lot first to organize the administration of the occupied Turkish territories and then to carry out the thankless task of watching over the inauguration of the system of self-government conferred upon Egypt, together with the establishment of the future relations between Great Britain and that country. He found Egypt in a state of turmoil and left it in profound peace.

VIRILE QUALITIES

A man of powerful physique and of determined will, a bold sportsman and a fearless rider, these were Lord Allenby's outward and dominant attributes. His resolute countenance and confident yet dignified bearing spoke truly of a tireless energy, boundless strength of purpose, and great moral and physical courage. Dependent on such qualities and of kindred nature were the professional characteristics which early in his career marked him out as a cavalry officer and military personality of far more than ordinary promise. He had come by the familiar nickname of 'The Bull.' But behind this massive exterior there lay a keen intellect, sharpened in later life by long study, that only revealed itself to those who had either intimate dealings with him or the ill-fortune to oppose him in purpose or in argument.

These virile qualities stand revealed in every one of his campaigns. In South Africa, the enterprise and energy of the successful column commander; in France, the skill and quick grasp of the cavalry leader who covered the retreat. Again in October, 1914, the supreme determination which enabled him for three weeks to hold a long line with totally inadequate forces; once more in 1917, the skill and patience during the advance at Arras in the teeth of abominable weather and other adverse circumstances. Then in Palestine, the sagacity with which he refused to be rushed into a great undertaking with inadequate resources. Lastly, the perspicacity, boldness, and knowledge that contributed to a series of unbroken successes in a campaign that may be justly regarded as a model for all time. These incidents make up the career of a truly great leader in war.

A CLEAR-CUT TEMPERAMENT

To his staff and to his subordinates in the field, Allenby's straightforwardness was his most striking characteristic; any form of prevarication or dissimulation was abhorrent to his nature. Such a direct and clear-cut temperament could not bear a grudge; his disapproval, freely and forcibly expressed on occasion, was reserved for disobedience or slipshod execution of orders, still more for want of frankness; these big faults he would not overlook. Those who served Allenby honestly or to the best of their ability might rely on receiving generous recognition of success and on a very human allowance being made for errors committed in good faith.

Closer acquaintance revealed in him a shrewd judgment of men, a wide knowledge of matters apart from his own profession, a sense of humour, and a faculty of enlightening conversation on a multitude of varied topics. He was remarkably well read and well informed. His receptive memory was well stored with a comprehensive historical knowledge relating to all countries and periods, and he possessed a, familiarity with scientific questions surprising in a layman. He was an enthusiastic naturalist and botanist, the study of animals, birds, and plant life constituting the favourite recreation of his leisure moments. These lighter, and by many unsuspected, qualities rendered Allenby an admirable host and a delightful guest.

Edward Henry Hynman Allenby, the elder son of Mr. Hynman Allenby, of Felixstowe House, Suffolk, was born on April 23, 1861. From Haileybury College he passed into the Royal Military College, and was gazetted to the 6th (Inniskilling) Dragoons on May 10, 1882. In 1884 he was employed with his squadron for some months in quelling an insurrection in Bechuanaland. Again, in 1888, he was engaged with his regiment in repressing the armed disturbances which had broken out in Zululand. At that time he was adjutant. In 1889 he was promoted captain, and in May, 1897, major.

Meanwhile, in 1896, he had passed into the Staff College, gaining a high place in the open competitive examination. At Camberley he excelled both at study and at sport; for he won high praise for his work, while he became Master of the Drag Hounds, and stood out as a prominent and popular figure among his fellow-students. From March, 1898, until October, 1899, he held the now obsolete appointment of adjutant to a cavalry brigade.

IN SOUTH AFRICA

It was after the outbreak of the South African War that Allenby first came to the fore. His regiment formed part of the Cavalry Division under Major-General French (later Field-Marshal the Earl of Ypres), and was first engaged in the Colesberg district of Cape Colony, and then took part in the successful relief of Kimberley and the advance to Pretoria. In April, 1900, Allenby obtained temporary command of the 6th Dragoons, and in November of the same year, in recognition of his excellent work, received a brevet lieutenant-colonelcy. After the fall of Pretoria in June he had been employed in the Eastern Transvaal, and after the collapse of the organized Boer forces he received in January, 1901, the command of an independent column, which was active first in the Western Transvaal, next on the Natal frontier, and lastly in working back south and east along the Orange River Valley.

At the end of the war, in which he had gained the reputation of being an enterprising, persevering, and able column commander, Allenby received a brevet colonelcy, was created CB, and was given the command of the 5th Lancers. In October, 1905, he became substantive colonel and brigadier-general, and was appointed to command the 4th Cavalry Brigade, then stationed in the Eastern Counties. It thus fell to his lot to play an appreciable part in reforming the training of cavalry as a result of the lessons learnt in the South African War. He was promoted major-general in September, 1909, after 27 years' service, and had to relinquish the command of his brigade.

THE GREAT WAR
FRANCE AND FLANDERS

In the following April he was appointed Inspector of Cavalry, and it was this position that he was holding on the declaration of war against Germany. No little of the credit may thus be attributed to him for the superiority which British mounted troops displayed, both individually and collectively, over the enemy's horsemen during the opening phases of the great conflict.

As Inspector of his arm, Allenby assumed the command of the Cavalry Division which formed part of the original Expeditionary Force. During the retreat from Mons he covered the exposed left flank of the British Force. On the Marne the cavalry preceded the crossing of the river by the British right wing. Then on the Aisne it covered the advance of Haig's Corps. In the subsequent advance to the Marne and the Aisne, the effect of the cavalry did not fulfil expectations, and with the more static conditions of war that set in during that fighting, the opportunities for the cavalry, now reorganized into two divisions – the second being commanded by Major-General Hubert Gough – grew limited.

The transfer of the British Expeditionary Force to Flanders afforded Allenby and his men a brief period of open fighting, during which it covered the advance of the II and III Corps. Next the cavalry was called upon to distinguish itself in a different role, the defence against overwhelming odds of a large and important section of the British line. The two cavalry divisions, comprising five brigades, had been formed on October 10 into a Cavalry Corps, of which Allenby had been given the command with the rank of lieutenant-general.

During the protracted struggle before Ypres, the Cavalry Corps, posted on the Messines-Wytschaete ridge, filled the gap between the I Corps at Ypres and the III Corps at Armentières. There, with his brigades and a few battalions of infantry, which were lent to him, he held on to the ground between Messines and the Menin Canal against no fewer than six German cavalry divisions, supported by many battalions of Jägers.

For the better part of three weeks, heavily outnumbered, without trenches or adequate artillery support, the British mounted troops clung desperately to their ground. In the end the villages of Messines and Wytschaete were lost only a few hours before the arrival of French reinforcements, and even then this occurred only when the German cavalry had been relieved by an entire infantry corps. To Allenby himself this success must principally be ascribed, owing to the resolute and fearless spirit he manifested throughout the crisis; he refused even to admit the possibility of failure during that long, monotonous struggle.

THE THIRD ARMY

Trench warfare now set in, and the cavalry was condemned to a period of complete inactivity. Allenby was transferred to the command of the V Army Corps, in succession to Sir Herbert Plumer, who was promoted to command the Second Army. Six months later, in October, 1915, he was given the command of the newly formed Third Army near the Somme with the rank of temporary general; this command he was to hold for over 18 months.

During 1916 the Third Army was given little scope. Having been shifted north to make room for the Fourth Army, it did not participate in the battles of the Somme, beyond carrying out the minor and disastrous attack on Gommecourt. But in the spring of 1917 the Allies determined to attempt a great effort to break through the German front. The principal attack was to be delivered by the entire French Army, then recently placed under the chief command of General Nivelle, while on the British front these French efforts were to be seconded by an attack delivered near Arras by Allenby's Army.

Here Allenby wished, for surprise, to have a preliminary bombard-ment of only 24 hours, but a prolonged bombardment was then custom-ary, and he was induced to forgo his desire. The original attack, carefully planned and well carried out realized an immediate success; it broke into the German front on a width of eight miles. But with a forewarned enemy the exploitation was soon checked, and Nivelle's great assault, on which far-reaching hopes were founded, turned into a complete and expensive failure. The French Army became so entirely disorganized by the reverse as to be incapable for the time being of any further effort. So the main burden fell on the British; the Battle of Arras was accordingly continued under unforeseen and unfavourable conditions, and the fighting after the first advance grew costly and inconclusive. For this Allenby incurred some blame, owing to the methods employed, but he also carried an unforeseen handicap. The British plan had been based on a successful continuance of the French attack; it was never anticipated that the Germans would be left free to turn with such a weight of numbers against the Third Army. Allenby conscientiously, if clumsily, carried out an operation which, it was recognized, could hardly be decisive, and had been continued mainly with a view to giving the French time in which to recover from their unexpected reverse.

PALESTINE
A CRUSHING VICTORY

Meanwhile events in other theatres of war had led the War Cabinet to decide on a fresh offensive against the Turkish forces in Palestine.

The two British failures before Gaza suggested the advisability of finding a new leader for the enterprise; and the choice fell upon Allenby, who assumed the command of the Egyptian Expeditionary Force in July, 1917. Almost his first act was to order the removal of G.H.Q. from Cairo to the front, where he could be in closer touch with the troops. This move, and his own constant presence along the front, immediately revived the spirit of the Army, somewhat depressed by its recent failures, and the stagnation of trench life in hot, uncomfortable surroundings. As Lawrence wrote of him in 'The Seven Pillars':- 'The good cheer and the conscious strength of the C-in-C was a bath of comfort to a weary person after long, strained days.' Reinforcements, especially of heavy artillery, were demanded by Allenby. All these, owing to the trend of policy at home, he was able to obtain, and the next three months were spent in reorganizing the entire Army and in hard training for the coming offensive.

FIRST SUCCESSES

Basing his plan on an appreciation made before his arrival by Sir Philip Chetwode, he determined to seize Beersheba, then strongly entrenched and held by the Turks as a detached post to protect their left flank. The next move was to strike at the enemy's left flank, keeping the mounted troops ready to pass behind and cut the Turkish lines of retreat. A subsidiary attack on Gaza was to deceive the enemy of the real direction of the main blow. The true obstacles to an advance lay in the nature of the country as much as in the strength of the Turkish defences. Beersheba and the Turkish left lay 15 to 20 miles from the nearest British posts, while in the intervening desert there existed neither roads nor water.

These difficulties were overcome by careful engineer work and appropriate dispositions. After a skilful night march Beersheba was captured with practically its entire garrison on October 31. A pause then became necessary before the Turkish left could be assaulted. Accordingly an attack on the other flank was delivered against some of the outlying defences of Gaza so as to deceive the enemy. The real blow on the left of the Turkish main line at Hareira and Sheria was struck on November 6 after some delays. Although the pursuit failed to cut off the Turkish retreat the advance was steadily pushed on.

After the occupation of Jaffa, Allenby boldly resolved to advance without further delay into the hills and to attack Jerusalem, although barely half his force as available owing to difficulties of supply and the enemy had received large reinforcements. Leaving only a small force to protect his communications in the plain, Allenby struck eastwards at the difficult passes of the Judean range with the remainder of his available troops. This first effort was checked by the enemy within sight of Jerusalem, but the capture of the passes more than justified the boldness of the attempt.

After a delay rendered necessary for the improvement of communications, which also allowed the remainder of his troops to arrive, Allenby ordered a fresh attack, to which Jerusalem surrendered on December 9. He made his formal entry on foot into the Holy City on December 11. To a certain extent Allenby had found the materials for this great success already prepared, especially the organization of the communications across the Sinai Desert, which alone rendered practicable the offensive movement of such a large force. But the audacity with which the scheme of operations was carried through, and, above all, the resolution which animated the whole were the outcome of Allenby's own power as a commander and leader of men. He continued the personal contact with his command which had been characteristic of him in France.

Throughout the campaign he was (to quote from the Official History of the operations) constantly up and down his line, so that there can have been few commanders in modern warfare who were so well known to their troops ... blessed with strength and endurance which made little of very long drives in intense heat and on dusty, bone-shaking tracks, he was enabled to communicate his will, his determination to conquer, directly also to subordinate officers and the rank and file themselves. In the advance to Nablus he was seen up in front of his car urging on tired men at a moment when his personal influence was the strongest stimulant they could have had.

The victory achieved the great object of drawing into Palestine all available Turkish reserves and of eliminating the danger to Baghdad; and it had an equally great moral effect, not only in Britain but throughout the world. The success attending this series of well-conceived movements leading to so important a result in Palestine did much to counteract the depression caused by the long-drawn-out agony of the more strenuous fighting in Flanders.

The early part of 1918 was spent by Allenby in improving his position by means of a series of small operations. A further great movement had been authorized by the War Cabinet for the spring, but the success of the German offensive in France led to a request being made to Allenby for a surrender of all the troops he could spare. Two complete divisions, comprising 24 additional British battalions, nine Yeomanry regiments, 5^1/$_2$ heavy batteries, and some machine-gun companies, were consequently sent to France. For these units Indian troops were substituted during the summer. This change necessitated a complete reorganization of the Army, but ultimately the British superiority in mounted men remained unimpaired.

In March and April two advances into Trans-Jordan had ended in failure, but they served to make the Turks anticipate a renewed move in this direction. Meanwhile Allenby had decided that when the time for the final advance should come he would make his main effort on the coastal plain, where his advantage in mounted troops could be exploited. With great foresight he utilized the period of waiting, while his Army was being prepared for the final thrust, in luring the Turks into a position best suited to his purpose. By keeping a large force of cavalry throughout the summer in the stifling Jordan valley, he aimed at persuading the enemy that the British command was contemplating a stroke against the vital railway junction of Deraa behind the Turkish left flank. This was supplemented by a series of ruses concerted by Lawrence. Through their combined effect Allenby's strategic object was fully secured. By the autumn he had induced the Turks to move into the precise position which best favoured his plan of operations. Large forces had been transferred to the enemy's left flank east of the Jordan, and the right flank had been correspondingly weakened. So, when the moment proved opportune, Allenby adroitly concentrated five divisions and three cavalry divisions (three-quarters of his entire force) against the Turks.

On the morning of September 19, 1918, the infantry broke away for the cavalry to dash through the gap thus created and so ride straight north over the Pass of Megiddo into the Plain of Esdraelon; within 24 hours of the opening of the battle three mounted divisions were in the rear of the Turkish Seventh and Eighth Armies, and held all lines of retreat. The enemy Commander-in-Chief, Liman von Sanders, escaped capture only by accident. It remained for the infantry only to drive the bewildered Turks into the arms of the cavalry. No more dramatic and crushing victory has been recorded in military history.

The capture of Damascus and the break-up of the Fourth Turkish Army, harassed to extinction in its retreat by Feisal's Arabs, soon followed. From Damascus the pursuit was pushed with extreme boldness to Aleppo, which was captured by a single weak division of cavalry far beyond reach of support and in face of greatly superior Turkish forces. The Turks then asked for an armistice.

Though the fighting qualities of the Turkish troops had unquestionably deteriorated by this period of the War, nothing can belittle the quality of Allenby's achievement. In little over a month an advance of 500 miles was made, while 75,000 prisoners and nearly 400 guns were captured. The original conception, the patience in preparation, the rapidity and audacity in execution, prove that Allenby was a true master of war.

HIGH COMMISSIONER IN EGYPT
MODERATE POLICY

After the Armistice Allenby showed by his handling of the difficult problems of the control of the captured territories that he was as able an administrator as he had been a commander. Consequently, when a sudden outbreak of disorder occurred in Egypt in March, 1919, he was appointed by his Majesty's Government to be British High Commissioner in that country. In addition, he continued for some time to exercise command of the Expeditionary Force and to control the administration of Palestine. But the task of governing Egypt under martial law and of preparing the way for the settlement of the delicate problems of the country's future status was claiming his full attention, so that by the autumn he had abandoned the task of administering Palestine and of commanding the British forces remaining in those regions.

The problem of the future relations between Great Britain and Egypt was beset with grave difficulties. The obstacles to the discovery of a practical settlement which, while safeguarding the essential needs of British Imperial defence would still satisfy the aspirations of the Egyptians to control their own affairs, seemed almost insuperable. Allenby's conduct of affairs in Egypt was much criticized at the time by British residents in Egypt, who considered that he was sacrificing British interests by the concessions that he advised.

Allenby was firm in suppressing disorder, but he was ready to gratify the growing desire of Egyptian Nationalists for a larger measure of self-government. He endeavoured to pursue a middle course which, while pacifying Egyptian aspirations, maintained the safety and prestige of the British Empire. Throughout his six years in Cairo he upheld the dignity of his high office, and his personality alone did much to restore the name and word of an Englishman to the high pinnacle on which they stood in the East before the War.

THE CADET FORCE

With the conclusion of his term of office in Egypt, his opportunities of public service seemed at an end. But on the withdrawal of official recognition of the Cadet Force by the Labour Government in 1930 he gladly accepted the office of President of the British National Cadet Association, which was formed to maintain by voluntary action all cadet units throughout the country. In a letter to *The Times* published on November 1, 1930, the day when the official connexion between the Cadet Force and the Government ceased to exist, Lord Allenby declared that the movement, which had for years steadily grown, had exercised great influence for good in the mental, moral, and physical training of our youth, and the new body had been formed to ensure its continuance. He threw himself into the work with great energy, and his experience and knowledge proved invaluable.

No account of Allenby would be complete without some reference to him as a model of filial devotion. His mother lived to the age of 92; she died in March, 1922, having had the satisfaction of seeing her son arrive at the zenith of his career. His own married life proved intensely happy. A grievous blow fell on these devoted parents when they lost their only son, a lieutenant in the Royal Horse Artillery, who had already won the MC, and who died at the age of 19 of wounds received in action in 1917.

Lord Allenby was promoted to K.C.B. in 1915. and created a GCMG in 1917 and a GCB. in 1918. He was appointed colonel of the 1st Life Guards in January, 1920; he received the honorary degrees of D.C.L., Oxford, and LL.D., Cambridge. In October, 1919, he received the thanks of Parliament for his services, together with a grant of £50,000; was promoted Field-Marshal, and raised to the peerage as Viscount Allenby of Megiddo and Felixstowe, with the honour of a special remainder to his brother and his heirs male. He also possessed a great many foreign decorations, and was a Knight of Grace of St. John of Jerusalem.

He married in 1896 Adelaide Mabel, daughter of Mr. H. E. Chapman, of Donhead House, Salisbury. Lady Allenby became a Lady of Grace of the Order of St. John of Jerusalem, and held the Grand Cordon of the Order of El Kemal of Egypt. His only brother, Captain Frederick Claude Hynman Allenby, R.N., died in August, 1934, leaving two sons, of whom the elder, Mr. Dudley Jaffray Hynman Allenby, 11th Hussars, succeeds to his uncle's peerage. He was born in 1903, was educated at Eton, and married in 1930 Molly, daughter of Mr. Edward Champneys, of Otterpool Manor, Kent, and has a son.

While the description of 'No more dramatic and crushing victory has been recorded in military history' is a risky accolade to award to Allenby's victory at Megiddo, there is no doubt that it was an outstanding success. Use of dummy camps and horse lines to deceive the Turks into expecting his attack on the east side of their positions allowed him to achieve surprise for his attack on the west. Once the five-mile-wide gap had been torn in the enemy's front, he was free to release his cavalry horde. In the pursuit stage of the latter action, the cavalry were supported by aircraft, bombing and straffing the fleeing Turks from the air, in a manner of the German blitzkrieg against the British and French armies two decades later.

Allenby had a proper understanding of the use of cavalry, indeed of mobile forces in breakthrough and pursuit, and is one of the best – if not the best – of British commanders of horsed cavalry.

* * *

TRENCHARD

Father of the Royal Air Force

11 FEBRUARY 1956

LORD TRENCHARD, FIRST Marshal of the Royal Air Force and the prime architect of British air power, died yesterday at his home in London. He had celebrated his eighty-third birthday a week ago.

He was one of the earliest – and, by any measure, the greatest – Air Force officers of any nationality. Seldom can a man have made a more lasting mark in so short a time. In 1914 he was an unknown major of The Royal Scots Fusiliers seconded to the Royal Flying Corps; yet little over three years later, when he was only 45, the news of his resignation from the newly created post of Chief of the Air Staff, after a difference of opinion, on a matter which he regarded as one of vital principle, with the Secretary of State, Lord Rothermere, caused a wave of dismay to pass over the country. The stature he had acquired in so short a time may be judged, too, by the intensity of feeling which manifested itself in a debate in the House of Commons in 1918 arising out of his resignation.

Yet his work in the war of 1914–18 was destined to be only a beginning- the earliest foundations of a reputation which was not to reach its pinnacle even in his massive services to British air power during his 11 years' tenure of the office of Chief of the Air Staff, when he preserved the integrity and built the basic structure of the great Service which was to save the free world in the Battle of Britain and have so predominant a share in the second victory over Germany. Opinions may differ about his work as Commissioner of Police of the Metropolis from 1931 to 1935, but there are many who rate it as not inferior to his service to the Air Force. However, his unflagging enthusiasm, his never-fading vision, and his deeply understanding wisdom were continually devoted to the Service he had done so much more than anyone to create – whether in the House of Lords, or behind the scenes in Whitehall or as elder statesman, guide, philosopher and friend to a long line of successors in the Air Ministry.

QUALITIES OF GREATNESS

It is not easy to define the quality of real greatness. Self-confidence without a trace of arrogance; a contemptuous yet not intolerant disregard for anything mean or petty; the capacity to shuffle aside non-essentials and put an unerring finger on the real core of a problem or the real quality of a man – a sort of instinct for the really important point: a selfless devotion to the cause of what he believed to be right; Trenchard had all these qualities, and above all a shining sincerity. Many people have disagreed with him. He was not always right – that would be too much to expect of any man. His single-minded steadfastness of purpose had its own defects. In his later years, especially, his refusal to compromise with what he believed to be unsound led him sometimes to extremes into which his warmest admirers were unable to follow him. But most of those who challenged his views lived to admit with the passage of time that he was right and they wrong. None of his critics would ever suggest that he was anything but transparently disinterested and intellectually honest: and all of them – however hotly they might disagree – regarded him with some affection. He was the most modest of men and hated being referred to as the 'Father of the Air Force.' He always protested that he did not invent these ideas of air power – they became as inevitable as sunset on the day Orville Wright made his first controlled power-driven flight. That may be true. It is none the less also true that this rather inarticulate soldier was not only the first man to give expression to those principles of air power which are to-day a commonplace but also, by his single-minded energy and drive, his burning faith in his own vision, created and preserved the Service that saved England in 1940. One of his most striking characteristics was his deep humanity and understanding of the point of view of the young officer and the non-commissioned ranks – a quality enriched by his long regimental service in many countries and with a wide variety of units. There can be few officers in history who have commanded so many different types of troops.

EARLY FIGHTING EXPERIENCE

The Right Hon. Sir Hugh Montague Trenchard, GCB, OM, GCVO, DSO, first Viscount Trenchard and Baron Trenchard, of Wolfeton, in the County of Dorset, in the Peerage of the United Kingdom, and a baronet, was born on February 3 1873 the son of Captain Henry Montague Trenchard, The King's Own Yorkshire Light Infantry. Unable to pass the examinations for Dartmouth or Woolwich – a fact which has since brought comfort to other lesser men – he came through the back door of the Militia to The Royal Scots Fusiliers in October, 1893, receiving his commission from the great-great-grandmother of our present Queen whom he regarded with such affectionate respect and pride. His early service was on the Indian Frontier, but the outbreak of the South African War gave him his first experience of action and his first acquaintance with irregular troops – Imperial Yeomanry, the Australian Bushmen Corps, and the Canadian Scouts. He was promoted to captain in February, 1900, but a dangerous wound in the lung during the operations west of Pretoria laid him low for many months: but before the end he was back again, this time with the Mounted Infantry in the Transvaal, Orange River Colony, and Cape Colony. Like many other good infantry soldiers, he dearly loved a horse and polo was a passion with him in those years before 1914.

In 1903 he was seconded with a brevet majority to the West African Frontier Force and began a new chapter of adventure which was to give him an abiding and understanding interest in the problems of Africa. For the first three years he was in Southern Nigeria where he saw much active service and played a notable part in bringing that great area under control and administration. He was awarded the DSO and was twice mentioned in dispatches for his work there, and then passed to the command of the Southern Nigeria Regiment from 1908 to 1912.

ROYAL FLYING CORPS

Invalided home in 1912, in trouble with his old wound, he was soon besieging the War Office for another appointment overseas with mounted troops. While his applications were being considered his thoughts turned to the Royal Flying Corps – which had just taken its place in the Army list – and he determined to become a pilot. From the little grass airfield within the oval of the motor-racing track at Brooklands, where he learnt to fly, Trenchard passed to the Central Flying School at Upavon to complete his instruction; in 1912 he became an instructor and in the following September was appointed Assistant Commandant under Captain Godfrey Paine, RN. Two years later, after the outbreak of war, he went to command the 1st Wing in France, working with the Indian Corps and IV Corps, whence after eight months he was promoted to the command of the Royal Flying Corps in the field. In the years that followed it was his duty and good fortune to build up this new service from small beginnings and to hammer out on the anvil of battle experience the new theory and practice of air warfare.

He built on foundations well and truly laid by David Henderson and he had many able lieutenants. He had also splendid human material to work on; excellent junior commanders from the pre-War RFC, and a swelling stream of adventurous young spirits that soon began to flow into the squadrons from the newly formed training schools at home. None of them would deny that through those long and terrible months of Loos and the Somme, Arras and Messines, third Ypres and Cambrai, the main inspiration and driving force was Trenchard himself.

Trenchard's greatest service to the Army in that war, the priceless legacy that he bequeathed to the RAF of to-day, is the policy which soon developed into an article of faith, that air mastery can be gained and maintained only by the offensive. It became the fighting doctrine of the RAF, as instinctive as 'engage the enemy more closely' in the Royal Navy.

In January 1918, the year in which he was promoted KCB, he was recalled from France to be the first Chief of the newly formed Air Staff in London. Sir Douglas Haig protested strongly at his loss; and his trust in his subordinate was matched by the highest devotion on Trenchard's part. His first tour of duty as C.A.S. did not last long. In April he resigned over a difference of opinion with the Secretary of State, Lord Rothermere. Whether he was right in doing so can always be argued. But the action was typical of his refusal to compromise on a matter of principle as also was his entire lack of self-interest in an issue which he regarded as one of right or wrong. For some time the possibility of forming an Inter-Allied force for the bombing of Germany had been under consideration, and in May the Air Council proposed to the War Cabinet the formation of an Independent Air Force to bomb Germany, with Trenchard in command responsible direct to the Air Ministry. In August it was eventually decided to form the Inter-Allied Independent Air Force with Trenchard in command answerable direct to Foch; the war ended before it had time to take shape; but the 1919 programme was of an ambitious scale and provided for large contingents of bombers from all the principal allies. His war services were rewarded with a baronetcy, and by a grant of £10,000 by the House of Commons.

CRANWELL OPENED

He was not destined to be long out of active employment. By April 1919, he was back as C.A.S. and began the great work of reorganization and building up the regular Air Force. The problem which faced him was to build up from the bottom a permanent Regular Service out of the ruins of our wartime air power. His policy was that the first charge on our resources should be the training of officers and men, to lay the foundations of a highly trained and efficient cadre capable of subsequent expansion should the need arise. The Cadet College at Cranwell was opened in 1920 followed by the school for apprentices at Halton and the Staff College at Andover.

Well-equipped permanent stations began to rise, to replace the wartime hutted camps which were all there was in the way of accommodation, so that when in 1923 the expansion to the Home Defence Air Force of 52 squadrons was authorized, he had the foundations on which to build. His far-seeing wisdom in those early days was finally and triumphantly vindicated by the vast expansion to over a million men in Hitler's war. Without the invaluable cadre of Cranwell-trained officers from Halton and the other apprentice schools that followed it we could never have achieved that culmination of British air power which was such a decisive factor in the Second Great War.

Trenchard's period as Chief of the Air Staff is now a matter of history. How well and fruitfully he laboured the story of the RAF in Hitler's war bears witness. He was C.A.S. for over 10 years – abnormally long in ordinary circumstances, but the conditions of his time were not normal, and in his case it was amply justified. Many features of the RAF which are commonplace today were innovations under Trenchard's regime, among them the short service commission, the auxiliary squadrons and university air squadrons, the introduction of airmen pilots and the system of technical specialization by General Duties list officers. Most have stood the test of time. One other major innovation – air control – for which he was responsible deserves special mention.

It was in Iraq that the system was first evolved and proved itself. Based on a widespread and intimate tribal intelligence network, the essence of air control was that the ultimate sanction of force was provided by a few squadrons centrally located, instead of by the large garrisons involved in the traditional method of controlling these wild and undeveloped territories. If force became necessary it was exercised, after due warning, by the bomber instead of by the old method of battle by a column of troops on the ground.

On January 1, 1930, he relinquished his appointment as Chief of the Air Staff. He had been made Colonel of his old regiment in 1916 and on transfer to the Royal Air Force had been given an honorary commission as a major-general in the Army. He was appointed Principal Air ADC to King George V in 1921 and became the first Marshal of the Royal Air Force in 1927.

COMMISSIONER OF POLICE

He became Commissioner of Police of the Metropolis in November 1931. The responsibilities of the Commissioner are always heavy, but Trenchard added to them activities of unprecedented scope and intensity in connection with his schemes of reform and reorganization. These plans were laid before Parliament in a White Paper 18 months after his appointment and received legislative sanction in the Metropolitan Police Act of 1933. The principal feature of the Trenchard reforms were the Police College at Hendon, opened by the Duke of Windsor, then Prince of Wales, in 1933 and closed on the outbreak of war in 1939, and the short service scheme for recruiting a substantial proportion of the police on a 10-year engagement. Among his special achievements were the forensic science laboratory at Hendon, and the many steps taken to extend and improve the application of scientific methods to police work. No commissioner ever probed so deeply into the relations of the police with the public and with criminals, or dealt more faithfully with misdoings and shortcomings. The Metropolitan Police owe him a great debt for his many contributions to their welfare – notably better housing and more facilities for recreation – and for the steps he took to rescue their provident fund from financial disaster.

When he left the police in 1935 a new vista of service opened before him. Several companies engaged in the West African trade had recently come together in the United Africa Company, within the Unilever Group. The purpose of those who formed the United Africa Company was to put the trade in West Africa on a better basis, both in the commercial sense and in the wider context of national and international relations. They were looking for a leader with the strength and prestige to secure recognition for this policy from Governments and from the public. Lord Trenchard, with his great interest in West Africa, was an ideal person. He joined the board in 1936, and accepted the chairmanship three months later, retiring from the position in 1953 after 17 years.

He married, in 1920, Katherine Isabel Salvin, second daughter of the late Edward Salvin Bowlby, of Gilston Park, Hertford, and Knoydart, Inverness-shire, and widow of Captain the Hon. James Boyle, and there were two sons of the marriage. The elder son Hugh, born in 1921, was killed in action in North Africa in 1943, and the surviving son, Captain Thomas Trenchard, MC, succeeds his father,

Trenchard may have hated being known as 'The Father of the Air Force' but the sobriquet has stuck and with good reason. Autonomous air forces were not inevitable; the RAF is the world's oldest air force of any significant size to become independent of army or navy control. Notably, the United States Army Air Force was the aviation component of the US Army until the establishment of the US Air Force proper in 1947. On the day of its formation, April 1, 1918, Trenchard's RAF also absorbed the Royal Naval Air Service, the Royal Navy only recovering control of its Fleet Air Arm in 1937.

This splendid obituary is a little thin on the nine years that Trenchard served in West Africa, earning the DSO and three of his total of ten mentions in despatches. There he was engaged in pacification and settlement operations in the Protectorate of Southern Nigeria, unpleasant and dangerous stockade and ambush work where, in the words of a typical citation to the Secretary of State for the Colonies in 1906, Brevet Major Trenchard 'commanded a column of 800 men in the field for five months and showed energy, resource and powers of organisation far above the average'.

MANNERHEIM

Marshal of Finland, patriot and statesman

29 JANUARY 1951

FIELD MARSHAL BARON MANNERHEIM, one of the outstanding figures of Finland and a great soldier, died in a hospital at Lausanne, Switzerland, on Saturday. He was 83. Carl Gustaf Emil Mannerheim was born on June 4, 1867. He was a Swedo-Finn, or 'Finlander,' of a noble house prominent in Sweden from the mid-seventeenth century and in Finland for some 150 years. His paternal ancestors for three generations had been outstanding figures. The most remarkable of them was his great-grandfather, Count Carl Erik, the eminent statesman who founded the system of free institutions granted to Finland after the Russian conquest of 1808, and who served for some years as Prime Minister of his country.

Gustaf Mannerheim, who was to distinguish himself in five wars, was early apprenticed to the profession of arms, entering the Corps of Cadets at Fredrikshamm in 1881. Six years later he joined the Nicolaevsky Cavalry School at St. Petersburg. At the present day a word of comment on his 30 years' loyal service in the Russian Army may be of interest. Russian rule, with some unfortunate lapses, was mild and almost beneficent in Finland until shortly before the beginning of this century. The less narrowly nationalistic Finns did not desire complete independence for Finland. The Finns were well enough pleased that members of the leading families should enter the Russian Army because the Russian authorities recruited their administrators in Finland from this source.

In 1889 Mannerheim was gazetted ensign in the 15th Alexandrinsky Dragoon Regiment, but transferred soon afterwards to the more fashionable Chevalier Guards. His good looks and a certain rather aloof charm, his brilliant horsemanship, and enthusiasm for life made him a popular figure. In late 1904, a lieutenant colonel aged 37, he went east to take part in the war with Japan, arriving after the Russians had suffered defeat in the battle of Liao-Yaung. On the losing side an officer of his rank often finds opportunities of proving his worth as good as those which present themselves to the victor, and Mannerheim on that occasion showed that there were in him the makings of an exceptional commander.

Between that war and the next the most important episode in Mannerheim's career was his famous trans-Asiatic expedition, which lasted two years, from the summer of 1906 to that of 1908. In that period, though he made several halts, he averaged about 11 miles a day on horseback, covering over 8,000 miles. The ride started at Andijan, and led through Sinkiang, Kansu, Shensi, Honan, and Shansi to its terminus at Peking. Its official object was to obtain military, and especially cartographical, intelligence, and that was fulfilled. But the scientific and artistic strain in Mannerheim, undeveloped till now, made itself felt; he constituted himself archaeologist and ethnologist, and brought back not only an immense amount of lore but also a notable collection of antiquities, works of art, and manuscripts which is now treasured by his country. Perhaps the most precious was a fragment of manuscript in a north Asiatic language believed to have been in use about the time of the birth of Christ.

In 1910 Mannerheim was appointed to command the Regiment of Uhlans of the Life Guards, and the following year, at the age of 44, was promoted major-general. On July 31, 1914, he led the Guard Cavalry Brigade to the San with the task of covering the mobilization of a Russian Army at Lublin. From the very first he showed his calibre, carrying out a brilliant flanking movement from Krasnik with a force of all arms and inflicting on the Austrians a sharp local reverse which had a considerable effect upon the main operations. During the next few months he took part in the heavy fighting in Poland, and continued to distinguish himself. In February, 1915, he was appointed to the command of the 12th Cavalry Division, and was engaged in all the fluctuating fighting in Poland until the end of 1916. He was then transferred to the Carpathians, where he took over the Wrancza Group, containing Rumanian as well as Russian troops. After the revolution broke out Mannerheim went home. By the time he reached Helsingfors Finland had proclaimed her independence. In January, 1918, he was appointed Commander-in-Chief of a non-existent Finnish Army.

In the War of Liberation Mannerheim displayed military genius, but his first act was one of almost incredible daring, when he attacked well-equipped Russian troops with a few half-trained peasants. The Russians, however, anxious only to get home, made no serious resistance. It was otherwise with the Red Finns whom they had equipped and to whom they sold their arms, and these proved most determined foes.

Mannerheim, however, looked upon further Russian intervention as possible and was therefore careful to cut communications across the Karelian isthmus as soon as he had made his own base of operations secure.

It is impossible even to outline the course of his campaign or to attempt to unravel the tangle of interests which extended into Finland from the rest of warring Europe and brought German troops to Mannerheim's aid, though not until he had already gained substantial success. By May opposition had come to an end. On the 16th Mannerheim entered Helsingfors at the head of 16,000 men. The aftermath of the war was accompanied by difficult and often distressing problems, and the harsh treatment of the imprisoned revolutionaries, which resulted in thousands of deaths, brought obloquy on the head of Mannerheim, though he had in fact opposed the Government's measures. He served as Regent in the confused days of constitution-making, as mediator with foreign States. His work for child welfare was of particular importance, and he would be remembered for it alone had he accomplished nothing else. With the leisure of retirement he travelled a great deal and was able to indulge his love of sport, especially shooting and fishing. In younger days he had been one of the finest horsemen in Russia and largely instrumental in the development of Russian military show riding, which achieved triumphs at Olympia and elsewhere.

In 1939 came the Russian attack upon Finland, and once again Gustaf Mannerheim took command of his country's forces. Once again Mannerheim, now supported by efficient commanders and staff officers trained under his own eye, displayed remarkable skill. His defence might, indeed, provide matter for a text-book on winter warfare in the far north. The breaking of the 'Mannerheim line,' however, rendered the Finnish situation hopeless, and it was on his advice that the Government decided to submit to the terms of the Soviet. In Finland's ill-advised second war against Russia, Mannerheim again acted as Commander-in-Chief. In this war the Finns largely confined their efforts to the recovery of what they had lost in the first, and it was not marked by many outstanding incidents. In the end they had to submit to taking action against their former German allies and driving them out of the country.

Mannerheim, who had been President of Finland in 1944, did not have to undergo trial, as at one moment seemed likely, and after residing abroad for some time was able lo return home. At the age of 25 Gustaf Mannerheim married Anastasie Arapov, daughter of a Russian Guard officer. He had two daughters, the elder of whom became a Carmelite nun.

Speaking fluent English, French, German, Russian and Swedish, Mannerheim was a shrewd and rational cosmopolitan in a country lacking – certainly in the first half of the 20th century – any real understanding of the outside world. He showed sharp political and strategic instinct at the start of the War of Liberation, a civil conflict between the Finnish communist 'Reds' and establishment 'Whites' in 1918, by quitting the capital to establish a base at Vaasa. Situated in a staunch conservative community on the Gulf of Bothnia, this provided a rallying point for those joining his cause and a port to receive material aid from Sweden. As his military strength and capabilities increased, he methodically beat the more numerous but poorly-led Reds until he could make a triumphant return to Helsinki.

In 1939, he alone perceived Moscow's demand for use of Finnish islands in the Gulf of Finland and bases for the Soviet fleet on her southern seaboard, as Russian defensive preparations for a possible German attack. He advised his Government to lease the islands, which were indefensible, and move back the frontier until Leningrad was out of artillery range from Finnish territory. The Government's refusal led to the Winter War. The Finns were finally forced to sue for peace, but Mannerheim's strategy of concentrating his military strength in Karelia, leaving the winter, the forests and ski troops to decimate the Red Army divisions invading the north and centre, prevented a walkover and Soviet occupation of the entire country.

Criticism of Mannerheim for the 'ill-advised' second war against the Soviet Union, in concert with Nazi Germany in June 1941, ignores the fact that Germany was everywhere undefeated at the time, the United States still neutral and it appeared that Europe's post-war frontiers would be dictated from Berlin. When the time for retribution came in 1944, he persuaded Finnish President Risto Ryti to get essential supplies from Germany against a promise to Hitler not to make a separate peace, then replaced Ryti as President and negotiated a deal with Stalin that kept Finland's independence, albeit initially tenuous in nature.

RUNDSTEDT

*Orthodox strategist and father figure of the
German officer corps.*

25 FEBRUARY 1953

FIELD-MARSHAL GERD VON RUNDSTEDT, who has died at the age of
77 at Hanover, was one of the ablest German commanders of the Second
World War. The epithet 'brilliant' does not fit him, because he lacked the
unconventional qualities which it summons up, but his orthodoxy was
never narrow. The Army ranked him high, and since the war the younger
school has treated his military reputation with respect. Cautious by
temperament, he could act very boldly and lent a sympathetic ear to
bold plans put up to him by competent subordinates. He was an accomplished soldier with his profession at his fingers' ends; but his ideas were
strategic rather than tactical and, unmindful of well-known advice, he
preferred small-scale to large-scale maps. For tactics he relied heavily
upon his staff. He served in the principal European campaigns:
Poland, France in 1940, Russia, and North-west Europe. He was strongly
opposed to war with Russia and feared it would turn out ill. Accused
of war crimes, he was, after long delay, released on grounds of ill health,
and proceedings against him were dropped. To many people in Britain
they had been unwelcome.

Karl Rudolf Gerd von Rundstedt came of an ancient family in the
Altmark of Brandenburg. He was born on December 12, 1875, and was
posted to the 83rd Infantry Regiment in 1893. In the 1914–18 war he
served in France, Russia, and Hungary, ending as chief staff officer of
XV Corps. He rose at moderate speed, though he held most of the staff
appointments and several commands. The last in peace, in Berlin, was
notable because, Fritsche and Beck being recluses, receptions and social
intercourse fell to him. Though grim and laconic, he became a man
of the world – at least the political and military world – and well known
outside Germany. In the autumn of 1938, having angered Hitler over
the celebrated Fritsche and Beck 'affairs,' he retired, but was brought
back next year for the offensive against Poland. He was six years the
senior of his superior, Brauchitsch, Commander-in-Chief of the Army,
though regarded as the more capable soldier and the stronger man.

DEFEAT OF POLAND

The role of Rundstedt's forces on the southern flank was decisive. His armour trapped the main Polish forces about Warsaw, though the supreme command believed that they had escaped south-eastward. He next took over Army Group A, which was to attack in the west. The final plan bore little resemblance to the original. The former was the work of Manstein, his chief staff officer in Poland, who had accompanied him to his new command. Rundstedt supported and slightly modified it. It was adopted, though its author was relegated to the command of an infantry corps in reserve.

The thrust through the Ardennes, the essential feature, was carried out by Rundstedt's group. When Guderian's armour was ordered to halt on the Meuse to await the infantry and that headstrong man proffered his resignation in a passion, Rundstedt sent Colonel-General List to bid him stay at his post; Guderian was allowed to make 'reconnaissances in force' and interpreted this directive so vigorously that he drove on to the Channel coast. Rundstedt had clearly been in two minds over the affair. In the last phase, the passage of the Aisne and the drive to the Swiss frontier, his group played an equally vital part. The commander was promoted to the rank of field-marshal.

THE RUSSIAN CAMPAIGN

Against Russia Rundstedt commanded Army Group South, which included Hungarian and Italian troops. Farther south lay the Rumanian forces, over which he had general strategic control. Experience in the Carpathians in the earlier war had taught him how to deal amicably with foreign troops. He handled the offensive with skill, determination, and success. At the end of November, however, he decided that his worst fears were being realized and that a halt, and even a withdrawal, were necessary to save the army from being engulfed in the Russian winter. On December 1 he was relieved of his command.

In March, 1942, he was appointed to a command in the west extending from Holland to the Italian frontier. By 1944 his chief subordinate, the commander of Army Group B, which would have to face invasion from Britain, was Field-Marshal Rommel. The strategic ideas of the two were opposed. Rundstedt advocated a classic system of defence, keeping the armoured forces well back from the coast and disposed so that they could strike at an invader wherever he might land. Rommel, deeply impressed by the difficulty of movement resulting from the complete British-American command of the air, thought this plan too risky and relied on defeating invasion on the coast. He was supported by Hitler, and Rundstedt does not appear to have fought very hard for his views. He was perhaps by now beginning to feel his years; indeed, henceforward his conduct, admittedly in the most difficult circumstances, seems to have become less vigorous. The upshot was that the armour was committed more or less piecemeal and there was no counter-offensive on a great scale.

THE ARDENNES OFFENSIVE

Rundstedt was relieved in early July and served as president of the 'court of honour' set up after the attempt on Hitler's life, but on September 5 returned as commander-in-chief in the west. His last great action was the counter-offensive in the Ardennes, but he considered the plan extravagant in view of the land and air resources available. He advocated an offensive, but with limited aims. Though this has been called the 'Rundstedt offensive,' it was Hitler's, and Hitler dealt directly with the group commander, Model. Soon afterwards Rundstedt was relieved once more. He must have got used to the process by then.

On May 2, 1945, he was arrested in the house in which he was living near Munich. From early 1946 till July, 1948, he was incarcerated at Bridgend in Glamorgan and Diss in Norfolk. In May, 1949, he was released in Germany. Brauchitsch, who was to have stood trial with him and Manstein, was dead, so the last-named was tried alone. Rundstedt represented the old Army and, where he was concerned, its alliance with Hitler was uneasy. Some thought that his opposition to Hitler would take active form, but his temperament and character in fact rendered this unlikely. He was in any case in temporary retirement when the bomb exploded in Hitler's headquarters.

> Despite his uneasiness about the German Army's alliance with Hitler, Rundstedt co-operated in the programme of clandestine rearmament in the 1930s. This reflected his old Prussian-style absolute loyalty to the German head of state, to whom he had given his oath of allegiance. It was on this basis that he not only accepted without question his removal from command, but actually courted it in Russia, where he considered Hitler's 'no withdrawal' orders lacking in tactical awareness and military judgement.
>
> Just who was responsible for ordering Guderian to pause, when he might have cut off virtually all the British Expeditionary Force from the Channel ports in 1940, is unlikely ever to be decided

with certainty. It would have been the sound thing to do if the French Army had been capable of launching a counter-offensive, as the German armoured units were nearing the limit of their attack capabilities, in terms of physical endurance of the men, ammunition and fuel. As it was, the French had no such ability and a great opportunity was lost to Germany.

The Rundsted-Rommel dispute over the dispositions of the German armoured divisions, prior to the Allied invasion of Normandy, became largely academic when Hitler refused to release those held ready to confront an expected Allied second invasion force in the Pas de Calais – which never came – to go to Normandy. Nevertheless, the course of the Normandy campaign suggests that Rommel would have been right. American and British formations advanced from the beachhead less swiftly than planned in the very early days, when vigorous armoured counter-attacks might well have thrown them off balance.

* * *

GUDERIAN

*Germany's dynamic panzer commander of
the Second World War*

17 MAY 1954

GENERAL HEINZ GUDERIAN, who had one of the most creative military minds of the 1939–45 War, has died at Fussen, in Bavaria, at the age of 65. He was born at Kulm, in west Prussia, later the Polish 'Corridor,' in 1888, the son of an army officer. Kurt Schumacher, the late Socialist Democrat leader, came from the same small town, and though Guderian was older the two men knew each other from youth. His father expressed the wish that he should become an officer and he was sent, with his brother, to the Karlsruhe cadet school in Baden. From there he was later transferred to the chief cadet school at Gross-Lichterfelde, near Berlin.

During the 1914–18 War his career alternated between regimental and staff duties, and by 1922 he had a wide knowledge of the army and its organization which stood him in good stead when he came to build up a formidable new arm of the service. It was Hitler, in the 1930s, who gave him the opportunity to put into practice the idea of a mobile armoured army which will stand as his contribution to the theory of war. Other men had the same idea, or a similar one: General Fuller, General Martel, and Captain Liddell Hart in Britain, and General de Gaulle in France, to all of whom he made acknowledgment. Some are apt to say, therefore, that he owes his place in military history merely to the fact that he alone found a political ruler to back him.

But there was more to it than that. He joined to his creative imagination a dynamic energy and opportunism. As chief of staff to the inspectorate of motorized troops and later as chief of staff to the armoured troops command, he was given the authority and the resources to build up a powerful mobile armoured force. Then, in 1938, he was appointed chief of mobile troops and promoted general of Panzer troops, and within a year could test his new model army in battle – in the invasion of Poland. The accuracy of his conception was immediately proved by the speed with which he broke through the Polish 'Corridor' and drove through Wizna to Brest.

But it was the campaign in the west which was his most remarkable achievement. Here his unorthodox method of leading his armoured and motorized forces – giving them the 'green light to the very end of the road' – was as successful as the original conception. In the Russian campaign the Panzer army was at first even more successful. But soon they had to contend with a new and dangerous enemy – space and depth. 'The very end of the road' was now a very long way away. Moscow did not fall – and he fell out of favour.

When he was finally reinstated, after the conspiracy of July 20, in which he had no part, he was given the wholly unsuitable post of Chief of Staff (of the German Army), in which his fighting qualities could not help him. This last phase of the war was the phase, too, through which it was difficult for a high German officer to pass with moral credit, unless with risk to his life. He remained attached to Hitler, though not without hesitation and doubts, for which he had to pay in the last months of violence and defeat with utterances which did him no credit. Yet it must be said that he had dared to oppose Hitler when his sense of decent soldierly behaviour was affronted.

As his volume of recollections, *Panzer Leader*, showed, he was a typical product of his Prussian traditions. He never pretended to have conspired against Hitler or to have quarrelled with him, except to prevent him making mistakes. But the German general who in 1944 extorted from Hitler permission to withdraw two S.S. brigades which had committed monstrous atrocities in Warsaw – and it was not an isolated act – deserves the tribute as well as the blame for the qualities nourished by his upbringing and his background.

'Schneller Heinz' to his German contemporaries was not just a theorist on armoured warfare but, unlike Fuller, Martel and Liddell-Hart, a highly successful practitioner on the battlefield. It is often overlooked, however, that his victories in France depended on the close support the German armour received from the Luftwaffe, hindering redeployment of British and French infantry and artillery and leaving the panzers free rein. British and French air commanders refused to acknowledge that bombing interdiction targets would have minimal effect on ground forces operating across a wide front. Instead, they should have directed their attention specifically against the German dive bombers, that were acutely vulnerable to fighter attack in the air but the principal cause of chaos on the ground.

Guderian and fellow exponents of armoured warfare in the German Army wisely eschewed the British theory of developing different tanks for different circumstances – for instance the British 'I' tank for support of infantry – concentrating instead on speed and firepower for all models. In consequence, American and British tanks were consistently out-gunned even in the final stages of the war in Europe.

Although an acknowledged favourite of Hitler for his successes early in the war, he did not allow this to inhibit his opinions. He argued resolutely against faulty strategic or tactical instructions issued by the Führer and was relieved of his command on Christmas day 1941 after he had ordered a militarily sound withdrawal against a dogmatic prohibition. Despite his moral stand on atrocities by SS troops in Poland, he appears not to have questioned the political objectives of the National Socialist regime.

WAVELL

Soldier and Man of Letters

25TH MAY 1950

FIELD-MARSHAL LORD WAVELL, who died in a nursing home in London yesterday morning at the age of 67, had a full, and diverse career as a soldier before becoming Viceroy of India in a period of danger and violent flux. He was well known to the Army long before the 1939–45 war brought him into the public eye and for a time surrounded him with a blaze of admiration and renown. He was then, indeed, more celebrated than any British soldier had ever been, since to-day the Press and wireless spread fame faster and more widely than it moved in the days of Marlborough, Wellington, or even Haig. But Wavell's success did not endure, and, as so often happens to officers who are senior in rank at the opening of long wars, he did not remain in high command until the end.

Known to his profession as keen and promising even before the 1914–18 war, Wavell held staff appointments during it, gaining valuable experience on the Western Front, with the Russian armies, at Versailles, and in Palestine. After the war he was notable for keeping abreast, if not ahead, of his times and for his open-mindedness and originality of thought. He was popular as a staff officer and as a commander, though he lacked personal magnetism and was deficient in social qualities. In a small and congenial circle he would talk well for a time, but his silence in company he did not know, and especially in that of women on social occasions, was notorious, and he did not know how to conceal boredom. Yet his fine presence and rugged good looks were an asset far outweighing this shortcoming, if such it can be called. In one of his own books he put physical and mental toughness as the first quality of the general, and he not only possessed this quality but also looked the part in every respect.

THE 1914–18 WAR

The Right Hon. Sir Archibald Percival Wavell, PC, GCB, GCSI, GCIE, CMG, MC, first Earl Wavell, Viscount Wavell, of Cyrenaica, and Viscount Keren, of Eritrea and of Winchester, in the County of Southampton, in the

214

Peerage of the United Kingdom, was born on May 5, 1883, son of Major-General Archibald Graham Wavell. He went to Winchester before passing into Sandhurst. In 1901 he was gazetted to The Black Watch and joined the 2nd Battalion during the war in South Africa, to serve with it until the peace in May, 1902. He went through the operations in the Zakka Khel country, on the North-West Frontier of India in 1908. Graduating from the Staff College in 1910, while still a subaltern, Wavell took a year's leave to study Russian. In 1912 he was appointed G.S.O. 3 in the Directorate of Military Training at the War Office.

After the outbreak of war in 1914 he was sent to France as a G.S.O. 2 at G.H.Q., but in a few months he became brigade major of 9 Brigade. In June, 1915, he was wounded, losing an eye. He was awarded the Military Cross for his service in France. On resuming duty he served for a short time with the home forces, but then went out to G.H.Q. as G.S.O.2 in the operations branch. His next appointment was attachment to the Russian armies in the Caucasus, from October, 1916, to June, 1917. He was then appointed liaison officer between the War Office and' the Egyptian Expeditionary Force in Palestine.

Early in 1918 he went for a short time to the new Supreme War Council at Versailles, returning in March to Allenby's headquarters in Palestine as G.S.O. 1. In April he became Brigadier-General, General Staff, to Chetwode's XX Corps and as such took part in Allenby's final victorious offensive.

After service with his regiment in the Rhine Army Wavell returned in 1921 to the War Office as AAG in the Directorate of Organization and from 1923 to 1926 he was G.S.O.1 in the Directorate of Military Operations. After spending most of 1926 on half pay he was appointed G.S.O.1 of 3 Division and in 1930 he took over the command of one of its brigades, which had been selected for experiments in tactical organization and training. Promoted major-general in 1933, he gave up his brigade early the next year and after nearly another year on half pay was appointed to command 2 Division. He was created C.B. in 1935.

In 1937 and the following year Wavell had a disagreeable spell in command of the troops in Palestine, when that country was disturbed. Promoted lieutenant-general in 1938, he was appointed G.O.C-in-C., Southern Command, the most important in the country in view of its training facilities. He did not, however, hold it for the normal period owing to the approach of war, and in 1939 became Commander-in-Chief, Middle East, with headquarters in Cairo, to enter upon the most eventful phase of his career.

NORTH AFRICA

To start with, however, all was quiet, and it was not until the defeat of France and the entry of Italy into the war in June 1940, that active operations began in the Middle East. Wavell drew first blood in daring actions against the Italians on the frontier of Cyrenaica, but his forces did not represent a fraction of theirs, and when they crossed the frontier he could only withdraw his advanced troops to a fortified position at Matruh. On reaching Sidi Barrani the enemy halted and sat down in a belt of entrenched camps. Wavell paid a visit to London to plead for some reinforcements and equipment from the slender store available. As the result of a decision which must be described as extremely gallant in view of the imminent danger of invasion which overhung the United Kingdom, he obtained them.

On December 9 he attacked the Italians by surprise, rolled up their front, and utterly routed them. The Italians fought by no means ill, but the handful of heavy Matilda tanks, completely impervious to their anti-tank weapons, dominated the battlefield and ended by demoralizing each successive garrison. Emboldened by his quick success, Wavell went on to capture the port of Bardia. On January 20, 1941, he stormed Tobruk and the garrison surrendered next day. Finally, the British light tanks, after an advance of some 150 miles along the boulder-strewn inland route which formed the chord of the arc of the coast of Cyrenaica, reached the Gulf of Sirte just ahead of the retreating Italian remnant, which had followed the good but longer coast road.

The intercepting force was heavily outnumbered, but held the Italian attack on February 6. Next day after all but effecting a break-through, the Italian force surrendered. In this campaign the British had captured in all some 120,000 prisoners, including 19 general officers, and 1,416 guns. It was almost an annihilation of the Italian forces in North Africa. Simultaneously forces under Wavell's command had operated against the Italians in East Africa, beginning on January 19 with the reoccupation of Kassala, a Sudanese frontier post captured by the enemy. This campaign was an outstanding example of operations on 'exterior lines,' the main columns being directed from the Sudan eastward and from Kenya northward and starting over 800 miles apart. Again the victory was complete, though Wavell had actually left his command when the last Italian force surrendered in the autumn of 1941.

The manner in which he swung his scanty reserves between the Libyan and East African theatres was masterly. The action of the Government in withdrawing a detachment from Wavell's command to the aid of Greece when attacked by Germany was fatal to his chances of maintaining his grip upon Cyrenaica. The expeditionary force sent to Greece was driven into the sea by the Germans in April, 1941, and the remnant left in North Africa was unable to withstand the attack of the first German forces to arrive in that theatre. The policy of splitting a force scarcely adequate for one task to do two, resulted in the heavy defeat of both sections. In mid-April the force in Cyrenaica was pushed back, with loss, to the Egyptian frontier. Wavell took the bold decision of dropping a garrison in Tobruk during the retreat, with the intention of maintaining it from the sea.

The Government now decided that the time had come for a change in the command. Wavell was relieved by General Sir C. J. Auchinleck and appointed to Auchinleck's former post that of Commander-in-Chief of India, which he took over on July 11. From this post also he assumed responsibility for the campaign in Syria, which he had initiated as Commander-in-Chief, Middle East, but in that theatre an armistice was signed a few days later. He had to direct the occupation of southern Persia, which began on August 25. But his gravest commitment was the ever more insistent threat of Japanese aggression, which kept him constantly flying to conferences and inspections. On December 28, three weeks after the Japanese attack on Pearl Harbour; it was announced that Wavell had taken over the defence of Burma. On January 4, 1942, he was appointed Supreme Commander, South-west Pacific Area.

DEFENCE OF INDIA

The new command was known as 'A.B.DA.,' these letters standing for the American, British, Dutch and Australian forces which were to operate under its orders; but, though Wavell formed a staff and moved to Java, the command never functioned in the sense of establishing effective control and making an entity of the scattered and ill equipped forces. The Japanese did not allow it time to do so. In March, after the loss of Malaya and the first landings of the Japanese in the Netherlands East Indies, this was recognized and Wavell was directed to his old post of Commander-in-Chief, India. It was an unspoken acknowledgment that the Netherlands East Indies were doomed and that India itself was in danger of invasion.

To the task of preparing to meet this threat and later on after the Japanese had halted in Burma, to organizing the first minor offensives against them – which achieved no durable success – Wavell devoted the next 15 months. On June 19, 1943, he was appointed Viceroy and Governor-General of India, and on July 23 was created a viscount. His three and a half years as Viceroy and Governor-General rank among the most strenuous and critical of his whole career. He made a good initial impression by immediately taking in hand the amelioration of the great Bengal famine and insisting on food distribution being placed on an all-India basis.

Genuinely devoted to India and striving hard to promote her interests as he saw them, he lacked those qualities of sympathy and imagination which were needed. The emotional foundation of current Indian nationalism disconcerted his cool and logical mind and, though he showed himself an admirable administrator with a first-rate grasp of practical problems and a high capacity for planning far-reaching schemes for the economic rehabilitation of the country, his repeated efforts to resolve the complicated political deadlock were unsuccessful. Throughout the remaining years of war, however, his services were invaluable; his grasp of military problems enabled him to mobilize the resources of India for her own defence and for the final assault upon the Japanese forces in Burma as no other man could have done.

In the sphere of domestic politics, his principal preoccupation was to arrange an accommodation between Hindus and Muslims which would enable him to reconstitute his Executive Council on a basis affording representation to the main political parties. The conference which he convened at Simla in June, 1945, nearly succeeded in bringing this about; it failed through the obduracy of Mr. Jinnah and the Muslim League, but characteristically he put the blame on himself. Shortly afterwards Wavell was recalled to London for consultations with Mr. Attlee's new administration; and it was decided to hold the long-postponed elections for the central and provincial legislatures and to convene as early as possible a constitution-making body.

The Labour Government refused to be stampeded into hasty action over Indian affairs; and Wavell's relations with Downing Street were perfectly cordial. The political deadlock remained, however: the Hindu and Muslim communities drifted farther and farther apart as a result of the elections, while both alike blamed Wavell and the British Government for the frustration from which they suffered. They were united only in determination to free themselves from British control. Mr. Attlee's announcement in February, 1946, that no obstacle would be placed in the way of India's leaving the British Commonwealth if she desired to do so gave the Cabinet mission which went to Delhi in the next month a real chance of success. The plan which it produced owed much to Wavell himself, whose industry and acumen greatly impressed his Ministerial colleagues; but differences of interpretation of the complicated provisions of the plan served further to accentuate Hindu-Muslim differences, and Wavell's refusal to constitute a Muslim League Government drove it into 'direct action' and touched off dangerous communal rioting.

In September, 1946, a Government of Congress views was formed and a few weeks later Wavell scored his principal political success by inducing the Muslim League to join the Congress in a coalition Government.

HINDUS AND MUSLIMS

But the coalition was uneasy, and as each side endeavoured to secure the support of the Governor-General against the other dissatisfaction grew. Wavell discharged his difficult task with complete impartiality, but became more and more unpopular with both sides. There were signs that he was losing the confidence of the British Cabinet; his frequent visits to England for consultation failed to clear the air. While he did not differ from the Cabinet in holding that a British withdrawal from India in the near future was inevitable, his ideas regarding the time and measure of the process were not in agreement with theirs.

In February, 1947, Mr. Attlee announced that the Government were irrevocably determined to withdraw from India by June, 1948, and gave the news of Wavell's recall. To the British public, ignorant of the growing differences between the Viceroy and the Cabinet, Wavell's supersession by Lord Mountbatten came as something of a shock which was not lessened by the curt and ungenerous terms in which the change was signified to the world at large. It was characteristic of the man that he kept silent and made no attempt to put his views on the matter before the public.

Wavell, who was advanced to an earldom in February, 1947 was the recipient of many honours, including the Grand Crosses of the Orders of the Bath, the Star of India, and the Indian Empire, and a number of foreign decorations. He received honorary degrees from St. Andrews, Cambridge, and Oxford universities. He was a notable writer, with a style sparing of ornament yet intensely characteristic, indeed unmistakable to those who had come to know it. His widely read volume on The Palestine Campaign became a standard military manual. His life of his old master, Lord Allenby, appeared, owing to the exigencies of war, in two parts,

Allenby, a Study in Greatness and *Allenby in Egypt*, and was hailed as a brilliant biography. His essays *Generals and Generalship*, published in *The Times*, made an original contribution to their subject.

His anthology *Other Men's Flowers* was attractive not only for its choice of material but also for a delightful commentary. In 1915 he married Eugenie Marie, only child of the late Colonel Owen Quirk, and they had one son and three daughters. The heir to the earldom and viscountcy is his son, Archibald John Arthur, Viscount Keren, born May 11, 1916, who entered his father's regiment, The Black Watch, and was awarded the Military Cross while serving under Wingate in Burma.

It came to be widely held that Wavell had been forced by political direction from London to divert two divisions to Greece after his successful campaign against the Italians in Cyrenaica in February 1941, leading to defeat in Greece and a set-back in the Western Desert. In a lecture after the war, Wavell explained that the decision was made by the 'men on the spot', that is to say by him, and that doubts over the wisdom of the deployment came from London. The initial outcome appeared near disastrous for the Commonwealth forces but, also after the war, General Alfred Jodl, the Wehrmacht Chief of Operations Staff, stated that Germany had lost the war by being obliged to divert divisions to counter the British landing in Greece, thereby delaying the attack on Russia, 'so losing Moscow, Stalingrad and the war'.

ALANBROOKE

One of the greatest soldiers of his generation

18 JUNE 1963

FIELD MARSHAL VISCOUNT ALANBROOKE, who died yesterday at his Hampshire home at the age of 79, held high command in the field for only a brief period in 1940, but has been universally recognized as one of the greatest – intellectually and in military knowledge probably the greatest – soldiers of his generation. As Chief of the Imperial General Staff during the greater part of the Second World War he exercised behind the scenes a profound influence upon its course. He possessed a gift for lucid explanation and exposition which was an invaluable asset at international conferences and also enabled him to succeed in the task in which so many soldiers have failed, of talking convincingly to the politician. He was as much at home in Whitehall as with his fellow soldiers and the leaders of the other fighting services.

Alan Francis Brooke, Field Marshal Viscount Alanbrooke, KG, GCB, OM, GCVO, DSO, was the sixth son of Sir Victor Brooke, third baronet, of Brookeborough, Co. Fermanagh, and of Alice Sophia, daughter of Sir Alan Bellingham, third baronet. He was born in the south of France at Bagnères de Bigorre, where his parents were then living, on July 23, 1883. Sir Victor Brooke was a warm friend of James Roosevelt, father of Franklin Delano, and this friendship was always borne in mind by the future President of the United States. Alan Brooke's early education was obtained at a French lycée, with the result that he grew up virtually bilingual. He afterwards passed through the Royal Military Academy Woolwich, and was gazetted second lieutenant in the Royal Artillery in December, 1902. His early service was spent in Ireland. In 1906 he went to India and was posted to N Battery, R.H.A. and when war with Germany broke out in 1914 he was commanding the R.H.A. Ammunition Column at Secunderabad.

PROMISING STAFF OFFICER

In September of that year be landed at Marseilles with the Secunderabad Cavalry Brigade in the Indian Cavalry Corps. A few weeks later, during the Battle of la Basée, he was promoted captain, and in

January, 1915, became Staff Captain – subsequently Adjutant – R.H.A., 2nd Indian Cavalry Division. In November he went to the 18th Division as Brigade Major R.A., and in this capacity he served through the Battle of the Somme, having been promoted major in April, 1916. He became Staff Officer R.A. at the headquarters of the Canadian Corps in February, 1917, and later in the year G.S.O.2 R.A, remaining with the Canadians through all their battles until nearly the end of the war. In September, 1918, however, he was transferred to the First Army as G.S.O.1 R.A. He was awarded the D.S.O. in 1917 and a bar to this decoration in 1918. In January, 1919, he was made a brevet lieutenant-colonel.

Brooke had emerged from the war with the reputation of a most capable and promising staff officer, and he was selected to attend the first post-war course at the Staff College. In 1920, after graduation, he became G.S.O.2 of the Northumbrian Division, Territorial Army. In 1923 he returned to the Staff College as an instructor, remained there for four years, and then studied for a year at the Imperial Defence College. After a year on regimental duty he was appointed Commandant of the School of Artillery at Larkhill, his promotion to colonel being antedated to 1923. From 1932 to 1934 he was Army Instructor at the Imperial Defence College. He then received command of the 8th Infantry Brigade at Plymouth. In June, 1935. he was promoted to major-general, and later that year became Inspector of Artillery. He vacated this post in 1935 on appointment to that of Director of Military Training at the War Office.

In 1937 Brooke became commander of an experimental formation known as the 'Mobile Division', but passed on in the following year to become Commander of the Anti-Aircraft Corps, an appointment which was enlarged to that of G.O.C.-in-C. Anti-Aircraft Command in 1939. Once again he was scarcely given time to settle down, becoming G.O.C.-in-C., Southern Command in 1939, in succession to General Wavell. The Southern was the most important of the home commands at the time, and it was understood that the appointment carried with it the command of an army corps in any expeditionary force which might be sent abroad in the event of war with Germany. And in 1939, on the outbreak of war, he went out to France in command of the II Corps. He had been promoted to the rank of lieutenant-general the previous year.

In the retreat to Dunkirk and the operations covering the evacuation from that port in 1940 Brooke displayed consummate ability. Almost immediately after his return to England he was selected to go back to France and to take command of British troops still in the country, that

is, south of the Somme. There was still some slight hope of French resistance continuing, in which case the British Government intended to send
the maximum assistance. That hope was rapidly dispelled by the situation which Brooke discovered after landing at Cherbourg on June 12. The
French armies were in dissolution. He strongly advocated a second evacuation, but remained in France until the French Government asked the
Germans for an armistice.

A DAUNTING RESPONSIBILITY

Back in England Brooke returned for a period of a few weeks to the
Southern Command, but was then appointed Commander-in-Chief
Home Forces. This was a position of serious and indeed daunting
responsibility. Almost all the equipment of the expeditionary forces had
been lost and the troops in the United Kingdom had to be provided with
obsolete weapons, while in many cases weapons were altogether lacking.
All the Commander-in-Chief's great energy, ability, and experience
were devoted to the task of re-equipment, training, and preparation of
defence against invasion. The air victory in the Battle of Britain removed
the danger for 1940, though there still seemed to be a possibility of its
recurrence. Brooke was in that year promoted to the rank of general and
awarded the K.C.B., his C.B. dating from 1937.

At the end of 1941 he was appointed to succeed his old friend and
fellow-Ulsterman, General Sir John Dill, as Chief of the Imperial General
Staff. He took over that office at a black moment, when the Japanese were
in the full flood of victory and Singapore already appeared doomed to
fall. In some quarters regret was expressed that he should have given
up his command, since he was considered to be of all British soldiers
of his generation the most likely to shine in the field. But as the war
developed it is certain that his services could not have been more
valuable in any capacity than they were at the War Office from now to the
end of hostilities and during the period of the immediate aftermath. He
established the best possible relations with the Americans and exercised
a strong influence upon the future course of allied strategy, especially
before the military expansion of the United States had reached its greatest height and the American commanders had acquired experience.

After that the Americans were naturally less inclined to accept advice
as a matter of course from any foreigner, however experienced and able,
but they still paid great respect to his views, knowing that these always
had a firm basis. It has been suggested that he was inclined to overrate
the progress made by the gun in the unending duel with the tank and to

consider that the opportunities of the latter would henceforth prove to be much more limited against a first-class enemy than proved to be the case in the invasion of north-west Europe. If so, he was not alone in this mistake. It is certain, however, that both on the Chiefs of Staffs Committee and in his relations with commanders-in-chief or allied supreme commanders in the field his personality, strategic insight, and knowledge were elements of strength.

He worked very long hours without showing undue fatigue. He also travelled immense distances and as the war progressed was more and more often absent from London, knowing that the affairs of Whitehall and the War Office itself could safely be left for considerable periods in the hands of the Vice-Chief, Lieutenant-General Nye. He liked to obtain his information and 'briefing' from the same small group of men, so that though he was the dominant personality in the War Office, he was hardly known by sight to the majority of its inmates and there were people on the same floor who never caught sight of him for months on end; but those who served him had no reason to complain of any lack of gratitude or regard. The immense burden that fell on Brooke's shoulders, and the skill and determination with which he shouldered it, are convincingly described in Sir Arthur Bryant's *The Turn of the Tide*, which is based on Brooke's war diaries. This book created a considerable stir when it was published in 1957, chiefly because it portrayed the irritations as well as the glories that fell to those who worked under Sir Winston Churchill in the direction of the war – although Lord Alanbrooke made it clear in his foreword to the book that any irritations or impatience at the defects that arose out of Sir Winston's very greatness were insignificant when set against the magnitude of his achievement.

The book shows how Brooke gradually developed his own technique for dealing with the Prime Minister by steady argument from facts to prevent Britain's strategy from outrunning her resources. In his diary Brooke records his disappointment in August, 1943, when the Prime Minister handed over to the Americans, during the Quebec conference, the appointment of Supreme Commander for the invasion of Europe. Brooke had earlier voluntarily given up the chance of taking over the North African Command before El Alamein because he thought he could serve a more useful purpose by remaining with the Prime Minister, and he had been promised the Supreme Commander's appointment by Churchill. It was, he records, 'a crushing blow' and it was delivered without sympathy or regrets. But Brooke survived it to record his final judgment on Churchill: 'He is quite the most difficult man to work with that I have ever struck, but I would not have missed the chance of working with him for anything on earth.'

CRITICAL COMMENTS

Two years later a sequel was published, *Triumph in the West*, once again written by Sir Arthur Bryant and based on Alanbrooke's diaries. As well as chronicling, as its title indicates, the victories of the allied forces, it provoked renewed controversy by critical comments on American strategic thinking and particularly on General Eisenhower's technical military capacities as a commander. Brooke was advanced to G.C.B. in 1942, in which year he also became A.D.C. General to the King. He was created a field marshal on January 1, 1944. In 1945 he was created Baron Alanbrooke, of Brookeborough, County Fermanagh, in the peerage of the United Kingdom and later advanced to a viscounty. He was awarded the Order of Merit and made K.G. in 1946. He also received a number of the highest foreign decorations, and received honorary degrees from many British universities. He was appointed Colonel Commandant R.A. (1939–1957), R.H.A. (1940–1957), Glider Pilot Regiment (1942–1951) and H.A.C. (1946–1954). He left the War Office in the summer of 1946 after the most memorable tenure of the appointment of C.I.G.S. in the history of that office.

After retirement from the Army he continued to lead an active life, assuming many directorships in the City and holding a number of public offices. He was Master Gunner, St. James's Park from 1946 to 1956; Constable of the Tower of London from 1950 to 1955; and H.M. Lieutenant for the County of London from 1950 to 1957. At the Coronation in 1953 he was Commander of the Parade and Lord High Constable of England in the Abbey ceremonies. In 1949 he became Chancellor of Queen's University, Belfast. Alanbrooke was also a former president of the Zoological Society of London, holding office from 1951 to 1954. He was made G.C.V.O. in 1953.

Coming from a family devoted to sport, Lord Alanbrooke was a keen shot and fisherman. Later in life he took to bird-watching, an interest which he pursued in his scanty leisure all through the war and in which he found welcome refreshment of mind. He was a remarkably good and amusing conversationalist, and when he relaxed no respecter of persons or indeed of reputations.

He married first, in 1914, Jane Mary, elder daughter of Colonel John Richardson, Rossfad, Ballinamallard, County Fermanagh. She was killed in a motor accident in 1925. In 1929 he married Benita, widow of Sir

Thomas Lees, second baronet, eldest daughter of Sir Harold Pelly, fourth baronet. There were one son and one daughter of each marriage. His elder son, the Hon. Thomas Brooke, now succeeds to the peerage.

Alanbrooke was unusual for a man of superior intelligence in recognizing the intellectual shortcomings of less gifted men, rather than just dismissing them as lazy or plain fools. He showed great patience in explaining what was required of them, but was ruthless in moving those in positions beyond their capabilities. He showed compassion, however, in letting them down as lightly as possible.

His belief that artillery would eventually triumph over the tank, held by other senior artillery officers, was born of experience in the First World War when tanks were slow and vulnerable to accurate gunfire. The success of fast and well-armoured vehicles moving in open order, as first demonstrated by the Germans in Poland, the Fall of France and the Western Desert disposed of the contention.

His career was extraordinary for the little time he spent on regimental service, almost always being a staff officer or at a staff college as a student or an instructor until commanding an infantry brigade. Despite this apparent handicap, such was his reputation for competence, he was never criticised for being 'just a staff wallah'. His *War Diaries 1939–1945* demonstrated not only his relentless schedule of travel in the war years but the manner in which he was able to concentrate his mind on an astonishing variety of topics in the course of one morning, afternoon or evening without trace of blunted perception.

AUCHINLECK

Architect of a defensive strategy that led to
victory in the desert

25 MARCH 1981

FIELD-MARSHAL SIR CLAUDE AUCHINLECK, GCB, GCIE, CSI, DSO, OBE, who died on March 23 in Marrakesh, was one of the most striking and attractive figures among modern British soldiers. He was 96.

His force of personality, high-mindedness and charm were acknowledged by all who met him. During politically troubled times in India he was liked and trusted by Indian leaders who had little that was good to say of most of the other Britons with whom they came in contact. As Commander-in-Chief in India in critical years his influence was strong, beneficent and popular, and he will be remembered as one of the ablest who ever held that honourable post. In the final phase of British control in India he suffered bitter disappointment and lost some of his vast prestige, but this should not be allowed to dim a great record.

As a commander in the field he achieved a most meritorious victory in Africa against a hostile army far better equipped than his own. In a subsequent stage of the campaign he had to endure a crushing defeat. Yet after that defeat he saved Egypt from being overrun and held up an opponent in full course for Alexandria and the Nile Delta.

Indeed he laid the basis from which Britain's eventual strategic victory was achieved. However, his political master at the time failed to perceive this, and responding more to fashionable currents than military analysis, decided to change the command in North Africa. Auchinleck was sacked, and spent the best part of a year kicking his heels in the hills of India before he was allowed to return to the Indian task he understood so thoroughly.

He was a fine and accomplished soldier and a fine spirit, a great general and an idealist. Auchinleck's refusal to engage in the battle of the generals' memoirs while many others succumbed (and did not always do great service to their reputations) was very much in character. However in December, 1967, he presented 20 folders of his personal papers, covering the period 1939–47, to Manchester University library where they were to be made freely available to students of military history.

Claude John Eyre Auchinleck, who came of an old Scots family established in Ulster, was born on June 21, 1884, the son of Colonel John Claude Auchinleck, RHA. He was educated at Wellington and Sandhurst and was posted in 1904 to the 62nd Punjabis, later the 1/1st Punjab Regiment. Having got his captaincy in 1912, he went with his regiment to Egypt on the outbreak of the 1914–18 War. He served at Aden in 1915 and in Mesopotamia from 1916 to the end of the war. He saw the heavy fighting of Aylmer's successive attempts to relieve Kut-el-Amara. He was also present at the Battle of Kut in January, 1917, and the advance to Baghdad. In September of that year he became brigade major of 52 Brigade and was promoted major. He was appointed GSO 2 after the Turkish Armistice so that his promotion on the staff ladder was slow by comparison with that of several of his contemporaries; Dill, for example, one year older, was at that time chief General Staff officer of an army corps. Auchinleck had, however, been awarded the DSO in 1917, was thrice mentioned in dispatches, and created OBE in 1919. His career already appeared promising.

He was an early student at the Imperial Defence College in 1927. In February, 1929, after promotion to lieutenant-colonel, he assumed command of his regiment. In 1933 he took over command of the Peshawar Brigade and immediately distinguished himself in the operations against the Upper Mohmands, for which he was credited CB and again mentioned. Mountain warfare is of all forms that demanding most insistently the professional competence which can be learnt, and the most brilliant man finds himself in difficulties without it. Auchinleck both knew the ropes and had a flair for war. In the further Mohmand operations of 1935 he was mentioned once more and made CSI. In 1935 he was promoted major-general and next year became Deputy Chief of the General Staff at headquarters (India).

At the time of the allied intervention in Norway in 1940 Auchinleck was in England and was placed in command of the forces in the Narvik area, though not until after the original landing. Narvik was duly recovered from the enemy and his forces were pushed back until they were on the point of crossing the Swedish frontier, which would have involved their internment. However, the calls of the western front, where the German offensive had been launched, necessitated withdrawal from northern Norway. Auchinleck had done his work well, but it was a disappointing start.

Shortly after his return he was entrusted with the Southern Command in England, but in January, 1941, he became Commander-in-Chief in India. Before the end of 1940 he had been promoted first to the rank of Lieutenant-General, then to that of General, within the year, and had been created a GCIE. The appointment, for which he was eminently fitted, did not last more than six months. On July 2, 1941, it was announced that he had been appointed GOC-in-C Middle East in succession to Sir Archibald Wavell, who took over Auchinleck's post in India.

The record of Auchinleck's command in Egypt would be virtually the history of a whole phase of the war. Two secondary offensives carried out by Wavell had been sharply checked soon before the change in command took place, and his successor refused to be hurried into another. He had also considerable responsibilities outside the theatre, including the winding-up of the campaign in East Africa. On November 18 began the British advance round the southern flank of the Axis force's position on the Italian frontier. There followed a long and extraordinarily confused battle in which, after initial successes, the signs at one moment pointed to a defeat. By sheer grit and pertinacity the Commonwealth forces of the Eighth Army fought down their better-armed foe and compelled him to retreat into Cyrenaica, leaving some 20,000 prisoners; with masses of material and raising the siege of Tobruk. It was a handsome victory and remained so on balance even after Rommel, having received reinforcements, pushed the Eighth Army out of Benghazi and back to a position known as the Gazala Line with right flank on the sea some 35 miles west of Tobruk. The influence of Auchinleck upon the battle had been great, perhaps decisive, and he had taken the drastic step of changing his Army commander in the midst of the fighting.

A renewed offensive, which was to have been undertaken mainly for the salvation of Malta, was forestalled in May 1942, by Rommel, whose armoured strength had vastly increased owing to our inability to interfere seriously with his shipping. Auchinleck had warned the Prime Minister that, if he suffered defeat in Cyrenaica, he would be unable to hold the prepared positions in rear for lack of armour and would have to fall back all the way to Alamein.

In the event the outcome of the battle at Gazala was a defeat for the British, the loss of Tobruk, its garrison and stores and a precipitate withdrawal to the line at El Alamein. But it would be hard to apportion too much blame for this to Auchinleck. His own appreciation of

Rommel's choices had been faultless, but in the battle which ensued his Eighth Army commander General Ritchie disregarded Auchinleck's advice to hold back his armour and concentrate it in a counter-attack against Rommel and instead dissipated his armour in penny packets, enabling Rommel to destroy it. Misunderstandings certainly then seemed to follow between Auchinleck and Ritchie. Auchinleck became increasingly perturbed at the deliberate nature of Ritchie's command and the lack of urgency with which he seemed to be viewing the battle and which only too soon resulted in the loss of Tobruk. Once again he had to come up from his headquarters in Cairo and assume direct command of the battle. Once this happened he held up the enemy on the new line at Alamein, blunted the last of his repeated attacks and made certain that Rommel would advance no further in Africa.

The authors of the third volume on the Mediterranean and the Middle East in the *History of the Second World War* series, vindicate Auchinleck's major decisions. They give him full credit for turning retreat into counter-attack in the fighting of July, 1942 and point out that the success of the offensive at El Alamein in October that year 'should not be allowed to overshadow the earlier achievements of those who made it possible.'

In June, 1943, Auchinleck succeeded Wavell who had formerly succeeded him, as Commander-in-Chief in India. He was not surprised by his supersession, which he had in fact suggested, but he was hurt by the brusque attitude of the Prime Minister, who carried it out on the spot. Direct responsibility for the conduct of operations against the Japanese was withdrawn from him but he bore the heaviest weight since India had to provide bases, troops, and supplies for the campaign in Burma. Recruitment, training, administration, relations with Chinese and American forces fell to him, together with a great deal of semi-political work, in which he excelled.

His prestige in India, much enhanced by his earlier brief spell as Commander-in-Chief and untouched by his ill fortune in North Africa, proved invaluable in the great expansion of the Indian Army and of war industry in India, which occurred during the latter part of the war. He gave the Supreme Commander, South-East Asia, able and ungrudging support. He was created G.C.B. in 1945 and promoted to the rank of Field Marshal in 1946, and both these high honours were earned by splendid service.

The last phase in India was less happy. His one concern was now the future of the Indian Army, of the war record of which he was intensely proud. The partition of India into two dominions led to the splitting; of the Army, in itself a crippling blow to its efficiency and made still worse by the virtual civil war which broke out in Punjab. Whether wisely or not, Auchinleck determined to stay on, in his new appointment as 'Supreme Commander' to reconstitute the forces of the two dominions; but in November, 1947, it was announced in unusually blunt terms that the task had been made impossible by the absence of a spirit of good will and cooperation between them. Despite grave differences with political leaders, he left, after 44 years' service, to the deep regret of many Indian friends and above all of the Indian soldiers. In a lecture in London he revealed that his grievances were against India, not Pakistan, from which he had obtained a large measure of support. He had been the most popular of all Indian Commanders-in-Chief.

After his retirement he lived an active and busy life, constantly travelling by air between this country and India., where he had impor-tant, and in general, successful business interests. He eventually retired to live in Morocco.

To his friends he was always the best of company over the dinner table, amusing, inspiring and critical, though never cruel or self-pitying. He was a very fine character and a very attractive one.

Auchinleck married in 1921 Jessie, daughter of Alexander Stewart of Innerhadden, Kinloch-Rannoch, Perthshire, but obtained a divorce in 1943. There were no children of the marriage.

A calm and imposing crag of a man, Auchinleck generated confidence in his subordinates by his very presence. He had impressed Churchill by his preparation of Southern Command in England to resist the threatened German invasion in the autumn of 1940 and again when, as C-in-C India, he despatched a force to crush the pro-Axis Rashid Ali rebellion in Iraq, from where Britain bought much of her oil. It was therefore ironic that he should have been replaced in command of the Middle East for lack of progress against Rommel shortly after going forward to take personal command of the 8th Army and stopping the Africa Corps at a point when Rommel believed the Nile Delta was within his grasp.

He was criticised for poor judgement when choosing his subordinates, which was justified in his appointment of Ritchie to command the 8th Army in November 1941 who was insufficiently experienced at that stage of the war. More controversial, was his employment of Major-General Eric 'Chink' Dorman-Smith as his chief of staff 'in the field' during the desert fighting in the summer of 1942. In fact, ideas Dorman-Smith put forward for the defensive battle at 'First Alamein', in early July 1942, played a significant part in repelling Rommel with severe losses in his armour. A man of quick mind but little tact, Dorman-Smith made enemies without trying but Auchinleck had faith in his tactical ideas.

Auchinleck's greatest contribution to the Commonwealth war effort was delivered following his return to India as Commander-in-Chief in June 1943. The Japanese threat on India's north-east frontier did nothing to calm the outbreak of nationalist – nor to say anti-British – sentiment of the 'Quit India' campaign and inter-factional tensions always underlying the political scene of the sub-continent. His sure grasp of the religious antagonisms and prejudice, together with the political ambitions of the Indian political leaders helped to maintain sufficient control to see through the reforms and reorganisation of the Indian Army required for the provision of fighting troops for the Burma campaign.

He was deeply distressed by the horrific loss of life in the rioting and massacres that followed Partition of India in 1947, while he was still C-in-C but unable to intervene on a sufficient scale to prevent the slaughter. It is believed that he declined the peerage granted to all field marshals who had taken part in the war as an indication of his disapproval of the haste with which Partition was implemented.

CUNNINGHAM

The greatest Royal Navy commander of the Second World War

13 JUNE 1963

ADMIRAL OF THE FLEET Viscount Cunningham of Hyndhope, GCB, OM, DSO, the outstanding leader of the Second World War, died in London yesterday at the age of 80, as reported on another page. In the early part of the war he held major command at sea as Commander-in-Chief of the Mediterranean Fleet and subsequently of the Anglo-American expedition to North Africa. Later, as First Sea Lord from 1943 to 1946, he shared responsibility for the central direction of the war.

Cunningham was an officer whose name, until he reached the highest ranks of the Navy, was hardly known outside it. Though his merits and abilities fully justified his selection for the high posts he held, actually he owed his tenure of them to a large extent to luck. After his promotion to Vice-Admiral in 1936 he was unemployed for a year, and in view of the state of the flag lists at that time he himself hardly expected to hold more than perhaps one more minor command before concluding his career by retirement. Within three years, however, owing to unexpected retirements or deaths of flag officers senior to him, he found himself, as Commander-in-Chief of the Mediterranean Fleet, holding one of the two great sea commands, with the acting rank of Admiral and well in the succession for promotion to Admiral of the Fleet. He held the Mediterranean Command at the outbreak of war in 1939 and few could have been more suitable for it. Essentially a man of action rather than an administrator, it was the general feeling in the Mediterranean Fleet that their Commander-in-Chief was the man to seize every opportunity that might present itself of conducting the war with vigour; and so indeed it proved when, in 1940, Italy joined our enemies. Faced with a pronounced material superiority, he himself remarked that a vigorous offensive was the only possible policy.

It was fortunate that the command of the Mediterranean Fleet in that dark hour should be held by one who every officer and man under him could feel was the right man in the right place. Under his inspiring leadership, complete ascendancy over the Italian Fleet was quickly established, and maintained even when the loss of both north and south coasts of the Eastern Basin enabled strong land-based air forces to dominate the narrow seas. After an interlude in Washington, Cunningham returned to the Mediterranean command in 1942 as Allied Naval Commander-in-Chief, when the Anglo-American recovery of North Africa redeemed the balance once more. The next year he had the satisfaction of receiving the surrender of the Italian Fleet; and when Sir Dudley Pound died in harness in 1943, there was by common consent but one officer to succeed him as First Sea Lord. A man of florid and smiling countenance, with the blue eyes of the born sailor and the genial manner of one whose naval career had been passed chiefly in small ships, Cunningham was never one to insist on rigid formalities or precedents, and though he would excuse no failure in courage or seamanship, he would ever turn a blind eye to faults arising from dash or excess of zeal.

TORPEDO BOATS

Andrew Browne Cunningham was the son of Professor D J Cunningham, of Dublin and Edinburgh, and brother of General Sir Alan Cunningham. He was born on January 7, 1883 and educated first at Edinburgh Academy and later at Mr Foster's School at Stubbington. He passed into the *Britannia* as a naval cadet in January 1897.

His first command, which he held from May 1908 to January 1910 was torpedo boat No14 in the Home Fleet, one of the first oil-burning ships in the Navy, known by those serving in them as the 'oily wads'. They were small and fast, but handy and seaworthy craft, carrying only one warrant officer besides the lieutenant in command. There could be no better training for a young officer in seamanship, self-reliance and initiative than such a command; it was hard work, but it was a much sought after job. From *T.B.14* Cunningham graduated to a bigger ship, taking command of the destroyer *Vulture* in reserve for a year until, in January, 1911, he achieved the aim of every young destroyer officer of the day, a command in the 'running flotilla', the destroyer *Scorpion*, of the 1st Flotilla, Home Fleet. That command he held for the very unusually long period of seven years. In 1912, on the rearrangement of the flotilla consequent on the delivery of new ships, she was transferred to the 3rd Flotilla, Home Fleet. The next year she was transferred to the 5th Flotilla, then a unit of the Mediterranean Fleet and Cunningham was still in command of her at the outbreak of war.

In the history of the Dardanelles campaign, the name of the *Scorpion* is constantly occurring – she was ever in the forefront. On October 30, 1914, she and the *Wolverine* opened the campaign against Turkey by running into the Gulf of Smyrna and sinking a Turkish minelayer which was sitting alongside the pier at Vouriah. On March 4, 1915, she was part of the force supporting the landing on the south side of the straights, and it is on record that she ran right into the mouth of the river Mendere and silenced a battery which was holding up the advance of the Marines ashore. Time and again the *Scorpion* was in action, supporting the flank of the Army with her fire, assisting in the landing or evacuation of troops. On June 30, 1915, Cunningham was promoted to commander, remaining in command of the *Scorpion*, and on March 3, 1916, he was awarded the D S O for his services off the peninsula.

In February 1918 he transferred to the command of the *Ophelia* in the Dover Patrol, coming again under the command of Sir Roger Keyes who had been Chief of Staff at the Dardanelles and he transferred a month later to the *Termagant*. In her he took part in numerous engagements including the Zeebrugge expedition and after the Armistice he was awarded a Bar to his D S O for his services. In February 1919 he transferred to the *Seafire*, of the 5th Destroyer Flotilla in which he again saw active service in the operations in the Baltic under the command of Rear Admiral Sir Walter Cowan, commanding the 1st Light Cruiser Squadron; for this, in the next year, he was awarded a second bar to his D S O. He was promoted to Captain at the end of 1919 and on the conclusion of the Baltic operations returned to Rosyth with his flotilla.

In September 1920 he was put in charge of Sub-Commission 'C' of the Naval Inter-Allied Commission of Control, and in that capacity he supervised the demolition of the fortifications of Heligoland – an appointment in which his prolonged contact with German officers and officials gave him a knowledge of the people and language which was of great value to him in later years when he came to occupy a high position in the Admiralty. In 1922, he returned once more to destroyer service, becoming Captain (D) of the 6th Flotilla in reserve, transferring later to the command of the 1st Flotilla in the Home Fleet with his pendant in the *Wallace*, flotilla leader. In 1924 he went ashore, but continued his connexion with the destroyer flotillas as he was Captain-in-Charge of the destroyer base at Port Edgar, Firth of Forth, for a year and a half. Thence he returned to sea service as Flag Captain to Sir Walter Cowan, Commander-in-Chief of the America and West Indies Station, first in the *Calcutta* and later in the *Despatch* cruisers, for more than two years in all. In 1929 he was selected for a course at the Imperial Defence College, on the conclusion of which he took command of the battleship *Rodney*, one of the most sought-after of captain's commands. In accordance with the practice prevailing at that time he held it only for a year, and after a few months unemployed he became Commodore of the Naval Barracks at Chatham, a command which he continued to hold for four months after his promotion to flag rank in September, 1932.

REMOTE PROSPECT

In January, 1934, he was made CB and took command of the destroyer flotillas of the Mediterranean Fleet – Rear-Admiral (D) with his flag in the *Coventry* – which he held throughout the period of the Italo-Abyssinian War until March, 1936. Three months later he was promoted to Vice-Admiral, and the prospects of his further employment, except perhaps in a shore command at home, seemed remote. A year later, however, he was suddenly appointed Second-in-Command of the Mediterranean Fleet and Vice-Admiral Commanding Battle Cruiser Squadron, temporarily, in the vacancy caused by the illness of Vice-Admiral Sir Geoffrey Blake, and on that officer being invalided Cunningham's appointment was made permanent. He held it until August, 1938, and three months later was appointed Deputy Chief of the Naval Staff at the Admiralty – a post which it was generally expected would have gone to Sir Geoffrey Blake but for his enforced retirement – under Admiral Sir Roger Backhouse, who had just become First Sea Lord and Chief of the Naval Staff. In that position great responsibility was thrown on him when illness in turn incapacitated Sir Roger Backhouse early in 1939, in the middle of the international tension, which eventually developed into war. For some six months Cunningham acted as substitute for his chief on the Committee of Imperial Defence and at the Admiralty Board; and when it was finally decided that Admiral Sir Dudley Pound should succeed Sir Roger Backhouse. Cunningham, who had been promoted KCB at the beginning of the year, replaced him as Commander-in-Chief, Mediterranean, in June 1939, as an acting Admiral, to which rank he was promoted in January 1941.

On the outbreak of war in September, 1939, as Italy remained 'non-belligerent' the Mediterranean seemed liable to prove a backwater, and practically all the Mediterranean Fleet was withdrawn for service in other seas. It was brought up to strength the following year, however, when it became clear that Mussolini was bent on war, only to be left in marked inferiority by the defection of its French contingent; on that melancholy occasion, Cunningham showed himself a skilled diplomatist as well as a war leader, and was able to secure the effective neutralisation of Admiral Godefroi's squadron – which had been part of the Allied Fleet under his command – without rancour or bloodshed. Within a few weeks of Mussolini's declaration of war, Cunningham, in the Battle of Calabria, had chased a superior Italian Fleet back into the shelter of its bases; a few months later the Fleet Air Arm attack on Taranto put half the Italian Navy out of action; and in March 1941, in the brief night action known as the Battle of Cape Matapan, three of the largest Italian cruisers were destroyed in a few minutes. The arrival of the Luftwaffe on the shores of the Mediterranean at the end of 1941, and the loss of Cyrenaica, Greece and Crete made it impossible for the British Fleet, lacking support in the air, to operate freely or to keep the sea route fully open. When Cunningham handed over the Mediterranean Command to Sir Henry Harwood in May, 1942, to go to Washington as the British representative with the Joint Chiefs of Staff, there was little left for it to do within the Mediterranean itself until the recovery of North Africa again gave it sea room.

ALLIED COMMAND

Cunningham was away no more than six months. When the Anglo-American descent on French North Africa in 'Operation Torch' of November, 1942, began the expulsion of the Axis from Africa, he returned there as Allied Naval Commander-in-Chief under General Eisenhower as Supreme Commander of the invading forces. Two months later he again took over, as Commander-in-Chief of the whole Mediterranean Fleet, and was promoted Admiral of the Fleet. He had the satisfaction of completely regaining control of the Mediterranean, and, in September, 1943, of receiving the surrender of the whole Italian Fleet. The death of the First Sea Lord, Admiral of the Fleet Sir Dudley Pound, in October brought him back to the Admiralty in his place. He was at the head of affairs for the rest of the war.

Cunningham, who retired in 1946, was created GCB while holding the Mediterranean command in 1942, and baronet on relinquishing it. On the break-up of the coalition government in 1945, he, together with his brother Chiefs of Staff, Field Marshal Sir Alan Brooke and Marshal of the RAF Sir Charles Portal, was created a baron, taking the title of Lord Cunningham of Hyndhope, which he retained on promotion to a viscountcy in the New Year Honours of 1946. In the Birthday Honours of that year he was made OM.

In 1950 and again in 1952 he was Lord High Commissioner to the

General Assembly of the Church of Scotland. His memoirs, *A Sailor's Odyssey*, were published in 1951.

His marriage to Nona Christine, daughter of Horace Byatt, of Midhurst, Sussex, took place in 1929.

During the Boer War, having wangled his way to the front, Cunningham, aged sixteen, came under fire for the first time when manning the guns of the Naval Brigade before Pretoria.

Cunningham's 'diplomacy' in neutralising French naval forces in July 1940 was achieved by appealing to his sailors over the head of Admiral Godfroy and was made easier by the fact that those French ships were in Alexandria under the guns of the British. Diplomacy failed at Oran, resulting in the necessary but always-to-be-regretted British bombardment of the French ships in harbour, causing 1,147 French dead.

While the air attack on Taranto sank or disabled three Italian battleships – not 'half the Italian Navy' – and the description of Matapan is inaccurate, the premier tests of Cunningham's leadership were the continuous need to fight convoys through to Malta – 'the Verdun of the Mediterranean campaign' as the historian Corelli Barnet has described it – and the desperate actions to prevent German forces reaching Crete by sea and the subsequent evacuation. For Cunningham, Crete was 'a period of great tension and anxiety such as I have never experienced before or since' prompting his famous remark that in the context of grave naval losses versus the 16.000 British and Imperial troops that were rescued, 'it only took two or three years to replace a ship but three centuries to create a tradition'.

Cunningham's 'blue eye of the born sailor' was more often described as 'steely blue' and there are innumerable accounts of his often ferocious disciplinary attitudes. But he also had a rare humanity; when Commander-in-Chief, he told his new flag lieutenant, (later Captain) Hugh Lee, 'I shall be extremely rude to you at least once a day, but don't mind that, it's part of the job'.

HORTON

An Architect of victory in the Battle of the Atlantic

9 AUGUST, 1951

ADMIRAL SIR MAX HORTON was first and foremost a fighting man and a leader of fighting men. His unerring judgement, inflexible determination to see through that which he had started, be the end bitter or sweet, and his indomitable courage marked him for high command from his earliest service. His absolute sense of justice and readiness to praise and reward, criticize or punish, as occasion demanded, won him the respect, though not perhaps the affection, of all. His natural gift for grasping detail was further developed by his service in submarines. There can have been few flag officers who were, and who were acknowledged to be, such complete masters of their particular branch of the service.

His exploits in the 1914–18 war have been dealt with elsewhere, but it is not generally known that he proposed the one-man submarine, presenting the design in detail and volunteering to be the first to operate it in action. The idea was turned down at the time but became a reality in the last war. In the years between the wars Max Horton was one who never lost sight of the grim possibilities of the future, and the units with which he was associated or commanded were invariably brought up to and maintained at the highest pitch of efficiency. As Flag Officer Reserve Fleet, in 1937 he strove to have his ships with their scanty crews ready for the moment when they would be required. Due to the pressure he brought to bear and the reliance placed on his judgement the ships were manned and worked up long before mobilization had to be ordered, and the day that war was declared saw them at sea as part of the main Fleet.

His first appointment in the war was that of Vice-Admiral, Northern Patrol. There will be many even then elderly officers and men recalled to serve who will remember him in those days, visiting them at any hour of the day or night when they returned to Kirkwall in their hastily converted armed merchant cruisers, cheering them and inspiring them in their dangerous duty. Early in 1940 he was called back to the submarine service as Flag Officer, Submarines, which appointment he held for nearly three years. His work, in that branch of the service which was always nearest to his heart, can best be summarized in the words of a message sent to him by the Admiralty when he relinquished his command: 'The outstanding successes achieved by the British submarines both in Home and Mediterranean waters bear striking witness of the morale of the submarine service and to the efficiency of the training and skilful planning of operations carried out under your supervision. The prestige of the submarine service has never stood higher than it does at this moment and for this their lordships feel you are entitled to feel a very just satisfaction.'

In November, 1942, Admiral Horton was appointed Commander-in-Chief, Western Approaches. Here was the appointment for which the whole of his experience and personality had fitted him, here was scope for his administrative genius, his gift of leadership, and his knowledge of his own and the enemy's weapons. He united the many and varied units at his disposal into a weapon with which to defeat the enemy and, developing the intimate cooperation with Coastal Command which had been initiated by his predecessor, he attacked the enemy from below, on, and above the surface till they were ultimately forced to surrender. In a letter to him when the Command was dissolved in 1945 the Admiralty said: 'The Command has participated in virtually every form of Naval activity and in most on a large scale. In the campaign against the U-boats and in trade protection it has been pre-eminent, and its record in this vital sphere will form one of the enduring chapters of naval history of the kingdom. Never has the existence of the nation encountered so grievous a maritime threat as the German attack on its shipping during the years 1939–45, and with the triumph over that threat the name of Western Approaches Command will always be prominently associated. Their lordships desire me to convey to you their appreciation of the service which you have rendered as the leader and organizer of the Western Approaches Command during the period of its greatest activity and fullest development.' Max Horton never spared himself or made excuses. He judged all men, high and low, by the standard by which he judged himself: 'Have I done my best ? 'Some may remember his sternness, many will remember his winning smile of appreciation, none will forget his skill and courage. His friendship was something to be proud of; his company something to be enjoyed. He has left us now, but left us the happier for having known him.

Horton commanded submarines from 1905 to 1920; his exploits during the First World War were remarkable and included penetrating Heligoland harbour to sink a cruiser (the first warship ever to be sunk by a British submarine) and protracted operations in the Baltic. For these he was awarded the DSO and two bars, the Légion d'Honneur and three Russian medals.

As C-in-C Western Approaches from November 1942 he unquestionably inherited a thorough-going concern from Admiral Sir Percy Noble, bringing to the task a new energy and drive. He was the right man to pit against Dönitz at the point when the Battle of the Atlantic was reaching a climax. U-boat production was accelerating and their 'wolf pack' tactics were a serious threat. On the Allied side, despite Air Chief Marshal 'Bomber' Harris' mistaken policy, very long range aircraft were at last becoming available to fill the mid-ocean 'air gap' and Enigma signals intelligence was increasingly effective.

Profiting from the increase in available escorts, Horton instituted 'support groups' that often saved the day for embattled convoys. Under his command, in a campaign described by Churchill as one of 'science and stratagem', war-gaming, tactical innovation and intensive training were combined with the intelligent integration of new weapons and sensors finally to defeat the U-boat.

* * *

DÖNITZ

Architect of German wartime U-boat strategy

27 DECEMBER 1980

GRAND ADMIRAL KARL DÖNITZ, the former Commander in Chief of the German Navy and the man whom Hitler nominated as his successor, died in Auhmühle, West Germany, on December 24. He was 89. For a short period after the death of Hitler he had served as President of the Third Reich and C-in-C of its armed forces

Karl Dönitz personified the gravest threat to Britain of all Hitler's forces during the Second World War. As the brilliant and ruthless commander of the U-boats he was responsible for the direction of the Battle of the Atlantic, which could well have had a different outcome, had his advice been paid greater heed by Adolf Hitler. Dönitz was one of the most experienced and distinguished of the former U-boat commanders available to the German Navy, in 1935, when, as a result of the London Naval Agreement, it became possible for Germany to build a fleet of submarines. Accordingly, he was placed in charge of the development of the new arm. The treaty permitted Germany to build 70 U-boats, but despite the intense efforts of Dönitz initial progress was slow, and at the outbreak of the war, only 25 boats capable of employment in the Atlantic had been built.

The main difficulty with the U-boat construction plan was the shortage of materials. Göring, who had already fought the Army High Command on this question, was able to exploit his influence with Hitler to obtain priority for the Luftwaffe, over and above that which Germany's strategic situation warranted. None the less, by the end of the war, 1,168 U-boats had been built, and placed into service. However, the high loss rate, whereby 630 U-boats were sunk, prevented the Germans from attaining sufficient strength in the Atlantic completely to cut Britain's supply lines.

Dönitz was also responsible for the development of new tactics for the employment of submarines. German tactics in the First World War had not gone beyond the use of individual submarines. Dönitz set to work to develop some principles for the deployment of submarines in packs, with various submarines fulfilling different roles, such as surface reconnaissance, air reconnaissance, under-water attack, surface attack, stand-by and mutual support. He also was keenly aware of the advantages to be achieved by co-operation between submarines and aircraft, and the exercises carried out by the U-boat Command before the war stressed these new developments.

The high standards achieved by Dönitz's training methods, and the abilities of his subordinate commanders were dramatically illustrated by the daring raid on Scapa Flow. Dönitz himself had planned this operation against the very heart of the Royal Navy, and it was executed by U 47, under the command of Kapitanleutnant Prien. On October 14, 1939, the U 47, whose maximum under-water speed was seven knots, succeeded in negotiating the narrow entrance passage of Kirk Sound whose waters rushed and swirled between great rocks at speeds of up to

10 knots, *U 47* then sank the *Royal Oak*, and made its escape back to Kiel.

As the war advanced into 1941 and 1942, the U-boat menace became steadily worse. The enormous shipbuilding programme of the United States prevented the U-boats from gaining the upper hand, although for a few months the situation was extremely critical. In April, 1941, 640,000 tons of British shipping were sunk, while the British replacement rate was only of the order of 1m tons per annum. During this time Dönitz pressed Hitler repeatedly for higher priorities for the U-boat construction programme, but he was never given what he wanted until it was too late. In the meantime the combined resources of Allied might had been working to make the operation of submarines more dangerous and less fruitful. The use of aircraft and the convoy system kept Allied losses to a minimum, while German losses became ever greater. Dönitz attempted to counter these new threats by the introduction of devices such as Schnorkel, so that U-boats could charge their batteries without coming to the surface, where they were vulnerable to sudden attack. The development of better batteries enabled U-boats to remain submerged for as long as four days, creeping along at five knots. While the types I to XIV all had an underwater range of less than 100 nautical miles, the types XXI and XXIII could move 285 and 175 nautical miles without having to come to the surface. However, the Allied superiority eventually became such that with the loss of the French bases to the Germans, the operation of the U-boats became inordinately expensive in terms of the results which it achieved. Out of 39,000 men who served aboard the German submarines, 27,082 perished.

In January, 1943, Dönitz was selected by Hitler to replace Grand Admiral Raeder as Commander in Chief of the German Navy. Hitler and Raeder had reached impasse over the future of the capital ships still remaining to the fleet. Hitler wanted to scrap them, while Raeder thought them to be necessary to the maintenance of what German sea communications there still were. Perhaps Hitler thought that Dönitz would not be so well disposed towards capital ships as his predecessor who had spent most of his service above the waves. Dönitz asked for three weeks to consider the matter, and in his report he gave the same conclusions as Raeder had done. Hitler was prepared to accept this from Dönitz, and so he came to serve directly under the Führer.

Hitler developed a very high regard for Dönitz. While this is partly due to Dönitz's constant obedience to his wishes, it was also influenced by Hitler's total lack of experience in dealing with naval affairs, so that the Navy was left alone to a large extent and spared the tirades of abuse which the Air Force and, especially, the Army had to bear. Furthermore, the U-boat war had been a consistently greater success than any of Hitler's other military ventures. In these circumstances, Dönitz came to play a political role as the nominated successor to Hitler, after the latter had committed suicide. This appointment came to Dönitz as a complete surprise. The Army and the Air Force were both discredited in Hitler's eyes. Clearly the situation called for a military man, and so Dönitz was chosen. For 20 days he ruled the remnants of the Third Reich from Flensburg, until he was arrested by the Allied Control Commission on May 22, 1945.

He was then placed on trial at Nuremberg for his part in the 'conspiracy against the peace', and for his conduct of U-boat operations, particularly the unrestricted sea warfare which he introduced. He was found guilty, and sentenced to 10 years' imprisonment in Spandau jail. It is far from easy to reach a clear view of his case. His decisions that survivors were not to be rescued by U- boats were motivated by fear for the safety of the U-boats themselves. The case of the *Laconia* must not be forgotten in this regard. Here the *U 156* was bombed by an American aircraft while it was on the surface, in the process of rescuing 200 survivors, by towing their lifeboats to a rendezvous with ships of the Vichy French Navy. However, there were other incidents in which this outlook was used as an excuse for barbarous conduct on the part of individual German submarines, and Dönitz must bear some responsibility for this. He served his full sentence after the Nuremberg trials. He accepted this philosophically, and when asked if he felt any bitterness as a result, he would show the inquirer two volumes of letters, written as tributes to him on his release, by some hundreds of Allied statesmen and senior military officers. With such regard among those who had shared his problems from the other side of the hill he felt no rancour towards those who did not hold him in high regard. He was first and foremost a naval commander, educated in the spirit and tradition of patriotic duty and obedience to his superiors. Secondly, he was a Nationalist in his political sympathies. In times past, when coupled with a good government, this has been the ideal combination of views for a military man. When coupled with a bad government, however, the result, as so many German officers have learnt to their cost, is catastrophic. His fault was that he followed an outdated form of ideology in circumstances to which it was never meant to apply to its logical, and tragic conclusions.

Karl Donitz was born at Grünau, Berlin; on September 16, 1891. He entered the German Navy in 1910, and went to sea in the cruiser

Breslau. When the *Breslau* had been bottled up in the Dardanelles by the Royal Navy in 1914, he returned to Germany for U-boat training. He was given command of the coastal U-boat *UB68*, and operated in the Mediterranean in 1917 and 1918. On October 4, 1918, his U-boat was blown out of the water in the midst of an Allied convoy. The submarine had to be abandoned, and he was left swimming about while the convoy sailed on. Eventually a destroyer returned and rescued him and his crew. After a year of imprisonment he returned to Germany, and continued his naval career as commander of a torpedo boat, commander of a torpedo boat flotilla, Navigation Officer on board the Flagship of the Commander of the Baltic Sea Fleet, and as commander of the cruiser *Emden*, in which he made several long voyages to Africa and the Indian Ocean. In 1935 he was promoted from Kapitan to Kommodore, and made Commander of U-boats. He held this position until the end of the war, rising to the rank of Grand Admiral, after by-passing the rank of General Admiral, in January, 1943. He occupied both the post of Commander of U-boats and the Commander-in-Chief of the German Navy until the surrender. He was married and had two sons. His wife died shortly after his release from Spandau. Both sons were killed during the war.

While in the *Breslau*, Dönitz was awarded the Iron Cross First Class for an action against the Russians in the Black Sea. *UB68* was his third submarine command. While commanding *UB25* he was awarded the Knight's Cross of the Order of Hohenzollern for an attack inside Augusta harbour in Sicily.

Dönitz was never a member of the National Socialist party although he saw himself as a loyal member of the German state and supported Hitler without question throughout the war. Despite the perennial lack of U-boats properly to fulfil his strategic aim, he would never compromise the arduous and lengthy training programmes that he had instituted and for which he was noted, a price that showed itself well worth paying. His leadership is manifested by the extraordinary level of morale exhibited by his crews right to the end of the war, by which date 785 U-boats had been sunk from all causes.

At the Nuremberg trials, Fleet Admiral Chester W Nimitz, CinC of the US Pacific Fleet, furnished an affidavit in support of the practice of unrestricted submarine warfare, a practice that he himself had employed. This evidence is widely credited as a reason why Dönitz was only sentenced to ten years imprisonment. Both

Dönitz's sons were submariners. He also had a daughter who in 1937 married Günter Hessler, a very successful U-boat captain who survived the war.

* * *

ROMMEL

A masterly tactician and aggressive exploiter of success

16 OCTOBER 1944

FIELD-MARSHAL ERWIN ROMMEL, whose death was announced by the German wireless yesterday, was an able general, whose spell of success in Africa enabled German propaganda to build him up as a military figure second only to Hitler himself. This exaggerated reputation was exploded in the battle of El Alamein, but Rommel's conduct of the Axis retreat to Tunisia proved beyond doubt his professional competence. Ruthless and resourceful, Rommel had been connected with the Nazi Party since its inception, and was completely identified with its fortunes; his death will be as much a political as a military blow to the enemy.

Erwin Rommel was born in 1891 and was educated at Tübingen University. In the 1914–18 war his career was one of extraordinary distinction for a young and very junior officer. He started off as an ensign in the 124th Infantry Regiment, first came to notice for a brilliant exploit on the French front, and afterwards won the order 'Pour le Mérite' – for one of his rank the equivalent of the Victoria Cross – for his skill, leadership and personal bravery in Italy. After the war he taught at the Dresden Military Academy before joining the National-Socialist Party. He became a storm-troop leader, attached to Hitler's bodyguard and organized the campaign of terror in Coburg (in which Socialists and Communists were killed) which Hitler described in 'Mein Kampf' as the turning-point of his career.

GANGSTER METHODS

Rommel's qualities of leadership – and perhaps also his taste for the methods of a gangster in civil war – brought him the personal favour of Hitler. He took part in the occupation of Austria, the Sudetenland and Czechoslovakia. In the present war he served in the Polish campaign and in 1940 commanded a Panzer division in France. He received the Knight's Cross for his part in breaking the French front in the region of Maubeuge, and it is believed to have been his division which reached the sea at St. Valery-en-Caux and cut off the British 51st Division.

When Hitler realized that he would have to go to the support of his Italian allies in North Africa or see them driven right out of the continent, he entrusted Rommel with the organization of the Afrika Korps. This force was extremely well trained and equipped, and on being transported to Libya it won an instant success against the depleted and relatively ill-armed British forces. In April, 1941, General Wavell was forced to abandon Benghazi. Advancing with extreme rapidity, Rommel drove his opponent across the Egyptian frontier and laid siege to the isolated garrison which had been dropped off in Tobruk.

A long period of comparative lull followed. Rommel – the real commander-in-chief of the Axis forces, though he had a nominal Italian superior – was building up a strong force, but was always short of certain essential supplies. His attacks against Tobruk were fruitless, but he was contemplating one on a bigger scale when he was attacked on November 18, 1941, by the British Eighth Army. The long and extremely confused battle which followed went against Rommel, though the German armoured tactics were, at least to begin with, superior to the British, and the German armour was very much better in quality. By sheer persistence and pluck the British, in spite of almost catastrophic losses in tanks, wore down the enemy, or perhaps rather the enemy's commander. By the end of December, 1941, he had retreated headlong to Jedabia, leaving his forces on the frontier to be mopped up. In all he had lost 20,000 prisoners, but he had saved the personnel of his two crack armoured divisions, which was what he chiefly cared about. Having received some reinforcements in tanks. he succeeded in pushing the Eighth Army back to the line Gazala-Bir Hakeim, some 40 miles west of Tobruk.

BACK AT TOBRUK

This campaign had gone against Rommel on balance, but he made up for it in a resounding victory in May and June, 1942. Outflanking and rolling up the Eighth Army's position from the south, he drove it back in fierce fighting to the frontier, then suddenly turned upon Tobruk, left isolated once again, and carried it by storm. The British were unable to call a halt until they reached El Alamein, 80 miles west of Alexandria. They had lost 50,000 men and vast quantities of material, and were no longer sure of even being able to hold Egypt. Rommel had been aided by superior material, notably in tanks, but his tactics had been masterly. However, he made no headway in his attacks on the El Alamein line; in fact, the Eighth Army began to launch local counter-offensives.

So the stage was set for the final trial, one of the most vital in the war. Rommel's last attack, begun on August 31, failed after sharp fighting. And then, in the last week of October and the first week of November General Montgomery inflicted a heavy defeat upon the Axis forces. Rommel was in hospital in Germany when the offensive began, but hurried back to his post. He succeeded in extricating once more a large proportion of his best German forces, leaving the rest and the Italians to their fate. Though outmanoeuvred in the battle, he conducted the long retreat to Tunisia with skill. But his African career ended with another disaster. His last attack on the Eighth Army at Medenine in March. 1943; was a complete failure, and he then returned home, leaving not only the troops which he had led back across North Africa but also those which had been landed in Tunisia to meet their inevitable end.

His first European appointment after his return, on completing further hospital treatment, was apparently an inspectorship of the western coast defences. But before the allies landed in Normandy on June 6, 1944, he had been made commander of an army group defending the Low Countries and France north of the Biscay coast. He was wholly unable to prevent the landing, which took the Germans largely by surprise, but he made vigorous efforts to confine the allied holding by means of armoured divisions which he concentrated from all points. The Germans have announced that it was on July 17 that he sustained the injuries from which he has now died.

Rommel was undoubtedly a tactician of genius, but with some weaknesses. Restless. arrogant, and difficult to work with, neglectful of the administrative side of the forces which he commanded, he was too apt to repeat himself. But he brought to modern large-scale warfare the methods of bluff and ambush which had begun to appear unattainable in present-day conditions. This strange figure, master of tank warfare without knowing anything about a tank or even understanding the inside of a car, was in fact full of contradictions. Disliked by those with whom he came in contact, he yet exercised an amazing influence over the troops from whom he exacted so much. Brutal in speech and sometimes in action, he treated British wounded prisoners in Africa with consideration. Boundless in daring it would seem that his nerve was liable to break suddenly. He will be remembered as a brilliant though uncertain and uneven commander in the field rather than as a commander-in-chief.

Although there is some merit in the final assessment of Rommel in the last sentence of this obituary, it should be borne in mind that he never had opportunity to exercise authority as a commander-in-chief free of restraint by his superior in north-west Europe, Rundstedt, and of Hitler over control of the panzer divisions held in reserve to counter the threat – that never materialised – to the Pas de Calais. Published when the Allies had just suffered a serious setback at Arnhem in September 1944, effectively extending the war in Europe well into 1945, this assessment of Rommel's character and military performance in North Africa reflects obvious elements of British wartime positive reporting – not to say propaganda – so as not to allow morale either in the armed forces nor on the Home Front to suffer any damage.

Of all the German commanders of the Second World War, Rommel was the best known and most highly respected by the British Army and public. Known as 'The Desert Fox' for his tactical successes in Libya, news or even rumour of the arrival of his panzers out of the desert dust and haze was enough to send shivers of apprehension down the spines of those about to face them. It was his resilience in regrouping tank units after they had suffered losses and his attack at unexpected times and from unexpected directions that so often gained him the initiative, even over forces with overall greater strength than his. He concentrated his armour to deliver devastating and often decisive punches in battle, rather than spreading tanks piecemeal over the battlefield simply to support the infantry – never the critical arm in the open desert – as was the wasteful way of most British commanders.

To describe him as 'neglectful of the administrative side of the forces he commanded', ignores the fact that he was always obliged to fight in the desert on a logistic shoestring, because of the vulnerability of his lines of supply across the Mediterranean. Indeed, credit is due to him for the extent he refused to be confined by this limitation, relying on the German soldier's ability to improvise and utilize captured enemy resources, especially for the armoured exploitation of his breakthroughs in the desert.

Although his death was attributed by German radio broadcast to a relapse following recovery of his injuries sustained by air attack by an RAF fighter on his staff car on July 17, 1944, he had actually been persuaded by two German generals to take poison rather than face the consequences of investigation into his implication in the July 20, 1944 Hitler assassination attempt. After the war, it emerged that he had been approached by the plotters and had agreed it would be wise to remove Hitler and his immediate Nazi entourage and try to negotiate a separate peace with the Western Allies. No evidence was produced to implicate him in the actual assassination plot, but mention of his name was enough.

* * *

MONTGOMERY

Victor of El Alamein and a legend
in his own lifetime

25 MARCH 1976

FIELD-MARSHAL VISCOUNT MONTGOMERY of Alamein, KG, GCB, DSO, whose great victory in the Western Desert in 1942 made him famous throughout the world in the course of a few days, has died at the age of 88, as announced on another page. Later in the war he was British Commander-in-Chief in the final victory over Germany in North-west Europe in 1944 and 1945.

It has been said that Montgomery never lost a battle. In its most literal sense this judgement is valid, although there were two occasions, at Enfidaville in Tunisia and on the Sangro in Italy when offensives which he conducted were checked; and it is of course true that in the airborne landing at Arnhem he failed to crown with final success an otherwise well-conceived and skilfully conducted offensive. History will almost certainly judge Montgomery amongst the great British generals. Although there were notable deficiencies in his political and strategic armoury, his skill and judgment on the battlefield, together with his unique qualities of leadership were beyond question. His technical expertise and his capacity to inspire total confidence in his troops have been universally recognized. No one admired him more than the German soldiers and officers who were his enemies in battle.

After the campaign in the Western Desert he became a national figure. His stature grew throughout the Second World War and when it ended and he began to visit London from time to time from his post in Germany, crowds used to form in Whitehall and outside theatres in the hope of catching a glimpse of the great man. 'Monty' was one of the rare breed that become a legend in their own time. It is no exaggeration to say that the British, not always disposed to love their generals, took Montgomery to their hearts in the heady atmosphere of après-Alamein. Those who lived through the Second World War will recall that whereas up to the autumn of 1942 it had seemed to be a series of strategic withdrawals, if not outright disasters, now, at long last, there was a resounding, incontestable battle victory that all had yearned for.

Winston Churchill, who not infrequently sensed what ordinary people felt, judged the mood rightly in Volume IV of his book *The Second World War*: '... the Battle of Alamein will ever make a glorious page in British military annals. There is another reason why it will survive. It marked in fact the turning of "the Hinge of Fate". It may almost be said "Before Alamein we never had a victory. After Alamein we never had a defeat".'

An Ulsterman, Bernard Law Montgomery was born on November 17, 1887, a son of the Rev Henry Montgomery, who became Bishop of Tasmania in 1889. Montgomery's childhood holds the key to the complex and often abrasive character which he became in later life. The Montgomery family were worthy respectable stock, pillars of Victorian society, guardians of the high standards of unselfish devotion to public service in the Church and in the Empire. The personal philosophy of Montgomery's father is summed up in one of his remarks to his children 'You come of a family of gentlemen. You know that word does not signify mere outward refinement. It tells of a refined and noble mind to which anything dishonourable or mean or impure is abhorrent and unworthy.'

Montgomery's mother was Maud, third daughter of Dean Farrar, sometime Dean of Canterbury and author of *Eric, or Little by Little*. She married Henry Montgomery when she was 16 and she was a strict and often harsh disciplinarian. Bernard suffered most from her rigid routine and lack of demonstrative affection perhaps because his character was so similar to that of his mother. At a very early age his stubborn and inflexible character began to emerge, and clashes between his mother and himself were inevitable.

He began to seek compensation for his mother's lack of affection in the satisfaction of authority and leadership. Even as a child he showed a strong desire to be the leader and the winner at all games. It was only in his relationship with his father that Montgomery displayed the normal childish qualities of affection and love. Henry Montgomery was a remote and intensely spiritual man, and his turbulent son worshipped him almost as a saint; but fundamentally Montgomery's childhood was unhappy and emotionally deprived.

He was born at Kennington but he was only two years old when his father was consecrated Bishop of Tasmania. It was there that he spent the most formative years of his life. Bishop Montgomery's nature and the circumstances of his mission dictated that the head of the household and of all domestic arrangements was the mother. The regime was a fearsome one, sweets were forbidden, the children rose at dawn and began lessons at 7.30 in a schoolroom built outside the house.

It was therefore a strange complicated and unhappy child who returned to England in 1901, at the age of 13, when his father was appointed to the Society for the Propagation of the Gospel in London. The family went to live in a large house in Chiswick, and in January, 1902, Montgomery and his brother Donald entered St. Paul's School as day boys. Within three years Bernard Montgomery was Captain of Rugby and a member of the cricket XI and the swimming team. All his formidable qualities of concentration and determination were harnessed to the pursuit of athletic excellence – not for its own sake, but as an activity in which his intense desire for personal power could find expression. As an ordinary member of a team he was often a nuisance – argumentative, uncooperative, obstructive – as captain he was perfectly happy. His skill at games was not matched by his academic record. He was, indeed, described as backward for his age; and a 1905 report on his English sums up perceptively not only the schoolboy but the man he was to become: 'Tolerable; his essays are sensible, but he has no notion of style'.

Even in this field, however, his inflexible determination and unshakable self-confidence were not to be undermined by intellectual deficiency. He had chosen the Army class at school and intended to go to

Sandhurst. He was told by his masters that to have any serious chance of getting there he must give more time to work. He therefore got down to work and passed into Sandhurst halfway down the list (or as he would prefer it, halfway up) at the age of 19. At the Royal Military College his career was distinguished only by his athletic preoccupations and a taste for the kind of rough horseplay that was characteristic of the Sandhurst of those days. This combination almost ended in disgrace. As a notable games player he could always command a following among the more hearty and impressionable of his fellow cadets; and he became something of a leader of a clique who did as little work as they could get away with, and who filled their leisure time in beating up people whose views or personal appearance displeased them.

After an episode in which a cadet suffered serious injury Montgomery, who was a lance-corporal was reduced to the rank of gentleman cadet. This was the first serious reverse in Montgomery's military career and, as at St Paul's, the effect upon him was sobering and decisive. He began to work, and although his graduation from the college had been put back by six months, when he eventually passed out he was 36th out of 150 cadets – a creditable if not exactly brilliant performance. The young officer who was gazetted to The Royal Warwickshire Regiment in 1908 was a strange and not altogether attractive figure. He lacked polish and personal charm; he was irritatingly self-confident and greedy for only one thing in life – success and the power that brings with it.

BRAVERY IN THE FIRST WORLD WAR

Almost at once Montgomery was posted to the 1st Battalion of his regiment on the North West Frontier of India at Peshawar. Here he began to lose some of his rough edges. His obsessive desire to excel at sport led him to enter the local point-to-point, although he was an indifferent horseman. After falling off at the start Montgomery remounted and charged through the field like a demented Lord Chiltern. After winning the race he fell off again; but he had won, and the Army loves a winner. After two years of Frontier life in the course of which he discovered, without losing an invincible belief in his own superiority, how to live harmoniously in an officers' mess – the most claustrophobically gregarious institution in the world – he emerged as the embryonic general, a dedicated, industrious soldier, with resilience, a certain Jack Russell pose and an ability to accept life in the same spirit as the celebrated lady who decided to accept God – because on the whole it was more prudent to do so.

At the end of 1912 the 1st Royal Warwickshire Regiment returned to England and Montgomery began to take the first small steps in his advance to the military summit. He passed out top of the musketry course at Hythe and played hockey for the Army. Until 1914 his life was well ordered, predictable and dedicated. When the war came Montgomery fought with his regiment at the Marne and the Aisne: and at the first battle of Ypres, while leading his platoon in a bayonet charge he was seriously wounded and came near to death. For his bravery in this action he was awarded the Distinguished Service Order and promoted to the rank of captain. The DSO for a subaltern is a rare decoration, regarded by most soldiers as a 'near miss' for a Victoria Cross. This was another of the decisive moments in Montgomery's life. He had faced danger and death and conquered both.

When he left hospital he returned to France and by the end of the war he had experience of staff work and operational command; he had reached the rank of lieutenant-colonel at the age of 30 – an impressive achievement in the Army of those days, even in war. He had also been awarded the French Croix de Guerre and been mentioned in dispatches six times. The revulsion against militarism which led the intellectuals of the 1920s towards pacifism predictably left Montgomery untouched. In 1920 he went to the Staff College at Camberley, an establishment at that time virtually innocent of any element of intellectual inquiry. He passed out successfully although he never knew whether he had earned a good report as, according to the custom of the day, no one ever told him. However he was posted as brigade major to the 17th Infantry Brigade stationed in Cork. In 1926, after a variety of staff appointments (including one at H.Q., 29th West Riding Division, where he ran tactical courses for officers at which he was the sole lecturer and fount of all military wisdom), he returned to the Staff College as a member of the directing staff; his industry and single minded preoccupation with the profession of arms was beginning to pay dividends.

It was at this time that another event took place that was to have a crucial impact on the character of Montgomery. He met Betty Carver, whose husband had been killed at Gallipoli in 1915. In July, 1927, they were married. Their son David was born in 1928 and in October, 1937, after being stung by an insect on the beach at Burnham-on-Sea, Betty Montgomery died of septicaemia after her leg had been amputated. Montgomery's short marriage had been successful and happy and his wife's death was a terrible blow. Although, with the help of close friends, he was able in time to return to the normal routine of his Army life, it is possible to say that in a very real sense, he never recovered from it.

In the meantime he had left Camberley again and succeeded to the command of the 1st Battalion of his own regiment – the first ambition of every infantry soldier of his generation. He took them to the Middle East, first to Palestine and then to the Suez Canal. Here he had a series of minor clashes of temperament with his colleagues and superiors, but won a reputation as 'an officer of great military ability who delights in responsibility ... definitely above average and should attain high rank in the Army. He can only fail to do so if a certain high-handedness, which occasionally overtakes him, becomes too pronounced.'

APPOINTED TO THE EIGHTH ARMY

From 1934 after his battalion had been moved to India until 1937, Montgomery was Chief Instructor at the Staff College in Quetta with the rank of Colonel, and after three happy and busy years he returned to England to take over command of the 9th Brigade at Portsmouth. Here he maintained his reputation as a thorn in the side of the military establishment by letting War Department land to a fairground proprietor and using the rent for garrison amenities. If the General Officer Commanding-in-Chief Southern Command had been a less urbane and tolerant soldier than Archibald Wavell, Montgomery's star might have waned from that moment, such is the sacred power of Army Regulations; but in spite of his crime, Montgomery was promoted to Major-General in 1938 to command a division formed to deal with the Palestine troubles. While there, he heard the news which was to open the door to all his future success; he had been selected to command the 3rd Division, one of the regular divisions of the Army and part of the British Expeditionary Force formed to go to Europe when war began. After a short but fierce illness which brought him back to England he was told plans had changed and that he was to go into a pool of temporarily unemployed major-generals. Characteristically he pestered the War Office into submission and on August 28. 1939, Montgomery assumed command of the 3rd Division.

The division was part of the II Corps, commanded by Lieutenant-General A. F. Brooke, later Field Marshal Lord Alanbrooke, who formed a high opinion of Montgomery and was to be his collaborator and occasionally his saviour in the years to come. Montgomery regarded 'Brookie' as the best soldier that any nation had produced for many years. Inevitably Montgomery got himself into trouble in the first winter of the war by writing a somewhat hair-raising confidential minute to his subordinate commanders on the subject, in those un-permissive days, extremely delicate, of venereal disease. Like the masters at St Paul's, Gort, the Commander-in-Chief at GHQ, and Brooke, the Corps Commander, thought little of Montgomery's literary style and less of his tact. However, thanks largely to Brooke's sympathetic handling of the matter, the turbulent divisional commander escaped with a reprimand.

After the evacuation from Dunkirk he commanded V and XII Corps and in late 1941 became General Officer Commanding-in-Chief South Eastern Command. It was during this period of his career in England that the Montgomery legend began to take root. From these years come most of the stories of the lectures at which not only smoking but coughing was forbidden; of the contemptuous and icy reprimands; of the sudden, brutal dismissals – the endlessly repeated anecdotes that fused together over the years into the familiar picture of the austere, dedicated autocrat, monastic, spartan and single-minded. Yet it was also in these years that Montgomery began to take hold of the imagination of the British soldier, who liked his colourful eccentricities, his informality, his impatience with the more fatuous rituals of martial protocol. By the summer of 1942 Montgomery was ready for what lay ahead. In August, with disastrous news arriving from Egypt General Gott, a Desert Corps Commander, was appointed to command the Eighth Army: at the moment ot taking up his appointment he was killed when his aircraft was shot down by the Germans. Montgomery flew out to take over command of the Eighth Army, then holding the position at El Alamein to which it had been driven back by the Axis forces. He arrived on August 12, 1942.

At once he had to meet an attack by the German commander, Rommel, launched on August 31. The Germans were halted in front of the Alam el Halfa ridge where Auchinleck had stopped them dead the previous month. Rommel was compelled to break off the action on September 4. Montgomery permitted no major counter-attack because he did not wish to interrupt preparations for his own offensive or to use troops whose general standard of training was still not high. The defensive victory, however, raised the Army's spirit and gave it confidence in its new commander.

Churchill and the War Cabinet now began to press Montgomery to expedite his own offensive, but he firmly refused and was backed by his superior in the Middle East Command General Alexander. The Battle of El Alamein began on the night of October, 23. The enemy's strongly fortified position, covered by thick minefields, lay between the sea and the impassable Qatara Depression, so that only frontal assault was possible. Montgomery's skill and the determination of his newly inspired troops combined to open a gap in Rommel's defences through which the British armoured forces were to pass. With impressive flexibility Montgomery changed the direction of his thrusts whenever he met strong opposition. The breach was fully opened by November 2, and the enemy was then heavily defeated in an armoured battle. In the northern sector Rommel began a hasty retreat under air bombardment, which cost him thousands of vehicles. In the centre and south the greater number of his forces, here chiefly Italian, were captured.

A rapid pursuit followed in which the Eighth Army's progress was governed almost entirely by the factor of supply. It reached Tripoli on January 23, 1943, just in time to make use of the port; if it had failed to take the place within another two days it would probably have been compelled to draw back on its supplies. Meanwhile the enemy forces made their way back over the Tunisian frontier to join hands with the other Axis forces opposing the British and Americans in that theatre. Montgomery fought four more battles in North Africa; Medinine, on March 6, when Rommel attacked his forward corps and was beaten off with serious loss in tanks; the Mareth Line, the old French frontier defences, which began on March 20; Wadi Akarit on April 6, and Enfidaville, where he was partially checked in the mountains. Troops were then withdrawn from the Eighth Army to aid the First in the area of Tunis where the terrain was easier. The victory which First Army then gained completely crushed the German and Italian forces and brought about a general capitulation. Montgomery had been promoted to the substantive rank of lieutenant-general on October 17, 1942. A few weeks later, on November 11, he was promoted general for service in the field. On the same day he was created K C B.

His next task was the invasion of Sicily, in which the Eighth Army operated in concert with the United States Seventh. Indeed one of the features of the campaign was the personal rivalry between Montgomery and Patton. Although the American reached Messina first, Montgomery won the battle behind the scenes. Though he was only one of the Army commanders and had over his head a land force commander-in-chief in General Alexander and a supreme allied commander in General Eisenhower, he succeeded in getting the whole plan recast and in arranging that the Americans should land side by side with his own troops in the Gulf of Gela instead of at the north-west corner of the island. Though there was fierce fighting in the plain south and south-west of Etna and on both flanks of the mountain, the campaign lasted only 38 days after the landing on July 10.

THE ALLIES RETURN TO EUROPE

The Eighth Army began the Italian campaign by landing near Reggio in the early hours of September 3. An armistice with Italy was announced five days later, but the Germans had large forces in the country and were determined to fight for it. Having made contact with the United States Fifth Army, which had been heavily engaged on the Salerno beaches, Montgomery switched over to the Adriatic coast, where he took under his command other forces which had landed at Taranto and Bari. He fought his way up the coast, exploiting small seaborne landings behind the enemy's flank with great skill, won a fierce and bloody battle on the Sangro, but was checked by the winter at the end of the year a short distance north of the river. Montgomery believed that the Allies had only themselves to blame for the delay – no master plan, no grip on operations; administrative muddle – the classic 'dog's breakfast' of Monty's colloquial vocabulary. He was not sorry to leave Italy on appointment to command the 21st Army Group for the invasion of north-west Europe from England.

Montgomery was placed in command of all British and American forces for the landing and the battle to secure the foothold, but it was understood that as soon as the allies broke out from their bridgehead the Supreme Commander, General Eisenhower, would assume direct command of the land forces and Montgomery would revert to the post of British Army group Commander. Again he exercised influence in modifying the plan, which was considerably strengthened by his intervention. Establishing his headquarters in the High Master's room at St. Paul's – which although an Old Pauline he entered for the first time as Commander-in-Chief – he began to impress his incisive mind and personality on the planning for the invasion. As one disenchanted general put it, the gentlemen were out and the players were coming in. Although he had mellowed and expanded during his triumphant days with the Eighth Army, Montgomery was still determined that the European campaign should be a Montgomery campaign – cold, clinical and meticulously thought-out. One of his outstanding characteristics was that no commands, no persuasion, no pressure would induce him to act upon a plan in which he did not believe or with resources he did not consider adequate.

Though the landing on June 6 was bitterly opposed by the enemy under the command of Montgomery's old adversary Rommel, and though there were anxious moments at the outset the operation was a full success. It was the intention of Montgomery to contain the largest possible numbers of the enemy, especially the German armour, in front of the British Army group – on the left, while the Americans broke through from the Cotentin peninsula. The whole front, pivoting on Caen, was then to make a great right wheel and drive the enemy up against the Seine.

This programme was in its broad lines adhered to, though some of the individual British attacks were disappointing and costly. The long-drawn-out fighting aroused anxiety at home and even among some senior officers in the field. Many believed, and said, that Montgomery had failed; but he never lost his nerve. The American break-out duly took place on July 25, and was completely successful. The Germans then launched a desperate counter-offensive on August 7 at Mortain in the direction of the coast at Avranches, with the object of cutting the American forces in two. It played into the hands of Montgomery who mounted what was probably the last of the great classic land battles ever to be seen in Europe. He at once ordered the American right to wheel north and the Canadian Army to accentuate its thrusts southward in order to envelop the enemy force in a sack. After a fierce struggle this was achieved, and the Germans in the 'Falaise pocket' were largely destroyed.

This operation had not held up the allied advance on the Seine. Eisenhower now decided that the moment had come for him to take over operational command of the land forces and for Montgomery to step down. This would in any case have been demanded by American public opinion in view of American strength now in the theatre, but it was disappointing to Montgomery, who had confidence in his ability to continue the rout of the enemy. It was all the more disappointing because the strategic ideas of the two differed, Eisenhower proposing a general advance on a broad front, whereas Montgomery believed that he could end this war with one bold decisive stroke. He wanted to mass a striking force of a million men on the narrowest front possible on the left wing, provide it with the maximum transport and fuel, and drive it forward to the Rhine in the region of the Ruhr.

After long and bitter controversy, ending in a meeting between Eisenhower and Montgomery in Monty's caravan, the supreme Commander had his way. The armies dashed forward from the Seine, Montgomery's armour penetrating within a few days into Holland through Belgium. But an airborne operation conducted by him with

American and British forces to cross the great rivers of Holland failed to secure the passage of the third, the Lower Rhine. The armies were now at the end of their tether, and Montgomery was directed to devote his energies to opening the port of Antwerp, captured intact, but useless while the Germans clung to its approaches from the sea. Meanwhile, American progress to the Rhine had been almost halted though it continued by slow steps through the worsening November weather.

In December the enemy struck back. His thrust cut deep into the Ardennes, and a very awkward situation arose. Montgomery was given command of the American forces north of the German-made salient, though many senior American officers strongly objected. Monty's bearing was not, to say the least, tactful. This was the culmination of a long period of friction and controversy – of which Montgomery was inevitably, the centre. There were those who believed that he had failed in the Normandy fighting – and it is true that when Eisenhower took over the supreme command, Monty lost much of his elan and dash. Now he returned to his finest form and utterly destroyed the German offensive. His public relations operation, however, was less successful and a festering Anglo-American quarrel began which ended in another show-down between Montgomery and Eisenhower. Eisenhower, of course, won; but he was as magnanimous in his victory as Monty was gracious in accepting it. As soon as the German offensive had been routed, the salient smoothed out and the 'misunderstandings' with the Americans removed, Montgomery returned to his own efforts to reach the Rhine.

This led to some of the hardest fighting of the campaign, but once it was achieved the rest proved relatively easy. For the second time the Germans had fought their battle with a great river behind them and could not renew the struggle on the far bank. The passage of the Rhine was not difficult, except as a problem of engineering and administration. Once it had been accomplished the 21st Army Group headed north-east towards the Baltic. On May 2 troops of the 21st Army Group reached Wismar, on the Baltic, and made contact with the Russians the next day. On the 4th, on Luneburg Heath, all the German forces in north-west Germany, Holland, and Denmark surrendered to Field Marshal Montgomery. His own account of his campaigns has appeared in his two books *El Alamein to the Sangro* and *Normandy to the Baltic*.

BRITISH C-IN-C IN POST-WAR GERMANY

Montgomery was appointed Commander-in-Chief of the British Forces of Occupation, Military Governor of the British Zone, and British

Member of the Allied Control Council of Germany, which held its meetings in Berlin. He met the Russians on friendly terms and got on particularly well with the genial Soviet Marshal Rokossovsky. He threw himself energetically into the task of restoring communications, re-opening the Ruhr mines and demobilizing German land workers to get in the harvest. He was a capable Military Governor, leaving, in his customary style, the administration to able subordinates under broad directives. His chief interest was in the armed forces, now being rapidly demobilized and going through the difficulties, material and moral, which such a situation inevitably entails.

He remained in Germany for about a year, and in June 1946 entered the War Office as Chief of the Imperial General Staff in succession to Alanbrooke. Many doubted the wisdom of the choice – believing that he was not as well fitted for this appointment as for high command in the field. They disliked his mannerisms; they found his eccentricities undignified; they feared that be would be at loggerheads with the other two services that he would seek personal glorification. Alanbrooke remarked to a friend: 'People seem to think that dreadful things will happen if Monty becomes CIGS; I am perfectly sure they will not '.

A peerage had been conferred on Montgomery in the New Year Honours of 1946. He bad taken the title of Viscount Montgomery of Alamein, of Hindhead in the County of Surrey. In 1945 he had been advanced from KCB to GCB. In December 1946 he received a distinctive mark of royal favour when he was installed a Knight of the Garter.

THE CONTROVERSIAL AUTOBIOGRAPHY

Montgomery was indeed far from being as good a CIGS as he had been a commander, but his qualities were such that they enabled him to do valuable work in spite of his inability to act as a member of a team instead of as its captain. He came under criticism about the number and length of his tours abroad, but he felt that in those years of confusion he ought to see all he could on the spot. His relations with the Minister of Defence, the then Mr A. V. Alexander, were appalling, and Montgomery later savaged the unfortunate politician in his memoirs.

Alexander, for his part, distrusted and disliked Montgomery, who, late in 1948, was 'released' to take up the international appointment of Military Chairman of the Western Union Commanders-in-Chief. In face of the threatening attitude of Soviet Russia, he had fought a hard battle in favour of a 'continental' strategy in which the British Army should take the maximum part, and won it. Thus, in the formation of

Western Union his role had been almost as vital as that of his ally, Mr Ernest Bevin.

The start was good. Nations which had appeared to be thoroughly disheartened and without defence policies, still less a united policy, became more confident. Coordination of ideas and information, frequent inspections and exchanges of visits, tactical study on the ground – all these proved invaluable. The organization was, however, at best a stoppage, and an insecure one at that.

In a lecture in 1949 Montgomery said significantly that the real difficulties of such an organization began when generalities were left behind and the hour for decisions arrived. He hinted that the machinery of western defence needed fresh fuel, What actually happened was that it was absorbed into a system far more powerful and dynamic and with far stronger powers of command, in the initiation of which Montgomery again played a big part. In March 1951, he became Deputy Supreme Commander to General Eisenhower, commander of the allied forces of Nato in Europe.

In this new role Montgomery accomplished some of his best peacetime work. The role was not, however, precisely that which its title implied. It was what Montgomery decided it should be. He was more inspector-general than deputy. He made constant visits to member states, and his reputation was such that he could make comments which from anyone else would have been unthinkable.

In 1958, shortly after his retirement, his autobiography, *The Memoirs of Field Marshal the Viscount Montgomery of Alamein*, KG, aroused even more controversy. Though it was touched by his old weakness of egotism tinctured with arrogance; and though it contained passages marked by prejudice and at least one (that referring to A. V. Alexander), which could only be considered grossly unfair, it was a remarkable work, making up in clarity of thought what it lacked in distinction of style. The most violent reactions came not from his own country but from allies. They bore witness to resentment in the United States and still more in Italy, though in the latter case he was writing of a country which had been an enemy under a Fascist dictatorship in war. The memoirs will occupy a permanent place in the records of the Second World War.

Montgomery's time was now his own and it was not to be expected that he would withdraw into a hermit's cell in Hampshire. Hardly had the cheers and counter-cheers over the autobiography subsided when his acceptance of an invitation to visit Russia created more excitement. this time, however, condemnation was more prevalent than approval –

not because he was visiting Russia but because of the circumstances and some of his comments on them. The visit was labelled 'private', but it was a visit to the Government and the General Staff. It coincided with preparations for a conference designed to lessen tension between the western and the communist worlds. It caused the British Government a certain embarrassment at a time when the United States, France, and the German Federal Republic were inclined to think that the British Prime Minister was going too far in the direction of appeasement. The Field Marshal's own views had become distinctly more inclined to compromise. It was a curious turn of the wheel which led some unbalanced and strident American commentators to picture him as 'a stooge of Macmillan's' for selling the pass to the Reds, an accusation that reveals a good deal more about American political psychology than it does about Montgomery's character. His visit to the Soviet Union in 1959 was followed by visits to India in January, 1960; to China in May, 1960 and September, 1961; to Africa in November, 1959, and January, 1962, and to Central America in December, 1961. His account of these travels was contained in his *Three Continents*, published in 1962. Two of the more significant judgements of this book were that the key to the peace of the world lies in China; and that Britain should not become entangled in the political systems of Europe by joining the Common Market.

At the beginning of 1963 Montgomery saw the beginning of a military reform which he had consistently advocated for many years, and which is now virtually complete – the reorganization of defence planning under a single central Ministry, and the abolition of the three separate service Ministries. In a speech in the House of Lords he remarked characteristically that it had come too late. By this time Montgomery was deeply involved in preparing his *History of Warfare*. This was a monumental work of research – understandably not all Montgomery's own. Indeed, he was in the habit of telling friends to concentrate on the first two chapters and the last – 'I wrote those myself'. The book was published in 1968 and although its critical reception was mixed it sold well. Meanwhile in 1967 Montgomery returned to the battlefields of the Western Desert to celebrate the twenty-fifth anniversary of Alamein. He was warmly received by the Egyptians and his week-long tour ended with a lecture to about 150 generals and senior officials at the Nasser Higher Military Academy in Cairo.

Montgomery spent the last years of his life quietly in his converted mill at Isington in Hampshire, tending his garden, which he loved, ruling his small household and his visitors with a firm military hand.

From time to time he emerged for some engagement which he considered important enough to disturb the routine of his evening years. Although he had to refuse on medical advice an invitation to be a pall-bearer at Sir Winston Churchill's state funeral in 1965, he was present in 1969 at St George's Chapel, Windsor, at the funeral of his old chief, Field Marshal Lord Alexander. In the same year, at the age of 82, he carried the Sword of State at the State Opening of Parliament and no defence debate in the House of Lords was complete without his trenchant contributions, delivered from somewhere near the exact centre of the Conservative benches, but often turning his own front bench colleagues pale with apprehension.

A GREAT BATTLEFIELD COMMANDER

By the most exacting standards, Montgomery was an outstanding general. Asked once to name the three greatest generals in history he answered with impish precision: 'The other two were Alexander the Great and Napoleon.' It will be for military historians and biographers to judge the validity of this half-serious, half-mocking remark. Certainly he was unique in the parade of great commanders. His military thinking combined immense conviction with clarity of expression and great simplicity. His method was to reduce a problem to its bare essentials – indeed he often over-simplified in a manner alien to the more sophisticated academic mind; but he went straight to the heart of the matter, and if in doing so he sometimes missed the subtleties of emphasis that might have avoided personal friction, just as often he reached by intuition solutions which his staff officers had failed to reach after hours of study. They were solutions of the sort which, once reached, appeared obvious to everyone.

He made some enemies along the way – and they were not all Germans and Italians. Many of his colleagues – political and military – found his flamboyant personality distasteful. They thought his eccentricities of dress, his preoccupation with personal publicity and his florid evangelical messages to his troops exaggerated and contrived. But Montgomery knew what he was about. He had grasped the importance to the soldier in the ranks of good public relations, and he exploited it coldly and deliberately. Few troops who served under his command were not inspired by 'Monty', who knew what he wanted and went all out to get it.

In his mature years he was obsessively neat and punctual himself and deplored untidiness or unpunctuality in others. His unhappy childhood;

his early lack of rapport with his mother; and the tragedy of his wife's death made him a difficult, lonely and complicated man. But he was, above everything, a soldier. It was, in the mud, the snow or the dust, in the fear, the pain and the blood that he was at his greatest. He killed the enemy coldly and efficiently; but for the lives of his own soldiers he cared intensely. He was meticulous in preparation, in administration and in execution. He knew his dark trade better than anyone else in his time.

Perhaps his greatest single virtue as a soldier was his sense of 'balance'. Like the great athlete he would have liked to be, he was always poised in battle, able to work out his plans however the enemy reacted; and if afterwards he was ready too often to say that everything had gone exactly as he had planned, there was more truth in the boast than literal minded critics have been ready to admit. The essence of his personal philosophy was that true freedom was having the liberty to do what you ought, not what you want. History will in time deliver its verdict on Montgomery the soldier; until it does, he will be mourned not only as a national figure, but, even by those far removed in spirit or in sympathy from the profession of arms, as the last of the great battlefield commanders.

Montgomery's acclaimed insistence on a feasible plan and meticulously thorough preparation was not apparent in Operation 'Goodwood', the offensive east of the Orne in mid-July 1944. Eisenhower and his deputy, Air Chief Marshal Tedder, understood it to be an intended breakout from the eastern end of the Normandy bridgehead and massive air support was supplied. The launch of three armoured divisions with inadequate infantry support achieved little for loss of 150 tanks on the first day. Afterwards, Montgomery claimed 'Goodwood' had 'mounted the threat to Falaise' and forced the enemy to react. That alone did not justify the air support supplied or the ground force losses sustained

Criticism of Montgomery in aiming for 'a bridge too far' at Arnhem is not valid, as the whole purpose of Operation 'Market Garden' was to capture a Rhine bridge giving access to the Ruhr with a chance of ending the war in a few months. The operation failed for two reasons: 1st Airborne Division landed too far from the Arnhem bridges, allowing time for the enemy, in particular the 9th ss Panzer Division, to react. Second, by allowing Patton's 3rd (us) Army to advance beyond the Meuse, Eisenhower was unable to give sufficient logistic support to the American 1st and British 2nd

Armies that would have allowed the former to create a diversion around Aachen and, probably, the latter to reach the Rhine in time.

* * *

EISENHOWER

Modern America's soldier statesman

29 MARCH 1969

GENERAL DWIGHT D. EISENHOWER, thirty-fourth President of the United States, who died yesterday at the age of 78 will always be remembered in Europe as Commander-in-Chief of the allied armies of liberation in the West. The task called for qualities of mind and character which Eisenhower possessed to a unique degree and which gave him, in 1952, an easy election to the presidency.

His charm was well attested: even so harsh a critic as General de Gaulle could find no hard word to write of him. He was considerate of his allies' and colleagues' susceptibilities and bore with equanimity the tasks laid on him by Mr. Roosevelt and Mr. Churchill. He was quite capable of firmness: how else could he have successfully commanded Generals Patton and Montgomery? He could also be ruthless on occasion and did not always care to show delicacy towards his subordinates.

His presidency was in many respects a disappointment. Some of the crucial developments of the following decade first emerged during his time in the White House, including the space race, American involvement in Indo-China, civil rights agitation, and the détente with Russia. But it cannot be said that Eisenhower gave the lead in tackling any of them, except perhaps relations with Russia.

AN IDEALIST

He took to the presidency the techniques of command he had learnt and practised in the United States Army. He established a firm chain of command and delegated his responsibilities to people he trusted. The result was that he never gave to his presidency the firm personal imprint Roosevelt, Truman and Kennedy did. The most notable of his appointments in his first term were Secretary of the Treasury, Mr. George Humphrey, and Mr. John Foster Dulles, Secretary of State American foreign policy in the Eisenhower years was Dulles's, not Eisenhower's, and the Administration's financial policy followed the rigidity of Humphrey's orthodoxy.

Yet whatever his weaknesses may have been as a statesman, he proved himself one of the most formidable vote-winners in American politics this century. Nor was his appeal confined to his own country. His personality inspired trust and confidence among the peoples of many nations Nobody could rival him in a good-will mission overseas. The slogan 'I like Ike' was more than a publicist's gimmick; it reflected what very many people felt about this warm-hearted, friendly, idealistic man. He managed to remain above the partisan political battle for so much of his time in Washington because he was a figurehead and a symbol – a symbol of all that is best in intention in American public life.

Dwight David Eisenhower was born in Texas on October 14, 1890, of a family which had left Germany for Switzerland in the seventeenth century and settled in America about a century later. When he left Abilene High School, Kansas, his father could not afford to send him to college, and young Eisenhower, who was very powerfully built, set himself to earn the necessary money by working as ditcher, cow-puncher, and baseball player. Then he received a nomination for the military academy of West Point, from which he passed out in 1915. In the following year he married Miss Mamie Geneva Doud. They had two sons, of whom one died young and the other followed his father to West Point, saw active service in the Army, and later was on the White House staff under his father.

Until he reached the rank of Lieutenant-General and Commander-in-Chief of the allied landings in North Africa in 1942, Eisenhower never commanded troops in the field. He had the professional misfortune to miss serving in Europe during the First World War, but unlike many veterans, he applied himself to study the lessons to be learnt from that war. He rose through the Army in a series of commands. The turning point in his career was his service from 1929 to 1933, as lieutenant-colonel, in the office of the Assistant Secretary of War and later in that of the Chief of Staff, General Douglas MacArthur.

MacArthur took Eisenhower to the Philippines with him in 1935 where he served as Assistant Military Adviser to the Philippines

Commonwealth. In February, 1940, he returned to an infantry regiment in the United States, but after holding a number of brief staff appointments became Chief of the War Plans Division two years later, with the temporary rank of major-general. In June, 1942, he was appointed to command the American Army in the European theatre and promoted to the temporary rank of lieutenant-general. Before his appointment as Commander-in-Chief, North Africa, he had been comparatively little known, but the success of that operation gave him a richly deserved reputation.

Eisenhower, who won the liking and the esteem of the British soldiers, sailors, and airmen with whom he came in contact, was an excellent coordinator and a good administrator, but for operations in the field he did not at that time appear to possess the necessary experience. At the Casablanca Conference it was, therefore, decided to place him in supreme command of all allied forces of sea, land, and air, while the British General, Sir Harold Alexander (later Lord Alexander of Tunis), took command of the allied army group engaged in the actual operations, in close cooperation with a tactical air force. These measures proved entirely satisfactory, and it was under this organization that the campaign was brought to a triumphant conclusion in early May with the destruction of the whole Axis force in North Africa. In this great victory Eisenhower played an honourable and valuable part, and was awarded an honorary G.C.B.

In North Africa he inevitably became involved in the disputes between General de Gaulle and his rivals. The American Government distrusted de Gaulle and, against Eisenhower's advice, supported first Giraud, then Darlan, former Vichy Vice-Premier, who happened to be in Algiers when the landings occurred, and then Giraud again when Darlan was murdered.

General de Gaulle easily outmanoeuvred Giraud and set up his provisional Government, with which allies had to deal. It was important, and typical of the man, that Eisenhower escaped unscathed through the storm, and also survived other difficulties with de Gaulle after the Normandy landings.

In December, 1943, he was appointed Supreme Commander, Allied Expeditionary Force, with the task of carrying out the invasion of France and Germany. By this time the United States was playing so preponderant a part in the war that the appointment of an American to this post had become inevitable, and in default of General Marshall, who could not be spared from Washington, Eisenhower was the obvious choice.

His appointment was well received on both sides of the Atlantic. A heavy responsibility fell upon him with respect to the date of the invasion, which he once postponed owing to unfavourable weather and then bade go forward when the prospects were more than doubtful. However, June 6, 1944, proved a fortunate day. The passage to the Bay of the Seine was made without loss and a foothold was obtained on the coast of Calvados. The earlier operations of both American and British forces were conducted by Field-Marshal (then General) Montgomery, but in September, after the break-out and the advance to the Seine, Eisenhower himself took over direct command of the land forces. There were sharp differences between him and Montgomery over the strategy of the campaign.

Montgomery advocated an attack on a narrow front into the heart of Germany, and Eisenhower favoured a simultaneous attack all along the line. In the event, the campaigns in Europe were led to a triumphant conclusion by Eisenhower, who showed complete mastery in commanding huge armies of several nations.

LAST DISPUTE

After the Normandy landings the greatest battles were the break-out from the bridgehead and the German counter-offensive through the Ardennes in mid-winter. Eisenhower rose to the crisis, and victory on both occasions owed much to his role. The last dispute of the war was whether the western Allies should attempt to reach Berlin and Prague before the Russians or whether they should drive south to prevent any Nazi last stand in the Alps. Eisenhower is often blamed for taking the decision, his alone, of directing Patton south, and ordering the British armies in the north to allow the Russians to finish the war in their own way. It is seldom asked what the western allies would have done with Berlin and the eastern zone had they conquered it before the Russians. The answer, almost certainly, is that they would have peaceably handed them over to their Russian allies.

Eisenhower remained for a few months as commander in the American zone of occupation in Germany, but before the end of 1945 was appointed Chief of Staff of the United States Army at Washington. His main task was now to demobilize that army, a process which his successor had to reverse owing to the threatening attitude of Russia. Early in 1948 he resigned his appointment and became President of Columbia University. On December 19, 1950, he was appointed Supreme Allied Commander, Europe. The moment was fateful. The campaign in Korea had brought home to many who had hitherto disregarded or underrated it the menace to Europe of Russian aggression. Prolonged efforts had already been made to meet the danger, but so far they had resulted in little but plans, without performance. It was felt that he now faced an opportunity but also a responsibility as great as any that had come to him in the course of the 1939–45 War, and the work that he did was of the greatest importance in starting Shape on a sound military and diplomatic footing.

Eisenhower displayed considerable hesitancy before he finally accepted the Republican invitation to run as presidential candidate in the election of 1952. Until the last moment, indeed, he had not only the general public guessing, but most of the 'inner circle' too. However, in the end he resigned his commission and accepted, to the great relief of the Republicans. General Eisenhower believed at first, it appears, that his popularity and the widespread demand that he should stand for the presidency would make it unnecessary for him to fight for the Republican nomination or descend to partisan politics. In this he was to be disappointed. The supporters of Senator Robert Taft of Ohio were entrenched in the party machine and had no intention of giving up the prize without a struggle to a non-partisan neophyte. A determined attempt by the highly professional Taft forces to pack the convention failed, but the rift between Mr. Eisenhower, the party's moderate and internationally minded candidate, and the conservative and nationalist right wing of the party was widened.

For the sake of the party Eisenhower accepted the foreign policy plank drawn up by Dulles favouring 'liberation' of the Soviet satellites, although his experience in Europe must have taught him that this could not be accomplished overnight without a major war and that the slogan was certain to alarm America's allies. The return to the states of tidelands oil – the resources lying under the water along the coasts – was pledged; and optimistic promises were made about balancing the Budget and reducing taxation. A meeting with Senator Taft was widely regarded as a capitulation to secure party unity although in domestic politics Eisenhower was in fact a conservative at that time. Finally, Eisenhower promised that if he was elected he would go in person to Korea to hasten a peace.

In the election he won an overwhelming victory over Mr. Stevenson, securing a majority of six million votes, and he broke open the solid Democratic South. Meanwhile, the party's congressional candidates, whom he had been at such pains to conciliate and assist, trailed far behind, securing the barest majorities in the Senate and House.

The new President, the first Republican to enter the White House since Mr. Hoover's election in 1928, was not only inexperienced, he also held certain preconceived and rather naive notions about the presidency. The most important was an extreme version of the separation of powers. The President, in his view, was to reign, not to rule, while Congress, if its functions were treated with respect and its members with consideration, would eagerly cooperate for the general good. This is an interpretation of the Constitution which no President has found tenable. Mr. Eisenhower was no exception, although for the first few months he found an unexpectedly able and devoted lieutenant in Congress in Senator Taft. It was particularly wide of the mark in 1953, for 20 years of opposition had nourished irresponsibility and extremism in the Republican ranks.

Inside his official family the President also favoured a wide delegation of powers and reliance on staff work which reflected his military training. Mr. Nixon, the Vice-President, was encouraged to play a more active part than had ever before fallen to a Vice-President. But the key figure was Mr. Sherman Adams, who had managed the election campaign, and then went into the White House as an assistant and almost deputy-President. This streamlining and institutionalising of the Presidency became extremely useful when the President suffered his heart attack in 1955, but it had the obvious drawback of protecting the President from responsibilities which nobody else could carry so effectively. It also meant that he did not deal personally with all the detailed information and the clash of opinion on which decisions must be based. His sessions on the golf course became increasingly the subject for wry humour, sometimes unfairly so. And there were critics who felt the President was encouraged to spend too much time away from his desk. Once elected, the President had lost no time carrying out his pledge to visit Korea and hasten a peace. After his retirement, he revealed in an interview that he persuaded the Chinese to conclude the armistice by letting it be known that America was contemplating resuming full-scale operations, and extending the war to include bombing Chinese bases across the Yalu and the use of tactical nuclear weapons.

In February the nationalist elements in Congress were delighted by the 'unleashing' of General Chiang Kai-shek, accomplished when the President rescinded Mr. Truman's order to the fleet to prevent any landings on the mainland of China. Other pledges, however, proved more difficult to honour. There was the impossibility of peacefully liberating the captive nations of Eastern Europe. The Budget was at first intractable, in spite of cuts in military spending and foreign aid; a deficit proved impossible to avoid, and tax relief had to be postponed for another year.

This was a bitter disappointment and the President's authority had to be exerted to force Mr. Reed, chairman of the House Rules Committee, to cooperate. The incident was a reminder of how few of the Republican chairmen of committees were Eisenhower men. Instead, Congress was ruled by conservative Republicans long accustomed to working with reactionary Southern Democrats. Polite suggestions from the White House clearly would not evoke from this coalition the progressive measures on education, health, and housing which were a vital part of the President's concept of dynamic or modern conservatism. On the other hand, there was a dangerous degree of support for such a measure as the Bricker Amendment to the Constitution, which came within one vote of success in the Senate and would have crippled the authority of the President in foreign affairs.

This is an extract from the obituary published in *The Times* of 29 March 1969.

Neither gifted strategist nor dynamic leader and with no battle experience before the Allied landings in North Africa in 1942, Eisenhower learned fast from the indifferent showing of poorly trained American commanders and troops in Tunisia, where they were repulsed by the Germans at the Kasserine Pass. He accepted some responsibility for the set-back in Tunisia, recognizing that he had failed to be sufficiently specific in his orders to immature US commanders and also failed to be sufficiently in touch with the battle to influence the outcome by reacting to events and issuing fresh and dynamic orders.

Despite this uncertain start, his exceptionally co-operative and friendly attitude – boosted to an extent by the American public relations machine – brought about a general acceptance of his appointment as overall commander for the invasion of Sicily. In the course of this brief campaign, he was to observe the unhealthy rivalry between Montgomery and Patton, fostered chiefly by the latter, that was to lead to problems during the North-west Europe campaign in 1944–1945.

By the time he was appointed to command Operation 'Overlord', the invasion of Normandy, his grasp of essential detail, calmness, moderation and above all patience and good humour had won him the confidence of the Western Allies. Montgomery may have derided him for failing to see that planning must extend much further than over the Normandy beaches, but was relieved that the execution of the initial battles was to be left to him. Subsequently, through a deft mix of insistence and diplomacy, Eisenhower kept his jostling Army commanders working towards the same ultimate objective. This was not easy as they were individuals, rather than a team, but he was unrivalled for that great responsibility.

Together with General Douglas MacArthur, he was appointed to the specially-created five-star rank of General of the Army towards the end of the Second World War.

* * *

PATTON

Brilliant American War Leader

22 DECEMBER 1945

GENERAL GEORGE S. PATTON, Junior, commander of the United States Fifteenth Army, whose death is announced on another page, was one of the most brilliant and successful leaders whom the war produced. It was he who led the American attack on Casablanca, forged his way through to effect a juncture with the Eighth Army near Gafsa, commanded the Seventh Army in Sicily, and then swept at the head of the Third from Brittany to Metz and onwards.

George Smith Patton, a cavalryman by training and instinct, became a tank expert. Brave, thrustful and determined in action, he was a remarkable personality, who taught his men both to fear and to admire him. At the same time he was a serious and thoughtful soldier. He was an early advocate of the employment of armour in swiftly moving masses to exploit the break-through, and was finally able, with the help of

American methods of mass-production, to realize his theories in practice. A great athlete in his earlier days, he had also a taste for philosophy, literature, and poetry. He was the son of a California pioneer, and was born at San Gabriel, in that State, on November 11. 1885. Soldiering was in his blood, for he was the great-grandson of General Hugh Mercer, who served under Washington, and his grand-father died in the Civil War. It was natural, therefore, that he should find his way to the United States Military Academy at West Point, where he graduated in 1909. After great achievements on the track at West Point he was to be placed fifth in the cross-country run of the Modern Pentathlon (in the main a military event) at the Olympic Games of 1912. He was also to be known as a fine horseman and show rider and a crack pistol slot. He developed a flamboyant and emotional character, for which his men found expression in the sobriquet 'Old Blood and Guts,' but he was a born military leader.

Commissioned in the cavalry, Patton served first at Fort Sheridan, Illinois. A little later he went to France to study the sabre there and after his return served as Master of the Sword at the Mounted Service School at Fort Riley, Kansas. In 1916 he was aide-de-camp to General Pershing on the punitive expedition into Mexico. Then, when America entered the 1914–18 war he, by that time a captain, went on Pershing's staff to France, where, in November, 1917, he was detailed to the Tank Corps and attended a course at the French Tank School and he was present when the British tanks were launched at Cambrai. After this he organized the American Tank Centre at Langres and later the 304th Brigade of the Tank Corps, which he commanded with much distinction in the St. Mihiel offensive of September, 1918. Having been transferred with his brigade to the Meuse-Argonne sector he was wounded on the first day of the offensive. For his services he was awarded the D.S.C. and D.S.M. and at the time of the Armistice was a temporary colonel.

Returning to the United States in early 1919, Patton in 1920 was given command as a permanent captain of a squadron of the 3rd Cavalry at Fort Myer. Then he was detailed to the general staff corps and served for four years at the headquarters of the First Corps area at Boston and in the Hawaiian Islands. After four more years at Washington he was ordered to Fort Myer, where as a permanent lieutenant-colonel, he remained on duty with the 3rd Cavalry until 1935.

Patton received command of the 2nd Armoured Division in October. 1940. with the temporary rank of brigadier-general, becoming in the next year commanding general of the First Armoured Corps. While he was thus employed Patton learned that they might be required in North Africa. He therefore set up a large desert training centre in California, where he built up a coordinated striking force.

At last his opportunity came and as commander of the Western Task Force he and his men succeeded in their swift descent in occupying Casablanca. He himself had a narrow escape, for the landing craft which was to take him ashore was shattered. Later, when the American Second Corps were in difficulties at Kasserine Pass, Patton was sent to retrieve the situation and, with timely British aid, not only did so but carried it on to Gafsa, near which it made contact with the Eighth Army. Thus it was that he was chosen to command the Seventh Army in the invasion of Sicily. It was while he was visiting a field hospital in that island that, suspecting a soldier of being a malingerer, he struck him. The incident was reported and General Eisenhower made it clear that such conduct could not be tolerated; but Patton, who made generous apology, was far too valuable a man to lose when hard fighting lay ahead, and a little later he was nominated to the permanent rank of major-general.

In April, 1944, he arrived in the European theatre of operations, and he took command of the Third Army, which went into action in France on August 1. With it he cut off the Brittany peninsula, played his part in the trapping of the Germans and drove on to Paris. In October he had another of his narrow escapes when a heavy shell landed near him but failed to explode. Driving on relentlessly towards the German frontier, it fell to Patton to re-conquer Metz, and in recognition of this victory he received the Bronze Star. His next outstanding performance was in late December when the Third Army drove in to relieve the First and helped to hold Bastogne. He was famous for the speed of his operations; but, surpassing himself on this occasion, he surprised the Germans, and slowed down and eventually checked the advance of Rundstedt's southern column. One of his most striking feats was when in the advance to the Rhine, he moved towards that river with his right flank on the Moselle. The Germans were apparently expecting him to force a crossing of the Rhine, but instead he suddenly crossed the Moselle near the confluence, taking the enemy 'on the wrong foot' and completely smashing up his array. In Germany his armoured divisions made the deepest advances of all, penetrating in the end into Czechoslovakia. A German staff officer, captured in the final stages, reported that his general had asked him each morning as a first question what was the latest news about Patton.

In April this year President Truman nominated Patton to be a full general. The Third Army occupied Bavaria last July, and in September Patton was ordered to appear before General Eisenhower to report on his stewardship of Bavaria. The summons was a result of Patton's statements to a Press conference that 'Nazi politics are just like a Republican and Democratic election in the United States,' and that he saw no need for the de-Nazification programme in the occupation of Germany. In October General Eisenhower announced that General Patton had been removed from the command of the Third Army and had been transferred to the command of the Fifteenth Army, a skeleton force.

Patton, in spite of many idiosyncracies. which included the free use of a cavalryman's tongue – 'You have never lived until you have been bawled out by General Patton' his men used to say – was a fundamentally serious soldier, offensively minded and bent on the single object of defeating his enemy. He affected a smart and sometimes striking turnout, and was insistent that those under him should also maintain a smart and soldierly appearance.

> This rodomontade piece ignores Patton's preoccupation with out-performing his allies to the detriment of team success. His insistence in driving 3rd (US) Army on to the Rhine at Coblenz, in defiance of Eisenhower's order, drew vital logistic support to him from 1st (US) Army which, otherwise, could have aided the British 2nd Army by creating a diversion around Aachen during Operation 'Market Garden'- the drive to the key point of the Rhine, north of the Ruhr.
>
> He could find words to inspire, none better than in his message to 3rd (US) Army on leaving for France in August 1944. 'You are not going there to die for your country, but to make some other goddam son-of-bitch die for his country.'

KESSELRING

One of Germany's most accomplished
commanders in the Second World War

18 JULY 1960

KESSELRING, ONE OF the ablest German generals of the Second World War, died on Saturday at Bad Nauheim at the age of 74. His *Blitzkrieg* methods in Poland and his long, stubborn campaign in Italy showed that he possessed, rarely among military commanders, an equal understanding of the command of air and land forces.

Albert Kesselring was born on November 30, 1885 of a middle-class family and was commissioned in a Bavarian artillery regiment in 1906. He served in the First World War, reaching the rank of captain and was quickly promoted in the post-war *Wehrmacht*. He served as a major in the Department of the Defence Ministry responsible for training, and as a lieutenant-colonel at Army headquarters. Under Hitler he was promoted in 1935 to major-general and transferred to the Luftwaffe.

The Luftwaffe was not then the effective weapon it later proved to be, and Kesselring was given much of the credit for its high state of training. He was responsible for many of its operations in the early phases of the war when aircraft and armour combined to make *Blitzkrieg* a terrifying and effective weapon. In the Polish campaign he commanded the First Air Fleet, and under his leadership the air attacks against Norway and on the western front were mounted. He was promoted to field marshal for these successes, and in 1942 assumed command of air operations in the Mediterranean and Africa.

He took over the armies in Italy in 1943, where he fought a bitter defensive campaign, and in March 1945 replaced von Rundstedt as Oberbefehlshaber West and assumed command of all forces on the western front. When the Soviet Army broke through south of Berlin his command was extended to all forces south of the breakthrough. He surrendered to the American armies on May 6, 1945.

Kesselring was held with the other Field Marshals in Dachau, and in the following year was extradited to Italy to face charges of responsibility for the murder of 335 Italian civilians and issuing orders for the shooting of civilians as reprisals against partisan activities. He was found Guilty by a British military court in Venice and sentenced to death, though it was said in evidence that it was Field Marshal Lord Alexander's opinion that Kesselring had fought fairly. The sentence was deplored by some of those who had fought against him, and was commuted to life imprisonment.

He was released in 1952, and afterwards became the president of the ex-service men's association, Stahlhelm.

'Smiling Albert' to thousands of German soldiers and airmen who served under his command, due to his irrepressible smile, was a master of the quick appreciation and lightning reaction to new circumstances. His technique was to throw his enemy off balance. Classic examples are his reinforcement by air of Tunisia with a parachute regiment of two battalions, backed by dive-bombers, to counter the Allied advance on Tunis in November 1942 and, in Italy, the rapid redeployment of elements of eight divisions to contain the Allied landings at Anzio.

He displayed outstanding strategic and tactical talent during the Italian campaign, for eighteen months forcing the American 5th and British 8th Armies to incur maximum casualties for every mile of ground gained. His time-consuming campaign was conspicuous for a series of well-prepared defensive lines, each based on the mountain ranges and rivers that make Italy ideal for the defensive battle, and for holding on to each until the Allies were obliged to mount a major assault, then skilfully slipping back to the next position with the bulk of his force still intact, always a testing manoeuvre.

While awaiting trial for war crimes in Germany after the war, he showed his British escorting officer some photographs of his family. 'This is my wife,' he explained, 'ach, she is an ambitious woman. After I had been a field marshal for three years she told me,' You'll never get anywhere Albert, you do not push yourself enough.'

MACARTHUR

Brilliant soldier and controversial strategist

6 APRIL 1964

GENERAL OF THE ARMY Douglas MacArthur, whose death is announced on another page, was a brilliant general and American military hero whose defiance of the civil authority during the Korean war led to his replacement, perhaps the most controversial episode of Mr. Truman's presidency.

MacArthur believed that Asia, not Europe, was the decisive battleground between the Communists and the free world, and he advocated an aggressive military policy. Inevitably he became the idol of the Asia-first school in the United States and the focus of Republican attacks upon President Truman's foreign policy. When the Republican Party chose General Eisenhower as its Presidential candidate in 1952 it finally rejected MacArthur's view of the world struggle, but even President Truman continued to proclaim his respect for MacArthur as a soldier. He will be remembered for his winning of the war against Japan, for his efforts, as military governor, to set Japan upon a democratic and pacific course, and for the energy and ability with which, as the first United Nations commander, he saved the situation in the early days of the Korean war.

MacArthur's greatest achievements came after he had retired from the United States Army. He was over 60 in 1941 when he was recalled to defend his country's interests in the Far East. Unquestionably he was the best equipped commander of his day for such immense responsibility. His ability and knowledge of the Far East were both exceptional.

He was born on January 26, 1880, at Little Rock, Arkansas, the son of Lieutenant Arthur MacArthur and Miss Mary Hardy. At 19 he was appointed to the United States Military Academy, and with characteristic intellectual ability, graduated head of his class. Early missions in the Far East, during the Russo-Japanese war, gave him a valuable insight into Japanese methods of warfare. When in 1917 the United States went to war, MacArthur became Chief of Staff of the Rainbow Division, in which, according to his own suggestion, every state in the union was represented. In France his personal courage was outstanding. Returning to the United States in 1919, MacArthur became the youngest man to be appointed commandant at West Point in 1930, once again the youngest man to hold so high a post, he was appointed Chief of Staff of the Army with the rank of general. His warnings about the need for preparedness were disregarded and five years later he retired at his own wish. but was detailed to assist the Philippines in military and naval affairs. In 1937 he retired with the rank of general.

In July, 1941, President Roosevelt recalled MacArthur to duty and appointed him commanding general of the Far East Command. When in December the Japanese mercilessly bombed Manila 10 hours after the attack on Pearl Harbour, all that MacArthur could hope to do was to gain time and his historic defences of Bataan and Corregidor were skilful and determined efforts to this end. Ordered to transfer his headquarters when further resistance became useless, he escaped to Australia in a motor torpedo boat. As he landed he proclaimed with a characteristic touch of egotism and flair for publicity: 'I have come through and I will return.'

As supreme commander of the allied naval, air and land forces of the entire South West Pacific, MacArthur became one of the greatest military figures of the war. In March, 1942, he was awarded the Congressional Medal and in 1944 he was made General of the Army. A year earlier he had been made honorary GCB. Once the Japanese offensive had been brought to a halt his 'island-hopping' return to the Philippines began. MacArthur's strategy was to use air power to neutralize a hostile strategic base and then to seize this point in a forward bound, usually through sea-power, by-passing the Japanese forces. By October 1944, MacArthur was able to announce at Leyte 'I have returned,' although it took until May 1945 to complete the re-conquest of the islands.

The capitulation of the Japanese after the dropping of the second atomic bomb made the planned invasion unnecessary, and instead MacArthur was appointed military governor of Japan and commander-in-chief of the forces of occupation. He remained in Japan six years, hastening the transformation of a feudal society into a modern democratic state. Not all observers believed that the revolution was as far-reaching as MacArthur insisted, but his sympathetic handling of the Japanese was a great asset to the free world. His power was immense; as John Gunther wrote, 'he imposes democracy like a dictator.'

When South Korea was attacked in June, 1950, MacArthur enthusiastically supported President Truman's decision to go to its aid in the name of the United Nations. His letter to the Veterans of Foreign Wars in August showed, however, that he was out of sympathy with the Administration's policy of neutralizing Formosa and avoiding a conflict with Communist China which might turn into a world war. MacArthur's views alarmed the other nations resisting aggression and endangered their unity. President Truman considered recalling MacArthur, but instead he was ordered to withdraw the message although it was too late to prevent its publication.

After the brilliant landing at Inchon, which displayed MacArthur's genius at its best, President Truman, anxious to discuss future plans and to meet his formidable subordinate, flew to Wake Island for an historic encounter. MacArthur never denied that he assured the President that the Chinese were unlikely to intervene in force and that victory was at hand. Later, however, he insisted that the Chinese moved only because they had been assured that in Manchuria they would enjoy a 'privileged sanctuary.'

This refusal of the Administration to allow MacArthur to bomb bases in China became an embittered political controversy as Chinese 'volunteers' poured over the Yalu and the United Nations forces were pushed back. MacArthur, frustrated by this limitation on his freedom of action, called on the United Nations to choose between withdrawal from Korea or a decision to use Nationalist troops, bomb Manchuria, and blockade the Chinese mainland. Criticisms of the Administration, leaking from his headquarters, inflamed the Republicans. In fact, early in 1951, the tide turned and plans were made for a negotiated settlement. On hearing this MacArthur issued a threatening call to the Chinese to lay down their arms. The effect was to destroy prospects of a negotiated settlement, which MacArthur viewed as appeasement of the Communists. It was this which finally convinced the Administration that MacArthur was a threat to civilian control which could not be tolerated, although another act of insubordination soon followed: a letter to the Republican minority leader criticizing the priority given to Europe in the Administration's plans.

Despite warm invitations from President Truman, MacArthur had refused to return to the United States until he was recalled. Then he had not seen his country for 14 years. He had become steeped in the Far East and out of touch with American opinion. Moreover, surrounded by supporters of an almost fanatical devotion, he had grown increasingly impatient of criticism or advice. Visitors were struck by the self-imposed isolation of the legendary viceroy of the Pacific.

MacArthur was relieved of all his commands on April 9, 1951. His homecoming released a tidal wave of emotion. Eloquent, articulate and histrionic, the General seemed likely to sweep the country off its feet. Congressmen wept when he addressed them; the demand for records of his speech reached two million. But the exhaustive inquiry of the Senate Foreign Relations and Armed Services committees drained the enthusiasm away. MacArthur, on the witness stand, gave cautious and evasive answers to many questions. His Republican sponsors, many of whom were isolationists, were dismayed to find that he favoured expanding rather than liquidating the Korean war. The Chiefs of Staff punctured, for most Americans, the delusion MacArthur had fostered that America could escape from the frustrations of the cold war by 'going it alone' and ignoring its allies.

MacArthur wrung many hearts when he told Congress that old soldiers never die, they only fade away. The prophecy was truer than he may have expected. MacArthur plunged into politics and probably would have welcomed the Republican presidential nomination. At the Republican convention, he was regarded as a Taft man because of his opposition to General Eisenhower, although there was a world of difference between Taft's isolationism and MacArthur's pronouncement that 'there is no substitute for victory.' This convention in 1952, which resulted in a victory for General Eisenhower and only a handful of votes for MacArthur, closed the door on either a political or a military job. MacArthur accepted the chairmanship of Remington Rand, Incorporated; and save for the brief opening of old controversies when the Truman memoirs and the Yalta papers were published, faded out of public life.

He was twice married. By his second wife, formerly Miss Jean Faircloth, he had one son.

Described as 'the bloodiest fighting man in the Army', Brigadier MacArthur, with two Distinguished Service Crosses, seven Silver Stars, a Distinguished Service Medal and two wounds, was the most decorated American officer of the First World War.

MacArthur's South-West Pacific campaign was mutually supported by Admiral Nimitz's primarily naval strategy in the Central Pacific. Over immense distances, his advance towards the Japanese mainland required eighty-seven amphibious landings, all successful, characterised by MacArthur's brilliantly adventurous judgement, often his personal courage in the front line and his ingenious fusions of land, sea and air power. Field Marshal Viscount Alanbrooke wrote: 'MacArthur outshone Marshall, Eisenhower and all the other American and British generals including Montgomery.' The influential military historian, Sir Basil Liddell Hart agreed: 'He was supreme among the generals. His combination of strong personality, strategic grasp, tactical skill, operative mobility and vision put him in a class above other allied commanders in any theatre'.

The verdict of history strongly supports MacArthur's achievement, opposed at the time by some United Nations governments, in designing and implementing Japan's liberal, de-militarised constitution, preserving the Emperor as a figurehead and bringing to the people freedoms and privileges which they had never known. But MacArthur's land reform programme was probably his greatest triumph, while his equally unsung industrial *wirtschaftswunder* was an economic miracle rivalling that of Germany.

MacArthur, contrary to some beliefs, never advocated using nuclear weapons against the Chinese during the Korean war. It was inept answers by President Truman to close questioning at a press conference on 30 November, 1950, that left journalists with the impression that nuclear weapons were being considered and that 'release' was in the hands of the field commander. This prompted a hurried flight to Washington by British Prime Minister Clement Attlee.

NIMITZ

The Mastering of Japanese Sea Power

22 FEBRUARY 1966

FLEET ADMIRAL CHESTER W. NIMITZ, perhaps the greatest of the galaxy of talented flag officers produced by the American Navy during the Second World War, died on Sunday at the age of 80, as reported briefly in later editions of *The Times* yesterday.

Although he had achieved flag rank only in June, 1938, 10 days after the devastating Japanese attack on Pearl Harbour on December 7, 1941, he was designated Commander-in-Chief, U.S. Pacific Fleet, by President Roosevelt. When on the last day of the year he hoisted his flag on board a submarine he was faced by a disastrous situation.

Not only was his country ill-prepared for war but a large part of the American battle fleet, though fortunately not its aircraft carriers, had been destroyed or disabled; the capital ships of the embryo British Eastern Fleet had just been sunk off Malaya and the survivors of that force, of the small American Asiatic Fleet originally based on Manila, and of the Dutch East Indies squadron together with some Australian warships were soon to be almost completely wiped out in the Java Sea. Allied sea power had virtually disintegrated throughout the vast area for which Nimitz had assumed responsibility. The Japanese Navy, and especially its formidable carrier striking force, was supreme over the whole of the central and western Pacific and was reaching down towards Australia in the south and Ceylon in the west.

But Nimitz quickly showed himself not only a resolute leader in adversity but a master of the organization of large naval forces, and a supremely successful strategist. Backed by Admiral E. J. King, the Chief of Naval Operations in Washington, in whose mind the Pacific war always held first place, and by the vast output of American industry, the American naval recovery was far more rapid than seemed possible at the close of 1941. It is true enough that Nimitz was aided in making his dispositions by virtually infallible intelligence derived from the breaking of the Japanese naval cypher; but he none the less accepted grave risks by sending two of his precious carriers thousands of miles from Pearl Harbour to meet an anticipated threat in the Coral Sea in May, 1942.

The resulting battle – the first between carriers in which the opposing ships never came within sight of each other – may be classed as a drawn fight: but the Japanese threat to New Guinea and northern Australia was eliminated. Almost exactly a month later, on June 4, the Americans won their decisive victory off Midway Island when four of the Japanese carriers were sunk and the rest of the invasion fleet intended for the seizure of the whole group of the Hawaiian islands withdrew.

SEIZING THE OFFENSIVE

If Coral Sea won Nimitz and his brilliant subordinates a breathing space, the battle of Midway transformed the whole strategic situation in a few hectic hours. Nor was Nimitz slow to take advantage of the change by assuming the offensive. From the beginning he had realized that only by the establishment of temporary advanced bases in the islands of the central and south Pacific, and by the organization of floating and mobile support and supply, could naval forces operate at the required distances from their home bases. It was also clear to him that the recovery of the lost territories could be achieved only by means of large-scale amphibious operations – always the most hazardous undertakings of war.

In August 1942, the first combined assault took place in the Solomon Islands and in the months of very hard sea-air fighting that followed losses were heavy on both sides. At one moment, in October 1942, Nimitz was left with only one carrier in the south Pacific, and she was considerably damaged. An appeal for help led to the British *Victorious* being sent out. The crisis was, however, surmounted and in November, 1943, Nimitz launched the first amphibious assault across the central Pacific – at the Japanese-held Gilbert Islands. This was soon followed by a succession of westward leaps organized, planned, and executed on the same pattern. In the autumn of 1944 the climax came with the junction of Nimitz's central Pacific forces with those of General Douglas MacArthur from the southwest Pacific in the Philippine Sea, and the total defeat of the Japanese Navy in the battle of Leyte Gulf in October. Although from time to time units of Nimitz's fleet were detached to serve under General MacArthur the great majority remained under the Admiral's direct control throughout the campaign. For the final stages of the approach to the Japanese homeland the strategy favoured by Nimitz, to seize the islands of Okinawa and Iwo Jima, was finally accepted. He moved his headquarters forward from Pearl Harbour to Guam and directed the vast naval forces allocated to those undertakings.

SUBMARINE SUCCESSES
Meanwhile Nimitz, himself a submarine specialist of long experience, had developed a steadily increasing offensive against Japanese merchant shipping. It was the submarine arm, fostered by him, which contributed the largest share to the blockade of Japan which, by August, 1945, had become virtually complete. At the signature of the Japanese surrender on board the U.S.S. *Missouri* on September 2, 1945, Nimitz represented the Government of the United States as well as his country's Army and Navy. Apart from his outstanding gifts as a strategist and as organizer and trainer of naval combat and support forces, Nimitz won the respect and affection of sailors of all nationalities who came under his command. He was that rare person in any fighting service – a leader of commanding presence who was yet naturally and entirely modest. Whenever a British ship called at Pearl Harbour he found time to board her and, insisting that work was not to be interrupted, would walk round the decks informally, chatting to officers and men in the most winning and intimate manner. He was always most generous to the part played by the British Navy and other allied forces in his campaigns, marginal though that part was. When early in 1945 the British Pacific Fleet under Admiral Sir Bruce Fraser arrived to take part in the final phase of the war, the warmth of Nimitz's welcome was in marked contrast to the attitude of those American naval men who had not wished to see the White Ensign return to the Pacific.

Chester William Nimitz was born in Fredericksburg. Texas, on February 24, 1885, and joined the Naval Academy, Annapolis, in 1901. He graduated with distinction (seventh out of 114) in 1905, and first served in the Asiatic fleet based on Manila. Early in 1909 he joined the submarine branch, and in the same year was appointed to command the First Submarine Flotilla. He continued to serve in command of submarines. or in a tanker in which diesel engines had been experimentally installed, until August, 1917. In the latter capacity he was instrumental in adapting and modifying diesel engines for use in the United States Navy. On his appointment as C.-in-C., Pacific Fleet, he was promoted Admiral. and when in December, 1944, Congress approved the introduction of the rank of Fleet Admiral he was one of the first officers nominated by the President to that rank. In November, 1945, his appointment as Chief of Naval Operations, in succession to Fleet Admiral E. J. King. was confirmed by the Senate for two years.

Having remained on continuous 'active duty' in the Navy up to the time of his death Nimitz was frequently called in for consultation by

Secretaries of the Navy and others concerned in defence problems. But his chief interest after completing his term of office as Chief of Naval Operations lay in the fields of education and international relations. From 1949 to 1954 he held the title of 'Plebiscite Administrator Designate' for Kashmir. Although disagreement between the parties concerned prevented the plebiscite being held, Nimitz's nomination was confirmed, and during this phase of his career he acted as roving 'goodwill ambassador' for the United Nations Organization, and made many speeches in explanation of its purposes and problems.

Nimitz's ability to pick the right man for the job was nowhere better illustrated than his selection of Raymond A Spruance – the thinking man's admiral but not an aviator – to command the three available carriers at Midway (one of which was sunk) after their nominal commander Halsey had fallen ill. Spruance's famous three cool and cerebral decisions won this pivotal battle.

Just one statistic illuminates the immense American war effort that backed Nimitz in what has been described as the most ingenious military campaign in history – between January 1943 and September 1945, American shipyards completed seventeen 30,000 ton fast carriers of the *Essex* class.

Born of a dubious command structure with weak demarcations wherein MacArthur controlled operations amongst the islands of the south-west Pacific and Nimitz the central Pacific, inter-service rivalry between Nimitz and MacArthur persisted to the end. MacArthur's pettiness obscured his genius and led him to see Nimitz as a competitor. It was noted that both Halsey and Nimitz showed infinite patience in dealing with the temperamental general and his 'navalophobia'. MacArthur was a critic of the tactics used by Nimitz's subordinate commanders in taking islands like Tarawa, Iwo Jima and Okinawa by frontal assault at huge cost in lives, compared to his own skilful envelopments.

The decision to invest the Philippines – MacArthur's preference – rather than bypass them required the personal involvement of President Roosevelt, who, almost on his death-bed, also designated MacArthur rather than Nimitz to be the overall commander-in-chief of Allied forces in Japan. But it was entirely appropriate that it should be Nimitz who signed the Tokyo Bay surrender instrument on behalf of all the Allies in the Pacific theatre.

MANSTEIN

An outstanding German soldier

13 JUNE 1973

AN OUTSTANDING GERMAN soldier. Field-Marshal Erich von Manstein, one of the outstanding soldiers of the Second World War died on Sunday at the age of 85. His influence and effect came from powers of mind and depth of knowledge rather than by generating an electrifying current among his troops 'putting over' his personality. Ice-cold in manner although with strong emotions underneath, he exercised command more in the style of Moltke than Napoleon and those who cultivate the Napoleonic touch.

The range and versatility of Manstein's ability was shown in the way that, after being trained as an infantryman, and then becoming pre-eminent as a staff planner, he proved a brilliant and thrusting armoured corps-commander in his first test run with mechanized troops. In his next big test he proved equally successful in directing the siege attack on a fortress. By the variety of his experience and qualities he was exceptionally well equipped for high command.

Erich von Manstein was born on November 24, 1887, the tenth child of his parents. His original surname was von Lewinski, but his parents agreed to his adoption by a childless aunt who had married a von Manstein. Both families had long-standing military traditions and 16 of the boy's immediate forebears had been generals; in Prussian or Russian service. After leaving a cadet school in 1906, he was commissioned into the 3rd Regiment of Foot Guards. Badly wounded in the autumn of 1914, he was given a staff post on recovery, and made his mark in a series of such appointments on the Eastern, Western and Balkan fronts.

After the war he was taken into the Reichswehr and by 1935 he had risen to be head of the operations section of the General Staff, while the next year he was advanced to *Oberquartier-meister 1* – deputy to the Chief of the General Staff, then General Beck.

Early in 1938, when Fritsch was dismissed from the post of Army Commander-in-Chief, Manstein was sent away to command a division, having come to be regarded in Nazi circles as an obstacle to the extension of their influence in the Army. But on mobilization, in 1939 he was made

Chief of Staff of Rundstedt's Army Group, which played the decisive role in the Polish campaign. He then moved with Rundstedt to the Western Front, and there soon began to advocate a change in the plan for the coming offensive. He urged that the main thrust, with the bulk of the armoured forces, should be shifted from the right wing in the Belgian plain to the hilly and wooded Ardennes – as the line of least expectation. His persistence in pressing for the change of plan deprived him of a hand in directing it, for he was honourably pushed out of the way by promotion to command a reserve corps, of infantry, just before the new plan was adopted under Hitler's pressure – after hearing Manstein's arguments.

In the crucial opening stage of the offensive, which cut off the Allies' left wing and trapped it on the Channel coast, Manstein's corps merely had a follow-on part. But in the second and final stage it played a bigger role. Under his dynamic leadership, his infantry pushed on so fast on foot that they raced the armoured corps in the drive southward across the Somme and the Seine to the Loire.

When the German plan of invading England was discarded in favour of an attack on Russia, Manstein was given the command of an armoured corps. With it he made one of the quickest and deepest thrusts of the opening stage, from East Prussia to the Dvina, nearly 200 miles, within four days. Promoted to command the Eleventh Army in the south, he forced an entry into the Crimean peninsula by breaking through the fortified Perekop Isthmus, and in the summer of 1942 further proved his mastery of siege warfare technique by capturing the famous fortress of Sebastopol, the key centre of the Crimea – being Russia's main naval base on the Black Sea.

He was then sent north again to command the intended attack on Leningrad, but called away by an emergency summons to conduct the efforts to relieve Paulus's Sixth Army, trapped that winter at Stalingrad, after the failure of the main German offensive of 1942. The effort failed because Hitler, forbidding any withdrawal, refused to agree to Manstein's insistence that Paulus should be told to break out westward and meet the relieving forces. Following Paulus's surrender, a widespread collapse developed on the German's southern front under pressure of advancing Russian armies, but Manstein saved the situation by a brilliant flank counterstroke which recaptured Kharkov and rolled back the Russians in confusion.

Then in the Germans last great offensive of the war in the East, 'Operation Citadel', launched in July 1943 against the Kursk salient,

Manstein's 'Southern Army Group' formed the right pincer. It achieved a considerable measure of success, but the effect was nullified by the failure of the left Pincer, provided by the 'Central Army Group'. Having checked the German offensive, the Russians now launched their own on a larger scale along a wider front, and with growing strength.

From that time onwards the Germans were thrown on the defensive, strategically, and with the turn of the tide Manstein was henceforth called on to meet, repeatedly, what has always been judged the hardest task of generalship – that of conducting a fighting withdrawal in face of much superior forces. His concept of the strategic defensive gave strong emphasis to offensive action in fulfilling it, and he constantly looked for opportunities of delivering a riposte, while often ably exploiting those which arose. But when he urged that a longer step back should be made – a strategic withdrawal – in order to develop the full recoil-spring effect of a counter-offensive against an over-stretched enemy advance, Hitler would not heed his arguments.

Unlike many of his fellows, Manstein maintained the old Prussian tradition of speaking frankly, and expressed his criticisms forcibly both to Hitler in private and at conferences in a way that staggered others who were present. That Hitler bore it so long is remarkable evidence of the profound respect he had for Manstein's ability, and a contrast with his attitude to most of his generals, and to the General Staff as a body. In March 1944, Hitler removed Manstein from command and thereby removed from the path of the Russians and their allies the most formidable individual obstacle in their advance to victory.

Manstein moved westward when the Russian tide of advance swept over Eastern Germany, and surrendered himself to the British in May, 1945. The Russians demanded that he, along with other generals who had served on the Eastern Front, should be handed over to them as war criminals. The British and Americans refused, but agreed to put them on trial in special military courts. Many questions were raised in England about the legality or justice of the procedure adopted, while a long delay occurred, during which most of the other British-held prisoners of war were released. But Manstein was eventually put on trial, at Hamburg, in August, 1949 – four years after the end of the war. A subscription list was opened in England, on the initiative of Lord De L'Isle, VC, and Major-General Lord Bridgeman, to provide the funds necessary for an adequate; defence, and Mr Winston Churchill was one of the first subscribers. Mr R. T. Paget, QC, offered to lead the defence without fee. The trial continued, with intervals, until the week before Christmas. In the end, Manstein was acquitted on the eight most serious charges, and convicted only on a number, of lesser, or modified charges.

The decision of the court followed Nuremberg Trial precedents, and he was sentenced to 18 years imprisonment, but this was later reduced, and in 1953 he was released. In a deeper sense, however, that period of imprisonment was penalty and retribution for his failure, in common with most of his fellow generals, to make a firm and timely stand against the Nazi regime and its abuses, despite the disapproval he early and often showed.

In 1955–56 he was chairman of a Military Sub-Committee appointed to advise the Bundestag Defence Committee on the organization, service basis, and operational doctrine of the new German forces of the Federal Republic.

In 1920 Manstein married Jutta Sibylle von Loesch, daughter of a Silesian land-owner; and had two sons, the elder of whom was killed in the war.

Sir Basil Liddell-Hart, the British military analyst and historian, described Manstein as the Allies' most formidable military opponent; a man who combined modern ideas of manoeuvre, a mastery of technical detail and great driving power. Unlike many army commanders of the 20th century, he kept his field head-quarters to a basic minimum of staff, communications and vehicles, giving it maximum mobility.

ROKOSSOVSKY

Master of the Counter-Offensive

5 AUGUST 1968

MARSHAL OF THE SOVIET UNION Konstantin Konstantinovich Rokossovsky, K.C.B., top Soviet war-time general and post-war Defence Minister of Poland, died in Moscow on Saturday at the age of 71.

His military career spanned two regimes in Russia, the Tsarist and the Soviet. In the span of 30 years, from 1914 to 1944, he rose from cavalryman in the Imperial Dragoons to Marshal of the Soviet Union. At the outbreak of the Soviet-German War, in 1941, he represented not only the survivors of Stalin's military purge of the mid-1930s but also the promising formation commanders who were about to be put to the acid test. From the outset he displayed ability and personal courage, and went on to join that relatively small group of senior Soviet commanders with whose names the growing Soviet successes came to be associated: Moscow 1941, Stalingrad 1942, Kursk 1943. Byelorussia 1944 and the final triumphs of 1945. His wartime career was the foundation of his reputation, while his post-war activity was linked more with the phase of the Stalinist domination of eastern Europe, in particular Poland. His career as a 'political soldier' came to an abrupt end in 1956; with the displacement of Marshal Zhukov in 1957 his own service began to draw to a close and ended in an extended phase of semi-retirement, a respected veteran of Stalin's great war.

In spite of widespread and officially fostered stories about his 'Polish origins', Rokossovsky was born in 1896 in Velikiye Luki: his father was a railway worker, and the young Rokossovsky went to work as a stone-cutter in his youth. At the outbreak of the 1914–18 War he was called up to the Imperial Russian Army. Tall and well-built, he was assigned for this reason to the Dragoons, serving with the 5th Dragoon Regiment, and thereby beginning his long connexion with the cavalry, an extended introduction to his work with mobile forces.

At the time of the outbreak of the Russian Revolution and the disintegration of the Imperial Russian Army, he attained the rank of junior N.C.O.; in October, 1917. Rokossovsky joined the pro-Bolshevik paramilitary organization, the Red Guard, and entered the Red Army when it was formally established in 1918. Rokossovsky's membership of the Communist Party dated back to 1919, by which time he was a section commander with the 30th Cavalry Division on the Eastern Front, operating against Admiral Kolchak. For the remainder of the period of the Russian Civil War, Rokossovsky continued to serve in the eastern theatre, against Admiral Kolchak in Siberia, against Ataman Semenov's forces and finally in Outer Mongolia against the troops of Baron Ungern-Sternberg. By this time he was a regimental commander.

At the close of the Civil War, Rokossovsky continued to serve with the Red Army as a regular officer (or 'commander', the term 'officer' being as yet rigorously eschewed) and proceeded, in the company of many more Civil War veterans, to undergo formal military education, attending the Frunze Military Academy and the 'Higher Red Banner Cavalry Courses' in Leningrad. With the activation and reinforcement of the Special Far Eastern Army (O.D.V.A.) for operations in 1929 against the Chinese, promoted by the dispute over Soviet rights in the Chinese Eastern Railway, Rokossovsky was sent back to the Soviet Far East where he assumed command of an independent cavalry brigade, and with which he fought in the brief operations in November, 1929, in the area of Manchouli. He remained with the Special Far Eastern Army, commanded by Blyukher, and by 1932 commanded the 5th Cavalry Division which was stationed in the valley of the Dauriya. At this time the Soviet Far Eastern forces were experimenting with tanks and Rokossovsky is reported to have had his first experience of them.

When, in 1938, the military purge finally broke over the Soviet Far Eastern command. Rokossovsky was a corps commander: he was arrested, extremely roughly handled and his 'case' investigated. (According to the most exact Soviet account. Rokossovsky did not 'confess' and the 'case', while being further probed by the NKVD, was finally dropped.) He was 'rehabilitated' and returned in the winter of 1938–39 to command a mobile formation in the west, which subsequently took part in the 'liberating drive' into Byelorussia and eastern Poland in September, 1939. In June, 1940, with the restoration of formal senior ranks into the Soviet command, Rokossovsky became a major-general and was posted to the Kiev Special Military District where he assumed command of the 9th Mechanized Corps, which he helped to form and train.

With this formation. he fought in the first engagements of the Soviet-German War (Great Patriotic War), proving himself from the outset a competent commander and a cool head. He was transferred in August. 1941, to the crucial Western Front, where he commanded the 16th Army covering the Minsk-Moscow highway. For the remainder of 1941 he fought on this front, first in the defensive battles before Moscow and then in the successful Soviet counter-stroke which saved the capital. These successes identified him with the rapidly rising Soviet commanders whose ability was proved. In the spring of 1942, Rokossovsky went to the Bryansk front, and in October to the Don front, which was vitally associated with the successful Stalingrad counter-offensive: in January, 1943, together with Voronov, he signed the ultimatum to Field Marshal Paulus and the encircled German Sixth Army. During the gigantic battles of 1943, where the German offensive against Kursk was broken, he commanded the central front (Kursk-Orel).

During the next great period of Soviet success and advance (the 'ten decisive blows' of 1944). Rokossovsky took command of the Ist Byelorussian Front for Operation Bagration, the plan to destroy the German Army Group Centre; in June. 1944, he was appointed Marshal of the Soviet Union and by August. 1944, his forces had reached the Vistula. He was, of necessity, implicated in the failure of the Red Army to support the Warsaw Rising (1944). Having finally moved into Warsaw, his forces in the winter of 1944–45 entered East Prussia and in February, 1945, Rokossovsky's 'East Prussian' campaign, one characterized by speed and swift mobile thrusts, opened; in April, he took command of the 2nd Byelorussian Front for the final phase of the operations against Berlin, covering Zhukov's flanks.

At the end of the war, Rokossovsky, now much advertised as 'Polish' in origin, remained to 'co-ordinate' Polish forces: in 1949, he was formally transferred to Poland, becoming Polish Defence Minister. Commander-in-Chief of the Polish forces and a Marshal of Poland. In addition, he was elected to the Polish Politburo and was a deputy to the Sejm. One more extension of his role came in 1955 when he was appointed a deputy commander of the Warsaw Pact organization. During the Polish excitements of 1956, however, he was removed from his position in the Polish armed forces and in Polish political life by Mr. Gomulka and he returned to the Soviet Union where he was reinstated in his Soviet Marshal's appointment and made a deputy Defence Minister, under Marshal Zhukov.

In October, 1957. he was posted away from Moscow as commander of the Trans-Caucasus Military District and his last official military appointment was that of January, 1958, as a deputy Defence Minister, this time under Marshal Malinovsky. From 1960 onwards he lived in semi-retirement, prominent only as a Deputy of the Supreme Soviet (to which he was first elected in 1946).

He was a Hero of the Soviet Union, was awarded the Order of Victory, several Orders of Lenin and all major Soviet military decorations and the decoration Builder of People's Poland.

Rokossovsky had the reputation of being cool-headed, personally brave, and loyal to the Communist Party. His speciality was the rapid mobile thrust and he became one of the foremost Soviet exponents of this and his reputation has continued to grow as a wartime commander. Rokossovsky, who was more than six feet tall, was known to his men as 'The Hammer of the Huns'.

Although blamed in Western capitals for failing to go to the aid of the Polish Home Army at the time of the Warsaw uprising in August 1944, Rokossovsky's army group was in dire need of replenishment. It was therefore convenient for Moscow to broadcast an appeal to the inhabitants to rise against their Nazi occupiers, knowing that Polish supporters of the Government in exile in London would be slaughtered while the Red Army paused to prepare for the final drive on Berlin

* * *

ZHUKOV

Leader of the Soviet Attack on Germany

20TH JUNE 1974

MARSHAL ZHUKOV, WHO prepared and carried out the final Soviet offensive against the German armies on the Eastern front and later commanded the Russian armies of occupation in Germany, has died at the age of 77.

Zhukov was perhaps the most brilliant of the Soviet soldiers who fought in the Second World War. Although, like Rokossovsky, he was not an outstanding veteran of the Russian Civil War, his victories over the

Germans at Moscow, on the Don, in the Ukraine, and finally in Berlin have guaranteed him a significant place in military history. A great popular hero, he bulked too large on the political scene to suit either Stalin's autocracy or Mr Khrushchev's brand of personal rule. At the end of the war Stalin moved him into a comparatively minor post and in 1957 in highly dramatic circumstances Mr Khrushchev removed him from the party praesidium and the Ministry of Defence. He was accused of resisting party control of the armed forces, of 'adventurism' in foreign affairs, promoting the cult of his own personality and was even blamed for the unpreparedness of the Soviet forces when the Nazis invaded in 1941.

It was not until May, 1965, on the occasion of a large military parade to mark the twentieth anniversary of the end of the Second World War, that he again made a public appearance standing with other leading commanders and being greeted with a special burst of applause.

Georgi Konstantinovitch Zhukov was born in 1896 in the village of Strelkova, near the spot where Kutozov defeated Napoleon. Of peasant stock, his early education was neglected and at the age of 11 he was apprenticed to a furrier in Moscow. During the 1914–18 War he served with the 10th Novgorod Dragoons as an NCO and was twice awarded the Russian George Cross for gallantry and daring. He was an ardent supporter of the October Revolution, and in the newly formed Red Army, he was elected to his regimental council and became the chairman of his squadron committee.

In 1919 he joined the Communist Party. During the civil war, as a young cavalryman, he took part in the defence of Tsaritsyn, under Voroshilov, where he was wounded. When internal peace was at last restored to Russia, he continued to serve in the Red Army, rising to command a cavalry corps. Between the wars he commanded the Stalin Cossack Corps and for his work in the field of military training he was decorated with the Order of Lenin. In 1939 he saw fighting at Khalingol, Mongolia, against the Japanese Sixth Army and his abilities as a general on this occasion won him the title of 'Hero of the Soviet Union'.

In February, 1941, Stalin appointed Zhukov Chief of the General Staff, in which post he was responsible for working out the Soviet defence plan in the spring of 1941, completed in outline by May; in this post Zhukov began his wartime service when Germany invaded the Soviet Union; he was dispatched almost at once to assist with the defence of the Ukranian frontiers, and when in August Shaposhnikov was installed once more as Chief of the General Staff, Zhukov was assigned to command of the Reserve Front, the main covering force for Moscow. On September 12 he was flown to Leningrad to organize the last-ditch defence of the city against Army Group North, and he was recalled from Leningrad on October 8 to take command of the Western Front when Army Group Centre broke through the centre of the Soviet forces and drove for Moscow.

In this post he was responsible for the defence of the capital, before which Army Group Centre was finally halted. Having taken part in planning the Soviet counter-blow, Zhukov commanded the Western Front armies until February 1, 1942, when he was appointed 'Commander of the Western Axis' to supervise the encirclement and destruction of Army Group Centre. This, however, was not accomplished and Zhukov remained in command at the centre before Moscow throughout the summer of 1942. The crisis developed not at the centre but in the south-west and in the autumn of 1942 Zhukov was dispatched to Stalingrad as 'Stavka (G.H.Q.) representative' to supervise the defence of the city and to take part in planning and supervising the counter-offensive where he coordinated the operations of the South-western and Don Fronts (while Vasilevski of the General Staff controlled the Stalingrad Front proper).

In January, 1943, he was appointed a Marshal of the Soviet Union and once again in the spring and summer of 1943 acted as planner and 'Stavka co-ordinator' of the giant battles at Kursk in 1943. Zhukov was also Stalin's 'deputy', a post later formalized as First Deputy or Deputy Supreme Commander. During the third winter campaign, 1943–44, Zhukov planned and coordinated the operations of the 1st and 2nd Ukrainian Fronts, but when General Vatutin was killed by anti-Soviet guerrillas in February, 1944, Zhukov assumed personal command of the 1st Ukrainian Front, which, in spite of considerable successes, failed to accomplish the total inner and outer encirclement of the German forces in the south-west.

Zhukov was also at this time associated with the planning of the major offensive operations in Belorussia: Operation Bagration, in which Zhukov and Vasilevskii again collaborated in planning and coordination, Zhukov assuming responsibility for the 1st and 2nd Belorussian Fronts, which expelled German forces from Soviet territory, and which reached into Poland. After the planning conference on operations in Germany (October, 1944), Stalin appointed his 'First Deputy' Zhukov on November 16 to command the 1st Belorussian Front, to which Stalin assigned the task of taking Berlin.

On January 26, 1945, Zhukov presented his plans for the offensive, while a certain delay was imposed by clearing the Soviet flanks, principally in Pomerania. At the end of March, after the conclusion of the first stage of operations in Germany, the General Staff worked out the final version of the Berlin attack plans; on April 16 Zhukov's 1st Belorussian and Koniev's 1st Ukrainian Fronts began their offensive on the Oder and Neisse respectively, Zhukov being held up for three days by the German defences. With Koniev moving on Berlin from the south-east, Zhukov's troops struck from the east and north-east, and the final battle for Berlin began on April 25, the encirclement of Berlin having been completed on April 21–22. On May 2 the Berlin garrison under General Weidling capitulated to Zhukov, whose troops had stormed the Reichstag and raised the Soviet flag over it. Soon afterwards he was appointed C-in-C of the Soviet occupation forces in Germany; he also became a member of Allied Control Commission.

In *The Memoirs of Marshal Zhukov*, which he published in 1971, he recounts how Stalin became hesitant, fearful and near despair when the German invasion became a certainty and how the Russians grew suspicious after the fall of Nazi Germany that the western allies were plotting against them. He also graphically described his early life in poverty when his family had to live for a while in a shed and his father, a cobbler, had to journey to Moscow in search of work.

Zhukov's reputation was established by his redoubtable battlefield success, although this was built on a loss of lives in his huge armies that would scarcely have found acceptance in a western nation, even one fighting to rid its territory of a barbaric invader. His attitude doubtless had origin in his harsh Russian peasant background and upbringing, where human life was cheaply held.

He was the first professional soldier to be appointed a member of the praesidium of the Central Committee of the Soviet Communist Party, a reward for siding with Nikita Khruschev against Malenkov and other supporters of Stalin and his methods.

DOWDING

Victor of the Battle of Britain

16 FEBRUARY 1970

AIR CHIEF MARSHAL LORD DOWDING, GCB, GCVO, CMG, victor of the Battle of Britain, died at his home in Kent yesterday at the age of 87. As Chief of Fighter Command from 1936 to 1940, he laid the plans for and directed the Battle of Britain when 'the Few' won imperishable glory. 'Stuffy' Dowding as he was always called – a nickname given him in the artillery though no one quite knew why – had grown up with the R.A.F., but that nickname 'Stuffy' completely belied his gift of charm and accessibility. One writer said of Dowding – 'Never in history has a commander won so signal a victory and been so little thanked by his country, and even in his own service. Even the barony was belated.'

Hugh Caswall Tremenheere, First Baron Dowding of Bentley Priory, in the county of Middlesex, in the peerage of the United Kingdom, was born on April 24. 1882, the eldest child of A J C Dowding. From the successful preparatory school run by his parents at Moffat he followed his father to Winchester, where he was not happy. A distaste for Greek verbs led him to the army class and the Royal Military Academy at Woolwich. Failing to qualify as a sapper, he was gazetted to the Royal Garrison Artillery. He served at Gibraltar, Colombo and Hongkong before obtaining a transfer to the Mountain Artillery and spending six agreeable years in India. After many unsuccessful requests to be allowed to sit for the staff college entrance examination he was granted a year's furlough to prepare for it.

At Camberley in 1912 and 1913, Dowding was struck by the prevailing ignorance of aviation. Attracted by flying and believing that ability to fly would further his career, he qualified for his pilot's certificate on the day of his passing-out from the staff college. After a short course at the newly-formed Central Flying School he applied for transfer to the Royal Flying Corps Reserve and rejoined the garrison artillery.

On the outbreak of war, Dowding was called from his battery to command the camp from which the first squadrons of the Royal Flying Corps left for France. In October, he went to Belgium with No. 6 Squadron, hastily dispatched on the eve of the fall of Antwerp. He served briefly at Royal Flying Corps headquarters in France and was thence posted to No. 9 (Wireless) squadron, where his technical bent stood him in good stead. On the disbandment of the squadron early in 1915 Dowding, who had succeeded to the command, was sent home to form a new unit with the same designation. Later in the year he commanded No. 16 squadron at La Gorgue. Electing to fly as observer on a particularly dangerous mission during the Battle of Loos, he narrowly escaped a forced landing behind the enemy's lines.

In 1916 he served with the administrative wing at Farnborough and afterwards as commander of the ninth wing at the Somme. In the meantime he had the congenial task of putting through its final training the first squadron of Sopwith aircraft armed with guns firing through the airscrew. Command of the ninth wing brought him directly under Trenchard, with whom he had had a disagreement caused by Trenchard's misunderstanding of a technical issue. During the battle Dowding was not convinced that his chief was wise to insist on frequent patrols over the enemy's lines at the cost of heavy casualties. Characteristically, he did not hide his views. His request that one of his squadrons should be relieved was granted, but he was deprived of his command and received no further appointment in France. Employed at home in various capacities, he rose to Brigadier-General and was awarded the CMG for his war services.

On the creation of the Royal Air Force, Dowding was not selected for a commission in the new service. Only after representations from his commanding officer was he granted a temporary attachment, afterwards made permanent. As a Group Commander at Kenley, as Chief of Staff at Headquarters, Inland Area, and afterwards at Baghdad, as Director of Training at the Air Ministry and later in command of Fighting Area at Uxbridge, he found limited scope for exceptional abilities. His chance came in 1929 when he was sent to report on service requirements arising from disturbances in Palestine. His observations on the spot confirmed views already formed by Trenchard, and his report found favour.

From 1930 to 1936 Dowding served on the Air Council as air member successively for supply and research and for research and development. No better choice was ever made. A fearless pilot, Dowding was never an outstanding one. But he had a good grasp of the practical side of airmanship and a rare understanding of the limitations of air power. His period of office saw the emergence of the all-metal monoplane fighter and of radar, whose possibilities he was among the first to recognize. Almost from the start he was keenly interested in the application of radar to night fighting, but he saw that defence against a massive onslaught in daylight must come first. Even had he not lived to win the Battle of Britain his work in the field of technical development would place him high among his country's saviours.

Within a month of his joining the Air Council, Dowding was asked to sanction the issue of a certificate of airworthiness to the ill-fated R101. His surrender to the insistence of others that the reconstructed ship should leave for India without full trials was a blunder due to inexperience misled by too-hopeful reports from the ship's designers. In 1936 Dowding was picked for the new post of Air Officer Commanding-in-Chief. Fighter Command, with overriding control of all branches of active air defence at home. He held it for more than four years. Passed over for preferment to Chief of the Air Staff in 1937, he was reserved for a more crucial role. In May, 1940, the Government contemplated sending to France a substantial part of his already-depleted force as a gesture of encouragement to the French. His advice that a sacrifice which could not save France would mean defeat for his own country was tendered with an authority no other airman could command. His squadrons were spared to fight the battle for which he had prepared them. A series of setbacks for the Luftwaffe culminated on September 15 in a hard-fought struggle over London which robbed the Germans of all colourable hope of achieving the right conditions for a landing in this country. Towards the end of the battle Dowding was accused of allowing his squadrons to be used in smaller formations than some critics thought desirable. At the same time the bombing of Britain after dark brought demands that certain day-fighter squadrons should be relegated to night fighting. He opposed them; predicting that only fighters with airborne radar would master the night bomber. Over-ruled on several issues, in November he was relieved of a post already held longer than the normal term. In 1941, after a visit to the United States and Canada and the writing of a brilliant report on the Battle of Britain, his name was placed on the retired list. Within a month he was recalled to suggest economies in manpower. He retired in 1942 without attaining the rank of Marshal of the Royal Air Force, then reserved for officers who had held the post of Chief of the Air Staff. Next year he received a barony. From 1937 he was Principal Air Aide-de-Camp to King George VI.

There was controversy surrounding Dowding's removal as chief of Fighter Command. Some of his admirers said it was because he had dared to question Whitehall.

In 1957, the controversy was revived by the publication of Dowding's authorized biography, *Leader of the Few*, by Basil Collier, whom Dowding had helped to write the book.

'To many members of the public', Collier wrote. 'Dowding's removal from his post immediately after he had won, brilliantly, a hard-fought battle, seemed an act of almost monstrous folly and ingratitude '.

In recent months there had been renewed controversy over Dowding's dismissal from his command in the second week of November, 1940, just after the Battle of Britain. He should, it was suggested, have been promoted to the most senior rank of Marshal of the Royal Air Force which would almost have doubled his income. Lord Balfour of Inchrye, wartime Under-Secretary of State for Air, last year pioneered a campaign pressing for Dowding's much-belated promotion to Marshal of the R.A.F. He denied that he connived to get rid of Dowding, and said that he 'yielded second place to none' in his admiration of the Air Chief Marshal. Last month Marshal of the R.A.F., Sir John Slessor, in a letter to *The Times*, called into question a passage in Robert Wright's book, *Dowding and the Battle of Britain*, about the removal of Dowding from his command. Slessor referred to the allegation attributed to Lord Dowding that just after the real Battle of Britain had been won, in the second week of November, 1940, he was summarily – and by implication unexpectedly – dismissed from his command in the course of a sudden and very brief telephone conversation by the Secretary of State for Air, Sir Archibald Sinclair (now Lord Thurso). While placing himself 'among the many who think he was shabbily treated at the end of the Battle of Britain', Slessor suggested 'that in connexion with this event, it is not impossible that Lord Dowding's memory may have let him down.' Slessor stated he had consulted a number of people in recent months, associated with the events in 1940, and all agreed that it was incredible that Sir Archibald Sinclair could have acted in the manner described.

Dowding wrote to *The Times* saying that there was no 'mystery' about the manner in which he was relieved of his command. In a matter as grave at that, the record of what he remembered could not fail him. But on January 20 this year, Mr. A J P Taylor wrote revealing a document indicating that Sir Archibald Sinclair had indeed met Dowding and not dismissed him on the telephone.

Last September Dowding, confined to a wheelchair because of arthritis, received a standing ovation to a trumpet fanfare at the premiere of the film, *Battle of Britain*. He took his place in the stalls among 350 of the pilots he had once commanded.

After his retirement Dowding became keenly interested in spiritualism, a subject which had long dwelt in the background of his mind. A confident speaker and a lucid writer, he did much selfless work for the spiritualist movement and wrote many books and articles, mostly on occult subjects. He was also interested in animal welfare and advocated strict control of vivisection. A keen shot, he gave up field sports and became a vegetarian. In his prime he was a skier of international standing and an enthusiastic polo player.

His first marriage in 1918 to Clarice Maud, daughter of Captain John Williams, was cruelly cut short by her death in 1920. His second marriage in 1951 to Muriel, widow of Pilot Officer Maxwell Whiting, who shared his interests and who survives him, brought him great happiness.

To intimates Dowding revealed himself as an affectionate and kindly figure for whom no effort on behalf of those in need of help was too much trouble. In his official dealings he was not an easy man. To him slackness, hypocrisy and self-seeking were not peccadilloes but scarlet sins. During his service career he was sometimes impatient with colleagues and subordinates whom he suspected of adopting standards lower than his own. In later years he radiated loving-kindness redeemed from mawkishness by a sense of fun and an undimmed eye for human foibles. As a public servant no man deserved better of his country. Thousands who never knew him as a public servant will mourn him as a servant of mankind.

He is succeeded by his only child, Wing Commander the Hon. Derek Hugh Tremenheere Dowding, born in 1919.

The importance of the Battle of Britain to the final outcome of the second world war is illustrated by the remarks of Field Marshal Von Rundstedt who, questioned about when he felt that the tide had begun to turn against the Germans – was it at Stalingrad or El Alamein? – replied, 'Oh no. It was the Battle of Britain. That was the first time I realized that we were not invincible.'

Having been a subaltern for 13 years, Dowding rose to brigadier within four years and was a General or Air Officer for 26, a highly unusual record.

He has been criticized for not settling the squabble, hinted at above, between his two fighter Group commanders, Air Vice Marshals Park and Leigh-Mallory, the one advocating attacking as far forward as possible by squadrons, the other advocating 'Big Wing' tactics. Dowding's judgement that both were doing well and could not be removed at that critical time must have been right.

His controversial dismissal, dwelt on at length here, was to a degree prompted by his age, 58, his lengthy tenure in post and, no doubt, his disinclination to be diplomatic with his superiors, several younger than he. Being right is not endearing.

* * *

GALLAND

The Luftwaffe's Fighter Commander

14 FEBRUARY 1996

A FLYER WHO WAS among Germany's top aces of the Second World War, Adolf Galland commanded the fighter arm of the Luftwaffe from the end of 1941 until 1945. Credited with 103 kills by Luftwaffe statisticians, he was a tactician skilled in the handling of fighter forces. He always attributed the Luftwaffe's defeat in the Battle of Britain to the fact that it was not properly deployed by Goering, who used its fighters as a strategic rather than as a tactical weapon.

Thus, the Messerschmitt Me109 was used as a bomber escort, a role for which its short range made it unsuitable, rather than being used to attack the RAF's fighters. The flawed German system of using *Luftflotten*, air fleets of mixed fighters and bombers, rather than organizing them as separate commands told against them when they were concentrated against the numerically inferior but tactically superior RAF in the summer of 1940.

Throughout the war Galland was a fearless critic of his boss, Hermann Goering, whom he regarded as being unfit for the command he held. With his thick, black hair and moustache, easy grin and cigar clamped between his teeth, even when airborne, Galland was a reassuring figure to his young pilots, and after he attained general's rank always remained 'one of the boys'.

Adolf Galland qualified as a glider pilot while in his teens. In 1932 he joined Germany's commercial airline, Lufthansa, and when it was formed, transferred to the Luftwaffe. He flew 300 missions for the Kondor Legion during the Spanish Civil War and gained much valuable experience of operations.

At the outbreak of the Second World War Galland was in a training post and took no part in the air operations of the Polish campaign. But by April 1940 he was back to active service in fighters and took part in the air attacks which supported the invasion of the Low Countries and France in May 1940. As an officer in the celebrated Jagdgeschwader 26 he played a prominent part in the Battle of Britain, making a name for himself along with Werner Molders and Helmut Wick as one of the most successful pilots on the German side. In August he was appointed to lead a fighter group in the battles which raged in the skies over the Channel and the South East of England. In the following year he was involved in countering the RAF's daylight fighter sweeps over France.

Much of Galland's success as a fighter pilot was due to his never underestimating his opponents; unlike Goering he did not make the mistake of disparaging the RAF's capacities at the outset of the Battle of Britain. Indeed, he is said jokingly to have told the latter when questioned as to Luftwaffe needs during the battle, that a squadron of Spitfires would benefit the performance of his Gruppe.

Molders had been made Inspector of Fighters in 1941 but was killed in an air crash later that year and in November Galland was appointed to succeed him. In the following year he was promoted to become, at 30, the youngest general in the German armed forces.

For the next two years it was his melancholy task to attempt to orchestrate an air defence for the Third Reich against the numerically and technically superior air forces of the Western allies, and to witness the total destruction of his command under the relentless night and day onslaught mounted by the RAF and the US 8th Army Air Force. It was a tribute to his qualities as a leader that he was nevertheless continually able to inspire his pilots whose numbers daily dwindled, especially heavy toll being taken of their attempts to break up the massive daylight raids of the American bomber squadrons with their powerful long-range fighter escorts.

Nevertheless he was always alert to make the latest technical advances available to his pilots and continually strove for tactical innovations which would offset the Luftwaffe's inferiority in numbers. Thus such novelties as rocket and even bomb attacks were experimented with, against the tightly packed American bomber formations.

Although rising to high command, he retained the mentality of, and sympathised with, the problems of the front line pilot with whom he was prone to side in the frequent arguments between the operational units and the Supreme Command. In particular, he was a severe critic of Hitler's initial decision to deploy the new Me262 jet fighter which would have given the Luftwaffe a perhaps decisive air superiority over the Allies only as a fighter bomber.

This stance made him enemies and in January 1945 he was relieved of his command when Goering ordered him on permanent leave without naming a successor. However, he did fly operationally again and was shot down in combat with an American Mustang fighter a fortnight before the end of the war.

After the war Galland pursued his interest in commercial and military aviation and was for a period a consultant and adviser to the Argentine Air Force.

Galland typified to a degree the chivalry which existed between combatants in the air and was a popular figure at the air force reunions of his old adversaries. He was, for example, a welcome figure at the thanksgiving service for the life of the legless RAF ace Sir Douglas Bader, in St Clement Danes Church in the Strand, in 1982.

Adolf Galland was born on March 19, 1912. He died on February 9, 1996 aged 83. He was married with two children.

General Galland, while only eighty-seventh amongst German fighter pilot aces, amassed all his victories against the Allies in the West, including 55 Spitfires and 30 Hurricanes. Many other German high-scorers gained over the inexperienced and under-trained Soviet pilots flying early marks of the Yak fighter on the Eastern front. But the Luftwaffe became outnumbered and outclassed in the East as well as in the West. With the exception of the excellent Focke-wulf Fw 190A fighter, the Third Reich's aircraft development, as in so much of its higher management of war under Hitler, was inadequate. Properly employed and if numbers surviving Allied bombing had allowed, the Me262 – vying with the British Gloster Meteor as the world's first operational jet warplane – might have delayed the inevitable. While flying the Me262, Galland made seven kills against American aircraft, two of them heavy bombers.

HARRIS

Executant of strategic air offensive against Germany

7 APRIL 1984

MARSHAL OF THE ROYAL AIR FORCE, Sir Arthur Harris. Bt, GCB. OBE, AFC, who died on April 5 at the age of 91, was as Commander-in-Chief of Bomber Command from 1942 until 1945 the executant of Britain's strategic air offensive against Germany, which though it suffered its reverses and had, and continues to have its critics, undoubtedly made a considerable contribution to the winning of the war in the West.

His own universally used nickname 'Bomber' is indicative of the single minded passion with which this iron-willed officer pursued the goals and the bombing policies in which he believed. In particular the 'area bombing' whose most devastating monument was the destruction of the city of Dresden by Bomber Command and the US 8th Air Force in February 1945 caused controversy at the time – one of its major critics was the Bishop of Chichester, the Right Rev George Bell – and continues to be the subject of intense dispute.

Harris could indeed be stubborn to the point of pig-headedness. He grudged the deployment of Bomber Command on the vital work of disrupting the French railway system in the months leading up to Overlord, though this produced decisive results. He was never enthusiastic about trying to disrupt German oil production. By this time his mind was too wedded to the policy of bombing cities on which Bomber Command had sustained its vision of itself during its bleaker years.

But his stance deserves to be seen against the fact that he took over a Command in 1942 which was badly demoralized, whose results, or lack of them were being severely criticized in the highest circles and whose very *raison d'être* came close to being called into question.

Above all, February 1942 was a bad time for Britain. Defeated almost everywhere on land and on sea, looking increasingly towards America for sustenance, the country had only one force with which it could independently take the fight to the enemy. This was Bomber Command, and it was this arm which Harris forged into an instrument whose operations eventually played their part in bringing German military resistance to an end.

And, whatever the tactical limitations of Bomber Command's performance in 1942 and 1943, the knowledge that Britain at least possessed a weapon with which to mete out reciprocal punishment put fresh heart into a civilian population whose own lot had been a diet of bombing for so long.

Arthur Travers Harris was born at Cheltenham on April 13. 1892. His father was in the Indian Civil Service. He was educated at Gore Court, Sittingbourne, and at Allhallows, Honiton, Devon. From 1910 to 1914 he was in Rhodesia, first gold mining, then driving a mail coach. and finally tobacco planting.

When the 1914–18 War broke out he joined the Ist Rhodesia Regiment, with which he served in the ranks in South West Africa. After the disbandment of the regiment in July, 1915, on the completion of that campaign, he came to England, learnt to fly at Brooklands, and joined the Royal Flying Corps as second lieutenant in November.

During 1915–17 he served in France, and in 1918, having risen to squadron commander, was in command of a home defence squadron. He was a pioneer in night flying and night fighting. The A F C was awarded him in November, 1918, and when the postwar R A F was established on August 1, 1919, he was granted a permanent commission as squadron leader.

In 1922 he received the thanks of the Air Council for the invention of an electric truck to facilitate the moving of heavy bomber aircraft on the ground which enabled two men to do the work of 16.

He commanded No 31 Squadron in India in 1921–22 and No 45 (troop carrier) Squadron in Iraq in 1922–24. This relegation to a support role was not to his liking, and he quickly improvised bomb sighting equipment and challenged the bomber squadrons to a competition which he won with ease, at the same time pointing out to headquarters that one of his aircraft could carry the bomb load of an entire bomber squadron and moreover deliver it further and with greater accuracy. Thus was demonstrated a belief in large aircraft. and in their direct employment against the enemy, and not as ancillaries to the other services.

In 1925 after a short course at the Army Senior Officers School, Sheerness, he commanded No. 58 (Bomber) Squadron for two years, during which he was instrumental in effecting great improvements in the methods of navigation and bombing by night.

He was appointed the O.B.E. in 1927.

From 1930 to 1932 he was on staff duties in the Middle East Command

and early in 1932 commanded the long-distance flight from Cairo to East Africa and back.

Staff service in Iraq followed, and in 1933 he gained more varied experience in command of a flying boat squadron at Pembroke Dock, dismaying the orthodox by insisting that a flying boat was an aeroplane and, therefore, perfectly at home over the land.

For the next four years he was at the Air Ministry as deputy director, operations and intelligence, and later director of plans where he played a significant part in inter-service planning.

Outspoken as always, his thinking was too advanced to be entirely acceptable to his colleagues, yet his opinions on aircraft in coast defence, on the vulnerability of big ships to air attack and on the type of aircraft which could best meet the needs of the Army were vindicated by war experience.

In July 1938, he was for 12 months Air Officer Commanding in Palestine and Transjordan where he instigated a novel form of air patrol which allowed the Air Force to give effective help to the Army in its difficult task of suppressing gang warfare.

On the outbreak of war in September 1939, he was given command of No 5 Bomber group until his appointment as Deputy Chief of the Air staff in November, 1940. Six months later he was chosen to go to Washington as the first Head of the RAF Delegation, and it was from this post that he was appointed in February 1942 to succeed Air Marshal Sir Richard Peirse as Commander-in-Chief, Bomber Command, and was made Air Chief Marshal in March. 1943.

At the point Harris took over Bomber Command the assumptions on which the concept of strategic air power were based had been exposed as totally fallacious. In August 1941 the Butt report had shown that only 10 per cent of the bombers in the Ruhr raids had got to within five miles of their target, a dismaying contradiction of the theory that average error in bombing was about 1,000 yards. Churchill himself became sceptical about the whole possibility of affecting the war's outcome by bombing. Losses, as in the November 1941 raid on Berlin sometimes ran as high as a completely unacceptable 12 per cent.

In this atmosphere 'area bombing' the wholesale devastation of cities, was born. Its first triumphant demonstration was the 1,000 bomber raid on Cologne in May 1942, and it was after that that Harris broadcast his grim message to the German people 'We are coming by day and by night ... We are going to scourge the Third Reich from end to end ...'

The proposition of the area offensive was not of course a purely vengeful or sadistic one. It had its roots in what was practical. If bombers could guarantee to hit no target smaller than a whole city then a whole city that target must be. And what was practical influenced what seemed strategically desirable. To destroy the will of the German working people, to make them homeless, to make them incapable of performing their manufacturing tasks, this might end the war as effectively as the struggle on the battlefield. The area offensive is viewed as a series of 'Battles' – Ruhr, Hamburg and Berlin, and it had its successes. After the virtual destruction of Hamburg in the summer of 1943 Speer remarked to Hitler that if the RAF could repeat this operation on six other major cities Germany would be finished.

But even with better radars, the introduction of the Pathfinder Force to mark targets and generally much improved accuracy in bombing, it was not invariably possible to repeat such spectacular and decisive destruction. (And such brilliant operations as the famous Dambuster raid, involved percentage losses – 42 per cent – which were quite unacceptable.)

Over Berlin between November 1943 and March 1944 Harris received a check and the Air Staff sceptical now of Harris's assertion that Bomber Command alone could subdue Germany, insisted on selective attacks against industry. Then in April 1944 this aim became the specific one of attacking the French rail network in the months before the Normandy landings.

In this Bomber Command was notably successful in spite of Harris's own perhaps illogical feeling that this was mis-deployment of his force. This success owed much to commanders such as Leonard Cheshire who had worked hard at precision marking techniques and produced bomb errors which were down to below 300 yards by the end of operations.

After the Normandy invasion Bomber Command was deployed in a number of spheres. Oil and communications rated higher than they had in 1943 but it may still be considered that the area offensive once again held sway to a greater extent that was necessary in the circumstances. Bomber Command entered the last months of the war able to strike at will over Germany in a way that would have seemed inconceivable in the dark days of 1941.

Whatever the ultimate verdict as the effectiveness of wartime strategic bombing, Harris may fairly be considered to have been treated somewhat churlishly in the aftermath of hostilities. He had after all been the architect of a role for Bomber Command when Britain's possession of a large bomber force seemed likely to prove an embarrassment. He had borne the mental burden of vast losses – over a thousand complete aircrew, the equivalent of the Command's entire strength during the Battle of Berlin alone – and had, by his command's example, put heart into the Americans to continue and develop their own efforts in the face of their own reverses in the air by day.

However, though promoted Marshal of the Royal Air Force in 1946, his name unlike that of other major war commanders was not on the list of peerages for the New Years Honours of that year. His sole reward was a baronetcy, created in 1953.

From 1946 to 1953 he was Managing Director of the South African Marine Corporation but latterly he had lived at Goring-on-Thames where he died.

He was twice married, firstly in 1916 to Barbara, daughter of E W K Money and secondly in 1938 to Therese Hearne. There were a son and two daughters of the first marriage and a daughter of the second.

Despite recent revisionist judgements, 'Bomber' Harris remains a controversial figure. However, he had no part in framing the famous Air Ministry Directive No 22 dated February 14, 1942, born of an influential Cabinet paper by Professor F W Lindemann, the British government's leading scientific adviser, justifying the use of area bombing to 'dehouse' the German workforce as the most effective way of reducing their morale and affecting enemy war production. Harris had little belief in the effectiveness of 'morale-breaking' but supported the campaign against major industrial centres.

After the German invasion of the Soviet Union in 1941, British bombing parried Stalin's constant complaints about Western inactivity. Bombing absorbed only 7 percent of the British war effort, rising to 12 per cent in 1944/45; while in Germany it produced debilitating strains in society and industry and, with the Americans, brought the war effort to crisis point by the winter of 1944/45. By 1944, German defences required a million men, 55,000 guns and over 70% of the fighter force.

Harris' much remarked single-mindedness and his dislike of what were known as 'panacea' targets may be thought to be justified by the fact that less than half the bomb tonnage went on Germany's industrial cities; Bomber Command was a jack-of-all-trades and the CinC had to prevent its dissipation.

Harris can be faulted, however, in his persistent refusal to allocate 'very long range' (VLR) aircraft to fill the 'air gap' in mid-Atlantic at a time when the U-boat campaign might have lost Britain the war. Writing to Churchill on June 17, 1942 that Coastal Command was 'merely an obstacle to victory', Harris' opinions about the anti-submarine battle proved to be wrong.

* * *

SLIM

Soldier of indomitable spirit who defeated the Japanese

15 DECEMBER 1970

FIELD MARSHAL VISCOUNT SLIM, KG, GCB, GCMG, GCVO, GBE, DSO, MC., died yesterday. He was 79. His name will be for ever associated with the victorious campaign of the Fourteenth Army in Burma during the Second World War. He was a soldier of the highest ability, with a keen eye for strategy, but perhaps his most remarkable quality was his influence over his troops. The campaign in Burma was of a kind that made particularly high calls upon the spirit of the troops, and especially of the European troops, to whom the country was in the popular phrase, 'a green hell'. It is no secret that to build up, and still more to maintain, the spirit of Europeans in these surroundings, with entire absence of any comfort, relaxation, society, or intercourse with civilians of their own race, was a most difficult task. Nor, indeed, can it be denied that in some cases the British units fell below their highest standards before the end of the campaign.

Even Slim could not achieve the impossible in the moral sphere. What can be said is that he worked wonders. The contact between an army commander and his troops is necessarily remote in modern warfare, and therein lies a serious moral danger. Like Montgomery in the Eighth Army, though by rather different methods, Slim contrived to impress his personality on the men he led, Indian as well as British, in one of the most trying and difficult campaigns of modern times. They felt complete confidence in him and indeed gave him their affection, which is something rarer. Yet it hardly needs to be said that personality alone, without generalship, would not have sufficed. The British soldier demands first and foremost of his commanders that he should be 'put in with a chance'. He always felt that he would be when commanded by Slim.

William Joseph Slim was born on August 6, 1891. There was nothing in his environment or upbringing to indicate that he would adopt the profession of arms and rise to great heights in it. He was educated at King Edward's School, Birmingham, and after leaving followed several avocations. He was a junior clerk, a school teacher, and an engineer. The outbreak of war in 1914 found him a Territorial non-commissioned officer, and on August 22 he was commissioned in The Royal Warwickshire Regiment. He first saw active service on the Gallipoli peninsula. In August 1915, he was seriously wounded in the Battle of Sari Bair, and on discharge from hospital graded as permanently unfit for first-line service. However, he reappeared in the firing line, this time in France. Next he served in Mesopotamia, where he was wounded again and awarded the Military Cross. On this occasion he was evacuated to India, where on recovery he served as G S O 3 in 1917 and G S O 2 in 1918. In 1919 he transferred to the Indian Army. He joined the 6th Gurkha Rifles. a regiment alongside which he had fought and the bearing of which had deeply impressed him. All his life he was to be an enthusiast about the military qualities of the Gurkha. He was promoted captain in the same year, received a brevet-majority in 1930, and became a substantive major in 1933. From 1934 to 1937 he was an instructor at the Staff College, Camberley, with the local rank of lieutenant-colonel. Between then and the outbreak of war in 1939 he attended the Imperial Defence College.

At an early stage of the war Slim found himself in Sudan, on the Eritrean frontier, in command of the 10th Indian Brigade. He took part in the first offensive against the Italians on that front at Gallabat, but was wounded in early 1941 before the decisive struggle at Keren. On recovery from this third wound of his career he was posted as brigadier-general staff to Lieutenant-General Quinan, but shortly afterwards obtained command of the 10th Indian Division, with which he served in Syria, Persia, and Iraq. He was awarded the D S O for his service during this year.

His next appointment in March, 1942 was far from a promising one. It was to the command of the First Burma Corps, which in fact represented practically the whole of the forces at General Alexander's disposal. At the end of the terrible fighting retreat through jungle and mountains, he was appointed to command the XV Corps in India. For his work in Burma he received the CBE and for that in command of the XV Corps the CB. Late in 1943 a new army designated the Fourteenth, was formed for operations in Burma, and Slim was appointed to command it. He had a great opportunity before him, but also a heavy responsibility. Never so far had British or Indian troops succeeded in defeating the Japanese. The morale of the latter was consequently very high and they went into battle supremely confident of success. Backed by General Giffard, who commanded the army group and was largely responsible for the training, Slim exerted his utmost efforts and ingenuity to implant in his formations the belief that they contained better and more intelligent soldiers than the Japanese and were capable of beating them.

It was only when he had succeeded in this task that he could contemplate a major offensive for the reconquest of Burma. Even then the difficulties were great, since Burma had perforce to be placed low on the list of British priorities as a theatre of war. A country with the slenderest possible military link in communications with India and itself possessing hardly any resources for modern war, so that it depended more than ordinarily upon importations from Britain and the United States, was thus starved by comparison with other theatres.

By cooperation with the Americans, who were interested less in Slim's campaign than in preventing free China from falling under the domination of the Japanese and were prepared to bring in material and supply administrative troops for that purpose, Slim partially overcame one side of this difficulty. The other was overcome by the use of air transport, which in this theatre was used with a skill and effectiveness not found in any other. In Burma all depended on the air, not only for the transport of supplies but for transferring whole divisions from one region to another. In February, 1944, when the British offensive was under way but was still being conducted on a relatively small scale, the Japanese struck back, first in the Arakan, the strip of territory on the west coast. Using their favourite simple methods of envelopment, the Japanese gained a temporary tactical success, but they were finally fought down and utterly defeated. This to some extend prejudiced the start of their second and main offensive in Manipur and Assam, directed against India itself, where they hoped to provoke a rising. The battles round Imphal and Kohima none the less developed into a struggle to be measured by months and with fluctuating fortunes. In the end the Japanese were worn out by the stress. Their army, having suffered heavy losses and already showing signs of disintegration, fell back across the Chindwin in the midst of the monsoon of 1944.

The Japanese Army did not disintegrate after all, though it was never again to be the same fighting instrument. Using the air for supply with the same effect as in the defensive battles, Slim launched a powerful offensive across the Irrawaddy. Mandalay fell at the end of the third week of March, 1945, and Rangoon not long afterwards. All was not yet finished, and there was in fact some sharp fighting with large bodies of Japanese trapped west of the Sittang and with other forces east of the river which endeavoured to make diversions with the purpose of rescuing these troops.

Slim himself, however, passed on to another task. He had been appointed commander-in-chief of the army group known as 'Allied Land Forces South-east Asia', which was to carry out the reconquest of Malaya. For that there was, as it proved, no need. September 9 was the date fixed for the landing, but by that time the unconditional surrender of the Japanese had taken place.

For his services with the Fourteenth Army Slim was promoted K C B, in September, 1944. He was also promoted to the rank of general in August, 1945. After his return to England in December. 1945, he was the recipient of further honours, being promoted G B E in 1946.

In 1946 he was allotted the task of reopening, as commandant, the Imperial Defence College at which he had attended as a student. The college was not only restarted but also established on a scale considerably greater than that of before the war. In this period Slim made himself known to the general public as a really admirable speaker and particularly as a broadcaster. In July, 1947, he was offered but refused the post of Commander-in-Chief of the Army of the Dominion of India. In the following September he was appointed a member of the Railway Executive and London Transport Executive set up under the Transport Act earlier in the year.

He became deputy chairman of the Executive, with special responsibility for stores, estates, police and public relations. In view of the war this was an important appointment, but it did not last long. In the following year Slim became Chief of the Imperial General Staff, the appointment taking effect on November 1. Three months later, on January 4, 1949, he received the baton of a Field Marshal.

On September 3, 1952. his appointment to be Governor-General of

Australia was announced. The Prime Minister, Mr. Menzies, had departed from the Labour policy of recommending an Australian for this high office. He naturally came under criticism, which in its turn involved for Slim something less than an ideal start. Again his personality and good humour served him well. Some ruffling of the water did occur; indeed, his very able Prime Minister must have known in advance that it would have been useless to put forward his name if the new Governor-General had to be extremely cautious, and still less if he were expected to utter platitudes. He was sworn in on May 8, 1953.

The publication of his admirable book of war memoirs, *Defeat into Victory*, in 1956 reinforced his position. His appointment was prolonged for two years, and before he left the country in January, 1960, he published another successful book of a very different sort, the lively, amusing and sometimes touching *Unofficial History*. Without exaggeration it may be said that he left in Australia an indelible impression of character, honesty and friendliness, as well as of a powerful mind. In January, 1950, he was promoted to GCB. Late in 1952, after his appointment as Governor-General had been announced, he was created GCMG. In 1954, in connexion with the Queen's tour, he was created GCVO. In his last year in Australia he received the Garter and in 1960 he was created a Viscount. He was Governor and Constable of Windsor Castle from 1964 until June this year. In his later years he held a number of directorships.

In person Slim was a big, bluff man with a jutting chin, which gave an air of determination to his countenance. Socially he was an attractive figure and good company at a dinner-table, though not normally talkative. He married in 1926 Aileen, daughter of the Reverend J. A. Robertson, and had one son and one daughter. The former followed his father's foot-steps in becoming an officer in the Gurkha Rifles.

Scant credit is given in this obituary to Slim's achievement in bringing fighting elements of 1st Burma Corps out to India in 1942. There appears to have been no contingency plan for an evacuation across the Chindwin river and precious little administrative support ordered forward, by GHQ India in Delhi, for the reception of the near-destitute troops when they reached Imphal and Kohima on the Indian side of the frontier. Slim was to be seen during this largely chaotic withdrawal, doing what he could to encourage his soldiers, fixing him in their esteem. The line of communication to Assam, to where 1st Burma Corps was withdrawn, was tenuous in the extreme but that was inadequate excuse for command and staff failures to organize administrative support and reinforcements for Slim's force.

Slim's eventual defeat of the Japanese in Burma owes much to his realistic approach to what could reasonably be expected of his troops, his exploitation of air supply and outmanoeuvring rather than outfighting the enemy. He took care to maintain close and friendly relationships with RAF and USAF commanders responsible for providing the 14th Army with close air support and air re-supply but he did not appear to have great faith in the impact that Wingate's long-range penetration operations would have on the overall strategic situation. He was also said to have under-valued the fighting capabilities of the African troops under his command, believing the high proportion of European officers and NCOs inhibited initiative by the rank and file.

His period as Chief of the Imperial General Staff from 1948 to 1952 presented him with problems that receive no mention in the obituary. As part of the post-war austerity programme, the infantry of the British Army had been halved in 1947. The onset of the communist insurrection in Malaya in 1948 raised a demand for infantry, a situation compounded by outbreak of the Korean War in 1950. As in Burma, he faced difficulties with inadequate resources, but persuaded the Government to re-raise some infantry battalions and expand the Malay Regiment to help plug the gap. His down to earth approach was a constant source of confidence to those around him.

WINGATE

Guerrilla Operations in Burma

1ST APRIL 1944

MAJOR-GENERAL O. C. WINGATE, D.S.O., late R.A., who was killed in an aeroplane accident in Burma on March 24, during an operational flight, had an unusual military career of exceptional distinction. He gained fame for his exploits in Palestine before the war as head of the Jewish counter-guerrillas, was sent to Abyssinia on special duty during the campaign which led to the restoration of the Emperor, and after that, until his death, was the leader of the two expeditions in Burma associated with his name.

Orde Charles Wingate, born on February 26. 1903, son of the late Colonel G. Wingate C.I.E., came of a well-known military family. He was educated at Charterhouse, and after passing through Woolwich was gazetted to the Royal Artillery in 1923. He was attached to the Sudan Defence Force from 1928 to 1933, was promoted captain in 1936, and the same year was sent to Palestine and Transjordan in a special appointment for which his profound knowledge of the Arab world particularly fitted him. At that time the Mufti of Jerusalem was giving his support to the bands of Arabs and disaffected Syrians who were causing the authorities so much trouble, and to counter their activities he organized, trained, and led a force of soldiers and supernumerary police which operated solely by night. The work he did was very arduous, entailing lying out in the open night after night, and he regularly led the parties themselves and acted as scout. The results achieved by his force were very important in the area of the oil pipe-line and on parts of the northern frontier. His sterling work was recognized in 1938 by the award of the D.S.O.

When the present war broke out Wingate was stationed in Kent in charge of anti-aircraft guns, but his successes in Palestine, fresh in the mind of the authorities, made him the obvious man to be selected for special service under Wavell as the organizer and leader of the Abyssinian partisans. The full story of his adventures there has not yet been told, but it is known that he was even more successful than in Palestine. By the time he went to Burma to take charge of guerrilla warfare there was probably no man in the allied forces more fitted than he to organize and lead the 'Jungle Commando.' His presence in Burma and the nature of his operations were among the best kept secrets of the war, until in May, 1943, it was officially announced that his long-range jungle force, which received its supplies entirely by air, had arrived in India from northern Burma after spending three months as wreckers in the midst of enemy-controlled country. Wingate's brigade, consisting of British and Gurkha columns with intelligence and reconnaissance detachments from the Burma Rifles, penetrated hundreds of miles across jungle ranges and valleys. The rivers Chindwin and Irrawaddy were crossed and the Myitkyina railway was cut in 80 places.

Skilfully infiltrating through the chain of Japanese outposts and garrisons, the force penetrated hostile territory as far as the Shan States; much destruction was done and the enemy was forced to divert troops; from more important and hard pressed points. Lord Wavell recommended Wingate to the Royal Central Asian Society for the award of the Lawrence of Arabia Gold Medal, which was presented to his wife in July, 1943. Mrs. Wingate before her marriage, which took place in 1935, was Miss Lorna E. Paterson, daughter of Mr. W. Moncreiff Paterson, of Tilliefoure, Monymusk, Aberdeenshire.

The death of Wingate at the height of his greatest campaign, a campaign which even from the first fired the imagination of the world for its blend of science and sheer daring, is a grievous loss to allied arms. There will be heavy hearts in the jungles of Upper Burma among the thousands of men who knew the exhilaration of his leadership. In his military outlook Wingate combined the qualities of a guerrilla leader and the scientist; he was a solitary, elusive figure, and his disregard for convention fitted ideally into his orthodox military caution. His feats in Abyssinia, which he entered almost alone, far ahead of the army, to round up thousands of Italians with mere handfuls of men, were becoming legendary when Wavell, with whom he had served in Palestine, called him to India at the time of the withdrawal from Burma. Woefully little was then known by British and Indian troops about jungle fighting, and Wingate was given the task of raising an expedition to lead against the Japanese on their own ground. He saw that against a fundamentally primitive enemy, like the Japanese, telling blows could be struck by a large employment of those two great developments of modern warfare, wireless and air power. He saw, too, that everything depended on the adequate training of his force. and having carefully chosen his column commanders – after his own heart filled with a spirit of adventure – he took them into the wilderness during the monsoon to make jungle fighters of them. Nor were the British battalion in any way crack troops, but men in their 30's engaged on second-line duties.

The lessons and mistakes of this first expedition, with its experiments in equipment, in dropping air supplies to columns on the move, and its wireless links with bases hundreds of miles behind them, were invaluable in mounting the present campaign on a far larger scale. It was not achieved without heavy loss, and Wingate was the first to admit its limited scope; but out of it came the long-range penetration column as a weapon of great possibilities when used far ahead of a following army, and not least the proof that the Japanese soldier can be outwitted and out-manoeuvred in the jungle.

There was a deceiving frailty about Wingate's appearance, at once belied not only by his endurance on the march but by his rapid recovery from a succession of illnesses. He came out of the jungle spent with fever, and was awarded a second bar to his D.S.O., and soon went ill again. This time he lay on the danger list at Delhi with typhoid. He was full of surprises and idiosyncrasies, a soldier who combined the scientific skill of an accomplished gunner with wide literary tastes. He was seldom without his Bible, and his military proclamations were often full of tags and biblical quotations which he was wont to use on occasion as a code. His column commanders swore by him and shared his joys.

After his first expedition Wingate returned to England, where he met the Prime Minister, it is said, in a bush-shirt, and accompanied him to the Quebec conference. Together with Admiral Lord Louis Mountbatten and his American colleagues he laid the plans for a second campaign which, as one of its essential features, has included the largest allied air landing of the war 200 miles in the rear of the enemy where no airfield existed. These plans were not received in all quarters without scepticism, but they cannot be seen in their true light until the whole story is told. By any measure Wingate was one of the thrilling figures of the war.

A loner in every sense, Wingate travelled with only a handful of local guides on several journeys in the Middle East in the 1930s, including into the Libyan desert. While in Palestine, he embraced the Zionist cause with all the fervour of a convert and made many friends in the Jewish community, among them the future General Moshe Dayan, then in his early twenties.

During the Second World War he characterized himself as 'a boot up the backside of mankind' in his advocacy of irregular warfare.

His first long-range penetration into Burma realized little in the way of disruption to the Japanese, but was a propaganda victory for the Commonwealth at a low point of the war against the Japanese out of all proportion to the lives lost effort or effort expended, as it exploded completely the dangerous myth of the invincibility of the Japanese soldier.

* * *

RIDGWAY

United Nations Supreme Commander in Korea

27 JULY 1993

GENERAL MATTHEW B. RIDGWAY, commander of the famous US 82nd Divison during the second world war and United Nations supreme commander in Korea from 1951, died yesterday in Pittsburgh aged 98. He was born on March 3, 1895. Ridgeway was an adventurous and resourceful soldier who pioneered the US Army's use of airborne troops in the second world war. He later went on to succeed Douglas MacArthur as head of the United Nations forces during the Korean war before reaching the top of his profession as US Army chief of staff. In all he did he had that capacity to inspire his men with a relentless desire to be at grips with the enemy.

From 1943 onwards he sought to convince a sceptical US high command that parachute operations could be the key to unlocking enemy positions, and by his personal example – he jumped with his men on D-Day – he carried his point beyond argument. He was, perhaps, continually involved in more fierce fighting during the war than any other allied general. Sicily, Salerno, Normandy, the Ardennes counter-offensive and the crossing of the Siegfried Line all felt his hand, and, as in the Ardennes, he was frequently called in to restore situations in which things were not going well.

When he went to Korea, first as commander of the US 8th Army, it was in a similarly fraught situation. After a retreat conducted in bitter weather, morale amongst the men was low and the situation was worsened by the fact that many of them had lost faith in commanders who they sensed were not interested in sharing their hardships. Ridgway got his subordinate commanders out of their jeeps and onto their feet. 'Get off your fat asses and get climbing hills' were his unambiguous instructions to one and two-star generals who had forgotten what marching was, and had hoped to keep matters thus. Very soon the new commander had converted a dispirited rabble into an aggressively minded and tactically canny force.

His colourful personality endeared him not only to his own men but to the British, Canadian and Australian troops who came under his aegis after he replaced MacArthur as UN supreme commander. Patton had had his pearl-handled revolvers; Montgomery his assorted headgear; Wingate his beard and battered pith helmet. But Ridgway, who never went anywhere without one, or sometimes two, primed grenades attached to his chest, surely outdid them all. The ear-splitting siren which he had fitted to his jeep made sure that his arrival in the lines was never unannounced. And there were few of his men whose spirits did not acquire new mettle when 'old iron tits' (as he was known from his grenade-adorned person) was near.

Matthew Bunker Ridgway son of Colonel Thomas Ridgway, was born at Fort Monroe, Virginia. From the beginning he led an army life at the various posts where his father was stationed. After attending the English High School in Boston, he entered West Point, and in 1917 was commissioned into the infantry. He served first with the 3rd Infantry in Texas, was an instructor at West Point and after a course at the Infantry School went overseas to command a company in China. After further overseas service in Panama and the Philippines, he went in 1933 to the command and general staff school. He then did a number of staff jobs until, in 1939, he was appointed to the general staff in Washington where he worked with the war plans division until 1942.

In March 1942 Ridgway became assistant divisional commander of the 82nd Division, and soon after took command. It became an airborne division in August 1942, and so began his close association with airborne operations, of which he became the US Army's leading exponent. He planned and led the airborne invasion of Sicily in July 1943. Here he displayed the front line leadership for which he became renowned. He fought his way with his own advance guard to Trapani in the west of the island and subsequently took his troops into mainland Italy at Salerno.

In spite of mistakes in Sicily, Ridgway's belief in airborne forces was vindicated when on D-Day in June 1944 he jumped with his division in the assault on the Cotentin peninsula. He was next appointed to command the 18th Airborne Corps. As such he was involved in the allied invasion of the Netherlands where fighting was still in progress when, on December 18, 1944, news came of the German breakthrough in the Ardennes. Ridgway's corps was immediately dispatched into the area and became involved in some of the heaviest fighting of the Northwest Europe campaign. In March 1945 he again distinguished himself, at the Rhine crossing where his corps broke through decisively in the Wesel area. He led it until it affected its junction with Soviet troops on the Baltic in May 1945.

In August 1945 he returned to the US and from October commanded in the Mediterranean until January 1946 when he went to be Eisenhower's representative on the military staff committee of the UN. Here he helped to produce the report which was a first step towards establishing an international police force. During this time he was also chairman of the Inter-American Defence Board, and then, after being C-in-C Caribbean Command in 1948–49 and deputy chief of staff in 1949–50, he once more embarked on active service.

In December 1950 Ridgway was appointed commander of the 8th Army in Korea. He took over at a time when it was defending roughly the line of the 38th parallel, and was virtually in command of all operations under MacArthur's direction. There followed a difficult period. The Communist offensive at the beginning of 1951 caused UN troops to withdraw and Seoul was evacuated for the second time. But in a war such as this one Ridgway was simply not interested in ground won or lost. His aim was to inflict as many casualties as possible on the enemy and he was able to convince his men that the Chinese superiority lay only in their numbers. 'All we've got to do is kill more of their guys than they do of ours. It's as simple as that. And we're going to win this war that's for sure.' It was an attitude which took the 8th Army back across the 38th parallel.

In April 1951 he replaced MacArthur as C-in-C UN Command, and in June began the negotiations which eventually led to the armistice. In these he displayed qualities which appeared to be antithetical to his character of battlefield fire-eater. As a negotiator he surprised many by his political wisdom and his far-sightedness. But in truth these qualities were merely a part of his view of the function of warlike operations as the hard-headed instrument of foreign policy goals. He was not a man to sacrifice life needlessly for aims which yielded diminishing returns.

Ridgway still had his two most responsible posts in front of him. In May 1952 he took over from Eisenhower as Supreme Allied Commander (SACEUR) in Europe. He held the post for only a year, but during this time held out resolutely for the strengthening of Nato's forces and refused to accept that nuclear weapons did away with the need for powerful conventional armies.

In July 1953 he handed over to General Gruenther, and returned to Washington to become Army chief of staff. In this, his last military post, he did not always see eye to eye either with the new doctrine of massive retaliation or with some of his military and political colleagues. But his restraining influence during the war in Indochina and the offshore island crisis made an indispensable contribution to the prevention of general war. In 1955 he retired from the Army, and from then until 1960 was chairman of the Mellon Institute of Industrial Research.

In his book, *The Korean War*, published in the 1960s when the Vietnam war was beginning to absorb America's military energies, Ridgway made comparisons with the two conflicts and expressed reservations later to be more widely shared in the US military about such a squandering of resources.

Three times married, he is survived by his third wife Mary and by two daughters of his first marriage.

This hard-fighting general learned a lot from his first operational experience – the Allied invasion of Sicily in 1943. Due to inadequate training of the American pilots of the towing aircraft many gliders ditched in the sea and others, together with some parachute troops, landed well away from their objectives. He never allowed such an ill-prepared approach to war again. He made a decisive impact – at a critical juncture – on the UN Force in Korea.

GORSHKOV

Mastermind of global Soviet seapower

16 MAY 1988

ADMIRAL SERGEI GORSHKOV, Commander-in-Chief of the Soviet Navy from 1956 until 1985, who died on May 13, aged 78, transformed Russia's Navy from a coastal defence force into an ocean-going navy with the capacity to inflict cataclysmic destruction with missiles from its submarines, and able to show the flag and influence the affairs of nations thousands of miles from the Kremlin. He had done more for Russia as a maritime power, it was said, that anyone since her navy was founded by Peter the Great.

Sergei Georgievich Gorshkov was born in the Ukrainian town of Kamenets-Podolsk in February, 1910. At the age of seventeen he joined the Red Navy, then in the doldrums. It had fallen into political disfavour after the Kronstadt mutiny of 1921, and in any case Soviet industry could not support a large shipbuilding programme.

His first command was of a patrol boat in the Black Sea. After seven years with the Pacific Fleet, where he commanded destroyers, he returned to the Black Sea, where he spent most of the war. In 1942–43, now a rear-admiral commanding the Azov Flotilla, he co-operated closely with the Red Army in the battle for the Caucasus; for a short time Gorshkov even commanded the 47th Army. At the end of 1943 he directed the landings that brought the Red Army back into the Crimea. In April 1944 his force helped to seize the Danube estuary and to take Belgrade and Budapest back from the Nazis.

After the war he took over command, in 1951, of the Black Sea Fleet. In July 1955 he moved to headquarters in Moscow and six months later was Commander-in-Chief. It was a difficult time. His predecessor's shipbuilding plans had been turned down by Khruschev, who thought that surface warships had had their day. The Soviet Armed Forces were going through what the Russians call a 'revolution in military affairs'. The roles of the different services were being called into question by the advent of nuclear weapons.

Gorshkov had to wage a long and difficult campaign to defend the Navy's interests and secure for it an important place in the new Soviet nuclear doctrine. But expanded shipbuilding programmes, and Soviet deployment on all the world's oceans, became evidence that Gorshkov was successful in his campaign. After Khrushchev's fall the Navy benefited from the new emphasis on balanced conventional forces. In 1976, Gorshkov set out his views in a book entitled *The Sea Power of the State*. It argued that the Navy had a key role in peace as well as war. It was a flexible instrument that could be used in limited conflicts and in support of state interests far from the Soviet frontiers. Above all, he argued, a strong navy was the indisputable mark of a great power. His philosophy was warmly praised in the House of Commons in 1981, by Mr Keith Speed, who had just been dismissed as a junior Defence Minister after controversy over the diminishing importance attached to the Royal Navy in the British defence pattern.

Gorshkov was evidently a very able manipulator of Soviet bureaucracy. Although he presided over an expansion in submarine power, he was never himself a submariner. (Khrushchev seems to have been under a misapprehension on this point and wrote in his memoirs that Gorshkov's submarine experience was an important reason for appointing him Commander-in-Chief.) He was also an effective publicist, and the attention the Western press gave to the new deployments of the Soviet Navy no doubt strengthened his case that naval presence would bring political benefits to the Soviet Union. Much of the press comment was sensationalist, but it should not obscure Gorshkov's real achievement in changing the character and the role of the Soviet Navy.

His decorations included five Orders of Lenin. He was made a Hero of the Soviet Union in 1965.

Gorshkov was promoted Kontr Admiral in 1941 aged 31, younger than Nelson or Beatty. In 1967 he was specially promoted to a new rank of Admiral of the Fleet of the Soviet Union. In 1955 he was appointed First Deputy CinC of the navy and CinC and First Deputy Minister of Defence in 1956, a post he held for thirty years. When he retired in 1985 his fleet comprised 64 ballistic-missile, 50 guided-missile and 67 attack submarines, all nuclear powered, as well as four aircraft carriers, 40 cruisers and 268 destroyers and frigates, many fitted with long range missiles. Supporting ancillary craft included a full armoury of highly sophisticated electronic eavesdropping ships and a well-resourced hydrographic and survey fleet. Latterly, some of his attack and missile-firing submarines were of very advanced design.

The obituary gives full credit to Gorshkov's political skills in persuading the politburo of an essentially land-based nation whose Second World War glories were only those won by the Red Army to think globally and invest accordingly. With its emphasis on nuclear-powered submarines, Gorshkov's navy for many years put the wind up the North Atlantic Treaty Organisation – a sea-based alliance with its major partner separated from the majority by an ocean, reliant upon a reinforcement strategy and hampered by treaty-based geographical boundaries. In short, NATO depended upon the sea, the Soviet Union didn't.

* * *

WALKER

Fighting General of uncompromising methods

14 AUGUST 2001

WALTER WALKER CREATED apprehension in the minds of his enemies and superiors alike. To hard fighting experience, meticulous staff work, skill in training men and interpreting intelligence, he added a clarity of thought which almost invariably led to his being proved right in the end. Whitehall thought him undiplomatic because he said things inconvenient to hear. He might have been more subtle, but he knew that polite criticism is easily smiled away. He was never content just to have his say: it was his unswerving purpose to win.

His career was punctuated by a series of remarkable military achievements, which were of increasing importance as he came to hold more senior commands. The first of his three DSOs came as a Gurkha commander in the Burma campaign, where his battalion took severe toll of the Japanese, thanks to his rigorous retraining of what had been an exhausted unit. His second came in the Malayan Emergency in the 1950s where, again, he greatly increased the effectiveness of his Gurkhas in operations against communist insurgents, thanks to a complete reappraisal of their training and tactics.

His third was awarded in 1965 when, as Director of Operations in Borneo, he devised and executed the tactics which thwarted President Sukarno of Indonesia's attempt to subvert the newly-formed Federation of Malaysia by military means. Clearly a victory of this geopolitical importance should have received greater reward. Describing Walker as 'our finest fighting general', the Defence Secretary of the day, Denis Healey, went on to describe the campaign to the House of Commons as 'one of the most efficient uses of military force in the history of the world'. Certainly it was one of the British Army's neatest and tidiest post-war operations.

But by that time Walker had made plenty of enemies among those senior to him. Widely admired as a man of resolution, he occasionally allowed himself to lapse into self-aggrandisement. His battles with authority on behalf of his beloved Gurkhas, whose numbers were con-tinually threatened with reduction, had led him into the political arena and into a direct collision with the Chief of the General Staff.

In retirement, Walker continued to be a stormy petrel. In the early 1970s his name was associated with what came to be thought of as a private army, raised to do battle with the trade unions. Though he denied this, he had not helped his cause by having previously given a newspaper interview in which he said that the Army might have to take over the country. After the collapse of this project he continued to advance robust opinions in letters to the press on the dangers to the country from relaxed vigilance against enemies without: principally the Soviet Union; and those within: among them trades unions and the acceptance of homosexuals within the armed forces.

Walter Colyear Walker was born in Tiverton, Devon, the son of an Assam tea-planter. His grandfather had led the 'Forlorn Hope' ladder party at the storming of Delhi's Water Bastion during the Indian Mutiny. He was educated at Blundell's and the RMC Sandhurst before entering the 8th Gurkhas in 1933. As battalion adjutant he was mentioned in dispatches during the second Mohmand campaign on the North West Frontier.

In 1942 he attended the Staff College, Quetta, subsequently joining 4/8th Gurkha Rifles as second-in-command following the battalion's successful defence of the 'Admin Box' in Arakan in February 1944. After further heavy fighting around Imphal they had earned a rest, but Walker felt that retraining was a higher priority. Walker drove his riflemen hard with the slogan 'move quickly, fight fiercely, shoot low'. When he took command in November, 4/8th Gurkhas were ready for General Sir William Slim's offensive into Burma. They began with an assault crossing of the Irrawaddy and an advance down the road to Prome.

As the Japanese began to pull out of Arakan, the 7th Indian Division – which included 4/8th Gurkhas – was ordered south to prevent the 28th Japanese Army escaping across the Irrawaddy towards the Thai border. For three days and nights Walker's battalion faced wave after wave of fanatical Japanese attempts to break through at Taungaw but the 4/8th held, killing hundreds of the enemy. For his undaunted leadership, Walker was awarded the DSO.

On the Partition of India in 1947, 8th Gurkhas remained with the Indian Army and Walker transferred to the 6th Gurkhas in British service, soon to be involved in countering the communist insurrection in Malaya. Walker's first task was to establish the Jungle Warfare School in South Johore, where units were trained before entering the jungle. His methods endured for a decade.

When he took command of 1/6th Gurkha Rifles in 1950 he found them keen but not especially successful in killing communist terrorists. As with the 4/8th in the war, he retrained them with ruthless efficiency. His methods, unpopular with some, brought success against the enemy, to which his perceptive use of intelligence owed much. He received a Bar to his DSO and, after a staff job in England, was appointed to command 99 Gurkha Brigade in South Johore, where the last hard-core terrorist group was holding out.

Intelligence on the terrorists was thin but Walker gained the confidence of Special Branch, always wary lest the Army compromise its sources. In three months, working from Special Branch information, his Operation Tiger accounted for the entire enemy group. On the last day of 1958 South Johore was declared 'white' – virtually ending the Malayan Emergency. Walker was appointed CBE, but a reduction in the Brigade of Gurkhas was now in the offing. After attending the Imperial Defence College in London, he was promoted major-general to command the 17th Gurkha Division – designated to counter any threat to Commonwealth interests in the Far East. He was consequently dismayed when informed by the Commander-in-Chief, General Sir Richard Hull, that to reduce defence costs the number of Gurkha battalions was to be halved.

Walker kept his counsel until, in his capacity as Major-General

Brigade of Gurkhas, he next briefed the King of Nepal on matters concerning his subjects under command. He revealed the reduction plan to the King and also took the American Ambassador to Kathmandu into his confidence. Both were seriously concerned; the King because he depended on Gurkha pay and pensions to help Nepal's economy and the ambassador because he regarded British-Nepali relations as important for regional stability. Walker's report to the King of Nepal reached London and Washington, and Sir Richard Hull, by then Chief of the General Staff, recalled him to London intending to sack him for deliberate breach of confidence. Warned by friends, Walker apologized, but Hull thereafter questioned his judgment.

Ironically the Gurkha battalions were saved, for the time being, by the outbreak of a totally unexpected conflict. President Sukarno of Indonesia declared his opposition to the newly formed Federation of Malaysia. The outcome was a three-year war in Borneo. The Gurkhas fought in it from the outset, with Walker as tri-service Director of Operations. Infantry were quickly diverted from the Malayan peninsula but artillery, helicopters and resources of all kinds were in short supply. Hull suspected Walker of playing up the Borneo campaign to keep his precious Gurkhas, but he was mistaken: the fighting became bitter and prolonged.

The campaign was virtually won during Walker's command, thanks to his skilled direction – particularly his boldly conceived cross-border operations. A KCB was widely expected in recognition of his achievements. Instead he received a second bar to his DSO, an honour for a less senior officer but clearly a snub to him. Worse was to follow. Appointed Deputy Chief of Staff Plans, Operations and Intelligence HQ Allied Forces Central Europe, he was informed he was to be retired at the end of his stint. Unwittingly, President de Gaulle came to his aid. Having taken France out of Nato's military structure, he demanded removal of the Alliance's installations from France by April 1, 1967. When planning of the move to Brunssum in The Netherlands became critically delayed, AFCENT's commander, General Johann von Kielmansegg, put Walker in charge. He ruthlessly substituted workers for drones and moved the headquarters on time.

So he was not retired on leaving AFCENT, but promoted lieutenant-general to become C-in-C Northern Command in England. The routine KCB followed, to the satisfaction of his friends. The Army was having recruiting difficulties at the time and Walker put his mind to this. A speech on recruiting attracted the interest of Tyne-Tees Television and an interview with Walker about the problem was filmed and shown. His selection as NATO C-in-C Allied Forces Northern Europe, based in Oslo, with promotion to full general gave rise to speculation. The appointment was coveted by Denmark and Norway. His reputation fathered the thought that Walker was being sent to 'stiffen up the Scandinavians'. The Norwegian Minister of Defence, Otto Tidemand, bitterly resented his arrival.

Undeterred by any of this, Walker set about training the staff to his way of working, and as improvements began he resumed his contact with Tyne-Tees Television. He suggested a film to portray NATO capabilities for public viewing and confidence-building. Meticulous care was taken to ensure that there was no breach of security but, amid rising apprehension as to political reactions, the alliance's Secretary-General, Manlio Brosio, condemned the production for depicting NATO as a warlike organization instead of a political one. As a result, the film was never screened. An interview for the Dutch newspaper, *De Telegraaf*, in October 1971 was also turned against Walker. His off-the-record comment that 'in wartime Norway would be lost *without reinforcement*' was quoted – without the qualifying phrase – outraging Oslo.

In retirement, in 1974, concerned by what he saw as the unbridled power of trade unions to damage the country's economy, Walker launched a countrywide appeal for public-spirited people to register for what he termed Civil Assistance, in case of need. His intention was benign but open to misinterpretation that he was trying to raise a private army of volunteers to challenge the unions, especially when it was stated that more than 100,000 people had pledged their support. In the event, the enterprise soon petered out. In his autobiography, *Fighting On*, published in 1997, Walker insisted that Civil Assistance was intended to do no more than support the authorities in a constitutional way.

The last 16 years of his life were beset by acute physical suffering brought about by two unsuccessful hip-replacement operations in service hospitals. He faced pain and disablement with the fortitude he had shown throughout his life, and in 1990 won substantial compensation from the Ministry of Defence after a four-year action.

In 1938 he married Beryl Johnston, the daughter of another Assam tea-planter. She predeceased him in 1990. He is survived by their twin sons and a daughter.

Every army needs a Walter Walker at least once in a generation. Few are fortunate enough to get one.

FIELDHOUSE

Falklands Conflict Commander-in-Chief

18 FEBRUARY 1992

ADMIRAL OF THE Fleet Lord Fieldhouse, GCB, GBE, who died yesterday aged 64 was commander-in-chief of the task force which recaptured the Falkland Islands after they had been seized by Argentina in 1982 and was later Chief of the Defence Staff from 1985 to 1988. He was born on February 12, 1928. Lord Fieldhouse was a sailor who reached the top of his profession as First Sea Lord and Chief of Naval Staff from 1982, and as Chief of Defence Staff from 1985.

For long his reputation was that of a staff man and in senior appointments he had tended to be thought of as something of a 'Whitehall warrior'. But this was hardly just as he had had good operational commands all the way up the line and in 1982 he came suddenly before the public as commander-in-chief of the task force which was charged with the recovery of the Falkland Islands after they had been invaded by Argentina in April. As such he was in charge of all the air, sea and land forces in the South Atlantic which he was able to control by satellite communications without having to leave his underground command headquarters at Northwood. In this vital role he much impressed the prime minister, Mrs Thatcher, who went frequently to his headquarters to be briefed by him on the progress of the campaign.

The deployment of a brigade group 8,000 miles from home made the Falklands operation a highly complex one. Much might have gone wrong against an enemy who was numerically superior, was fighting on his own doorstep and had the inestimable advantage of being able to operate under the umbrella of land-based air cover. That, in spite of some setbacks, the occupying forces had had enough and were ready to surrender by June 15 was a credit to Fieldhouse and planning which, though it owed much to strenuous improvization, functioned almost as if the campaign had been long foreseen and meditated in detail.

John David Elliott Fieldhouse was the son of Sir Harold Fieldhouse, who was secretary of the National Assistance Board from 1946 to 1959 and rose from humble beginnings to be a major and influential figure in the establishment of the State welfare system during and after the second

332

world war. John Fieldhouse joined the Royal Navy as a cadet in 1944 and served as a midshipman in the East Indies fleet in 1945–46. He volunteered for submarine service in 1948 and became the commanding officer of HMS *Acheron* in 1955. He was already marked out as an officer of promise and underwent extensive training in the newly-established department of nuclear science at Greenwich which culminated in the award of a postgraduate degree in 1961.

The Royal Navy at this time was beginning the deployment of nuclear-powered submarines, which was to be much enhanced by the decision, in December 1962, to procure a submarine-based deterrent force based upon the American Polaris weapon system. Fieldhouse became the commanding officer of the first British nuclear-powered submarine, HMS *Dreadnought*, in 1964. After a spell as the executive officer of an aircraft carrier, HMS *Hermes*, he was promoted captain in December 1967 and became the first Squadron Commander (SM10) of the Polaris submarine squadron.

A string of important appointments followed, including command of the Nato Standing Naval Force (Atlantic) in 1972–3, and it was no surprise when he was selected for early promotion to flag rank in January 1975. He became Flag Officer, Submarines (which carried with it a parallel Nato submarine command appointment) in 1976 and Controller of the Navy and a member of the Admiralty Board in 1979. This was the period during which both the development of new surface ships, including frigates and the new class of light aircraft carrier and a replacement for the Polaris submarines were matters of high policy. Apart from the strategic questions that were involved about what sorts of ships and what sorts of functions should be selected from a wide range of technological possibilities, the increasing cost of weapons material in a period of high inflation and deepening recession made the settlement of policy highly contentious.

The economic uncertainties of escalating costs and the political environment, in which there was more extensive questioning of Britain's future as a nuclear power, were only partially alleviated by the determination of the new Conservative government in May 1979 to give a higher priority to defence matters. Fieldhouse was a convinced advocate of Trident, selected by the government as a successor-system to Polaris, early in 1980.

He had become Commander-in-Chief, Fleet, in the summer of 1981, but with the Argentine invasion of the Falklands at the end of March 1982 he became the commander-in-chief of the task force which was dispatched immediately. He sat in the middle of the web in his shore headquarters at Northwood and was the operational director of what was undoubtedly a brilliantly improvized campaign.

The operational plans, for local sea control of the Falkland Island area for the assault and land campaign that would follow if force had to be used to expel the Argentines, had to be devised under emergency conditions which required a constant interchange between headquarters and the senior officers of the component forces. And then the plans had to be carried out. This involved taking political as well as military factors into account, which also meant a constant flow of advice and communication between London, the command centre at Northwood and the forces in the field. Fieldhouse's principal function in this respect was to provide clear directives to the operational commanders and shield them from the 'clutter' of unnecessary detail which modern communications can invite; but at the same time to provide comprehensive information to the Chief of Defence Staff and, through him, to the cabinet group that was in effect the War Cabinet, that would enable broad policy decisions to be made effectively.

Fieldhouse's plan of campaign envisaged four main objectives, to be achieved in phases: the establishment of a sea blockade round the Falklands; the repossession of South Georgia; the gaining of air and sea supremacy throughout the battle area and the eventual repossession of the islands. There were setbacks, notably the loss of some warships and a container ship which carried vital supplies, while there were also casualties among soldiers when two transports were bombed. But that the war plan's goals were all inexorably accomplished after a campaign which from day one of the Argentine aggression lasted only ten weeks was greatly to Fieldhouse's credit and added much to his reputation in professional circles.

The experience added weight to his very strong claims to become the Chief of the Naval Staff in due course and he was appointed First Sea Lord in 1982, having been created GBE for his services during the Falklands operation as well as the GCB, which was the normal award for his rank and appointment. His time as First Sea Lord was naturally preoccupied by the analysis of what lessons had been highlighted in the first campaign against a substantial opponent which the Royal Navy had fought for a quarter of a century; but it was also heavily flavoured by the taste of vindication which the Falklands brought to the navy, after its utility and organization had been challenged by the secretary of defence, Sir John Nott, in 1981.

..eldhouse's experience as an operational commander made him an obvious choice as Chief of the Defence Staff in 1985. But it still required a major break with tradition to enable this to happen. Since its creation the post of CDS had been rotated between the three services on the principle of 'Buggins's turn'. The army in the person of Field Marshal Sir Edwin Bramall had the job and in 1985 it was the RAF's turn, in the person of the Chief of the Air Staff, Marshal of the RAF Sir Keith Williamson. But the high regard in which the government of Mrs Thatcher held Fieldhouse went against the RAF's nominee and, out of turn, the sailor became CDS. In the event the appointment was doubly appropriate. With the defence reorganisation of 1982 and 1984 the post carried added operational responsibilities for which Fieldhouse was admirably well qualified.

In retirement from his service career Fieldhouse was a consultant to Vosper Thorneycroft (UK) Ltd and in 1990 he became chairman of the White Ensign Association. He was made a life peer in 1990.

He married, in 1953, Margaret Ellen Cull. They had one son and two daughters.

The British campaign to restore sovereignty to the Falklands islanders owed much to the American support that was given despite damage to their South American interests – particularly in the further supply of the excellent Sidewinder air-to-air missile without which the Sea Harriers could not have achieved what they did. A share in their satellite communications allowed Northwood a secure and high-data-rate channel to submarines. The runway at Ascension Island was invaluable.

There was irony in that the naval cuts proposed by Sir John Nott would have made the Falklands campaign impossible; after the conflict the cuts were impossible.

General Galtieri's oppressive junta having fallen, the ultimate beneficiaries were the Argentine people. On the morning after the loss of the destroyer *Coventry* and the critically important supply vessel *Atlantic Conveyor*, Fieldhouse addressed his staff; 'I can sense an atmosphere of gloom here. I do not like it'. Pointing to General Dick Trant and Brigadier Dunphie in their khaki uniforms, he said; 'The Army is used to taking casualties in battle. The Navy is not. I am prepared to lose more ships. What I will not accept is a staff with long faces. Straighten your backs and get back to work with smiles on your faces'.